Dr. Chase's Recipes

Or, Information for Everybody

by

Alvin Wood Chase

APPLEWOOD BOOKS
Bedford, Massachusetts

Dr. Chase's Recipes

was originally published in

1870

ISBN: 978-1-4290-1034-4

Thank you for purchasing an Applewood book.
Applewood reprints America's lively classics—
books from the past that are still of interest
to the modern reader.
For a free copy of
a catalog of our
bestselling
books,
write
to us at:
Applewood Books
Box 365
Bedford, MA 01730
or visit us on the web at:
For cookbooks: foodsville.com
For our complete catalog: awb.com

Prepared for publishing by HP

Respectfully,
A. W. Chancel. B.

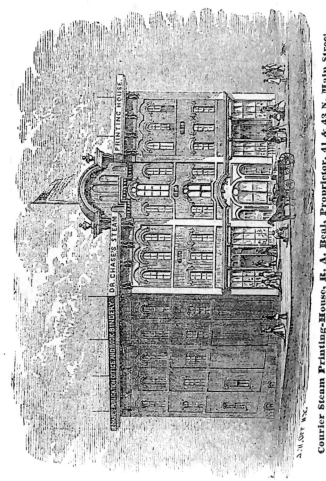

DR. CHASE'S STEAM PRINTING HOUSE.

PRINTING HOUSE.

DR. CHASE'S STEAM PUBLICATION OFFICE AND BOOK BINDERY.

Courier Steam Printing-House, R. A. Beal, Proprietor, 41 & 43 N. Main Street.

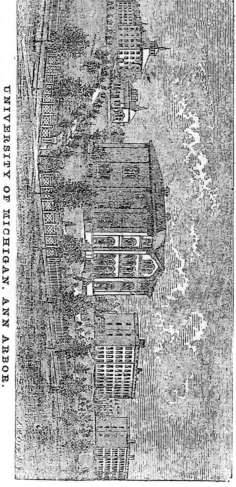

UNIVERSITY OF MICHIGAN, ANN ARBOR.

In this perspective view, from the North-West, we have an accurate representation of the University Buildings, in 1865. The centre one is occupied by the Law Department and Library; the two on the right by the Literary, Chapel, Museum, &c.; the first on the left is the Laboratory of Applied Chemistry; and the last, by the Medical Department. The number of Students for the year 1866-7 was 1255. For residents of the State, an entrance fee of only $10.—non-residents $25—with $10 yearly, pays for a full Literary, Law, Medical, or Civil and Mining Engineering Course; the first requiring four, the two next two, and the last, three years.

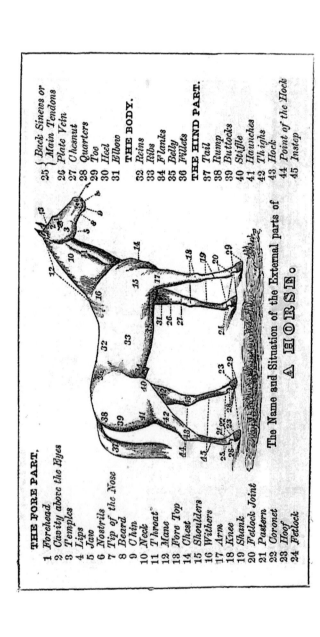

THE FORE PART.

1 Forehead
2 Cavity above the Eyes
3 Temples
4 Lips
5 Jaw
6 Nostrils
7 Tip of the Nose
8 Beard
9 Chin
10 Neck
11 Throat
12 Mane
13 Fore Top
14 Chest
15 Shoulders
16 Withers
17 Arm
18 Knee
19 Shank
20 Fetlock Joint
21 Pastern
22 Coronet
23 Hoof
24 Fetlock

25 { Back Sinews or
     { Main Tendons
26 Plate Vein
27 Chesnut
28 Quarters
29 Toe
30 Heel
31 Elbow

THE BODY.

32 Reins
33 Ribs
34 Flanks
35 Belly
36 Fillets

THE HIND PART.

37 Tail
38 Rump
39 Buttocks
40 Stifle
41 Haunches
42 Thighs
43 Hock
44 Point of the Hock
45 Instep

The Name and Situation of the External parts of

A HORSE.

DR. CHASE'S RECIPES;

OR,

INFORMATION FOR EVERYBODY:

AN INVALUABLE COLLECTION OF

ABOUT EIGHT HUNDRED

PRACTICAL RECIPES,

FOR

Merchants, Grocers, Saloon-Keepers, Physicians, Druggists, Tanners,
Shoe Makers, Harness Makers, Painters, Jewelers, Blacksmiths,
Tinners, Gunsmiths, Farriers, Barbers, Bakers, Dyers,
Renovaters, Farmers, and Families Generally,

TO WHICH HAVE BEEN ADDED

A Rational Treatment of Pleurisy, Inflammation of the Lungs.
and other Inflammatory Diseases, and also for General
Female Debility and Irregularities:

All arranged in their Appropriate Departments.

BY A. W. CHASE. M. D.,

STEREOTYPED

CAREFULLY REVISED, ILLUSTRATED, AND MUCH ENLARGED,
WITH REMARKS AND FULL EXPLANATIONS.

We Learn to Live, by Living to Learn.

IN CLOTH, $1.25; PAPER COVERS, $1.00;
MOROCCO GILT, $2.00.
THE GERMAN IN CLOTH ONLY, $1.25.

ANN ARBOR, MICHIGAN
PUBLISHED BY R. A. BEAL.
1 8 7 0.

FIFTY - SECOND EDITION—THREE HUNDRED AND NINETY-FIVE
THOUSAND—ENGLISH AND GERMAN.

PREFACE

———

Is bringing a permanent work, or one that is designed so to be, before the public, it is expected of the Author that he give his reasons for such publication. If the reasons are founded in truth, the people consequently seeing its necessity, will appreciate its advantages, and encourage the Author by quick and extensive purchases, they alone being the judges. Then:

FIRST.—Much of the information contained in "Dr. Chase's Receipes; or Information for Everybody," has never before been published, and is adapted to every day use.

SECOND.—The Author, after having carried on the Drug and Grocery business for a number of years, read Medicine, after being thirty-eight years of age, and graduated as a Physician to qualify himself for the work he was undertaking; for, having been familiar with some of the Recipes, adapted to these branches of trade, more than twenty years, he began in "Fifty-six," seven years ago, to publish them in a Pamphlet of only a few pages, since which time he has been traveling between New York and Iowa, selling the work and Prescribing, so that up to this time, "Sixty-three," over *twenty-three thousand* copies have been sold. His travels have brought him in contact with all classes of Professional and Business men, Mechanics, Farmers, and Farmers, thus enabling him to obtain from them many additional items, always having had his *note book* with him, and whenever a prescription has been given before him, or a remark made, that would have a *practical* bearing, it has been *noted*, and at the first opportunity *tested*, then if good, written out in *plain* language expressly for the next edition of

this work. In this way this mass of information has been col·
lected, and ought to take away an objection which some persons
nave raised : " It is too much for one man to know !" because
they did not realize that the work had been made up from *others*
as well as the Author's *actual every day experience*, instead of
from *untried* books. Yet from the nature of some of the Recipes,
one has occasionally found its way into some of the earlier edi·
tions, which have needed revision, or to be entirely dropped.
This, with a desire to add to the various Departments, at every
edition, has kept us from having it Stereotyped until the present,
tenth edition.

But now, all being what we desire; and the size of the work
being such that we cannot *add* to it without increasing the price

we have it Stereotyped, and send it out, just what we expect, and are willing it should remain.

THIRD.—Many of the Recipe books published are very large,
containing much *useless* matter, only to increase the number,
consequently costing too much—this one contains only about
eight hundred recipes, upon only about four hundred different
subjects, *all* of which are valuable in daily, practical life, and at
a very reasonable price—many of them are without arrangement—this one is arranged in regular Departments, all of a class
being together—many of them are without remark, or explanation—this one is fully explained, and accompanied with remarks
upon the various subjects introduced by the Recipes under consideration—those remarks, explanations, and suggestions accompanying the Recipes, are a special feature of *this* work, making
it worth double its cost as a *reading* book, even if there was not
a prescription in it.

FOURTH.—The remarks and explanations are in *large* type,
whilst the *prescriptive* and *descriptive* parts are in a little smaller
type, which enables any one to see at a glance just what they
wish to find.

FIFTH.—It is a well known fact that many unprincipled per·
sons go around " gulling" the people by selling single Recipes
for exorbitant prices. The Author found a thing, calling him·

self a man, in Battle Creek, Mich., selling a Washing-Fluid Recipe for two dollars, which he obtained of some; but if he could not obtain that, he would take two *shillings*, or any other sum between them. A merchant gave a horse for the "White Cement" Recipe. The late Mr. Andrews, of Detroit, Mich., gave *three hundred dollars* for a Recipe, now improved and in this work, to cure a bone spavin upon a race mare of his. He removed the spavin with it and won the anticipated wager with her. The Author has, himself, paid from twenty-five to fifty, and seventy-five cents, and one to two, three five, and eight dollars for single items, or Recipes, hoping thereby to improve his work; but often finding that he had much *better* ideas already embodied therein.

The amount *paid* for information in *this* work, and for testing by experiment, together with traveling expenses, and cuts used in illustrating it, have reached over two thousand dollars, and all for the purpose of making a book worthy to be found in "Everybody's" library, and to prevent such extortions in the *price* of Recipes. Yet any single Recipe in the work which a person may wish to *use*, will often be found worth *many* times the price of the book, perhaps the *lives* of those you dearly love, by having at hand the necessary information enabling you to *immediately* apply the means within your reach, instead of giving time for disease to strengthen, whilst sending, perhaps miles, for a physician. Much pain and suffering, also, will often be saved or avoided, besides the satisfaction of *knowing* how many things are made which you are constantly *using*, and also being able to avoid many things which you *certainly* would *avoid*, if you *knew* how they were made.

Sixth.—It will be observed that we have introduced a *number* of Recipes upon some of the subjects; this adapts the work to all circumstances and places; the reason for it is this; we have become acquainted with them in our practice and journeyings, and know that when the articles cannot be obtained for one way, they may be for some other way; as also that one prescription is better for some than for other persons; therefore, we give the variety that all may be benefitted as much as possible. For instance, there are twenty different prescriptions for different diseases, and conditions of the eye; there are also a dozen different liniments, &c., &c.; yet the Author feels well assured that the most perfect satisfaction will be experienced in them as a whole. And although it could not be expected that special advantages of particular Recipes could be pointed out to any great extent, yet the Author must be indulged in referring to a few, in the various Departments. All, or nearly all, Merchants and Grocers, as also most Families, will be more or less benefited by the directions for making or preserving butter, preserving eggs, or fruit, computing interest, making vinegar, and keeping cider palatable, &c. In ague sections of country, none should be without the information on this subject; and in fact, there is not a medical subject introduced but what will be found more or less valuable to every one; even Physicians will be more than compensated in its perusal; whilst Consumptive, Dyspeptic, Rheumatic, and Fever patients ought, by all means, to avail themselves of the advantages here pointed out. The treatment in Female Debility, and the observations on the Changes in female life are such that every one of them over thirteen or fourteen years of age should not be without this work. The directions in Pleurisy and other Inflammatory diseases cannot fail to benefit every family into whose hands the book shall fall.

The Good Samaritan Liniment, we do not believe, has its equal in the world, for common uses, whilst there are a number of other liniments equally well adapted to particular cases. And we would not undertake to raise a family of children without our Whooping Cough Syrup and Croup Remedies, knowing their value as we do, if it cost a hundred dollars to obtain them Tanners and Shoemakers, Painters and Blacksmiths, Tinners and Gunsmiths, Cabinet Makers, Barbers and Bakers will find in their various Departments more than enough, in single recipes, to compensate them for the expense of the work; and Farriers and Farmers who deal in horses and cattle, will often find that Department to save a hundred times its cost in single cases of disease.

A gentleman recently called at my house for one of the books.

saying: "I have come ten miles out of my way to get it, for I staid over night with a farmer, who had one, and had been benefitted more than $20, in curing a horse by its directions." A gentleman near this city says he had paid out dollars after dollars to cure a horse of spavin, without benefit, as directed by *other* books, of recipes; but a few shillings, as directed by *this*, cured the horse. Another gentleman recently said to me: "Your Eye Water is worth more than $20." I could fill pages of similar statements which have come to my knowledge since I commenced the publication of this work, but must be content by asking all to look over our References, which have been voluntarily accumulating during the seven years in which the work has been in growing up to its present size and perfection; and the position in society, of most of the persons making these statements is such, many of which are entire strangers to the Author and to each other, that any person can see that no possible complicity could exist between us, even if we desired it

Families will find in the Baking, Cooking, Coloring and Miscellaneous Departments, all they will need, without the aid of any other "Cook Book;" and the Washing-Fluid, which we have used at every washing except two for nearly eight years, is worth to every family of eight or ten persons, ten times the cost of the book, yearly, saving both in labor and wear of clothes.

SEVENTH.—Many of the articles can be gathered from garden, field or woods, and the others will always be found with Druggists, and most of the preparations will cost only from *one-half* to as low as *one-sixteenth* as much as to purchase them already made; and the only certainty, now-a-days, of having a good article, is to make it yourself.

FINALLY.—There is one or two things *fact* about this book; It is the biggest humbug of the day; or it is the best work of the kind, published in the English language. If a careful perusal does not satisfy *all* that it is *not the first*, but that it *is the last*, then will the Author be willing to acknowledge that Testing, Experimenting, Labor, Travel and Study, to be of no account in qualifying a man for such a work, especially when that work has been the long cherished object of his life, for a lasting benefit to his fellow creatures, saving them from *extortion*, in buying single recipes, and also giving them a reliable work, for every emergency, *more* than for his own pecuniary benefit. Were it not so, I should have kept the work smaller as heretofore, for the eighth edition of two hundred and twenty-four pages when handsomely bound sold for One Dollar,   but in this edition you get a Dollar's worth of *book*, even if common reading matter, besides the most reliable *practical* information, by which you will *often* save, not only *dollars* and *cents*, but relieve *suffering* and prolong *life*. It is, in fact, a perfect mass of the most valuable methods of accomplishing the things spoken of, an Encyclopedia upon the various branches of Science and Art, treated of in the work, which no family can afford to do without; indeed, young and old, "Everybody's" book. And the "Taxes" nor "Times" should be, for a moment, argued against the purchase of so valuable a work, *especially when we assure you that the book is sold only by Traveling Agents, that all may have a chance to purchase ; for if left at the Book Stores, or by Advertisement only, not One in Fifty would ever see it.*

Some persons object to buying a book of Recipes, as they are constantly receiving so many in the newspapers of the day, but if they had all that this book contains, scattered through a number of years of accumulated papers, it would be worth *more* than the price of this work to have them gathered together, carefully arranged in their appropriate departments, with an alphabetical index, and handsomely bound; besides the advantage of their having passed under the Author's carefully *pruning* and *grafting* hand.

"To uproot error and do good should be the first and highest aspiration of every intelligent being. He who labors to promote th. physical perfection of his race—he who strives to make mankind intelligent, healthy, and happy—cannot fail to have reflected on his own soul the benign smiles of those whom he has been the instrument of benefitting." The Author has recieved too many expressions of gratitude, thankfulness, and favor, in regard to the value of "Dr. Chase's Recipes; or Information for Everybody," to doubt in the least, the truth of the foregoing quotation: and trusts that the following quotation

may not be set down to " Egotism" or " Bigotry," when he gives
't as the *governing* reason for the continued and permanent publication of the work:

"I live to *learn* their story, who suffered for my sake ;
  To emulate their glory, and follow in their wake ;
Bards, patriots, martyrs, sages, and noble of all ages,
  Whose deeds crown History's pages, and Time's great volume make

"I live for those who love me, for those who know me true,
  For the heaven that smiles above me, and awaits my spirit too ;
For the cause that lacks assistance, for the wrong that needs resistance.
  For the future in the distance, and the *good* that I can do."

May these reasons *speedily* become the governing principles
throughout the world, especially with all those who have taken
upon themselves the vows of our "Holy Religion;" *knowing*
that it is to those *only* who begin to love God, and right actions,
here, with whom the glories of Heaven shall ever *begin*. Were
they thus heeded, we should no longer need coroborating testimony to our statements. Now, however, we are obliged to
array every point before the people, as a *Mirror*, that they may
judge *understandingly*, even in matters of the most vital importance to themselves; consequently we must be excused for this
lengthy Preface, Explanatory Index, and extended References
following it. Yet, that there are some who will let the work go
by them as one of the "Humbugs of the day," notwithstanding
all that has or might be said, we have no doubt; but we beg to
refer such to the statement amongst our References, of the Rev.
C. P. Nash, of Muskegon, Mich., who, although he allowed it
thus to pass him, could not rest satisfied when he saw the *relia-
bility* of the work purchased by his *less incredulous* neighbors;
then if you *will*, let it go by; but it is hoped that all *purchasers*
may have sufficient confidence in the work not to allow it to
lay idle; for, that the designed and greatest possible amount of
good shall be accomplished by it, it is only necessary that it
should be *generally introduced, and daily used*, is the positive
knowledge of the

                                            AUTHOR.

INDEX.

MEDICAL DEPARTMENT.

PAGE

INDEX.

WHITEWASH AND CHEAP PAINTS.

COLORING DEPARTMENT.

INTEREST DEPARTMENT.

GLOSSARIAL, EXPLANATORY, DEPARTMENT.

INDEX TO ILLUSTRATIONS.

REFE_.ENCES.

ANN ARBOR REFERENCES.

The following statements are given by my *neighbors*, to whom I had sent the eighth edition of my "Recipes," asking their opinions of its *value* for the people, most of whom had previously purchased earlier editions of the work, and several of them used many of the Recipes; and surely their *position* in society must place their statements above all suspicion of *complicity* with the author in palming off a worthless book; but are designed to *benefit the people by increasing the spread of genuine practical information* :

Hon. ALPHEUS FELCH, one of our first lawyers, formerly a Senator in Congress, and also ex-Governor of Michigan, says:—
Please accept my thanks for the copy of your "Recipes," which you were so good as to send me. The book seems to me to contain *much valuable practical information*, and I have no doubt will be extensively useful.

A. WINCHELL, Professor of Geology, Zoology and Botany, in the University of Michigan, and also State Geologist, says:—I have examined a large number of Recipes in Dr. Chase's published collection, and from my knowledge, either experimental or theoretical, of many of them, and my confidence in Dr Chase's carefulness, judgment, and conscientiousness in the selection of such only as are proved useful, after full trial, I feel no hesitation in saying that they may all be received with the utmost confidence in their practical value, except in those cases, where the Doctor has himself qualified his recommendations.

JAMES C. WATSON, formerly Professor of Astronomy, and now Professor of Physics, in the University of Michigan, author of a "Treatise on Comets," also of "Other Worlds, or the Wonders of the Telescope," says:—I have examined your book of practical Recipes, and do not hesitate to say that so-far as my observation and experience enable me to judge, it is a work which should find its way into every family in the land. The information which it contains could only have been collected by the most careful and long continued research, and is such as is required in every day life. I can heartily recommend your work to the patronage of the public.

Rev. L. D. CHAPIN, Pastor of the Presbyterian Church, says: Allow me to express to you my gratification in the perusal of your book. I do not regard myself as qualified to speak in regard to the whole book, for you enter into Departments in which I have no special knowledge, but where I understand the subject I find many things of much practical value for every practical man and house-keeper; and judging of those parts which I do not, by those which I do understand, I think that you have furnished a book that most families can afford to have at any reasonable price.

Rev. GEO. SMITH, Presiding Elder of the M. E. Church, Ann Arbor, says:—I take pleasure in saying that so far as I have examined, I have reason to believe that your Recipes are genuine, and *not* intended as a *catch-penny*, but think any person purchasing it will get the worth of their money.

Rev. GEO. TAYLOR, Pastor of Ann Arbor and Dixboro M. E. Church, writes as follows:—As per your request, I have carefully examined your book of Recipes, recently issued, and take pleasure in adding my testimony to the many you have already received, that I regard it as the best compilation of Recipes I have ever seen. Several of these Recipes we have used in our family for years, and count each of them worth the cost of your book.

Elder SAMUEL CORNELIUS, Pastor of the Baptist Church, writes:—I have looked over your book of "Information for Everybody," and as you ask my judgment of it, I say that it gives evidence of much industry and care on the part of the compiler, and contains information which must be valuable to all classes of business men, in town and country, and especially to all families who want to cook well, and have pleasant, healthy drinks, syrups and jellies; who wish to keep health when they enjoy it, or seek for it in an economical way. I thank you for the copy you sent to me, and hope you may make a great many families healthy and happy.

REV. F. A. BLADES, of the M. E. Church, and Pastor in charge, for two years, of Ann Arbor Station, says: Dr. Chase—Dear Sir— Your work of Recipes, I have examined—and used some of them for a year past—I do not hesitate to pronounce it a valuable work— containing information for the Million. I hope you will succeed in circulating it very generally—it is worthy a place in every house.

This gentleman speaks in the highest terms of the "Dyspeptic's Biscuit and Coffee," as of other recipes used.

EBERBACH & Co., Druggists, of Ann Arbor, say:—We have been filling prescriptions from "Dr. Chase's Recipes," for three or four years, and freely say that we do not know of any *dissatisfaction* arising from want of correctness; but on the other hand, we know that they give *general* satisfaction.

REV. S P. HILDRETH, of Dresden, O., a former neighbor, inclos- ing a recent letter, says: I have carefully examined your book, and regard it as containing a large amount of Information which will be valuable in every household.

REV. WILLIAM C. WAY, of the M. E. Church, Plymouth, Mich., says:—I have cured myself of Laryngitis, (inflammation of the throat,) brought on by long continued and constant public speaking, by the use of Dr. Chase's black oil, and also know a fever sore to have been cured upon a lady, by the use of the same article.

OPINIONS OF THE ANN ARBOR PRESS.

A NEW BOOK.—Dr. Chase, of this city, has laid on our table a new edition of his work entitled "Dr. Chase's Recipes, or Infor- mation for Everybody," for making all sorts of things, money not excepted. We would not, however, convey the idea that the Doctor tells you how to make spurious coin, or counterfeit bills, but by practicing upon the maxims laid down in this work, money-making is the certain result. Buy a book, and adopt the recipes in your households, on your farms, and in your business, and success is sure to follow. The work is neatly printed, elegantly bound, and undoubtedly embodies more useful informa- tion than any work of the kind now before the public.

Students, or others, wishing to engage in selling a *saleable* work, will do well to send for circulars describing the book, with terms to agents, &c., for it is indeed a work which "Everybody" ought to have.—*Michigan State News, Ann Arbor.*

DR. A. W. CHASE, of this city, has placed on our table a copy of his "Recipes, or Information for Everybody." Beginning with a small pamphlet, the Doctor has swelled his work to a bound volume of about 400 pages; an evidence tha* his labors are appreciated. The volume furnishes many recipes and much information of real practical value.—*Michigan Argus, Ann Arbor.*

DR. CHASE'S RECIPES.—The ninth edition of Dr. Chase's Recipes has been recently published, revised, illustrated and enlarged,—comprising a very large collection of practical information for business men, mechanics, artists, farmers, and for families generally. The recipes are accompanied with explanations and comments which greatly increase the value of the work. It is a handsomely bound volume, ⁓⁓⁓ ⁓⁓ ⁓.—*Ann Arbor Journal.*

DR. CHASE, of Ann Arbor, has favored us with a copy of his book of recipes, which has, in an unprecedented short time, reached the ninth edition, showing its popularity wherever it has been introduced. It contains " information for everybody," for making all sorts of things. It is a valuable work for every one—many single recipes being worth much more than the cost of the book. Rev. Mr. Frazer, the gentlemanly agent for the work, is now in the city, and will call upon our citizens giving them an oppprtunitv to secure a copy. The work is neatly printed, elegantly bound, and undoubtedly embodies more useful information than any work of the kind now before the public.
                    a better investment cannot be made by any one.—*Grand Rapids Eagle.*

DR. CHASE, of Ann Arbor, has favored us with a copy of Recipes which he has published, * * * * who claims that they have been made up from his own and others' every day experience. There are certainly a great many useful recipes in this work that be found to richly repay its cost to any family.—*Michigan Farmer, Detroit.*

The following wholesale dealers of Detroit, and others with whom I have dealt for years, say:—We have been acquainted with Dr. A W. Chase for several years in the Drug and Grocery business, and we are well satisfied that he would not do a business which he did not know was all right. His information in the form of recipes can be depended upon.

GEO. BEARD, Dealer in Oysters and Fruit, Detroit.
WM. PHELPS & CO., Confectioners, Detroit, Michigan.
JOHN J. BAGLEY, Tobacconist, Detroit, Michigan.
SAMUEL J. REDFIELD, M. D., Wyandotte, Michigan.
RICHARD MEAD, Merchant, Bark Shanty, Michigan.
JOHN ROBERTSON, Captain of Steamer Clifton.
H. FISH, Captain of Steamer Sam. Ward.
C. A. BLOOD, former partner, Belle River, Michigan.

THE COURIER

STEAM PRINTING-HOUSE,

ANN ARBOR, MICHIGAN,

Was first built in 1864, (22x70 feet, four stories, including the basement, which is used for the Press-room), mainly for the purpose of enabling the proprietor to meet the increasing demand for "DR. CHASE'S RECIPES," at which time one-half of one story gave ample room for one Department of the business. But in 1865 he purchased the PENINSULAR COURIER, and began to do

JOB PRINTING AND BOOK-BINDING.

Adopting the motto—GOOD WORK FOR THE LEAST POSSIBLE PRICE—it soon became necessary to occupy the whole of one story for each branch or Department; and ultimately finding our rooms too small for the work demanded at our hands, in the summer of 1868, we made an addition of 40x70 feet, finishing each story in one room, the Bindery, Compositors, Press-room and Office being each 39x68 feet, putting in a 22 horse Boiler and Engine, one of Hoe's largest "Jobbers," upon which a sheet 39x56 inches can be printed—no other Press in the State equal to it in size,—also another large Adams' Book Press, upon which SIXTEEN OCTAVO pages can be worked, (while nearly all other Western printing establishments can only work eight pages, our press-work costing only ONE-HALF as much as theirs), with much other machinery and furnishing employment for OVER FORTY HANDS, and

SEVEN POWER PRESSES

MAKING IT THE

MOST COMPLETE PRINTING-HOUSE IN THE WEST

Clergymen, Lawyers and others who may desire the publication of Books, Pamphlets, Briefs, Sermons, Reports, Minutes, By-Laws, &c., &c., will find it greatly to their advantage to correspond with us before contracting elsewhere. Estimates cheerfully and promptly furnished.

In sending for Estimates, please give the size of page, size of type, number of pages, number of copies and style of binding.

Since purchasing the PENINSULAR COURIER, we have changed its name to

THE PENINSULAR COURIER AND FAMILY VISITANT

BESIDES GREATLY ENLARGING IT, AND IT IS NOW ACKNOWLEDGED TO BE THE

LARGEST, CHEAPEST, AND BEST FAMILY NEWSPAPER IN THE STATE

In proof of this assertion we have only to state that at the time of its purchase the circulation was less than 300, now OVER SIXTEEN HUNDRED copies, *(being more than double that of any other paper in the County,)* and our subscription list is constantly increasing.—Devoted to News, Politics, Temperance, Morality and Religion—Soundly Republican, ALIVE, in all its Departmen's,

TERMS:

$2 00 a year in advance. DR. CHASE'S RECIPES, by mail post paid, $1 25.
THE JUDD FAMILY, $1 00; VOYAGE AROUND THE WORLD, $1 00.

Address all orders to

R. A. BEAL, Proprietor.

DR. CHASE'S RECIPES

MERCHANTS' AND GROCERS' DEPARTMENT.

VINEGAR.—Merchants and Grocers who retail vinegar should always have it made under their own eye, if possible, from the fact that so many unprincipled men enter into its manufacture, as it affords such a large profit. And I would further remark, that there is hardly any article of domestic use, upon which the mass of the people have as little correct information as upon the subject of making vinegar. I shall be brief in my remarks upon the different points of the subject, yet I shall give all the knowledge necessary, tha families, or those wishing to manufacture, may be able to have the best article, and at moderate figures. Remember this fact—that vinegar must have air as well as warmth, and especially is this necessary if you desire to make it in a short space of time. And if at any time it seems to be "Dying," as is usually called, add molasses, sugar, alcohol, or cider—whichever article you are making from, or prefer —for vinegar is an industrious fellow; he will either work or die, and when he begins to die you may know he has worked up all the material in his shop, and wants more. Remember this in all vinegars, and they will never die, if they have air. First, then, upon a small scale, for family use.

To MAKE IN THREE WEEKS.—Molasses 1 qt.; yeast 1 pt.; warm rain water 3 gals. Put all into a jug or keg, and tie a piece of gauze over the bung to keep out flies and let in air. In hot weather set it in the sun; in cold weather set it by the stove or in the chimney corner, and in three weeks you will have good vinegar.

When this is getting low, pour out some for use, and fill

2—DR. CHASE'S RECIPES.

up the jug in the same proportion as at first, and you will never have trouble for want of good vinegar.

2. A correspondent of the Dollar Newspaper says: "The cheapest mode of making good vinegar is, to mix 5 qts. of warm rain water with 2 qts. of Orleans molasses, and 4 qts of yeast. In a few weeks you will have the best vinegar you ever tasted." He might well say, "The best vinegar you ever tasted," for it would have double the necessary strength, and three or four times the strength of much that is sold; yet this strength would cost less to make, than to buy by the quart.

3. In Barrels Without Trouble.—Merchants and Grocers, who retail vinegar, can always keep a good supply on hand by having about two or three barrels out of which to sell, by filling the first one they sell out, before quite empty, with

Molasses 1 gal.; soft water 11 gals.

Keeping this proportion to fill the barrel; the vinegar and mother which is left in the barrel makes it work much quicker than if put into empty barrels; so pass around on the next barrel as it is nearly out, having three barrels, and unless you sell more than a barrel a week, you need never be out of vinegar. Some recommend to use alum, cream of tartar. &c., in vinegar, but I say, never. It is always advisable to have a hole in the top of the barrel, if standing on end; if on the side, the bung out and a gauze over it, to keep out flies and let air in.

4. From Sugar, Drippings from Sugar Hogsheads, &c.—Dealers who retail molasses, often have from five to fifty pounds of sugar left in the barrel after selling out the molasses. Each pound of this, or other sugar, dissolved in two gallons of soft water, makes that amount of good vinegar by either of the above plans. Rinsings of molasses barrels or drippings of sugar hogsheads brought to this degree of sweetness, is as good for vinegar as any other material. Small beer, lager beer, ale, &c., which have become sour, make good vinegar by reducing with water; small beer will need but little water; lager beer will need as much water as beer, or a little more; and ale, twice as much water as ale; they will all need yeast, a quart or two to each barrel, unless put into barrels which have some vin-

egar in them, and it will do no harm, but quicken the process in all cases if there is vinegar in the barrel.

5. FROM ACETIC ACID AND MOLASSES.—Acetic acid 4 lbs; molasses 1 gal.; put them into a 40 gallon cask, and fill it up with rain water; shake it up and let stand from one to three weeks, and the result is good vinegar.

If this does not make it as sharp as you like, add a little more molasses. But some will object to this because an acid is used: let me say to such, that acetic acid is *concentrated* vinegar. Take 1 lb. or 1 pt. or any other quantity of this acid, and add seven times as much soft water, and you have just as good vinegar as can be made from *cider*, and that *instantaneously*.

6. FROM APPLE CIDER.—As there are those who will not have any but cider vinegar, and have plenty of cider out of which to make it, I will give you the best plan of proceeding for manufacturers:

Have a room where it will not freeze; place on end as many barrels or large casks, witho ut heads, to hold as much as you wish to make; fill these one-third full of soft water, and the other two thirds with apple cider; yeast 2 q ts. to each cask.

In a few weeks you will have good vinegar; without the yeast it would be all the season in becoming good. Then fill up into barrels for sale, leaving a little, say one-eighth, in the open barrels, and fill them up with water and cider as before. and it will become good much quicker than before. If the water is objected to, use the cider without it, but pure cider makes vinegar too strong for any one to use, and requires much longer time in making. These barrels may have boards over them to keep out flies and dirt. If the retailer can give it his attention, by having a barrel of good cider vinegar to sell out of, he can always keep it up, if, when he draws out two or three gallons of the vinegar, he will go to his cider, kept for the purpose, and replace the vinegar with the cider; or if making with molasses and water or any other article, fill up with the same; but take notice, if you forget or neglect, and draw your vinegar nearly all out before you fill in, it does not keep to the point of sharpness desired, unless you have two or three barrels as mentioned in recipe No. 2

Persons who have old sour cider on hand can in this way, or as mentioned in No. 6, have good vinegar from it immediately, as it comes around into vinegar much quicker than new cider.

7. IN THREE DAYS WITHOUT DRUGS.—The philosophy of making vinegar quickly, is this : The means that will expose the largest surface of the vinegar fluid, of a certain temperature, to the air, will convert it into vinegar in the shortest time ; and as there is no way by which so great a surface can be exposed as by the shavings process, and at the same time control the temperature, that plan has been adopted, as explained in the wood cut accompanying, and in the descriptive note :

Main cover, or loose boards,...............
Vinegar Fluid Space,.....................
False top, with tubes ; and cords hanging
   through it,..........,..... ....

Center portion of the tub, which should
   be filled with the shavings to within an
   an inch or two of the false top........

Holes to le in air..,.....................

The square projections on the side of the
   Generator represent hoops.

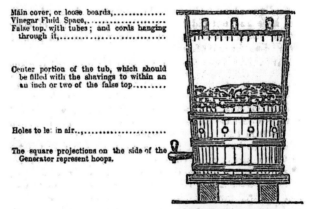

VINEGAR GENERATOR.

DESCRIPTIVE NOTE.—Those wishing to manufacture, to sell at wholesale, will prepare a tub, or square box, and arrange it as shown in the accompanying cut, knowing that the taller and larger the tub, the quicker will the vinegar become good. The air holes are bored through every other, or every third stave, around the whole tub. These holes are to be about one foot or eighteen inches from the bottom ; they must also be bored slanting down as you bore inward, othewise the vinegar would run out and waste as it drips down the side of the tub. These tubs ought to be from ten to twenty feet high, according to the quantity you desire to run off daily. Now take beech made or basswood boards—and they are valuable in the order named—cut them off about eighteen inches in length, and plane thick, heavy shavings from the edges; and if they do not roll up and stay in nice rolls, you must roll and tie them up with small cord; or clean corn cobs will do, but they will only last one season, whilst the shavings will last several years. If cobs are used, they must be put in layers, each layer crossing the other, to prevent their packing too close. Then wet or soak them thoroughly in water, and fill up the tub or tubs with them, until you are within two or three feet of the top, at which place you will nail a stout hoop around, upon the inside of the tub, which shall support the *false top*, which has been made and fitted for that purpose, through which false top you will have bored good sized gimlet holes about every two inches all over its whole surface, through each of which holes a small cord, about four or five inches in length, is to be drawn, having a knot tied upon its upper end to keep it in its place, and to prevent the vinegar-fluid from working out too fast. The size of these holes, and the size of the cord, must be such as to allow the amount of vinegar being made to run through every twelve hours, or if time can be given to put it up so often, it may run through every six hours. You will cork all around between the false top and the tub with cotton, which causes the vinegar-fluid, hereafter to be described, to pass through the gimlet holes and drip from the ends of the small cords, evenly, all over the shavings, otherwise, if the false top was not exactly level, the vinegar-fluid would all run off at the lowest point, down the side of the tub, and be a very long time in becoming good, whilst if it drips slowly and all over and down through the shavings, it soon comes around into good vinegar. The holes bored for that purpose, in warm weather, oxidizes or acetifies the vinegar-fluid, by affording the *two* essential points of quickly making good vinegar, that is, *air* and *heat*, without the expense of a fire to warm the fluid, or room in which the vinegar is made. Now bore five one-inch holes through the false top, one of them through the center, and the others two-thirds of the distance each way, towards the outside of the tub, into which holes drive as many pins, having a three-quarter inch hole bored through them lengthwise, which makes them tubes; cut the tubes off an inch below the top of the tub, so as to be out of the way of the main cover or loose boards which will be thrown over the top of the tub for the purpose of keeping out flies and dirt, and also to keep the *heated* air in, which comes up through the tubes; this air becomes heated by the chemical action of the air upon the vinegar fluid as it drips along down through the shavings in the tub, becoming so hot that it would be uncomfortable to hold the hand therein. The space between the false top and the cover is called the vinegar fluid space; and it must be sufficiently tight in the joints of the tub, or box, to hold the fluid when put in. Now take a barrel of good vinegar and pour it into the top or the tub, and let it drip through the gimlet holes, from the cords, over the shavings, two or three times, each time putting in one gallon of highwines, or two or three gallons of cider, as the case may be, which sours the shavings and greatly helps the starting process of the vinegar-making. Without the addition to the strength of the vinegar as it runs through, it would part with nearly all of its own strength or acidity, to the shavings and thus lose its own life. If you have not, nor cannot obtain, vinegar, to start with, you must begin with weak vinegar-fluid, and keep adding to it every time through until it becomes very sour; then you will consider yourself ready to begin to make vinegar in double quick time, by using any of the fluids mentioned in the foregoing vinegar recipes. But manufacturers generally use highwines thirty to forty per cent above proof, one gallon; water, eleven gallons; but persons living a great distance from market will find a cheaper plan by using ninety-eight per cent alchol, one gallon; water fifteen gallons; either of which make good vinegar, using yeast of course, with either article, from one pint to one quart to each barrel being made. Another tub or vat must be set in the ground, under the generator, or in a cellar, as the case may be, to hold as much vinegar as the space between the false and real top will contain, or as much as you wish to make at one time; from which it is to be carried up in buckets, (or a wooden pump having a leather sucker is quicker and easier to raise it,) to the top of the generator until it becomes good vinegar, which it will do in the time mentioned at the head of this recipe, if passed through the generator by the faucet every twelve hours which it must be; and if the tubs are fifteen or twenty feet high, it will only need passing through once, or *twice* at most.

Some will have no vinegar but that made from apple cider; then put in one-third water, and it makes vinegar as strong as anybody ought to use; but if they will have it at full strength, make it so, only it requires a little longer time to make.

If those who have cider which has been standing a long time, and does not become vinegar, will reduce it one third with water, and pass it through this machine, they will grind out first rate vinegar in one or two days' time. Sour beer or ale, the artificial cider, also, if it gets sour, make good vinegar when mixed with some other vinegar in making. Small beer, also drippings from sugar hogsheads in place of molasses, &c. Nothing having sugar or alcohol in it should be thrown away, as all will make good vinegar, which is as good as cash, and ought to be saved—if for no other purpose than to have the more to give the worthy poor.

J. was at first thought to be absolutely necessary to make the vinegar-fluid of about seventy-five degrees of heat, and also to keep the room of the same temperature; but it has been found that by keeping the heat in the tub by the false top and the loose cover, that in warm weather it does very well without heating up the fluid, although it would make a little quicker with it; and if desired to make in cold weather, you must heat the fluid and keep the room warm also.

If families choose to try this plan, they can make all they will need in a keg not larger than a common churn, whilst wholesalers will use tubs as tall as their rooms will admit.

The first merchant to whom I sold this recipe, made all the vinegar he could retail by placing strips of board across the centre of a whisky barrel, which supported the shavings in the upper half only, allowing the vinegar to stand in the lower half; as his room was so low, he could only use the one barrel and a wash tub at the top instead of the false-top and space as represented in our cut; it took him only a week to make it in this way. I used the vinegar over a year. The strength of the fluid he used was good common whisky, one gal.; water, four gals. So it will be seen that all kinds of spirit, or articles containing spirit, can be made into vinegar.

REMARK—If you wish to make *sugar* into vinegar, do not attempt to run it through the *generator*, as it forms mother in that way, and soon fills up the little holes; but make it by standing in a barrel, as mentioned under that head, No. 4.

8. QUICK PROCESS, BY STANDING UPON SHAVINGS.—Take 4 or 5 hogsheads or casks, and set them side by side, having a faucet near the bottom; then fill up the casks full of shavings prepared as in the foregoing recipe, or clean corn-cobs, putting some turning shavings over the top, after having put on an old coffee sack to keep the fine shavings from falling down among the coarse ones; this is to keep in the warmth; now sour the shavings with the best vinegar, by throwing it on the shavings and letting it stand half a day or so; then draw off by the faucet at the bottom, and throw it on again, adding 1 qt. of high-wines to each barrel each time you draw it off, as the shavings absorb the acid, and the vinegar would become flat, but by adding the spirit the shavings become soured or acetified, and the vinegar gets better also. When the shavings are right, take highwines 30 or 40 per cent above proof 1 gal.; molasses 1 qt.; soft water 14 gals.; (river or well water will do, but not as good

for any vinegar) and put it upon the shavings, and draw off and
put on again from one to three times daily, until sufficiently
sour to barrel up.

Mr. Jackson, a Grocer, of Jackson, Michigan, has been
making in this way for several years. He uses also, sour
ale, rinsings of sugar hogsheads, or the drippings, and
throws this fluid on the shavings, and draws off and returns
from one to three times each day until sufficiently sour to barrel up, which only requires a few drawings; he then fills his
barrels only two-thirds full, and leaves the bungs out summer and winter, and if he finds a barrel is getting weak in
strength, he puts in a quart of highwines, which recruits
the strength, or gives it work again, which, as I remarked
before, if you give him stock to work on, and air, he labors
—without both, he dies. *Bear this in mind*, and your vinegar will improve all the time, no matter how, or of what it
is made. He fills the tubs only one-third or one-half full
when making, does not heat, but uses yeast, and only works
them in warm weather, and in winter fills the tubs with
good vinegar, and lets them stand over until spring, when
they are ready for work again.

This man, with five casks thus managed, has sold over
three hundred barrels of vinegar in one season.

It might not be amiss, in closing this *long* subject, to say
that when you have no vinegar to begin with in *either* of
the processes, that if you commence with the fluid quite
weak at first, it begins to sour quicker than if begun with at
full strength, then as it begins to become sour, add more of
the spirit, cider, sugar, or molasses, &c., until you get the
desired point of strength. So you might go on until a swallow of it would strangle a man to death, and remove every
particle of skin from his throat.

BUTTER.—To Preserve any Length of Time.—First
—work out all the buttermilk. Second—use rock salt. Third
—pack in air-tight jars or cans. Fourth—keep in a cool place,
and you will have nice butter for years, if desired to keep so
long. A short recipe, but it makes long butter.

Merchants, who take in more butter than they can sell
during the warm months, can put it into jars and cover the
jar with about half an inch of lard over the top of the butter, and place it in the cellar; or they can put about an

inch or two of brine in place of the lard, and have it do well, first working out all the *buttermilk* which may remain, when bought in.   It would be well for them to have their regular customers to furnish them butter, to whom they furnish the right kind of salt, as the rock, or crystal salt, does not contain so much lime as the common, which is evaporated by artificial heat.   Let sugar, and saltpeter, and all other *peters*, alone, if you wish good butter, either for present use or long keeping.

2. MAKING—DIRECTIONS FOR DAIRYMEN.—If butter makers cr dairymen, will use only shallow pans for their milk—and the larger the surface, and the less the depth of the milk the better—then put into each pan, before straining, 1 qt. of cold spring-water to every 3 qts. of milk, they will find the cream will begin to rise immediately, and skim every 12 hours, the butter will be free from all strong taste arising from leaves, or coarse pasturage.

It is a fact, also, that high or up-land makes better butter than when the cows are kept on rich bottom pasturage.   The object of the cold water is double : it cools the milk, so that the cream rises before the milk sours, (for when milk becomes sour it furnishes no more cream,) and also improves the flavor.

3. STORING—THE (ILLINOIS) PRAIRIE FARMER'S METHOD.— First, work the buttermilk carefully from the butter; then pack it closely in jars, laying a thin cloth on top of the butter, then a thin layer of salt upon the cloth ; now have a dry cellar, or make it so by draining, and dig a hole in the bottom of it for each jar, packing the dirt closely and tightly around the jar, allowing the tops of the jars to stand only an inch or so above the top of the cellar bottom ; now place a board with a weight upon each jar to prevent removing by accident, and all is safe.

Merchants who are buying in butter, should keep each different lot separate, by using the thin cloth and salt, then another cloth over the salt before putting in the next lot, for mixed butter will soon spoil, besides not selling as well, and finally cover the top as before described.   If kegs or barrels are used, the outside must be as well painted as possible to prevent outside tastes, and also to preserve the wood.

FRUITS TO KEEP.—WITHOUT LOSS OF COLOR OR FLAVOR. —To each pound of rosin, put in 1 oz. of tallow, and 1 oz. of beeswax.   Melt them slowly over the fire in an iron kettle, and be careful and not let it boil.   Take the fruit separately and rub it over with whiting or fine chalk (to prevent the coating from adhering to the fruit,) then dip it into the solution once and hold it up a moment to set the coating; then pack away carefully in barrels or boxes in a cool place. When you dip oranges or lemons, loop a thread around to hold them; for pears or apples, insert a pointed stick to hold them by, then cut it off with a pair of sharp, heavy shears. Oranges or lemons cannot be put in boxes but must be placed on shelves, as the accumulated weight would mash them down.

It is now a well established fact that articles put up scientifically air-tight, may be kept fresh and fair for any length of time, or until wanted for use. This composition makes good sealing for air-tight cans or bottles, pouring it around the top of the can cover, and dipping the neck of the bottle into it. A *patent* has been secured for a composition for preserving fruit, of different proportions, however, from the foregoing, but the agent, at the Ohio State Fair in 1859, had such poor success in selling rights at three dollars that he reduced the price to twenty-five cents, and still but few would take hold of it, so that I think not much more will be done with the patent. I purchased twenty recipes for one dollar, but finding his composition to stick together and tear off pieces wherever they touched each other, I went to work to improve it, as above. The patented proportions are, rosin 5 lbs., lard or tallow 8 oz., beeswax 4 oz. The patentee is John K. Jenkins, of Wyoming, Pa., and the patent was issued December 8, 1858. It does not work well on peaches or other juicy garden fruits.

EGGS.—To Preserve for Winter Use.—For every three gallons of water, put in 1 pt. of fresh slacked lime, and common salt 1-2 pt.; mix well, and let the barrel be about half full of this fluid, then with a dish let down your fresh eggs into it, tipping the dish after it fills with water, so they roll out without cracking the shell, for if the shell is cracked the egg will spoil.

If fresh eggs are put in, fresh eggs will come out, as I have seen men who have kept them two, and even four, years, at sea. A piece of board may be laid across the top of the eggs, and a little lime and salt kept upon it, which keeps the fluid as strong at the top as at the bottom. This will not fail you. They must always be kept covered with the brine. Families in towns and cities by this plan can have eggs for winter use at summer prices. I have put up forty dozen   , with entire success

The plan of preserving eggs has undoubtedly come from a patent secured by a gentleman in England in 1791, Jaynes, of Sheffield, Yorshire, which reads as follows:

2. ENGLISH PATENTED METHOD.—"Put into a tub 1 bu. Winchester measure, of quick lime, (which is fresh slacked lime,) salt 32 oz.; cream of tartar 8 oz. Use as much water as will give that consistency to the composition as will cause an egg to swim with its top just above the liquid. Then put and keep the eggs therein, which will preserve them perfectly sound at least 2 years."

Persons who think it more safe can follow this English plan. I desire in all cases to give all the information I have on each subject. Consequently I give you the following also:

3. J. W. COOPER, M. D.'s, METHOD OF KEEPING AND SHIPPING GAME EGGS.—"Dissolve some gum shellac in a sufficient quantity of alcohol to make a thin varnish, give each egg a coat, and after they become thoroughly dry, pack them in bran or saw dust, with their points downwards, in such a manner that they cannot shirt about. After you have kept them as long as you desire, wash the varnish carefully off, and they will be in the same state as they were before packing, ready for eating or hatching."

This would seem to be from good authority, as Dr. Cooper has been engaged for the last thirty years in raising nothing but the best game fowls, and he has frequently imported eggs. He invariably directed them to be packed as above, and always had good success with them, notwithstanding the time and distance of the journey. He has also published a work upon *Game Fowls.* His address is Media, Delaware Co., Pa.

This last plan would be a little more troublesome, but still would not be very much to prepare all that families would wish to use through the winter, or even for the retailers; as the convenience of having them in a condition to ship would be one inducement to use the last method, for with the first they must be taken out and packed in oats or something of that sort, to ship; with the last they are always ready; and weather permitting, about Christmas or New Year's, fresh and good eggs in cities always command sufficient price to pay for all trouble and expense in the preservation and shipment.

THE SEX OF EGGS.—Mr. Genin lately addressed the Academy des Sciences, France, on the subject of the sex of eggs. He affirms that he is now able, after having studied the subject for upwards of three years, to state with assurance that the eggs containing the germ of males, have wrinkles on their smaller ends, while female eggs are smooth at the extremities.

While on the subject of eggs, you will excuse me for putting in a couple of items more which appropriately belong to other departments:

4. TO INCREASE THE LAYING.—"For several years past I have spent a few weeks of the latter part of August on the Kennebec river, in Maine. The lady with whom I have stopped is a highly accomplished and intelligent housewife. She supports a "hennery" and from her I derived my information in the matter. She told me that for many years she had been in the habit of administering to her hens, with their common food:

"Cayenne pepper, pulverized, at the rate of 1 tea-spoon each alternate day to 1 doz. fowls.

"Last season, when I was with her, each morning she brought in from twelve to fourteen eggs, having but sixteen hens in all. She again and again experimented in the matter by omitting to feed with the Cayenne for two or three days. The consequence invariably was that the product of eggs fell off five or six per day. The same effect of using the Cayenne is produced in winter as in summer."—*Boston Transcript.*

5. TO FRY—EXTRA NICE.—Three eggs; flour 1 table-spoon milk 1 cup.

Beat the eggs and flour together, then stir in the milk. Have a skillet with a proper amount of butter in it, made hot, for frying this mixture; then pour it in, and when one side is done brown, turn it over, cooking rather slowly; if a larger quantity is needed, it will require a little salt stirred in, but for this amount, the salt in the butter in which you fry it, seasons it very nicely.

BURNING FLUID.—BEST IN USE.—Alcohol, of 98 per cent 9 pts.; good camphene 1 qt., or in these proportions. Shake briskly, and it will at once become clear, when without the shaking it would take from 6 to 7 qts. of alcohol to cut the camphene, while with the least it is the best.

These proportions make the best burning fluid which can be combined. Many put in camphor gum, alum, &c., the first to improve its burning qualities, the last to prevent explosion, but they are perfectly useless for either, from the fact that campnor adds to the smoking properties, and nothing can prevent the gas arising from any fluid that will burn, from explosion, if the fire gets to it when it is confined. The only safety is in filling lamps in day-time, or far from fire or lights; and also to have lamps which are perfect in their construction, so that no gas may leak out along the tube, or at the top of the lamp; then let who will say he can sell you a recipe for non-explosive gas or fluid, you may set him down at once for a humbug, ignoramus, or knave. Yet you may set fire to this fluid, and if not confined it will not explode, but will continue to burn until all is consumed. Families cannot make fluid any cheaper than to buy it, as the profit charged on the alcohol is usually more than that charged on fluid; but they will have a better article by this recipe than they can buy, unless it is made from the same, and it is best for any one, even the retailer, only to make small quantities at a time, and get the freshest camphene possible. When made in large quantities, even a barrel, unless sold out very soon, the last part is not as good as the first, owing to the separation of the camphene from the alcohol, unless frequently shaken, whilst being retailed out.

INTEREST.—COMPUTING BY ONE MULTIPLICATON AND ONE DIVISION, AT ANY RATE PER CENT.—Multiply the amount by the number of days, (counting 30 days to each month.)

Divided by 60 gives the interest at 6 per cent.

do	45	"	"	8	"
do	40	"	"	9	"
do	36	"	"	10	"
do	30	"	"	12	"

EXAMPLE.—$150 at 3 months and 10 days, or 100 days, is 15000, divided by 60 gives $2,50 which is the interest at 6 per cent; or divided by 45 gives $3,33 interest at 8 per cent, &c.

I sold a gentleman, a miller, one of my books the second time, as some person stole the first before he became familiar with the foregoing rules, which he admired too much to lose.

2 METHOD BY A SINGLE MULTIPLICATION.—RULE.—To find the interest on any given sum of money for any number of years, months or days. Reduce the years to months, add in the months if any, take one-third of the days and set to the right of the months, in decimal form, multiply this result by one-half the principal, and you have the interest required.

EXAMPLE.—The interest required on $1,400 for 2 years, 8 months, and 9 days:

Interest on $1,400 for 2 years, 8 months, and 9 days.

$$27.3$$
$$700$$

Answer required, $191.10.0

The above example is at six per cent. Rule to obtain the interest at any other rate : For seven per cent increase the interest at six per cent by one-sixth, for eight per cent by one-third, for nine per cent by one-half, for ten per cent by two-thirds, for eleven per cent by five-sixths, for twelve per cent multiply by two. Twelve per cent is the highest rate of interest allowed by any State, except Minnesota, which, I believe, allows fifteen per cent.

In pointing off, persons will observe to point off as many figures in the product or answer as there are decimal points in the multiplicand. The balance, or remainder, show you the dollars and cents.

COUNTERFEIT MONEY.—SEVEN RULES FOR DETECTING.—FIRST—Examine the form and features of all human figures on the notes. If the forms are graceful and features distinct, examine the drapery—see if the folds lie natural; and the hair of the head should be observed, and see if the fine strands can be seen.

SECOND.—Examine the lettering, the title of the bank, or the round handwriting on the face of the note. On all genuine bills, the work is done with great skill and perfectness, and there has never been a counterfeit but was defective in the lettering.

THIRD.—The imprint, or engraver's name. By observing the great perfection of the different company names-in the evenness and shape of the fine letters, counterfeiters never get the imprint perfect. This rule alone, if strictly observed, will detect every counterfeit note in existence.

FOURTH.—The shading in the back-ground of the vignette, or over or around the letters forming the name of the bank, on a good bill is even and perfect, on a counterfeit is irregular and imperfect.

FIFTH.—Examine well the figures on the other parts of the note, containing the denomination, also the letters. Examine well the die work around the figures which stand for the denomination, to see if it is of the same character as that which forms the ornamental work surrounding it.

SIXTH.—Never take a bill that is deficient in any of the above points, and if your impression is bad when you first see it, you had better be careful how you become convinced to change your mind—whether your opinion is not altered as you become confused in looking into the texture of the workmanship of the bill.

SEVENTH.—Examine the name of the State, name of the bank, and name of the town where it is located. If it has been altered from a broken bank, the defects can plainly be seen, as the alteration will show that it has been stamped on.

INKS—BLACK COPYING, OR WRITING FLUID.—Rain water 3 gals.; gum arabic ¼ lb.; brown sugar ¼ lb.; clean coperas ¼ lb.; powdered nutgalls ¾ lb.; bruise all, and mix, shaking occasionally for 10 days, and strain; if needed sooner, let it steep in an iron kettle until the strength is obtained.

This ink can be depended upon for deeds or records which you may wish some one to read hundreds of years to come. Oxalic acid one-fourth oz. was formerly put in, but since the use of steel pens it does not work well on them. If not used as a copying ink, one-fourth the gum or sugar is sufficient as it flows more free without them.

2. COMMON BLACK.—Logwood chips 1 lb.; boil in 1¼ gals. of water until reduced to 2 qts.; pour off, and repeat the boiling again as before; mix the two waters, 1 gal. in all; then add bi-chromate of potash ½ oz.; prussiate of potash ¼ oz.; prussiate of iron (prussian blue) ¼ oz.; boil again about 5 minutes. and strain and bottle for use.

You will find none of the guminess about this ink that is found in that made from the extract of logwood; yet it is not presumed that this will be as durable as the gall inks, for deeds, records, &c., &c., but for schools and common use it is as good as the most costly inks. This copy was prepared with it, which was made two years ago.

3. RED—THE VERY BEST.—Take an ounce vial and put into it a tea-spoon of aqua ammonia, gum arabic the size of 2 peas, and 6 grs. No. 40 carmine, and 5 grs. No. 6 or 8 carmine also; fill up with soft water and it is soon ready for use.

This forms a beautiful ruling ink. I sold the book in the Pike County Bank, Ill., from the fact that this ink was so much better than what they could get of any other make. Speaking of banks, makes me think of what a gentleman of Michigan City, Ind., told me about a black ink for banking purposes which would never fade, composed of two articles only:

Iron or steel filings and simple rain water, exposing it to the sun for a good length of time; pale when first written with, but becoming very black.

I have never thought to try it, but now mention it, for fear it might be good, and lost to the world, unless now thrown to the public.

4. BLUE.—Take sulphate of indigo and put it into water until you get the desired depth of color; that sold in little boxes for blueing clothes is the article desired.

This does well for school children, or any writing not of importance to keep; but for book keeping it is not good, as the heat of a safe in a burning building fades away the color.

5. INDELLIBLE.—Nitrate of silver 11 grs.; dissolve it in 30 grs., (or about a tea-spoon) of water of ammonia; in 85 grs. (or 2¼ tea-spoons) of rain water, dissolve 20 grs. of gum arabic. When the gum is dissolved put into the same vial also 22 grs. of carbonate of soda, (sal-soda.) When all is well dissolved, mix both vials, or their contents, and place the vial containing the mixture in a basin of water, and boil for several minutes, or until a black compound is the result. When cold it is ready for use. Have the linen or other goods starched and ironed, and perfectly dry; then write with a quill pen.

If twice the amount is made at a time it will not cost any more, as the expense is only from the trouble of weighing, so little is used of the materials. Soft soap and boiling cannot efface it, nor years of wear. Use only glass vessels.

6. POWDER—BLACK.—Sulphate of copper 1 dr.; gum arabic ¼ oz.; copperas 1 oz.; nutgalls and extract of logwood 4 ozs. each; all to be pulverized and evenly mixed.—*Scientific American.*

About one oz. of the mixture will be required to each pint of boiling water used. It will be found a valuable color for boot, shoe and harness-edge, also. It should stand a couple of weeks before using, or it may be steeped a few hours if needed sooner.

HONEYS.—ARTIFICIAL CUBA HONEY.—Good brown sugar 10 lbs.; water 1 qt.; old bee bread honey in the comb 2 lbs.; cream of tartar 1 tea-spoon; gum arabic 1 oz.; oil of peppermint 3 drops; oil of rose 2 drops. Mix and boil 2 or 3 minutes and have ready 1 qt. more of water in which an egg is put well beat up; pour it in, and as it begins to boil, skim well, remove from the fire, and when a little cool, add 2 lbs. of nice bees' honey, and strain.

This is really a nice article, looking and tasting like honey. It has been shipped in large quantities under the name of "Cuba Honey." It will keep any length of time as nice and fresh as when first made, if sealed up. Some persons use a table-spoon of slippery elm bark in this amount, but it will ferment in warm weather, and rise to the top, requiring to be skimmed off. If it is to be used only for eating purposes, the cream-of-tartar and gum arabic may be left out, also the old bee-bread honey, substituting for it another pound of nice honey.

2. DOMESTIC HONEY.—Coffee sugar 10 lbs.; water 3 lbs.; cream of tartar 2 ozs.; strong vinegar 2 table-spoons: the white of 1 egg well beaten; bees' honey ¼ lb.; Lubin's extract of honey-suckle 10 drops.

First put the sugar and water into a suitable kettle and place upon the fire; and when luke-warm stir in the cream of tartar, and vinegar; then continue to add the egg; and when the sugar is nearly melted put in the honey and stir until it comes to a boil, take it off, let it stand a few minutes, then strain, adding the extract of honeysuckle last, let stand over night, and it is ready for use. This resembles candied honey, and is a nice thing.

3. EXCELLENT HONEY.—An article suitable for everyday use is made as follows:

Good common sugar 5 lbs.; water 1 qt.; gradually bring it to a boil, skimming well; when cool, add 1 lb. bees' honey and 4 drops of peppermint essence.

If you desire a better article, use white sugar and one-half pint less water and one-half pound more honey. If it is

COP

desired to give it the ropy appearance of bees' honey, put into the water one-fourth ounce of alum.

4. PREMIUM HONEY.—Common sugar 4 lbs.; water 1 pt.; let them come to a boil, and skim; then add pulverized alum ¼ oz.; remove from the fire and stir in cream of tartar ½ oz.; and water or extract of rose 1 table-spoon, and it is fit for use.

This took the premium at an Ohio State Fair. We use the recipes for common sugar and the one using Lubin's extract of honeysuckle, and desire nothing better.

JELLIES—WITHOUT FRUIT.—Take water 1 pt. and add to it pulverized alum ¼ oz., and boil a minute or two; then add 4 lbs. of white crushed or coffee sugar, continue the boiling a little, strain while hot; and when cold put in half of a two shilling bottle of extract of vanilla, strawberry, or lemon, or any other flavor you desire for jelly.

This will make a jelly so much resembling that made from the juice of the fruit that any one will be astonished and when fruit cannot be got, it will take its place admirably. I have had neighbors eat of it and be perfectly astonished at its beauty and palatableness.

BAKING POWDERS—WITHOUT DRUGS.—Baking soda 6 ozs.; cream of tartar 8 oz.; first dry them from all dampness by putting them on a paper and placing them in the oven for a short time, then mix and keep dry, in bottles or boxes.

The proper amount of this will be about one tea-spoon to each quart of flour being baked. Mix with cold water, and bake *immediately*. This contains none of the drugs generally used for baking powders; it is easy made, and does not cost over half as much as to buy them already made. This makes biscuit very nice without milk or shortening. Yet if milk is used, of course it would be that much richer. The main object of baking powders is for those who are " Keeping bach, " as it is called, or for those who are far from civilized conveniencies, and for those who prefer this kind of bread or biscuit to that raised with yeast or sour milk and saleratus. I stand among the latter class.

MOUTH GLUE—FOR TORN PAPER, NOTES, &c.—Any quantity of glue may be used, with sugar, only half as much as of the glue.

First dissolve the glue in water, and carefully evaporate as much of the water as you can without burning the glue;

then add the sugar; if desired to have a very nice article, use gelatine in place of the glue, and treat in the same manner; when the sugar is dissolved in the glue pour it into moulds or a pan and cut it into squares, for convenience, before it gets too hard. This dissolves very quickly by placing the edge of a piece in the mouth, and is not unpleasant to the taste, and is very handy for office or house use. Use to stick together torn bills, paper, &c., by softening the edge of a piece, as above, then touching the parts therewith and pressing together for a moment only.

SALOON DEPARTMENT.

REMARKS.—If saloon keepers, and grocers, who deal in wine, beer, cider, &c., will follow our directions here, and make some of the following articles, they, and their customers, will be better pleased than by purchasing the spurious articles of the day; and families will find them equally applicable to their own use. And although *we start* with an *artificial* cider, yet it is as healthy, and is more properly a small beer, which it should be called, but from its close resemblance to cider, in taste, it has been so named.

CIDERS.—ARTIFICIAL, OR CIDER WITHOUT APPLES.—To cold water 1 gal., put dark brown sugar 1 lb.; tartaric acid $\frac{1}{2}$ oz.; yeast 3 table-spoons, and keep these proportions for any amount desired to make; shake it well together. Make it in the evening and it will be fit for use the next day.

I make in a keg a few gallons at a time, leaving a few quarts to make into next time—not using yeast again until the keg needs rinsing. If it gets a little sour make more into it. In hot weather draw in a pitcher with ice; or if your sales are slow, bottle it and keep in a cool cellar according to the next recipe.

2. TO BOTTLE.—If it is desired to bottle this artificial cider by manufacturers of small drinks, you will proceed as follows:

Put into a barrel, hot water 5 gals.; brown sugar 30 lbs.; tartaric acid $\frac{1}{2}$ lb.; cold water 25 gals.; hop or brewers' yeast 3 pts.; work the yeast into a paste with flour $\frac{1}{2}$ lb.; shake or stir all well together; fill the barrel full, and let it work 24 to 48 hours, or until the yeast is done working out at the bung, by having put in a little sweetened water occasionally to keep the barrel full.

When it has worked clear, bottle it, putting in two or three broken raisins to each bottle, and it will nearly equal champagne. Let the bottles lay in a cool place on the side ---(observe also this plan of laying the bottles upon the side, in putting away apple-cider or wine)—but if it is only for your own retail trade you can make as follows in the next recipe, and have it keep until a barrel is retailed. The first recipe will last only three or four days in hot weather, and about two weeks in winter.

3. IN BARRELS FOR LONG KEEPING.—If retailers wish to keep this cider with the least possible loss of time, or families for their own drink or for the harvest field, proceed as follows :

Place in a keg or barrel, cold water 20 gals.; brown sugar 15 lbs., and tartaric acid ½ lb. only, not using any yeast, but if you have them, put in 2 or 3 lbs. dried sour apples, or boil them and pour in the expressed juice ; without the yeast it will keep, in a cool cellar, for several weeks, even in summer. The darker the sugar the more natural will be the color of the cider.

Dr. O. B. Reed, of Belle River, Mich., with whom I read medicine, drank of this cider freely, while sick with bilious fever, knowing its composition, and recommended it to his patients as soon as he got out amongst them again, as a drink that would allay thirst, with the least amount of fluid, of any thing with which he was acquainted. But some will prefer Prof. Hufeland's drink for Fever Patients, which see.

4. APPLE CIDER, TO KEEP SWEET, WITH BUT TRI-FLING EXPENSE.—Two things are absolutely necessary to preserve cider in a palatable state for any considerable time ; that is, to clear it of pomace, and then to keep it in a cool place, and the cooler the place the better. And then if kept air-tight, by bottling, it is also better, but farmers cannot take the time nor expense of bottling. Some persons leach it through charcoal, and others boil, or rather scald and skim, to get clear of the pomace. In the first place, cider, that is designed to keep over winter, should be

...de from ripe, *sound*, *sour* apples ly, and consequently t will be getting cool weather, and ,oss likely to ferment. *f*hen when made:

Stand in open casks or barrels, and put into each barrel about ι pt. each of hickory, (if you have them, if not other hard wood), ιshes and fresh slacked lime; stir the ashes and lime first into l qt. of new milk; then stir into the cider. It will cause all the pomace to rise to the surface, from which you can skim it as it rises, or you can let it remain about 10 hours, then draw off by a faucet near the bottom, through a strainer, to avoid the hardened pomace.

It is now ready for bottling, or barreling, if too much trouble to bottle. If you barrel it, it has been found essential to sulphur the barrel. The sulphuring is done by dipping cotton cloth into melted sulphur, and drying it; then cutting into strips about two by six inches. Put about three gallons of cider into the barrel; fire one end of the strip of the sulphured cloth, and introduce it into the bunghole, and hold it by means of the bung, giving it air sufficient to let it burn, keeping the smoke in as it burns, when you will push the bung in tight and shake the barrel until the sulphur-gas is absorbed into the cider; then fill up the barrel with cider, and if not already in the cellar, place it there, and you have accomplished the two points first spoken of. If the above plan is too much labor, get oil barrels, if possible, to keep your cider in, (as vinegar can scarcely be made in an oil barrel,)the oil coming out a little and forming an air-tight coat on the top of the cider in the barrel Or:

5. Make your cider late in the Fall, and when made, put into each barrel, immediately, ground mustard ½ lb.; salt 2 oz.; pulverized chalk 2 oz.; stir them up in a little of the cider, then pour into the barrel, and shake well.

I have drank cider, kept in this way, in August, which was made in early spring; it was very nice.

6. I have had cider keep very nice, also, by keeping in a cool cellar, and putting into each barrel:

Mustard seed 2 oz.; allspice 2 oz.; sweet oil ½ pt., and acohol 1 pt. only.

Always ship your cider, if you have cider to ship, late in the fall, or early in spring, for if taken out of a cool cellar

in hot weather it is sure to start fermentation. If wanted
for medicine, proceed as in the following recipe :

7. To PREPARE FOR MEDICINE.—To each barrel of
cider just pressed from rip=, sour apples, not watered :

Take mustard seed, unground, 1 lb.; isinglass 1 oz.; alum pul
verized 1 oz.; put all into the barrel, leave the bung out, and
shake or stir once a day for four days, then take new milk 1 qt.,
and half a dozen eggs, beat well together, and put them into the
cider and stir or shake again, as before, for 2 days; then let
it settle until you see that it is clear, and draw off by a faucet.

And if you wish to use in place of wine, in medicine,
put it into bottles; but if designed for family use you can
barrel it, bunging it tight, and keep cool, of course, and
you will have a *very nice article*, if the cider was not made
too near a well, or running stream of water; but it is found
that if made too near these, the cider does not keep.
Judge ye why!

In some parts of England, by using only ripe, sound apples, letting it work clear, racking off about twice, bottling,
&c., &c., cider is kept from twenty to thirty years. When
cider is drawn off and bottled, it should not be corked until
the next day after filling the bottles, as many of them will
burst. Then lay on the side.

SYRUPS.—To MAKE THE VARIOUS COLORS.—Powder cochineal 1 oz.; soft water 1 pt.; boil the cochineal in the water for
a few minutes, using a copper kettle; while boiling, add 30 grs.
of powdered alum, and 1 dr. of cream of tartar; when the coloring matter is all out of the cochineal, remove it from the fire,
and when a little cool, strain, bottle and set aside for use.

This gives a beautiful red, and is used in the strawberry
syrups only. Colored rather deep in shade. Pine apple is
left without color. Wintergreen is colored with tincture of
camwood, (not deep.) Lemon and ginger with tincture
of turmeric. (See Tinctures.) The two last named syrups
are not colored high—a light shade only.

2. ARTIFICIAL, VARIOUS FLAVORS.—The ground-work of all
syrups ought to be the same, i. e., Simple Syrup; to make it,
take 2½ lbs. of the best coffee sugar, which is found not to crystalize, and water 1 pt., or what is the same, 60 lbs. sugar, water
3 gals.

Dissolve the sugar in the water by heat, removing any

scum that forms upon it, and strain while hot. This can be kept in a barrel or keg, and is always ready to flavor, as desired.

3. RASPBERRY—Is made as follows:

Take orris root, bruised, any quantity, say ¼ lb., and just handsomely cover it with dilute alcohol, (76 per cent. alcohol, and water, equal quantities,) so that it cannot·be made any stronger of the root.

This is called the "Saturated Tincture;" and use sufficient of this tincture to give the desired or natural taste of the raspberry, from which it cannot be distinguished.

4. STRAWBERRY—Flavor is as follows:

The saturated tincture of orris, as above, 2 ozs., acetic-ether, 2 drs.; mix, and use sufficient to give the desired flavor—a very little only is required, in either case.

5. PINE APPLE flavor is made by using to suit the taste, of butyric-ether. If persons have any doubt of these facts simply, try them. Some think syrups even for fountains, charged with carbonic acid gas, that it is best to use about three-fourths oz. of tartaric acid to each gallon, but I prefer none unless the fountain is charged with the super-carbonate of soda, in which case it is necessary to use about three-fourths oz. of the acid to each pound of sugar. See Soda Syrups.

This, above plan, for making *simple syrup*, is the true way of making all syrups; but some people think they must use more water, that the syrup may be cheaper. Others will object to using artificial flavors. Oh! they say: " I buy the genuine article." Then, just allow me to say, don't *buy* the syrups nor the extracts, for ninety-nine hundredths of them are not made from the fruit, but are artificial. Rather make your own, as given under the head of Jams and Extracts. For the more watery syrups, see " Soda Syrups."

6. SARSAPARILLA—Is very nice as follows:

Simple syrup, as above, and nice golden syrup, equal quantities of each, and mix well; then use a few drops of oils of wintergreen and sassafras to each bottle, as used.

The amounts for the desired flavors cannot be given exactly to suit every one, but all will wish different flavors

in some towns, using very high flavor, and in others sufficient to percieve it, merely. All will soon get a plan of
their own, and like it better than that of others. This
mixture of golden syrup makes the sarsaparilla a beautiful
dark color without other coloring.

7. LEMON SYRUP, COMMON,—Was formerly made by dissolving four pounds of crushed sugar in one quart of water,
by boiling, and adding three ounces of tartaric acid and
flavoring with the oil of lemon; but it is best made as follows:

Coffee sugar 3 lbs; water 1½ pts.; dissolve by gentle heat, and
add citric acid 3 ozs., and flavor with oil or extract of lemon.
See "Extracts."

8. Or a very nice lemon syrup is made as follows: Take citric acid in powder ½ oz.; oil of lemon 4 drops; simple syrup 1
quart.

Rub the acid and oil in three or four spoons of the syrup,
then add the mixture to the remainder, and dissolve with
gentle heat. Citric acid is not as likely to cause inflammation of the stomach as the tartaric, hence, its better adaptation to syrups calculated for drinks, and especially in disease.

9. LEMON SYRUP—TO SAVE THE LOSS OF LEMONS.—Where
you have lemons that are spoiling or drying up, take the insides
which are yet sound, squeeze out the juice, and to each pint put
1½ lbs. white sugar, and a little of the peel; boil a few minutes,
strain and cork for use.

This will not require any acid, and one-half tea-spoon of
soda to three-fourths of a glass of water with two or three
table-spoons of syrup, makes a foaming glass. Some persons think they ought to put in water, but if water is added
the syrup will not keep as well, and takes more of it.

10. SODA SYRUP, WITH OR WITHOUT FOUNTAINS.—The common or more watery syrups are made by using loaf or crushed
sugar 8 lbs.; pure water 1 gal.; gum arabic 2 oz.; mix in a
brass or copper kettle; boil until the gum is dissolved, then
skim and strain through white flannel, after which add tartaric
acid 5½ oz.; dissolved in hot water; to flavor, use extract of
lemon, orange, rose pine-apple, peach, sarsaparilla, strawberry,
&c., ½ oz. to each bottle, or to your taste.

Now use two or three table-spoons of the syrup to three-
fourths of a tumbler of water and one-half tea-spoon of

.uper carbonate of soda, made fine; stir well and be ready to
irink, or use the soda in water as mentioned in the "Impe-
cial Cream Nectar;" the gum arabic, however, holds the
.arbonic acid so it will not fly off as rapidly as common
soda. The above is to be used *without* fountains, that is to
make it up as used, in glasses, or for the cheaper fountains
which have an ounce of super-carbonate of soda to the gallon of water; but for the fountains which are charged, in
the cities, with carbonic acid gas, no acids are used in the
syrups.

11. CREAM SODA, USING COW'S CREAM, FOR FOUNTAINS.—
Nice loaf sugar 5 lbs.; sweet rich cream 1 qt.; water 1½ gills;
warm gradually so as not to burn; extract of vanilla ¾ oz.; ex·
tract of nutmeg ¼ oz.

Just bring to a boiling heat, for if you cook it any length
of time it will crystalize; use four or five spoons of this
syrup instead of three as in other syrups. If used without
a fountain, tartaric acid one-quarter pound is added. The
tendency of this syrup is to sour rather quicker than other
syrups, but it is very nice while it lasts; and if only made
in small quantities and kept cool, it more than pays for the
trouble of making often.

12. CREAM SODA, WITHOUT A FOUNTAIN.—Coffee sugar 4 lbs;
water 3 pts.; nutmegs grated 3 in number; whites of 10 eggs
well beaten; gum arabic 1 oz.; oil of lemon 20 drops; or extract equal to that amount. By using oils of other fruits you
can make as many flavors from this as you desire, or prefer.

Mix all and place over a gentle fire, and stir well about
thirty minutes; remove from the fire, strain, and divide
into two parts; into one-half put supercarbonate of soda
eight ounces; and into the other half put six ounces tartaric
acid; shake well, and when cold they are ready to use, by
pouring three or four spoons, from both parts, into separate
glasses which are one-third full of cool water; stir each and
pour together, and you have as nice a glass of cream soda as
was ever drank, which can also be drank at your leisure, as
the gum and eggs hold the gas.

13. SODA WATER, WITHOUT A MACHINE FOR BOTTLING.—
In each gallon of water to be used, carefully dissolve ¼ lb. of
crushed sugar, and 1 oz. of super-carbonate of soda; then fill
half-pint bottles with this water, have your corks ready, now

drop into each bottle ½ dr. of citric acid in crystals, and immediately cork and tie down.

These bottles must be handled carefully without shaking,
and keep cool, until needed; a little more or less sugar can
be used to suit the taste of different persons.

OYSTER SOUP.—To each dozen or dish of oysters put ½
pt. water; milk 1 gill; butter ½ oz.; powdered crackers to
thicken. Bring the oysters and water to a boil, then add the
other ingredients previously mixed together, and boil from 3
to 5 minutes only.

Each one will choose to add salt, pepper, &c., to their own
taste. Keep about these proportions if you should have to
cook for an oyster supper, for parties, &c.

TRIPE—To PREPARE AND PICKLE.—First sew it up, after
it is turned inside out; be careful to sew it up tight, that no
lime gets into it; now have a tub of lime-water, the consistence of good thick white-wash; let it remain in from 10 to
20 minutes, or until when you take hold of it, the dark outside skin will come off; then put it into clean water, changing three or four times to weaken the lime, that the hands be
not injured by it; then with a dull knife scrape off all of the
dark surface, and continue to soak and scrape several times
which removes all offensive substances and smell. After this,
let it soak 20 or 30 minutes in 2 or 3 hot waters, scraping
over each time; then pickle in salt and water 12 hours, and it
is ready for cooking; boil from 3 to 4 hours, cut in strips to
suit, and put it into nice vinegar with the various spices, as
desired; renew the vinegar at the expiration of 1 week, is all
that will be required further.

Many persons stick up their *nose* when tripe is spoken of;
but, if nicely prepared, I prefer it to any dish furnished by
the beef.

MOLASSES CANDY AND POP-CORN BALLS—CANDY.
—Equal quantities of brown sugar and molasses, and put
them into a suitable kettle—copper is the best—and when it
begins to boil, skim it well, and strain it, or else pour it
through a fine wire sieve to free it of slivers and sticks which
are often found in the sugar; then return it to the kettle and
continue to boil, until, when you have dipped your hand in
cold water and passed one or two fingers through the boiling candy and immediately back to the cold water, what
adheres, when cold, will crush like dry egg shells, and does
not adhere to the teeth when bitten. When done, pour it on
a stone or platter which has been greased, and as it gets cool
begin to throw up the edges and work it by pulling on
a hook or by the hand, until bright and glistening like
gold; the hands should have a little flour on them occasion-

•llv; now keep the mass by a warm stove, (if much is made at one time), and draw it into stick size, occasionally rolling them to keep round, until all is pulled out and cold, then with shears clip a little upon them, at proper lengths for the sticks, and they will snap quickly while yet the stick will bend; no color no butter, no lard or flavor is used or need be, yet any oil can be used for flavoring, if desired, when poured out to cool.

Sugar left in molasses barrels works very nicely in this preparation. Pulverized white sugar sprinkled amongst it will prevent it from sticking together.

2. CANDY PERFECTLY WHITE.—If it is desired to have candy that is perfectly white, proceed as follows :

Best coffee sugar 2½ lbs.; the nicest syrup 1½ pts.; boil very carefully, until when tried as above, it crisps like egg shells, or flies like glass; then draw and work upon the hook until very white.

3. MOLASSES CANDY WITHOUT SUGAR.—Porto-Rico molasses boiled and worked as above, has a cream shade according to the amount of pulling, and most persons prefer it to the mixture of sugar and molasses, as in the first.

4. POP CORN BALLS.—Pop the corn, avoiding all that is not nicely opened; place ½ bu. of the corn upon a table or in a large dripping pan; put a little water in a suitable kettle with sugar 1 lb.; and boil as for candy, until it becomes quite waxy in water, when tried as for candy ; then remove from the fire and dip into it 6 to 7 table-spoons of thick gum solution, made by pouring boiling water upon gum arabic, over night, or some hours before; now dip the mixture upon different parts of the corn, putting a stick, or the hands, under the corn, lifting up and mixing until the corn is all saturated with candy mixture; then with the hands press the corn into balls, as the boys do snow balls, being quick, lest it sets before you get through.

This amount will make about one hundred balls, if properly done. White or brown sugar may be used. And for variety, white sugar for a part, and molasses or syrup for another batch. Either of these are suited to street peddlars.

5. ACTION OF SUGAR OR CANDY ON THE TEETH.—M Larez, of France, in the course of his investigations on the teeth, has arrived at the following conclusions:

First—that "refined sugar, either from cane or beet. is injurious to healthy teeth, either by immediate contact with these organs, or by the gas developed, owing to its stoppage in the stomach. Second—that if a tooth is macerated in a saturated solution of sugar, it is so much altered in the chemical composition that it becomes gelatinous, and its enamel opaque, spongy, and easily broken. This modification is due not to free acid, but to a tendency of sugar to combine with the calcareous basis of the teeth."

I have destroyed my own teeth, I have no doubt now, by constantly eating candies, while in the grocery business, before I knew its injurious effects, and I *believe* it to have destroyed the *first* teeth of all of my children which were bo.n during my candy-eating propensities. What say our candy-eating gentry to the above?

LEMONADE.—To CARRY IN THE POCKET.—Loaf sugar 1 lb.; rub it down finely in a mortar, and add citric acid ¼ oz.; (tartaric acid will do,) and lemon essence ¼ oz., and continue the trituration until all is intimately mixed, and bottle for use. It is best to dry the powders as mentioned in the Persian Sherbet, next following.

A rounding table-spoon can be done up in a paper and carried conveniently in the pocket when persons are going into out-of-the-way places, and added to half pint of cold water, when all the beauties of a lemonade will stand before you waiting to be drank, not costing a penny a glass. This can be made sweeter or more sour, if desired. If any however should prefer an effervescing drink, they can follow the directions given in the next recipe.

PERSIAN SHERBET.—Pulverized sugar 1 lb.; super-carbonate of soda 4 ozs.; tartaric acid 3 ozs.; put all the articles into the stove oven when moderately warm, being separate, upon paper or plates; let them remain sufficiently long to dry out all dampness absorbed from the air, then rub about 40 drops of lemon oil, (or if preferred any other flavored oil,) thoroughly with the sugar in a mortar—wedge-wood is the best—then add the soda and acid, and continue the rubbing until all are thoroughly mixed.

Bottle and cork tight, for, if any degree of moisture is ermitted to reach it, the acid and soda neutralize each ther, and the virtue is thus destroyed. A middling sized table-spoon or two tea-spoons of this put into a half pint glass and nearly filled with water and quickly drank, makes an agreeable summer beverage; and if three or four glasses of it are taken within a short time, say an hour or two, it has the effect of a gentle cathartic, hence for those habitually costive it would be found nearly or quite equal to the seidlitz powder, and for children it would be the pleasantest of the two. [The printers have tried it, and can bear testimony to its good qualities.]

BEERS.—ROOT BEER.—For each gallon of water to be used, take hops, burdock, yellow dock, sarsaparilla, dandelion, and spikenard roots, bruised, of each ¼ oz.; boil about 20 minutes, and strain while hot, add 8 or 10 drops of oils of spruce and sassafras mixed in equal proportions, when cool enough not to scald your hand, put in 2 or 3 table-spoons of yeast; molasses ⅔ of a pint, or white sugar ¼ lb. gives it about the right sweetness.

Keep these proportions for as many gallons as you wish to make. You can use more or less of the roots to suit your taste after trying it; it is best to get the dry roots. or dig them and let them get dry, and of course you can add any other root known to possess medicinal properties desired in the beer. After all is mixed, let it stand in a jar with a cloth thrown over it, to work about two hours, then bottle and set in a cool place. This is a nice way to take alteratives, without taking medicine. And families ought to make it every Spring, and drink freely of it for several weeks, and thereby save, perhaps, several dollars in doctors' bills.

2. SPRUCE OR AROMATIC BEER.—For 3 gals. water put in 1 qt. and ¼ pt. of molasses, 3 eggs well beaten, yeast 1 gill. Into 2 qts. of the water boiling hot put 50 drops of any oil you wish the flavor of; or mix 1 oz. each, oils sassafras, spruce and wintergreen, then use 50 drops of the mixed oils.

Mix all, and strain; let it stand two hours, then bottle, bearing in mind that yeast must not be put in when the fluid would scald the hand. Boiling water cuts oil for beers, equal to alcohol

3. LEMON BEER.—Water 30 gals.; ginger root bruised 6 ozs.; cream of tartar ¼ lb.; coffee sugar 13 lbs.; oil of lemon 1 oz.; or ¼ oz. of the oil may be used, and 6 good sized lemons, sliced: yeast 1½ pts.

Boil the ginger and cream of tartar, about twenty to thirty minutes, in two or three gallons of the water; then strain it upon the sugar and oils or sliced lemons, which have been rubbed together, having warm water enough to make the whole thirty gallons just so you can hold your hand in it without burning, or about seventy degrees of heat; then work up the yeast into a paste, as for the cider, with five or six ounces of flour. Let it work over night, skimming off the yeast, or letting it work over as the cider, then strain and bottle for use. This will keep fifteen or twenty days. The Port Huronites think it a splendid drink.

4. GINGER BEER.—White sugar 5 lbs.; lemon juice 1 gill; honey ¼ lb.; ginger, bruised, 5 ozs.; water 4½ gals.

Boil the ginger thirty minutes in three qts. of the water; then add the other ingredients, and strain; when cold, put in the white of an egg, well beaten, with one tea-spoon of lemon essence—let stand four days, and bottle. It will keep for months—much longer than if yeast was used; the honey, however, operates mildly in place of yeast.

5. PHILADELPHIA BEER.—Water 30 gals.; brown sugar 20 lbs.; ginger, bruised, 1¼ lbs.; cream of tartar ¼ lb.; super carbonate of soda 3 ozs.; oil of lemon, cut in a little alcohol, 1 tea-spoon whites of 10 eggs, well beaten; hops 2 ozs.; yeast 1 qt.

The ginger root and hops should be boiled twenty or thirty minutes in enough of the water to make all milk warm, then strained into the rest, and the yeast added and llowed to work over night; skimmed and bottled.

6. PATENT GAS BEER.—Ginger 2 ozs.; allspice 1 oz.; cinnamon ¼ oz.; cloves ¼ oz.; all bruised or ground; molasses 2 qts., cold water 7½ gals.; yeast 1 pt.

Boil the pulverized articles, for fifteen or twenty minutes, in the molasses; then strain into your keg, and add the water, then the yeast; shake it well together and bung down. If made over night it will be ready for use the next day. There ought to be a little space in the keg not filled with the beer. This beer is ahead of all the pops and mineral waters of the day, for flavor, health or sparkling qualities or speed in making. Be careful you do not burst the keg. In hot weather, draw in a pitcher with ice. I have sold this in the principal towns of Ohio, Indiana and Michigan, traveling with a caravan, and obtained two dollars for the recipe of the man who kept the inside stand, and blowed the head out of the first keg of it which he made.

7. CORN BEER, WITHOUT YEAST.—Cold water 5 gals.; sound nice corn 1 qt.; molasses 2 qts.; put all into a keg of this size; shake well, and in 2 or 3 days a fermentation will have been brought on as nicely as with yeast. Keep it bunged tight.

It may be flavored with oils of spruce or lemon, if desired, by pouring on to the oils one or two quarts of the water,
boiling hot. The corn will last five or six makings. If it
gets too sour add more molasses and water in the same proportions. It is cheap, healthy, and no bother with yeast.

8. STRONG BEER, ENGLISH IMPROVED.—Malt 1 peck; coarse
brown sug. 6 lbs.; hops 4 oz.; good yeast 1 tea-cup; if you
have not may take a little over 1 peck of barley, (twice the
amount of oats will do, but are not as good,) and put it into an
oven after the bread is drawn, or into a stove oven, and steam
the moisture from them. Grind coarsely.

Now pour upon the ground malt 3½ gals. of water at 170 or
172° of heat. The tub in which you scald the malt should
have a false bottom, 2 or 3 inches from the real bottom; the
false bottom should be bored full of gimlet holes, so as to act as
a strainer, to keep back the malt meal. When the water is
poured on, stir them well, and let it stand 3 hours, and draw off
by a faucet; put in 7 gals. more of water at 180 to 182°; stir it
well, and let it stand 2 hours and draw it off. Then put on a
gal. or two of cold water, stir it well and draw it off; you should
have about 5 or 6 gals. Put the 6 lbs. of coarse brown sugar in an
equal amount of water; mix with the wort, and boil 1½ to 2
hours with the hops; you should have eight gals. when boiled;
when cooled to 80° put in the yeast, and let it work 18 to 20
hours, covered with a sack; use sound iron hooped kegs or porter bottles, bung or cork tight, and in two weeks it will be good
sound beer, and will keep a long time; and for persons of a
weak habit of body, and especially females, 1 glass of this with
their meals is far better than tea or coffee, or all the ardent spirits in the universe. If more malt is used, not exceeding ¼ a
bushel, the beer, of course, would have more spirit, but this
strength is sufficient for the use of families or invalids.

9. ALE, HOME-BREWED—HOW IT IS MADE.—The following formula for the manufacture of a famous home-brewed
ale of the English yeomanry, will convey a very clear idea
of the components and mixture of ordinary ales. The middle classes of the English people usually make their ale in
quantities of two barrels, that is, seventy-two gallons.

For this purpose a quarter of malt, (8 bus.) is obtained at the
malt-house—or, if wished to be extra strong, nine bushels of
malt—are taken, with hops, 12 lbs.; yeast, 5 qts.

The malt, being crushed or ground, is mixed with 72 gals.
of water at the temperature of 160.°, and covered up for 3
hours, when 40 gallons are drawn off, into which the hops are
put, and left to infuse. Sixty gallons of water at a temperature
of 170° are then added to the malt in the mash-tub, and well

mixed, and after standing 2 hours, sixty gallons are drawn off The wort from these two mashes is boiled with the hops for 2 hours, and after being cooled down to 65°, is strained through a flannel bag into a fermenting tub, where it is mixed with the yeast and left to work for 24 or 30 hours. It is then run into barrels to cleanse, a few gallons being reserved for filling up the casks as the yeast works over.

Of course when the yeast is worked out it must be bunged If one-half a pint of this was taken each meal by men, and half that amount by females, and no other spirits, tea nor coffee, during the day, I hesitate not in saying that I firmly believe it would conduce to health. I know that this, which a man makes himself, or some of the wines mentioned in this work, home-made, are all that any person ought to allow themselves to use in these days when *dollars and cents* are the governing influences of *all* who deal in *such* articles.

10. PORTER, ALE, OR WINE, TO PREVENT FLATNESS IN PARTS OF BOTTLES FOR THE INVALID.—Sick persons who are recommended to use ale, porter, or wine, and can only take a small glass at a time, nearly always find the last of the bottle flat or stale.

To prevent this put in the cork firmly, and turn the cork and downwards, in a large tumbler or other vessel nearly filled with water.

This plan prevents communication with the external air.

11. CREAM NECTAR, IMPERIAL.—First, take water 1 gal.; loaf sugar 8 lbs., tartaric acid 8 oz.; gum arabic 1 oz.; put into a suitable kettle and place on the fire.

Second, take flour 4 tea-spoons; the whites of 4 eggs, well beaten together, with the flour, and add water ½ pt.; when the first is blood warm put in the second, and boil 3 minutes, and it is done.

DIRECTIONS : Three table-spoons of the syrup to a glass half or two-thirds full of water, and add one-third tea-spoon of super-carbonate of soda, made fine; stir well, and drink at your leisure.

☞ In getting up any of the soda drinks which are spoken of, it will be found preferable to put about eight ounces of super-carbonate, often called carbonate of soda, into one pint of water in a bottle, and shake when you wish to make a glass of soda, and pour of this into the glass until it foams well, instead of using the dry soda as directed.

12. GINGER POP.—Water 5¼ gals.; ginger root, bruised, ¼ lb.; tartaric acid ½ oz.; white sugar 2½ lbs.; whites of 3 eggs, well beaten; lemon oil 1 tea-spoon; yeast 1 gill.

Boil the root for thirty minutes in one gallon of the water, strain off, and put the oil in while hot; mix. Make over night, and in the morning skim and bottle, keeping out sediments.

13. SPANISH GINGERETTE.—To each gal. of water put 1 lb. of white sugar; ½ oz. best bruised ginger root; ¼ oz. of cream of tartar, and 2 lemons sliced.

DIRECTIONS: In making 5 gals. boil the ginger and lemons 10 minutes in 2 gals. of the water; the sugar and cream of tartar to be dissolved in the cold water, and mix all, and add ½ pint of good yeast; let it ferment over night, strain and bottle in the morning.

This is a valuable recipe for a cooling and refreshing beverage; compounded of ingredients highly calculated to assist the stomach, and is recommended to persons suffering with Dyspepsia or Sick Headache. It is much used in European countries, and persons having once tested its virtues will constantly use it as a common drink. And for saloons, or groceries, no temperance beverage will set it aside.

14. SHAM-CHAMPAGNE—A PURELY TEMPERANCE DRINK.—Tartaric acid 1 oz.; one good sized lemon; ginger root 1 oz.; white sugar 1½ lbs.; water 2½ gals.; yeast 1 gill.

Slice the lemon, and bruise the ginger, mix all, except the yeast, boil the water and pour it upon them and let stand until cooled to blood heat; then add the yeast and let it stand in the sun through the day; at night, bottle, tieing the corks, and in 2 days it will be fit to use.—*Mrs. Beecher.*

Be sure and not drink over three or four bottles at one time.

YEASTS—HOP YEAST.—Hops 1 oz.; water 3 pts.; flour 1 tea-cup; brown sugar 1 table-spoon; salt 1 tea-spoon; brewers' or bakers' yeast 1 gill.

Boil the hops twenty minutes in the water, strain into a jar, and stir in the flour, sugar, and salt, and when a little cool add the yeast, and after four or five hours cover up, and stand in a cool place or on the ice for use.

The above makes a good family yeast, but the following is the regular bakers' yeast, as they always keep the salt on hand.

3—DR. CHASE'S RECIPES.

2. BAKERS' YEAST.—Hops 2 oz.; water 1 gal.; wheat flour ½ lb.; malt flour 1 pt.; stock yeast ½ pt.

Boil the hops for thirty minutes in the water, strain, and let cool until you can well bear your hand in it; then stir in the flour and yeast; keep in a warm place until the fermentation is well under way, and then let it work in a cooler place six to eight hours, when it should be put in pint bottles about half full, and closely corked, and tied down. By keeping this in a very cool cellar, or ice-house, it will keep for months, fit for use. But as it is often troublesome to obtain yeast, to start with, I give you the "Distillers' Jug Yeast," starting without yeast.

3. JUG-YEAST, WITHOUT YEAST TO START WITH.—Hops ½ lb.; water 1 gal.; fine malt flour ½ pt.; brown sugar ½ lb.

Boil the hops in the water until quite strong, strain, and stir in the malt flour; and strain again through a coarse cloth, and boil again for ten minutes; when lukewarm, stir in the sugar, and place in a jug, keeping it at the same temperature until it works over; then cork tight, and keep in a cold place.

4. YEAST CAKE.—Good sized potatoes 1 doz.; hops 1 large handful; yeast ½ pt.; corn meal sufficient quantity.

Boil the potatoes, after peeling, and rub them through a cullender; boil the hops in two quarts of water, and strain into the potatoes; then scald sufficient Indian meal to make them the consistence of emptyings, and stir in the yeast and let rise; then, with unscalded meal, thicken so as to roll out and cut into cakes, drying quickly, at first, to prevent souring. They keep better, and soak up quicker, than if made with flour.

ICE CREAM.—Fresh cream ½ gal.; rich milk ½ gal.; white sugar 1 lb.; some do use as much as 2 lbs. of sugar to the gallon, yet it leaves an unpleasant astringency in the throat after eating the cream, but please yourselves.

Dissolve the sugar in the mixture, flavor with extract to suit your taste, or take the peel from a fresh lemon and steep one-half of it in as little water as you can, and add this—it makes the lemon flavor better than the extract—and no flavor will so universally please as the lemon; keep the same proportion for any amount desired. The juice of strawberries or raspberries gives a beautiful color and flavor to ice creams; or about ¼ oz of essence or extracts to a gallon, or to suit the taste. Have your ice well broken; 1 qt. salt to a bucket of ice.

About half an hours' constant stirring and occasional scraping down and beating together, will freeze it. The old-fashioned freezer which turns in a tub of ice, makes smoother and nicer ice-cream than all the patent freezers I have seen; and the plan of using the genuine cream and milk gives sufficient profit; but I will give you the best substitutes there are, in the following recipe, but the *less* you eat of *either* the better will it be for *health.*

2. ICE CREAM, VERY CHEAP.—Milk 6 qts.; Oswego corn starch ¼ lb.

First dissolve the starch in one quart of the milk, then mix all together and just simmer a little, (not to boil.) Sweeten and flavor to suit your taste, as above; or—

3. Irish moss 1½ oz.; milk 1 gal.

First soak the moss in a little cold water for an hour, and rinse well to clear it of sand and a certain peculiar taste; then steep it for an hour in the milk just at the boiling point, but not to boil; it imparts a rich color and flavor without eggs or cream. The moss may be steeped twice.

It is the Chicago plan. I have eaten it and know it to be very nice. A few minutes rubbing, at the end of freezing, with the spatula, against the side of the freezer, gives ice-cream a smoothness not otherwise obtained.

WINES.—CURRANT, CHERRY, AND OTHER BERRY WINES.—The juice of either of the above fruits can be used alone, or in combinations to make a variety of flavors, or suit persons who have some, and not the other kinds of fruit.

Express all the juice you can, then take an equal amount of boiling water and pour on the pressed fruit, let stand 2 hours, squeeze out as much as there is of juice, and mix, then add 4 lbs. of brown sugar to each gallon of the mixture; let stand until worked, or 3 or 4 weeks, without a bung in the keg or barrel, simply putting a piece of gauze over the bung hole to keep out flies; when it is done working, bung it up.

A cool cellar, of course, is the best place for keeping wines, as they must be kept where they will not freeze. Some persons use only one-fourth juice, in making fruit wines, and three-fourths water, but you will bear in mind that the wine will be good or bad, just in proportion to the water and sugar used. If care is used when you express the juice, to prevent the pulp or seeds from entering or remaining in the juice, no other straining or racking will be needed. Most persons also recommend putting in brandy, but if any spirit is used at all, let it be pure alcohol, from one gill to one-half pint only per gallon, but the strength of juice I recommend, and the amount of sugar, remove all necessity for any addition of spirit whatever. Bear in mind that all fruit of which you are to make wine ought to be perfectly ripe, and then make it as soon as possible thereafter, not letting the juice ferment before the addition of the sugar. If bottled, always lay them on the side.

2. RHUBARB, OR ENGLISH PATENT WINE.—An agreeable and healthful wine is made from the expressed juice of the garden rhubarb.

To each gal. of juice, add 1 gal. of soft water in which 7 lbs. of brown sugar has been dissolved; fill a keg or a barrel with this proportion, leaving the bung out, and keep it filled with sweetened water as it works over until clear; then bung down or bottle as you desire.

These stalks will furnish about three-fourths their weight in juice, or from sixteen hundred to two thousand gallons of wine to each acre of well cultivated plants. Fill the barrels and let them stand until spring, and bottle, as any wine will be better in glass or stone

3. Some persons give Mr. Cahoon, of Kenosha, Wis., credit for originating pie-plant wine, but that is a mistake; it has long been made in England, and has even been patented in that country. They first made it by the following directions, which also makes a very nice article, but more applicable for present use than for keeping.

For every 4 lbs. of the stalks cut fine, pour on 1 gal. of boiling water, adding 4 lbs. brown sugar; let stand covered 24 hours, having also added a little cinnamon, allspice, cloves and nutmeg, bruised, as may be desired for flavoring; then strain and let work a few days, and bottle.

4. TOMATO WINE.—Express the juice from clean, ripe tomatoes, and to each gallon of it, (without any water,) put brown sugar 4 lbs.

Put in the sugar immediately, or before fermentation

begins—this ought to be done in making any fruit wine. Something of the character of a cheese press, hoop and cloth, is the best plan to squeeze out the juice of tomatoes or other fruits. Let the wine stand in a keg or barrel for two or three months; then draw off into bottles, carefully avoiding the sediment. It makes a most delightful wine having all the beauties of flavor belonging to the tomato, and I have no doubt all its medicinal properties also, either as a tonic in disease, or as a beverage for those who are in the habit of using intoxicating beverages, and if such persons would have the good sense to make some wine of this kind, and use it instead of rot-gut whisky, there would not be one-hundredth part of the "snakes in the boot" that now curse our land. It must be tasted to be appreciated. I have it now, which is three years old, worth more than much pretended wine which is sold for three or four shillings a pint.

5. TOMATO CULTIVATION, FOR EARLY AND LATE.—The *Working Farmer* says of the tomato plant, "that it bears 80 per cent of its fruit within 18 inches of the ground, while more than half the plant is above that part. When the branches are cut they do not bleed, and they may therefore be shortened immediately above the large, or early-setting fruit.

"The removal of the small fruit on the ends of the branches is no loss, for the lower fruit will swell to an unnatural size by trimming, and both a greater weight and measure of fruit will be the consequence, besides obtaining a large portion five to fifteen days earlier. The trimming should be done so as to have a few leaves beyond the fruit, to insure perfect ripening. The importance of early manuring is too evident to need comment. The burying of the removed leaves immediately around the plant is a good practice, both by insuring full disturbance of the soil, and by the presenting of a fertilizer progressed precisely to the point of fruit making. The portions buried decay rapidly, and are rapidly assimilated." If wanted very early and large, trim off all except two or three upon each plant.

6. To ripen late tomatoes, pull the plants having green tomatoes on them, before the commencement of frosts, and hang them in a well ventilated cellar.

The fruit will continue to ripen until early winter, especially if the cellar is cool and damp.

7. THE TOMOTO AS FOOD.—Dr. Bennett, a professor of some celebrity, considers the tomato an invaluable article of diet, and ascribes to it various important medical properties.

First—that the tomato is one of the most powerful *aperients* for the liver and other organs; where *calomel* is indicated, it is probably one of the most effective and least harmful remedial agents known to the profession. *Second*—that a chemical extract will be obtained from it that will *supercede* the use of calomel in the cure of disease. *Third*—that he has successfully treated *Diarrhœa* with this article alone. *Fourth*—that when used as an article of diet, it is an almost sovereign remedy for *Dyspepsia* and *indigestion*. *Fifth*—that it should be constantly used for daily food, either cooked or raw, or in the form of catch-up; it is the most healthy article now in use.

Knowing personally the value of the tomato in disease, for food and wine, I freely give all the information regarding it which I can, that others may make as free use of it as health and economy demand, consequently, I give you the next item, which I have learned just as the type were being set, upon this subject in 1860.

8. TOMATOES AS FOOD FOR CATTLE.—Mr Davis, the editor of the "Michigan State News," Ann Arbor, Mich., says, "that he has fed his cow, this season, at least ten bushels of tomatoes."

His plan is to mix a little bran with them, (say 3 qts. to a half bushel of tomatoes, when fed;) they cause an excellent flow of rich and delicious milk.

He did not think of it until after the frosts, when ob serving them going to waste, he thought to see if she would eat them, which she did freely, from the commencement. I have also known pigs to eat them, but this is not common In 1862, I found my cow to eat them as freely as spoken of by Mr. Davis.

9. WINE, FROM WHITE CURRANTS.—Ripe, white currants, any quantity; squeeze out the juice, and put on water to get out as much more as there is of the juice, and mix the two, and to each gallon put 3¼ lbs. of sugar; let it work without boiling or skimming for 2 or 3 months, then rack off and bottle.

The white currant has less acidity than the red, and does not require as much sugar. I have never tasted currant wine equal to this.

10. GINGER WINE.—Alcohol of 98 per cent, 1 quart best ginger

root, bruised, 1 oz.; cayenne 5 grs.; tartaric acid 1 dr.; let stand 1 week and filter, or draw off by faucet above the sediment. Now add 1 gal. of water in which 1 lb. of crushed sugar has been boiled. Mix when cold. To make the color, boil ¼ oz. of cochineal, ¾ oz. of cream of tartar, ½ oz. of saleratus, and ¼ oz. of alum in 1 pt. of water until you get a bright red color, and use a proper amount of this to bring the wine to the desired color.

This wine is suitable for nearly all the purposes for which any wine is used, and a gallon of it will not cost more than a pint of many wines sold throughout the country for medicinal purposes, represented to be imported from Europe. Let a man, suffering with a bad cold, drink about half a pint of this wine hot, on going to bed, soaking his feet at the same time in hot water fifteen or twenty minutes, and covering up warm and sweating it out until morning, then washing off his whole body with cool or cold water, by means of a wet towel, and rubbing briskly with a coarse dry towel for four or five minutes, will not be able to find his cold or any bad effects of it in one case out of a hundred. Ladies or children would take less in proportion to age and strength. Females in a weakly condition, with little or no appetite, and spare in flesh, from food not properly digesting, but not yet ripened into actual *indigestion*, will find almost entire relief by taking half a wine-glass of this wine twenty minutes before meals, and following it up a month or two, according to their improved condition. For family use it is just as good without color, as with it.

11. BLACKBERRY WINE.—Mash the berries, and pour 1 qt. of boiling water to each gal.; let the mixture stand 24 hours, stirring occasionally; then strain and measure into a keg, adding 3 lbs. of sugar, and good rye whisky 1 pt., or best alcohol ½ pt. to each gal.

Cork tight, and let it stand until the following October, and you will have wine fit for use, without further straining or boiling, that will make lips smack as they never smacked under its influence before.

I feel assured that where this fruit is plenty, that this wine should take the place of all others, as it is invaluable in sickness as a tonic, and nothing is better for bowel disease. I therefore give the recipe for making it, and having tried it myself, I speak advisedly on the subject.

The *Dollar Times*, Cincinnati, O., first published this recipe, not using any spirits, but I find that it will often sour without it.

12. LAWTON BLACKBERRY—ITS CULTIVATION.- An editor at Coldwater, Mich., says of this fruit, " that where it is best known it is one of the most popular small fruits that has ever been cultivated. It has been known to pro-duce over one thousand full-grown ripe berries in one season on a single stalk ; the average size of fruit being from three-fourths to one and a half inches in diameter ; quality excel-lent, very juicy, seeds very small, and few in number. Five quarts of berries will make one gallon of juice, which, mixed with two gallons of water and nine pounds of refined sugar, will make three gallons of wine, equal in quality to the best grape wine. Professor Mapes and many others, who have tested the qualities of the same as a wine-fruit, speak of it in terms of the highest praise.

13. PORT WINE.—Fully ripe wild grapes 2 bu. ; best alcohol 3 gals. ; sugar 25 lbs. ; water to fill a barrel.

Mash the grapes without breaking the seed ; then put them into a barrel with the sugar and alcohol, and fill up with rain water, and let it lie a few weeks in the sun ; or if the weather has become cold, in a warm place ; then in the cellar until spring ; then rack off and bottle, or place in perfectly clean kegs or barrels, and you have a better article than nine-tenths of what is represented as imported Port.

14. CIDER WINE.—Prof. Horsford, a celebrated chemist, communicated the following recipe to the Horticultural Society of Massachusetts, and recommends it for general trial :

" Let the new cider from sour apples, (ripe, sound fruit pre-ferred,) ferment from 1 to 3 weeks, as the weather is warm or cool. When it has attained to a lively fermentation, add to each gallon, according to its acidity, from $\frac{1}{2}$ a lb. to 2 lbs. of white crushed sugar, and let the whole ferment until it possesses pre-cisely the taste which it is desired should be permanent. In this condition pour out a quart of the cider and add for each gallon $\frac{1}{4}$ oz. of *sulphite of lime*, not sulphate. Stir the powder and cider until intimately mixed, and return the emulsion to the ferment-ing liquid. Agitate briskly and thoroughly for a few moments, and then let the cider settle. Fermentation will cease at once

When after a few days, the cider has become clear, draw off carefully, to avoid the sediment, and bottle. If loosely corked which is better, it will become a sparkling cider wine, and may be kept indefinitely long.

This has been tried with varied success; those who do not think it too much to follow the directions, obtain a good article, but others, supposing it to do just as well without sugar, or drawing off, or bottling, have found but little satisfaction —they have no reason to expect any; and yet they might be well satisfied to obtain a good wine from the orchard, even with *all* the above requisitions.

15. GRAPE WINE.—"Ripe, freshly picked, and selected, tame grapes, 20 lbs.; put them into a stone jar and pour over them 6 qts. of boiling soft water; when sufficiently cool to allow it, you will squeeze them thoroughly with the hand; after which allow them to stand 3 days on the pomace with a cloth thrown over the jar, then squeeze out the juice and add 10 lbs. of nice crushed sugar, and let it remain a week longer in the jar; then take off the scum, strain and bottle, leaving a vent, until done fermenting, when strain again and bottle tight, and lay the bottles on the side in a cool place."

This wine is the same as used by the Rev. Orrin Whitmore, of Saline, Mich., for sacramental purposes. I have tasted it myself, and would prefer it for medicinal uses to nine-tenths of the wines sold in this country. With age, it is nice. I am of the opinion that it might just as well remain in the jar until it is desired to bottle, and thus save the trouble of the extra straining. For I have now wine, four years old in my cellar, made in Evansville, Ind., from the grape, which was made without the addition of any particle of matter whatever. Simply, the juice pressed out, hauled in from the vinery, put into very large casks in a cool cellar, not even racked off again under one year from the time of making. It tastes exactly like the grape itself; this, you will perceive, saves much trouble in racking, straining, &c I am told by other wine makers also, that if care is observed when the juice is pressed out to keep clear of the pomace, that wine is better to stand without racking or straining, and that nothing is found in the barrels, after the first year, save the crude tartar or wine-stone, as some call it, which all grape wine deposites on the sides of the cask. These wines are every way appropriate for sacramental and medicinal purposes, and far more pure than can be purchased once in a hundred times, and if one makes their own, they have the satisfaction of *knowing* that their wines are not made of what is vulgarly, yet truly called, "*Rot-gut whisky.*"

16. COLORING FOR WINES.—White sugar 1 lb.; water 1 gill; put into an iron kettle, let boil, and burn to a red black, and thick; remove from the fire and add a little hot water to keep it from hardening as it cools; then bottle for use.

Any of the foregoing wines can be colored with this, as desired, but for family use I never use any color.

17. STOMACH BITTERS, EQUAL TO HOSTETTERS', FOR ONE-FOURTH ITS COST, AND SCHIEDAM SCHNAPPS EXPOSED.—European Gentian root 1½ oz.; orange peel 2½ oz.; cinnamon ¼ oz.; anise seed ¼ oz.; coriander seed ½ oz.; cardamon seed ½ oz.; unground Peruvian bark ½ oz.; gum kino ¼ oz.; bruise all these articles, and put them into the best alcohol 1 pt.; let it stand a week and pour off the clear tincture; then bo'l the dregs a few minutes in 1 qt. of water, strain, and press out all the strength; now dissolve loaf sugar 1 lb. in the hot liquid, adding 3 qts. cold water, and mix with the spirit tincture fist poured off, or you can add these, and let it stand on the dregs if preferred.

18. NOTE.—SCHIEDAM SCHNAPPS, FALSELY SO CALLED.—It is generally known that in Schiedam, Holland, they make the best quality of Gin, calling it "Schiedam Schnapps;" consequently it might be expected that unprincipled men would undertake its imitation; but hardly ceuld it have been expected that so base an imitation would start into existence under the guidance of a man, who, at least, calls himself *honorable.*

"Take gentian root, ¼ lb.; orange peel, ¼ lb.; puds, ¼ lb.; (but if this last cannot be obtained, poma aurantior, unripe oranges,) or agaric, ¼ lb.; best galangal, ¼ lb.; centaury, ¼ lb.;—cost $1,20. Put pure spirit, 10 gals., upon them and let them stand 2 weeks; stir it every day, and at the end of that time put 3 gals. of this to one barrel of good whisky; then bottle and label; and here follows the label:

AROMATIC SCHIEDAM SCHNAPPS, A SUPERLATIVE TONIC, DIURETIC, ANTI-DYSPEPTIC, AND INVIGORATING CORDIAL.—THIS MEDICAL BEVERAGE is manufactured at Schiedam, in Holland, and is warranted free from every injurious property and ingredient, and of the best possible quality.

Its extraordinary medicinal properties in Gravel, Gout, Chronic Rheumatism, Incipient Dropsy, Flatulence, Colic Pains of the Stomach or Bowels, whether in adults or infants. In all ordinary cases of obstruction in the Kidneys, Bladder and Urinary Organs, in Dyspepsia, whether Acute or Chronic, in general Debility, sluggish Circulation of the Blood, Inadequate Assimiation of Food, and Exhausted Vital Energy, are acknowledged by the whole Medical Faculty, and attested in their highest written authorities."

I purchased the foregoing recipe of an extensive dealer in Evansville, Ind.; he put up the *stuff* in quart bottles, and labeled it as I have shown you; his label was got up in splendid style, *bronzed letters*, and sent out to the world as *pure "Schiedam Schnapps" at $1 per bottle."*

I have given you the whole thing, that the *thousands* into whose hands this book may fall, shall know what confidence, or that *no confidence* whatever, can be placed in the "Advertised Nostrums" of the day, but that the only security we have is to *make our own*, or go to those whom we *know* to be scientific. *Obtain their prescription and follow their counsel.* Every person knows that *real* Holland Gin possesses diuretic and other valuable properties; and who would not suppose he was getting a *genuine* article from this *Flaming, Bronze-crested Label*, pointing out especially all the complaints that *Schiedam-lovers are wont to complain of?* And yet not one drop of gin to a barrel of it. And my excuse for this *exposure* is that *they* and *all* who may have an occasion to use such articles, may know that "good whisky" ought to be afforded at less than $4 per gallon, *even* if $1,20 worth of bitter tonics are put into 3¼ barrels of the *precious stuff*.

Then take our advice where gin or other liquor is needed, as mentioned in the first recipe in the Medical Department.

MEDICAL DEPARTMENT.

I would give an introductory word of *Caution* in this Department.

Whenever you buy an article of medicine which is not regularly *labeled* by the Druggist, have him, in all cases, *write* the name upon it. In this way you will not only save *money*, but perhaps *life*. Arsenic, phosphorus, laudanum, acids, &c., should always be put where children cannot get at them. And always purchase the best quality of drugs to insure success.

ALCOHOL—In Medicines, Preferable to Brandy, Rum, or Gin, of the Present Day. —There is no one thing doing so much to bolster up the tottering yet strong tower of Intemperance, as the old Fogy Physicians, who are constantly prescribing these articles to their patients, and one-half of the reason for it is to cover the faults of their own constant use of these beverages. This unnecessary call for these articles thus used as a medicine, keeps up a large demand ; and when we take into consideration the almost impossibility of obtaining a genuine article, the sin of prescribing them becomes so much the greater, when it is also known by all really scientific men that with alcohol (which is pure) and the native fruit wines, cider, and cider wines, (which every one can make for themselves, and can thus know their purity,) that all the indications desired to be fulfilled in curing disease can be accomplished without their use.

Then, when it is deemed advisable to use spirits to preserve any bitters or syrups from souring, instead of 1 qt. of brandy, rum or gin, use the best alcohol ½ pt., with about 2 or 3 ozs. of crushed sugar for this amount, increasing or lessening according to the amount desired in these proportions. If a *diuretic* effect is desired, which is calculated to arise where gin is prescribed, put 1 dr. of oil of juniper into the acohol before reducing with the water; or if the preparation admits of it you may put in from 1 to 2 ozs. of juniper berries instead of the oil. If the *astringent* effect is desired, as from brandy, use, say, ¼ oz. of gum kino or catechu, either, or a half of each may be used. If the *sweating* or opening properties are required, as indicated by the prescription of rum, sweeten with molasses in place of the sugar, and use 1 dr. of oil of carraway, or 1 to 2 ozs. of the seed for the above amount, as the juniper berries for gin.

If the strength of wine only is desired, use 1 qt. of the ginger wine, or if that flavor is not fancied, use any other of the wines as preferred by the patient

But no one should use any of the descriptions of alcohol as a constant beverage, even in medicine, unless advised to do so by a physician *who is not himself a toper.*

If families will follow the directions above given, and use proper care in making some of the various fruit wines as given in this book for medical use, preparing cider, &c., which is often used in prescriptions, they would seldom, if ever, be obliged to call for the *pretended* pure brandies, rums, gins, &c., of commerce, and intemperance would die a natural death for want of support.

And you will please allow me here to correct a common error, with regard to the presence of alcohol in wines. It is generally supposed that wine made from fruit, without putting some kind of spirits into it, does not contain any alcohol; but a greater mistake does not exist in the world. Any fruit, the juice of which will not pass into the vinous fermentation by which alcohol is produced, will not make wine at all; distillation will produce brandy or alcohol from any of these fermented liquors.

There is no wine, of any note, containing less than 10 parts of alcohol to 100 parts of the wine; and from that amount up to 25¼ parts; currant 20½; gooseberry 11¾; cider from 5 to 9 parts; porter 4½; even small beer 1¼ parts or qts. to 100 qts..

So it will be seen that every quart of fruit wine not made for medicine, or sacramental purposes, helps to build up the cause (intemperance) which we all so much desire not to encourage. And for those who take any kind of spirits for the *sake* of the spirit, let me give you the following :

2. "SPIRITUAL FACTS.—That whis-key is the *key* by which many gain entrance into our prisons and almshouses.

3. That *brandy brands* the noses of all those who can-n't govern their appetites.

4. That *punch* is the cause of many *unfriendly punches.*

5. That *ale* causes many *ailings,* while *beer brings* to the jar.

6. That *wine* causes many to take a *winding* way home.

7. That *cham*-pagne is the source of many *real* pains.

8. That *gin slings* have "*slewed*" more than *slings of* on it."

AGUE MEDICINES.—DR. KRIEDER'S PILLS.—Quinine 20 grs.; Dover's powders 10 grs.; sub-carbonate of iron 10 grs.; mix with mucilage of gum arabic and form into 20 pills. DOSE—Two, each hour, commencing 5 hours before the chill should set in. Then take one night and morning, until all are taken.

I cured myself of Ague with this pill after having it hang on to me for three years with all the common remedies of the day, five weeks being the longest I could keep it off, until I obtained the above pill. This was before I had studied medicine. I have cured many others with it also, never having to repeat the dose only in one case.

In attacks of Ague, it is best to take an active cathartic immediately after the first 'fit,' unless the bowels are lax, which is not generally the case, and by the time the cathartic has worked off well, you will be prepared to go ahead with the 'cure' as soon as you know its periodical return

2. For very young *children*, nothing is better than 5 or 6 grs. of quinine in a 2 oz. vial with 1 table-spoon of white sugar, then fill with water. Dose—a tea-spoon given as above, as to time. A thick solution of licorice, however, hides the taste of the quinine quite effectually.

3. AGUE BITTERS.—Quinine 40 grs.; capsicum 20 grs.; cloves ¼ oz.; cream of tartar 1 oz.; whisky 1 pt.; Mix. Dose—1 to 2 table-spoons every 2 hours, beginning 8 hours before the chill comes on, and 3 times daily for several days. Or, if preferred without spirits, take the following:

4. AGUE POWDER.—Quinine 10 grs.; capsicum 4 grs.; mix and divide into 3 powders. DIRECTIONS—Take one 4 hours before the chill, one 2 hours, and the third 1 hour before the chill *should* commence, and it will very seldom commence again. Or

5. AGUE MIXTURE WITHOUT QUININE.—Mrs. Wadsworth, a few miles south of this city, has been using the following Ague mixture over twenty years, curing, she says, more than forty cases, without a failure. She takes—

Mandrake root, fresh dug, and pounds it; then sqeezes out the juice, to obtain 1¼ table-spoons, with which she mixes the same quantity of molasses, is dividing into 3 equal doses of 1 table-spoon each, to be given 2 hours apart, commencing so as to take all an hour before the chill.

It sickens and vomits some, but she says, it will scarcely ever need repeating. Then steep dog-wood bark, (some call it box-wood,) make it strong, and continue to drink it freely for a week or two, at least.

6. AGUE CURE, BY A CLAIRVOYANT.—There is no doubt in my mind but what there is much virtue in the following clairvoyant prescription, for I have knowledge of the value of one of the roots. See Cholic remedy:

Blue vervain, leaf and top, 1 lb.; bone-set ¼ lb.; best rye whisky 1 gal.

The dose was not given, but most persons would take a wine glass five or six times daily.

7. AGUE CURED FOR A PENNY.—It has been discovered that nitric acid is of great value in the treatment of Intermittent Fever, or Ague. A physician administered the article in twenty-three cases of such fever, and it was successful in all but one, in interrupting the paroxysms, and there occurred no relapse.

in the majority of cases, 5 or 6 drops of the strong acid, given in a little gum mucilage, every 2 hours, until 60 drops had been taken, were found sufficient to break the fever, and restore the patient to health. The foregoing confirms the following:

8. AGUE ANODYNE.—Muriatic acid and laudanum, of each ½ oz.; quinine 40 grs.; brandy 4 ozs. Take 1 tea-spoon 9, 6, and 3 hours before the chill, until broken; then at 7, 14, and 21 days after, take 3 doses, and no relapse will be likely to occur.

I am well satisfied that any preparation of opium, as laudanum, morphine, &c., which effect the nerves, are valuable in ague medicine, from its intimate connection with, if not entirely confined to, the nervous system; hence the advantage of the first Ague pill, the opium being in the Dover's powder.

I have given this large number of preparations, and follow with one or two more, from the fact that almost every physician will have a peculiar prescription of his own, and are generally free to contribute their mite for the benefit of the world; and as I have seen about as much of it as most book-makers, I have come in for a large share. The nature of the articles recommended are such also as to justify their insertion in this work.

9. FEBRIFUGE WINE.—Quinine 25 grs.; water 1 pt.; sulphuric acid 15 drops; epsom salts 2 oz.; brandy 1 gill; loaf sugar 2 ozs.; color with tincture of red sanders. DOSE.—a wine-glass 3 times per day.

This is highly recommended by a regular practicing physician, in one of the ague holes (Saginaw) of the west. It, of course, can be taken without any previous preparation of the system.

10. TONIC WINE TINCTURE.—A positive cure for Ague without quinine. Peruvian bark 2 ozs.; wild cherry tree bark 1 oz; cinnamon 1 dr.; capsicum 1 tea-spoon; sulphur 1 oz.; port wine 2 qts. Let stand a week, shaking occasionally. All the articles are to be pulverized. DOSE—A wine-glass every 2 or 3 hours through the day until broken, then 2 or 3 times per day until all is used.

Always buy your Peruvian bark, and pulverize it yourself, as most of the pulverized article is greatly adulterated. This is the reason why more cures are not performed by it.

11. SOOT COFFEE—Has cured many cases of ague, after "everything else" had failed; it is made as follows:

Soot scraped from a chimney, (that from stove pipes does not do,) 1 table-spoon, steeped in water 1 pt., and settled with 1 egg beaten up in a little water, as for other coffee, with sugar and cream, 3 times daily with the meals, in place of other coffee.

It has come in very much to aid restoration in Typhoid Fever, bad cases of Jaundice, Dyspepsia, &c., &c.

Many persons will stick up their noses at these " Old Grandmother prescriptions," but I tell many " upstart Physicians " that our grandmothers are carrying more information out of the world by their deaths, than will ever be possessed by this class of " sniffers," and *I* really thank God, so do *thousands* of others, that He has enabled *me*, in this work, to reclaim such an amount of it for the benefit of the world.

12. Balmony ¼ of a pint basin of loose leaves, fill with boiling water and steep ; drink the whole in the course of the day, and repeat 3 or 4 days, or until well.

It has cured many cases of Ague. It is valuable in Jaundice, and all diseases of the Liver ; and also for worms, by the mouth and by injection. It is also valuable in Dyspepsia, Inflammatory, and Febrile diseases, generally.

NIGHT SWEATS.—To RELEIVE.—After Agues, Fevers, &c., and in Consumption, many persons are troubled with " Night Sweats ;" they are caused by weakness or general debility. For its relief :

Take Ess. of tansy ¼ oz. ; alcohol ¼ oz. ; water ¼ oz. ; quinine 15 grs. ; muriatic acid 30 drops ; mix. *Dose*—1 tea-spoon, in a gill of cold sage tea.

It should be taken two or three times during the day, and at bed time ; and the cold sage tea should be used freely as a drink, also, until cured. It will even cure Ague, also, by repeating the above dose every hour, beginning twelve to fifteen hours before the chill.

FEVERS—GENERAL IMPROVED TREATMENT FOR BILIOUS, TYPHOID, AND SCARLET FEVERS, CONGESTIVE-CHILLS, &c. ALSO VALUABLE IN DIARRHEA, SUMMER-COMPLAINT, CHOLERA-INFANTUM, AND ALL FORMS OF FEVER IN CHILDREN.—The symptoms of Fever are generally understood, yet I will give the characteristic features by which it will always be detected : cold chills, followed by a hot skin ; a quickened pulse, with a weak and languid feeling of distress ; also, loss of appetite, thirst, restlessness, scanty excretions ; in fact, every function of the body is more or less deranged. Of course, then, that which will restore all the different machinery to healthy action, will restore health. That is what the following febrifuge has done in hundreds of cases—so attested to by " Old Doctor Cone," from whose work on " Fevers and Febrile Diseases," I first obtained the outlines of the treatment, and it gives me pleasure to acknowledge my indebtedness to him through fourteen years of neighborhood acquaintance, always finding him as willing to communicate, as qualified to practice, and daring, in breaking away from " Medical Society Rules," to accomplish good.

FEBRIFUGE FOR FEVERS IN GENERAL.—Carbonate of ammo nia 2 drs. ; alum 1 dr. ; capsicum, foreign gentian, colombo root, and Prussiate of iron, all pulverized, of each, ¼ dr. ; mix, by putting into a bottle, adding cold water 4 ozs. DOSE—One tea-spoon to a grown person, every 2 hours, in common cases of fever. It may be sweetened if preferred. Shake well each time before giving, and keep the bottle tightly corked.

The philosophy of this treatment is, the carbonate of ammonia neutralizes the acidity of the stomach, and determines to, and relaxes the surface ; and with the capsicum is a hundred per cent more efficient. The alum constringes, soothes, and aids in relieving the irritated and engorged mucous membrane of the stomach, and finally operates as a gentle laxative. The colombo and gentian are gently astringent and stimulating, but chiefly tonic, and the Prussiate of iron is tonic ; and in their combination are, (as experience will and has proved) the most efficient and safe Febrifuge, in all forms and grades of fever, yet known. We therefore wish to state that, after twenty-five years' experience in the treatment of disease, we have not been able to obtain a knowledge of any course of treatment that will begin to compare with that given above, for the certain, speedy, and effectual cure of all forms of fever ; and all that is requisite, is, to have sufficient confidence in the course of treatment recommended ; to use it from three to five, and in extreme cases, seven days, as directed, and that confidence will be inspired in all who use it, whether Physician (if unprejudiced) or patient, or the heads of families; remember all processes in nature require time for their accomplishment.

After the patient has been twenty-four hours without fever, or if the patient be pale, blanched, with a cool sur face and feeble pulse, at the commencement of fever, prepare the following:

2. FEBRIFUGE TEA.—Take Virginia snake root and valerian root, of each 2 drs.; boiling water 1 pt. Pour the boiling water on the roots and steep ½ an hour, and give a tea-spoon of the Febrifuge and a table-spoon of this Tea together, every 2 hours, and after he has been another 24 hours without fever, give it every 3 or 4 hours, until the patient has good appetite and digestion, then 3 times daily, just before meals, until the patient has gained considerable strength, when it may be entirely discontinued; or he may continue the simple infusion to aid digestion.

A strong tea of wild cherry bark makes the best substitute for the snake root tea, and especially if mercury has been previously used in the case, and if it has, it is best to continue the cherry bark tea until the patient is entirely recovered.

A patient using this treatment, if bilious, may vomit bile a few times, or if there is conjestion of the stomach, he wil probably vomit occasionally for a few hours, but it will soon subside. It will not purge, except a patient be very bilious, in which case there will probably be two or three bilious discharges; but it gives so much tone to the action of the stomach and bowels as to secure regular operations; but if the bowels should not be moved in two or three days, give injections of warm water, or warm water with a little salt in it.

Give the patient all the plain, wholesome diet, of any kind, he will take, espcially broiled ham, mush and rich milk, boiled rice, milk or dry toast, hot mealy potatoes, boiled or roasted, with good fresh butter, &c., &c.; and good, pure, cold water, or tea and coffee, seasoned to the taste. as drinks, and keep the person and bed clean, and room quiet and undisturbed by conversation, or any other noise, and see that it is well ventilated.

If there should be extreme pain in the head when the fever is at the highest, or in the back or loins, and delirium at night, with intolerance of light and noise; in such cases.

in addition to keeping the room cool, dark and quiet, and giving the febrifuge regularly, as above directed, take the following :

8. FEVER LINIMENT.—Sulphuric ether and aqua ammonia, of each 1 oz.; muriate of ammonia ½ oz.; mix, and shake the bottle, and wet the scalp and all painful parts, every 2 or 3 hours, until the pain abates. Keep tightly corked.

After the application of the liniment, fold a muslin cloth four or five thicknesses, dip it in cold water, and apply it to the head or any part afflicted with severe pain ; or to the pit of the stomach, if there be much vomiting ; and it may be renewed every three or four hours.

Besides the above treatment, dip a towel in cold water, and rub the patient off briskly and thoroughly, and be careful to wipe perfectly dry, with a clean, hot and dry towel ; this may be repeated every three or four hours, if the skin be very hot and dry ; but if the surface be pale, cool, moist, livid, or lead-colored, omit the general sponging ; but the face, neck and hands may be washed occasionally, but be sure to wipe perfectly dry with a clean, hot and dry towel. But if he be very pale and blanched, with a cool or cold surface, or have a white circle around his mouth and nose, or be covered with a cold, clammy perspiration, give the Febrifuge every hour, until the above symptoms disappear, giving the patient hot coffee or tea, pennyroyal, sage, balm, or mint tea, as hot as he can sup them, and as freely as possible, and make hot applications to his person, and put a bottle of hot water to the soles of his feet ; and after this tendency to prostration is overcome, then give the Febrifuge once in two hours as before only.

Children will use the medicine in all respects as directed for grown persons, giving to a child one year old a fourth of a tea-spoon, or fifteen drops ; if under a year old, a little less, (we have frequently arrested Cholera Infantum with the Febrifuge, in children under six months old, and in some instances under a month old,) and increase the dose in proportion to the age above a year old, giving half a tea-spoon to a child from three to six, and three-fourths of a tea-spoon from six to ten years, old and so on ; and be sure to offer children some food several times a day, the best of which is broiled smoked ham, good stale wheat bread boiled in good rich milk, mush and milk, boiled rice, etc. ; but animal diet agrees best, and especially in cases of Summer Complaint, or Cholera Infantum, the diet had better be almost exclusively animal. It will be difficult to use the infusion of snake root with children that are too young to obey the mandate of parents, and the Febrifuge may be made sweet, with white or loaf sugar, for young children, so as to cover its taste as much as possible, but older children will be benefited very much by the use of the infusion of snake root and valerian, and should take it as prescribed for adults, of course adapting the dose to the age of the patient.

4. NOTE.—The above treatment, if persevered in for a short time, is effectual in arresting Diarrhea, Summer Complaint, Cholera Infantum, and all forms of Fever in children. Give it every two hours, or if the patient be very feeble and corpse-like, give it every hour until there is reaction, and then give it every two hours, as prescribed for fever in general, and you will be satisfied with the result after a short time.

5. TYPHOID FEVER.—If the patient be Typhoid, that is, if his tongue be brown or black, and dry in the centre, with glossy red edges ; if he have Diarrhea, with thin, watery, or muddy stools, and a tumid or swollen belly, he will probably have a rapid, or frequent, and small pulse, and be delirious and rest but little at night; under these circumstances, give the Febrifuge in the Tea, No. 2, as for fevers in general, every two hours, and give, also, the following :

6. FEBRIFUGE BALSAM.—Gum camphor 30 grs.; balsam copaiba, sweet spirits of nitre, compound spirits of lavender, of each ½ oz.

Shake the vial, and give forty drops every four hours, in with the other medicine, until the tongue becomes moist, and the Diarrhea is pretty well subdued, when you will discontinue this preparation, and continue the Febrifuge and snake root tea, as directed for fever in general.

NOTE.—We do not believe that one case of fever in a thousand will develope Typhoid symptoms, unless such cases have been injured in the treatment of the first stage, by a reducing course of medicine, as bleeding, vomiting, especially emetic tartar, purging, especially with calomel, and compound extract of colocynth or oil, salts, or infusion of senna, and the common cooling powder, which is composed of saltpetre or nitre, and tartar emetic or ipecac, all of which irritate the mucous membrane of the stomach and bowels, and consequently produce determination of blood to these parts, that results in irritation, engorgement, congestion, inflammation, and consequently Typhoid Fever.

If fever is attended with the Dysentery, or Bloody Flux, it should be treated in the same manner precisely as Typhoid Fever, as it is nothing but Typhoid Fever with inflammation of the large, and sometimes small bowels. The treatment given for Typhoid Fever above, will cure all forms of Dysentery as it does fever, but the bloody and slimy discharges will continue for two or three days after the fever is subdued and the appetite and digestion are restored, and at times, especially if the patient discharge bile, which will be green, there will be a good deal of pain at stool, which, however, will soon subside.

7. SCARLET FEVER.—If you have Scarlet Fever, treat it in all respects as fever in general, and if the patient's throat should show any indications of swelling, apply the Fever-Liniment No. 3, and make the application of cold water in the same manner as there directed; and it had better be repeated every three or four hours until the swelling is entirely subdued, when the wet cloth should be substituted by a warm, dry, flannel one; but if the patient's throat should ulcerate, give a few drops of the Febrifuge every half hour, or hour, until the dark sloughs separate, and the throat looks red and clean, when you need only give the medicine at regular intervals, as recommended for fever in general, that is, every two hours. If this treatment be pursued at the onset, the throat will seldom, if ever, ulcerate.

8. CONGESTIVE, OR SINKING CHILL.—In case of Congestive, or Sinking Chill, give the Febrifuge as directed for fever in general; but if the patient be insensible and cold, or drenched in a cold perspiration, give the Febrifuge in a tablespoon of the snake root and valerian tea every hour until the patient becomes warm, and then give it every two hours to within twelve hours of the time he anticipates another chill, when you will give the following

9. STIMULATING TONIC.—Sulphate of quinine 20 grs.; pulverized capsicum 30 grs.; pulverized carbonate of ammonia 90 grs.; mix and put into a bottle, and add 15 tea-spoons of cold water, and give a tea-spoon, together with a tea-spoon of the Febrifuge,

every hour, either alone, or what is better, in a tea-spoon of the snake root and valerian tea, for 15 hours.

The patient should lie in bed and drink freely of penny-royal tea, or hot coffee, or some other hot tea, and after the time has elapsed for the chill, give the same as for fever in general, until the patient is entirely recovered. The above treatment will arrest any form of Ague, and the after treat ment will, with any degree of care, prevent its return. Or the Ague may be arrested most speedily, by taking one grain of quinine in a tea-spoon of the Febrifuge every hour for six hours preceeding a paroxysm, and then pursue the above tonic course.

I have given the foregoing treatment for fevers, because I know that it is applicable in all cases, and that the articles are kept by all druggists. But there is a better, because quicker method of cure, and I am very sorry to say that for want of knowledge, in regard to the value of the medicine, it is not usually kept by Druggists. I mean the Tincture of Gelseminum. It is an unrivaled Febrifuge. It relaxes the system without permanent prostration of strength. Its *specific action* is to cloud the vision, give double-sightedness and inability to open the eyes, with distressed prostration; which will gradually pass off in a few hours, leaving the patient refreshed, and if combined with quinine, completely restored. To administer it:

10. Take the tincture of gelseminum 50 drops, put into a vial, and add 5 tea-spoons of water; quinine 10 grs. Shake when used. Dose—One tea-spoon in half a glass of sweetened water, and repeat every 2 hours.

Watch carefully its action, and as soon as you discover its specific action as mentioned above, give no more.

Dr. Hale, of this city, one of the more liberal class of physicians, (and I use the term, liberal, as synonymous with the term, successful,) prefers to add twenty-five drops of the tincture of veratrum viride with the gelseminum, and give as there directed. And in case that their full specific action should be brought on, give a few spoons of brandy, to raise the patient from his stupor, or what is preferable:

11. Carbonate of ammonia ¼ oz.; water 4 ozs.; mix. Dose—one table-spoon every 15 or 20 minutes, until revived.

If Dr. Hale's addition should be used, it will be found

applicable in all cases of fever, except in Typhoid accompanied with its own excessive prostration; without the addition of the veratrum it is applicable in all cases of fevers above described. Of course, in all cases where the fever is thus subdued, you will continue quinine, or some other appropriate tonic treatment, to perfect a cure, and prevent a relapse. And it might not be amiss here to give a plan of preparing a nourishing and agreeable lemonade for the sick, and especially for persons afflicted with fever:

12. LEMONADE, NOURISHING, FOR FEVER PATIENTS.—Arrowroot 2 or 3 tea-spoons rubbed up with a little cold water, in a bowl or pitcher, which will hold about 1 qt.; then squeeze in the juice of half of a good sized lemon, with 2 or 3 table-spoons of white sugar, and pour on boiling water to fill the dish, constantly stirring whilst adding the boiling water.

Cover the dish, and when cold, it may be freely drank to allay thirst, as also to nourish the weak, but some will prefer the following:

13. PROF. HUFELAND'S DRINK FOR FEVER PATIENTS OR EXCESSIVE THIRST.—Cream of tartar ½ oz.; water 3 qts.; boil until dissolved; after taking it from the fire add a sliced orange with from 1½ to 3 ozs. of white sugar, according to the taste of the patient; bottle and keep cool.

To be used for a common drink in fevers of all grades, and at any time when a large amount of drink is *craved* by the *invalid*. Neither is there any bad taste to it for those in health.

UTERINE HEMORRHAGES.—PROF. PLATT'S TREATMENT TWENTY YEARS WITHOUT A FAILURE.—Sugar of lead 10 grs.; ergot 10 grs.; opium 3 grs.; epicac 1 gr.; all pulverized and well mixed. DOSE—10 to 12 grs., given in a little honey or syrup.

In very bad cases after child-birth, it might be repeated in thirty minutes, or the dose increased to fifteen or eighteen grains; but in cases of rather profuse wasting, repeat it once at the end of three hours, will usually be found all that is necessary, if not, repeat occasionally as the urgency of the case may seem to require.

Prof. Platt is connected with Antioch College, O., and has been a very successful practitioner.

DYSPEPSIA.—In the good old days of corn bread and

crust coffee, there was but little trouble with Dyspepsia;
but since the days of fashionable intemperance, both in
eating and drinking, such as spirituous liquors, wines, beers,
ale, tea, and coffee, hot bread or biscuit, high seasoned food,
over-loading the stomach at meals, and constant eating and
drinking between meals, bolting the food, as called, that is,
swallowing it without properly chewing, excessive venery,
want of out door exercise, with great anxiety of mind as to
bow the means can be made to continue the same indulgen-
ees, &c., all have a tendency to debilitate the stomach, and
bring on, or cause, Dyspepsia.

And it would seem to the Author that the simple state
ment of its cause—the truth of which no one can reason
ably doubt—would be sufficient to, at least, suggest its cure
But I am willing to state, that, as a general thing, this over-
indulgence would not be continued, nor would it have been
allowed, had they *known* its awful consequences. I know
that this was true in my own case, in all its points; this
was, of course, before I had studied, or knew but little, of
the power of the human system, or the practice of medicine, and it was for the purpose of finding something to
cure myself, that I commenced its study; for it was by
years of over-indulgence at table, and between meals, in the
grocery business which I was carrying on, that I brought on
such a condition of the stomach that eating gave me the
most intolerable suffering—a feeling almost impossible to
describe; first a feeling of goneness or want of support at
the stomach, heat, lassitude, and finally pain, until a thousand deaths would have been a great relief; drink was
craved, and the more I drark the more intolerable the suffering—apple cider, vinegar and water made palatable with
sugar, excepted. It might be asked at this point, what did
I do? I would ask, what could I do? Eat, I could not,
drink I could not; then what else was to be done, only, to
do without either. What, starve? No.

TREATMENT.—Take,—no, just stop taking "Throw all
medicine to the dogs"—yes, and food also. What, starve?
No, but simply get *hungry;* whoever heard of a dyspeptic
being hungry? at least, those who eat three meals a day.
They eat because the victuals *taste* good—mouth-hunger,
only.

The last year or two of my dyspeptic life, I only ate because it was eating time, and supposed I must eat or die, when I only died forty deaths, by eating.

All physicians whose books I have read, and all whose prescriptions I have obtained, say: "Eat little and often; drink little and often." I say eat a little, and at the right time, that is, when hungry at the stomach; drink a little, and at the right time, that is, after digestion, and it is of just as much importance to eat and drink the right thing, as at the right time.

Persons have been so low in Dyspepsia, that even one tea-spoon of food on the stomach would not rest; in such cases, let nothing be taken by mouth for several days; but inject gruel, rice water, rich broths, &c.; but these cases occur very seldom.

FIRST.—Then, with ordinary cases, if there is much heat of the stomach, at bed time, wet a towel in cold water, wringing it out that it may not drip, and lay it over the stomach, having a piece of flannel over it to prevent wetting the clothes. This will soon allay the heat, but keep it on during the night, and at any subsequent time, as may be needed.

SECOND.—In the morning, if you have been in the habit of eating about two large potatoes, two pieces of steak, two slices of bread, or from four to six hot pancakes, or two to four hot biscuits, and drinking one to three cups of tea or coffee,—hold, hold, you cry; no, let me go on. I have many times seen all these eaten, with butter, honey, or molasses, too large in amount to be mentioned, with a taste of every other thing on the table, such as cucumbers, tomatoes, &c., &c., and all by dyspeptics; but,

You will stop this morning on half of one potato, two inches square of steak, and half of one slice of cold, wheat bread—or I prefer, if it will agree with you, that you use the "Yankee Brown Bread," only the same quantity; *eat very slow, chew perfectly fine, and swallow it without water, tea, or coffee;* neither must you drink any, not a drop, until one hour before meal-time again, then as little as possible, so as you think not quite to choke to death.

THIRD.—The question now to be settled is, did you *suffer* from the *abundance* of your breakfast, or from the *kind* of food taken? If you did, take *less* next time, or chav the *kind*, and so continue to lessen the *quantity*, or change the *kind* until you ascertain the proper quantity and kind which enables you to overcome this exceeding suffering after meals; nay, more, which leaves you perfectly *comfortable* after meals.

LASTLY—You now have the whole secret of curing the worst case of dyspepsia in the world You will, however, bear in mind that *years* have been spent in indulgence; do not therefore expect to cure it in *days*, nay, it will take *months*, possibly a whole *year* of self-denial, watchfulness and care: and even then, one over loading of the stomach at a Christmas pudding will set you back again for months. Make up your mind to eat only *simple* food, and that, in *small* quantities, notwithstanding an over-anxious wife, or other friend, will say, now do try a little of this *nice* pie, pudding, or other dish, no matter what it may be. Oh! now do have a cup of this nice coffee, they will often ask; but *no*, NO, must be the invariable answer, or you are again a "goner." For there is hardly any disease equally liable to relapse as dyspepsia; and indulgence in a variety of food, or over-eating any one kind, or even watery vegetables or fruit, will be almost certain to make the patient pay dear for the whistle.

Then you must eat *only* such food ar you know to agree with you, and in just as *small* quantities as will keep you in health. Drink no fluids until digestion is over, or about four hours after eating, until the stomach has become a little strong, or toned up to bear it, then one cup of the "Dyspepsia Coffee," or one cup of the "Coffee Made Healthy," may be used. But more difficulty is experienced from over-drinking, than over-eating. Most positively must Dyspeptics avoid *cold* water with their meals. If the saliva and gastric juice are diluted with an abundance of *any* fluid, they never have the same properties to aid, or carry on digestion, which they had before dilution; then the only hope of the *Dyspeptic* is to use no fluid with his food, nor until digestion has had her perfect work.

CAUTION.—I may be allowed to give a word of caution to Mothers, as well as to all others. *One plate of food is* anough for health—two, and even three, are often eaten. Most persons have heard of the lady who did not want a "cart load," but when she got to eating, it all disappeared, and the retort, " Back up your cart and I will load it again," was just what I would have expected to hear if the load had been given to a Dyspeptic, which it no doubt was; then learn the proper amount of food necessary for health, and when that is eaten, by yourself or child, stop. If pudding is on the table and you choose to have a little of it, it is all right —have some pudding; if pie, have a piece of pie; or cake, have a piece of cake ; but do not have all, and that after you have eaten twice as much meat victuals as health requires. If apples, melons, raisins or nuts are on the table, and you wish some of them, eat them before meal, and never after it; if surprise is manifested around you, say you *eat* to live, not live to *eat*. The reason for this is, that persons will eat all they need, and often more, of common food, then eat nuts, raisins, melons, &c., until the stomach is not only filled beyond comfort, but actually distended to its utmost capacity of endurance; being led on by the *taste*, when if the reverse course was taken, the stomach becomes satisfied when a proper amount of the more common food has been eaten, after the others.

Are you a Grocer, and constantly nibbling at raisins, candy, cheese, apples, and every other edible? Stop, until just before meal, then eat what you like, go to your meal, and return, not touching again until meal-time, and you are safe ; continue the nibbling, and you do it at the sacrifice of future health. Have you children or other young persons under your care? See that they eat only a reasonable quantity at meals, and not anything between them; *do this*, and I am willing to be called a *fool* by the younger ones, which I am sure to be, but do it not, and *the* fool will *suffer* for his folly.

You may consider me a hard Doctor—be it so then ; the drunkard calls him hard names who says give up your " cups," but as sure as he would die a drunkard, so sure will you die a Dyspeptic unless you give up your *over-eating* and *over-drinking* of water, tea, coffee, wine, beer, ale, &c. Now you *know* the consequences, *suit* yourselves; but I.

have paid too dearly for my experience, not to lift a warning voice, or spare the guilty.

In recent cases, and in cases brought on by over-indulgence, at some extra rich meal, you will find the " Dyspeptic Tea," made from "Thompson's Composition," will be all sufficient, as spoken of under that head, which see.

2. The wild black cherries, put into Jamaica rum, is highly recommended, made very strong with the cherries, and without sugar; but I should say put them into some of the domestic wines, or what would be still better, make a wine directly from them, according to directions under the head of " Fruit Wines."

3. Old " Father Pinkney," a gentleman over 90 years of age, assures me that he has cured many bad cases of Dyspepsia, where they would give up their over indulgences, by taking :

Blue flag root, washed clean, and free from specks and rotten streaks, then pounding it and putting into a little warm water, and straining out the milky juice, and adding sufficient pepper-sauce to make it a little hot. Dose—one table-spoon 3 times daily.

It benefits by its action on the liver, and it would be good in Liver Complaints, the pepper also stimulating the stomach. See " Soot-Coffee " No. 12, amongst the Ague medicines.

LARYNGITIS,—INFLAMMATION OF THE THROAT.— This complaint, in a chronic form, has become very prevalent, and is a disease which is aggravated by every change of weather, more especially in the fall and winter months. It is considered, and that justly, a very hard disease to cure, but with caution, time, and a rational course of treatment, it can be cured.

The difficulty with most persons is, they think that it is an uncommon disease, and consequently they must obtain some uncommon preparation to cure it, instead of which, some of the more simble remedies, as follows, will cure nearly every case, if persevered in a sufficient length of time.   First, then, take the :

ALTERATIVE FOR DISEASES OF THE SKIN.—Compound tincture of peruvian bark 6 ozs. ; fluid extract of sarsaparilla 1 lb. ; extract of conium ¼ oz. ; iodide of potash, (often called hydriodate) ¼ oz. ; iodine ½ dr. ; dissolve the extract of conium and the powders in a little of the fluid, and mix all. DOSE—Two teaspoons 3 times daily, before meals, until all is taken. Shake the bottle well before using.

In the next place, take the :

2. GARGLE FOR SORE THROAT.—Very strong sage tea ½ pt., strained honey, common salt, and strong vinegar, of each 2 tablespoons; cayenne, the pulverized, one rounding tea-spoon; steeping the cayenne with the sage, strain, mix, and bottle for use, gargling from 4 to a dozen times daily according to the severity of the case.

This is one of the very best gargles in use. By persevering some three months, I cured a case of two years standing where the mouths of the Eustachian tubes constantly discharged matter at their openings through the tonsils into the patients mouth, he having previously been quite deaf, the whole throat being also diseased. I used the preparation for "Deafness" also as mentioned under that head.

Remembering always to breath through nature's channel for the breath, the nose.

Besides the foregoing, you will wash the whole surface twice a week with plenty of the "Toilet Soap," in water, wiping dry, then with a coarse dry towel rub the whole surface for ten minutes at least, and accomplish the coarse towel part of it every night and morning until the skin will remain through the day with its flushed surface, and genial heat; this draws the blood from the throat and other internal organs, or in other words, equalizes the circulation; know, and act, upon this fact, and no inflammation can long exist, no matter where it is located. Blood accumulates in the part inflamed, but let it flow evenly through the whole system, and of course there can be no inflammation.

You will also apply to the throat and breast the following :

3. SORE THROAT LINIMENT.—Gum camphor 2 ozs.; castile soap, shaved fine, 1 dr.; oil of turpentine 1 table-spoon; oil of origanum ½ oz.; opium ¼ oz.; alcohol 1 pt. In a week or ten days it will be fit for use, then bathe the parts freely 2 or 3 times daily.

This liniment would be found useful in almost any throat or other disease where an outward application might be needed. If the foregoing treatment should fail, there is no alternative but to bring in *emetics* with the other treatment, and continue them for *a long time.*

I mention the emetic plan last, from the fact that so many people utterly object to the emetic treatment. But when everything else fails, that steps in and *saves* the patient, which goes to show how *unjust* the prejudice. By the phrase, a long time, I mean several weeks, twice daily at first, then once a day, and finally thrice to twice a week, &c A part of this course you will see, by the following, is cor roborated by the celebrated Lung and Throat Doctor, S. S. Fitch, of New York, who says " it is a skin disease, and that purifying medicines are necessary to cleanse the blood—taking long, full breaths," &c. This is certainly good sense. His treatment of throat diseases is summed up in the following:

NOTE.—" Wear but little clothing around the neck—chew often a little nut-gall and swallow the juice—wear a wet cloth about the throat at night, having a dry towel over it—bathe freely all over as in consumption, and especially bathe the throat with cold water every morning, also wash out the inside of the throat with cold water—avoid crowded rooms—gargle with a very weak solution of nitrate of silver—chewing gold thread and swallowing the juice and saliva from it—borax and honey occasionally, and gum arabic water, if much irritation—use the voice as little as possible until well, also often using a liniment externally."

I had hoped for very much benefit from using croton oil externally, but time has shown that the advantage derived from it is not sufficient to remunerate for the excessive irritation caused by its continued application.

4. Smoking dried mullein leaves in a pipe not having been used for tobacco, is said to have cured many cases of Laryngitis. And I find in my last Eclectic Medical Journal so strong a corroboration, taken from the Medical and Surgical Reporter, of this fact, that I cannot refrain from giving the quotation. It says: " in that form of disease in which there is dryness of the trachea, *with a constant desire to clear the throat,* attended with little expectoration, and considerable pain in the part affected, the mullein smoked through a pipe, acts like a charm, and affords instant relief. It seems to act as an anodyne in allaying irritation, while it promotes expectoration, and removes that gelatinous mucus

which gathers in the larynx, and, at the same time, by some *unknown power*, completely changes the nature of the disease, and, if persevered in, will produce a radical cure."

We read in a certain place of a gentleman who was walking around and through a great city, and he came across an inscription "To the *unknown* God"—and directly we find him explaining that unknown Being to the astonished inhabitants. And I always feel, like this old-fashioned gentleman, to cry out, upon every convenient occasion, my belief, that it was *that* God's *great* wisdom, seeing what was required, and His *exceeding* goodness, providing according to our necessities, this wonderful, and to some, that *unknown* power in the thousands of plants around us. What matters it to us how it is done? If the cure is performed, it is sufficient.

Since the publication of the foregoing, in the ninth edition, I have been smoking the dried mullein, and recommending it to others. It has given general satisfaction for coughs and as a substitute for tobacco in smoking, exhilerating the nerves, and allaying the hacking coughs from recent colds, by breathing the smoke into the lungs. In one instance, after retiring, I could not rest from an irritation in the upper portion of the lungs and throat, frequently hacking without relief only for a moment; I arose, filled my pipe with mullein, returning to bed I smoked the pipeful, drawing it into the lungs, and did not cough again during the night.

An old gentleman, an inveterate smoker, from my suggestion, began to mix the mullein with his tobacco, one-fourth at first, for awhile; then half, and finally three-fourths; at this point he rested. It satisfied in place of the full amount of tobacco, and cured a cough which had been left upon him after inflammation of the lungs. The flavor can hardly be distinguished from the flavor of tobacco smoke, in rooms.

It can be gathered any time during the season, the centre stem removed, carefully dried, and rubbed fine, when it is ready for use. It gives a pipe the phthysic, as fast as it cures one on the patient; but the clay pipe, which is to be used, can be readily cleansed by burning out.

Here is the "Substitute for Tobacco" for which the French have offered 50,000 francs.

It can be made into cigars by using a tobacco-leaf wrapper
Catarrh is often more or less connected with that disease.
In such cases, in connection with the above treatment, take
several times daily of the following :

CATARRH SNUFF.—Scotch snuff 1 oz.; chloride of lime, dried
and pulverized 1 rounding tea-spoon; mix, and bottle, corking
tightly.

The snuff has a tendency to aid the secretion from the
parts ; and the chloride corrects unpleasant fetor.¹

CANCERS.—To CURE—METHOD OF DR. LANDOLFI,
(SURGEON-GENERAL OF THE NEAPOLITAN ARMY) AND SEV-
ERAL SUCCESSFUL AMERICAN METHODS.—The principle
upon which the treatment is based, consists in transforming
a tumor of a malignant character, by conferring upon it a
character of benignity, which admits of cure. This trans-
formation is effected by cauterization with an agent looked
upon as a specific, viz : chloride of bromine, combined, or
not, with other substances, which have already been tried,
but have hitherto been employed separately. The internal treatment is merely auxiliary. (Cancers may be known
from other tumors by their shooting, or lancinating pains ;
and if an open sore, from their great fetor.—AUTHOR.)
The formulas for the caustics are, with the exception of a
few cases, the following :

Equal parts of the chlorides of zinc, gold, and antimony,
mixed with a sufficient quantity of flour to form a viscid paste.

At Vienna, he used a mixture of the same substances in different proportions, chloride of bromine 3 parts ; chloride of zinc 2
parts; chloride of gold and antimony, each 1 part; made into a
thick paste with powdered licorice root. This preparation
should be made in an open place, on account of the gases which
are disengaged.

The essential element is the chloride of bromine, which has
often been employed alone; thus, chloride of bromine from 2½
to 4 drs., and put licorice root as much as sufficient.

The chloride of zinc is indispensable in ulcerated cancers,
in which it acts as a hemastatic, (stopping blood.) The
chloride of gold is only useful in cases of encephaloid
(brain-like) cancers, in which it exercises a special, if not a
specific action. Cancers of the skin, (epitheliomas,) lupus,
and small cystosarcomas, (watery or bloody tumors,) are
treated with bromine mixed with basilicon ointment in the

proportion of one part of bromine to eight of the ointment; the application should not extend to the healthy parts, its action being often propagated through a space of one or two lines. The paste is only allowed to remain on about twenty-four hours; on removing the dressing a line of demarkation is almost always found separating the healthy from the morbid parts. The tumor is itself in part whitish and part reddish, or marbled with yellow and blue. The caustic is replaced with the poultice, or with compresses smeared with basilicon ointment only, which are to be removed every three hours until the scar is detached; the pain progressively diminishing in proportion as the mortification advances, the line of demarkation daily becomes more evident; about the fourth or fifth day the cauterized portion begins to rise, and from the eighth to the fifteenth day it becomes detached, or can be removed with forceps, and without pain, exposing a suppurating surface, secreting pus of good quality and covered with healthy granulations. If any points remain of less satisfactory appearance, or present traces of morbid growth, a little of the paste is to be again applied, then dress the sore as you would a simple ulcer; if the suppuration proceeds too slowly, dress it with lint dipped in the following solution :

Chloride of bromine 20 or 30 drops; Goulard's Extract from 1 to 2 drs.; distilled water 16 ozs.

In the majority of cases healing takes place rapidly, cicatrization progresses from the circumference to the center, no complications supervene, and the cicatrix (scar,) resembles that left by a cutting instrument. His internal remedy, to prevent a relapse, is,

Chloride of bromine 2 drops; powder of the seeds of water fennel 23 grs.; extract of hemlock (Conium Maculatum) 12 grs.; mix and divide into 20 pills; one to be taken daily for 2 months, and after that, 2 pills daily for a month or two longer, 1 night and morning, after meals.

In any case of Cancer, either the foregoing, internal remedy, or some of the other Alteratives, should be taken two or three weeks before the treatment is commenced, and should also be continued for several weeks after its cure.

2. DR. H. G. JUDKINS' METHOD.—This gentleman, of Malaga, Monroe Co., O., takes :

Chloride of zinc the size of a hazel nut, and puts enough water with it to make a thin paste, then mixes with it equal parts of flour, and finely pulverized charcoal, sufficient to form a tolerable stiff paste.

He spreads this on a soft piece of sheep skin, sufficiently large to cover the tumor, and applies every two days until it is detached, then dresses it with "Judkins' Ointment," which see. Again—

3. L. S. HODGKINS' METHOD.—This gentleman is a merchant, of Reding, Mich. The method is not original with him, but he cured his wife with it, of cancer of the breast, after having been pronounced incurable. Some would use it because it contains calomel—others would not use it for the same reason; I give it an insertion from the fact that I am well satisfied that it has cured the disease, and from its singularity of composition.

Take a white oak root and bore out the heart and burn the chips to get the ashes, ¼ oz.; lunar caustic ¼ oz.; calomel ¼ oz., salts of nitre (salt petre) ¼ oz.; the body of a thousand-legged worm, dried and pulverized, all to be made fine and mixed with 1 lb. of lard.

Spread this rather thin upon soft leather, and apply to the Cancer, changing twice a day; will kill the tumor in three or four days, which you will know by the general appearance; then apply a poultice of soaked figs until it comes out, fibres and all; heal with a plaster made by boiling red beech leaves in water, straining and boiling thick, then mix with beeswax and mutton tallow to form a salve of proper consistency. To cleanse the system while the above is being used, and for some time after:

Take mandrake root. pulverized, 1 oz.; epsom salts 1 oz.; put into pure gin 1 pt., and take of this 3 times daily, from 1 tea to a table-spoon, as you can bear. He knew of several other cures from the same plan.

4. The juice of pokeberries, set in the sun, upon a pewter dish, and dried to a consistence of a salve, and applied as a plaster, has cured cancer.

5. Poultices of scraped carrots, and of yellow dock root, have both cured, and the scraped carrot poultices, especially, not only cleanse the sore, but remove the very offensive smell or fetor, which is *characteristic* of cancers.

6. A gentleman in Ohio cures them by making a tea of the yellow dock root, and drinking of it freely, washing the sore with the same several times daily for several days, then poulticing with the root, mashed and applied twice daily, even on the tongue.

7. Rev. C. C. Cuyler, of Poughkeepsie, N. Y., says he has known several cases cured as follows:

Take the narrow-leaved dock root and boil it in soft water until very strong, wash the ulcer with this strong decoction 3 times in the 24 hours, fill the cavity also with the same 2 minutes, each time, then bruise the root, and lay it on gauze, and lay the gauze next to the ulcer, and wet linen cloths in the decoction and lay over the poultice; and each time let the patient drink a wine-glass of the strong tea of the same root, with ½ of a glass of port wine sweetened with honey.

8. Dr. Buchan's work on Medicine, gives the case of a person who had cancer of the tongue, cured in fourteen days, as follows:

Dilute nitric acid 1 oz; honey 2 ozs.; pure water 2 pts.; mix. DOSE—Three table-spoons frequently; to be sucked past the teeth, through a quill or tube.

Opium was given at night, simply to keep down pain.

9. GREAT ENGLISH REMEDY—by which a brother of Lowell Mason was cured, is as follows:

Take chloride of zinc, blood-root pulverized, and flour, equal quantities of each, worked into a paste and applied until the mass comes out, then poultice and treat as a simple sore.

The Rural New Yorker, in reporting this case, says, in applying it, " First spread a common sticking-plaster *much* larger than the cancer, cutting a circular piece from the center of it a *little* larger than the cancer, applying it, which exposes a narrow rim of healthy skin; then apply the cancer plaster and keep it on twenty-four hours. On removing it, the cancer will be found to be burned into, and appears the color of an old shoe-sole, and the rim outside will appear white and parboiled, as if burned by steam.

" Dress with slippery-elm poultice until suppuration takes place, then heal with any common salve."

10. ARMENIAN METHOD.—In Armenia, a salve, made by boiling olive oil to a proper consistence for the use, is reported by an eastern traveler to have cured very bad cases.

11. Figs boiled in new milk until tender, then split and applied hot—changing twice daily, washing the parts every change, with some of the milk—drinking 1 gill of the milk also as often.

And continueing from three to four months, is also reported to have cured a man ninety-nine years old by using only six pounds, whilst ten pounds cured a case of ten years' standing. The first application giving pain, but afterwards relief, every application.

12. RED OAK BARK—A salve from the ashes, has long been credited for curing cancer, and as I have recently seen the method given for preparing and using it, by Isaac Dillon, of Oregon, published in a paper near him, I cannot keep the benefit of it from the public.. The directions were sent to him by his father, John Dillon, Sen., of Zanesville, O., and, from my knowledge of the Dillon family, I have the utmost confidence in the prescription. It is as follows :

Take red oak bark ashes 1 peck; put on to them, boiling water 6 qts.; let it stand 12 hours; then draw off the ley and boil to a thick salve; spread this, pretty thick, upon a thick cloth a little larger than the cancer, and let it remain on 3 hours; if it is too severe, half of that time; the same day, or the next, apply again 3 hours, which will generally effect a cure; after the last plaster, wash the sore with warm milk and water; then apply a healing salve made of mutton tallow, bark of elder, with a little rosin and bees-wax, (some root of white lilly may be added,) stewed over a slow fire; when the sore begins to matterate, wash it 3 or 4 times daily, renewing the salve each time; avoid strong diet, and strong drink, but drink a tea of sassafras root and spice-wood tops, for a week before and after the plaster.

13. PROF. R. S. NEWTON, of Cincinnati, uses the chloride of zinc, a saturated solution, (as strong as can be made,) or makes the chloride into a paste, with thick gum solution.

In cases of large tumors he often removes the bulk of them with a knife, then applies the solution, or paste, as he thinks best, to destroy any remaining roots which have been severed by the knife.

14. PROF. CALKINS, of Philadelphia, prefers a paste made from yellow-dock, red-clover, and poke, using the leaves only, of either article, in equal quantities.

Boiling, straining, and simmering to a paste, applying from time to time, to cancerous growths or tumors, until the entire mass is destroyed, then poultice and heal as usual

But Dr. Beach, of N. Y., who is a man of much experience in cancers, says beware of the knife, or any plaster which *destroys* the cancer or tumor; but first use discutients (medicines which have a tendency to drive away swellings,) unless already ulcerated, then, mild poultices to keep up a discharge from the ulcer, with alteratives, long continued. keeping the bowels regular, &c., &c. The Vienna physicians, as well as Dr. Beach, allow the inhalation of a few drops of chloroform where the pain is excruciating. And I would say, apply a little externally, also, around the sore.

Cancers should not be disturbed as long as they do not grow nor ulcerate, but as soon as *either* begins, then is the time to *begin* with them.

COSTIVENESS—To Cure.

—Costive habits are often brought on by neglecting to go to stool at the usual time for most persons have a regular daily passage, and the most usual time is at rising in the morning, or immediately after breakfast; but hurry, or negligence, for the want of an understanding of the evil arising from putting it off, these calls of nature are suppressed; but let it be understood, *nature* like a good workman or student, has a time for each duty; then not only let her work at her own time, but if tardy go at this time and not only aid but solicit her call, or in other words:

> When nature *calls*, at *either* door, do not attempt to bluff her :
> But *haste-away*, night or day, or *health* is sure to suffer.

The above with attention to diet, using milk, roasted apples and if not dyspeptic, uncooked apples, pears, peaches, &c., at meal time, "Yankee Brown Bread," or bread made of unbolted wheat, if preferred, and avoiding a meat diet, will in most cases soon remedy the difficulty. However :

2. In very Obstinate Cases—Take extract of henbane ½ dr., extract of colocynth ½ dr.; extract of nux vonica 3 grs.; carefully work into pill mass, and form into 15 pills. Dose—one pill night and morning.

Continue their use until the difficulty is overcome, at the same time, following the previous directions, faithfully.

With many persons, the following will be found all sufficient:

3. BRANDY.—½ pt.; and put into it rhubarb-root, bruised, 1 dr.; hiera-picra 1 oz.; and fennel seed ¼ oz.

After it has stood for several days, take a table-spoon of it three times daily, before eating, until it operates, then half the quantity, or a little less, just sufficient to establish a daily action of the bowels, until all is taken. Or, the second pill under the head of Eclectic Liver Pill may be taken as an alterative to bring about the action of the liver, which is, of course, more or less inactive in most cases of long continued costiveness.

4. CORN MEAL—1 table-spoon stirred up in sufficient cold water to drink well, and drank in the morning, immediately after rising, has, with perseverance, cured many bad cases.

5. A FRESH EGG—Beat in a gill of water and drank on rising in the morning, and at each meal, for a week to ten days, has cured obstinate cases. It might be increased to two or three at a time, as the stomach will bear.

CHRONIC GOUT—To CURE.—" Take hot vinegar, and put into it all the table salt which it will dissolve, and bathe the parts affected with a soft piece of flannel. Rub in with the hand, and dry the foot, &c., by the fire. Repeat this operation four times in the 24 hours, 15 minutes each time, for four days; then twice a day for the same period; then once, and follow this rule whenever the symptoms show themselves at any future time.'

The philosophy of the above formula is as follows: Chronic gout proceeds from the obstruction of the free circulation of the blood (in the parts affected) by the deposit of a chalky substance, which is generally understood to be a carbonate and phosphate of lime. Vinegar and salt dissolve these; and the old chronic compound is broken up. The carbonate of lime, &c., become acetate and muriate, and these being soluble, are taken up by the circulating system, and discharged by secretion. This fact will be seen by the gouty joints becoming less and less in bulk until they assume their natural size. During this process, the stomach and bowels should be occasionally regulated by a gentle purgative. Abstinence from spirituous libations; exercise in the open air, and especially in the morning; freely bathing the whole surface; eating only the plainest food, and occupying the time by study, or useful employment, are very desirable assistants.

2. GOUT TINCTURE.—Veratrum viride, (swamp hellebore) ½ oz.; opium ¼ oz.; wine ½ pt.; let them stand for several days. DOSE—15 to 30 drops, according to the robustness of the patient, at intervals of two to four hours.

M. Husson, a French officer, introduced this remedy in gout some sixty years ago, and it became so celebrated that it sold as high as from one to two crowns a dose. It is considered valuable also in acute rheumatism. In gout it removes the paroxysms, allays pain, and procures rest and sleep, reduces the pulse and abates fever.

3. Coffee has recently been recommended, not only for gout, but gravel also. Dr. Mosley observes, in his " Treatise on Coffee," that the great use of the article in France is supposed to have abated the prevalence of the gravel. In the French colonies, where coffe is more used than in the English, as well as in Turkey, where it is the principal beverage, not only the gravel but the gout is scarcely known. Dr. Faur relates, as an extraordinary instance of the effect of coffee on gout the case of Dr. Deveran, who was attacked with gout at the age of twenty-five, and had it severely till he was upwards of fifty, with chalk stones in the joints of his hands and feet; but for four years preceeding the time when the account of his case had been given to Dr. Faur to lay before the public, he had, by advice, used coffe, and had no return of the gout afterward.

PARALYSIS,—IF RECENT—TO CURE.—When paralysis, (numb palsy) has existed for a great length of time, but little benefit can be expected from any treatment; but if recent, very much good, if not a perfect cure will be the result of faithfully governing yourself by the following directions with this:

PARALYTIC LINIMENT.—Sulphuric ether 6 ozs.; alcohol 2 ozs.; laudanum 1 oz.; oil of lavender 1 oz.; mix and cork tightly. In a recent case of paralysis let the whole extent of the numb surface be, thoroughly bathed and rubbed with this preparation, for several minutes, using the hand, at least 3 times daily, at the same time take internally, 20 drops of the same, in a little sweetened water, to prevent translation upon some internal organ.

It may be used in old cases, and, in many of them, will undoubtedly do much good; but I do not like to promise what there is no reasonable chance to perform. It is well

in very recent cases to keep the parts covered with flannels
with a large amount of friction by the hand ; also, electricity
scientifically applied, that is by a Physician or some one who
has studied the nature and operations of the electrical ma
chine.

This liniment should be applied so freely, that about an
ounce a day will be consumed, on an arm or leg, and if a
whole side is palsied, proportionolly more.   In cases of pains
in the stomach or side a tea-spoon will be taken with unusual
success ; or for pain in the head, apply to the surface, always
bearing in mind that some should be taken internally whenever an external application is made.   In sprains and bruises
where the surface is not broken it will be found very efficacious.   It may be, successfully, rubbed over the seat of any
internal disease accompanied with pain.

ENLARGED TONSILS—To Cure.—Where the tonsils
are enlarged from colds, or epidemic sore throat.

Take No. six 1 oz. ; molasses 2 ozs. ; and hot water 4 ozs .
mix and sip a little into the throat often, swallowing a little also ;
it keeps up a discharge of saliva from those parts and thus relieves their swollen condition ; and stimulates to renewed healthy
action.

It has proved very efficacious in the above epidemic cases,
which leave the tonsils much indurated (hardened), as well
as swollen, with a tendency to chronic inflammation of the
whole larynx, or throat, often with little ulcers.   In that
case :

Put 10 grs. of nitrate of silver to 1 oz. of water with 3 or 4
drops of creosote, and swab the throat with it, and lay a flannel
wet with turpentine upon the outside.

The worst cases will shortly yield to this mild treatment.
Should there, however, be a disposition to fever, you might
also put the feet into hot water fifteen or twenty minutes
with occasional sponging the whole surface.

SICK HEAD ACHE—To Cure.—Sick head ache, pro-
per, arises from acidity, or over-loading the stomach ; when
it is not from over eating, all that is necessary, is to soak the
feet in hot water about twenty minutes, drinking at the same
time some of the herb-teas, such as pennyroyal catnip, or
mint, &c., then get into bed, cover up warm and keep up a

\weating process for about an hour, by which time relief will have been obtained; but when food has been taken which remains in the stomach, it is much the best way to take an emetic, and the following is the:

2. ECLECTIC EMETIC.—Which is composed of lobelia, and ipecacuanha, equal parts, and blood root half as much as of either of the others, each pulverized separately, and mix thoroughly. DOSE—·Half a common tea-spoon every 15 or 20 minutes in some of the warm teas, for instance, camomile-flowers, pennyroyal, or boneset—drinking freely between doses of the same tea in which you take it; continue until you get a free and full evacuation of the contents of the stomach.

After the operation, and when the stomach becomes a little settled, some nourishment will be desired, when any of the mild broths, or gruel, should be taken, in small quantities, without fear of increasing the difficulty.

"There is, probably, no emetic surpassing this, either in efficacy of action, or efficiency in breaking up morbid, unhealthy conditions of the system generally; and exciting healthy action. It is excellent in croup, chronic affections of the liver or stomach, &c., and in fact, when and where ever an emetic is needed."—*Beach.*

But after a full trial of both, upon my own person and others, I prefer lobelia seed alone, pulverized when used. The manner of administering them has been the cause of bringing the lobelia emetic into disrepute. I take "Thompson's Composition" tea, made as there directed and drink two saucers of it, fifteen minutes apart, and with the third I stir in one rounding tea-spoon of lobelia seed, pulverized, and drink it; then every fifteen minutes I take another saucer of the tea until free vomiting takes place, not taking any more of the lobelia; by this course I think it more efficient and thorough than the mixed emetic, and entirely free from danger of the "alarming symptoms," as they are called, brought on by continuing to give the lobelia every few minutes instead of waiting its action, and all for want of knowledge as to what that action should be; but if you give it its own time, continuing the stimulating tea, it will have its *specific* action, which is to vomit, no matter at which end it is introduced. When it begins to vomit it will generally continue its action until it empties the stomach, then I begin to substitute the composition with:

3. BREAD TEA, USED IN TAKING EMETICS.—Made by taking a piece of dry bread and crumbing it into a bowl, with a little salt, pepper, and butter, to suit the taste, then pouring boiling water upon it; this soon allays the retching, and strengthens the stomach to renewed healthy action.

PERIODICAL HEADACHE.—There are those who have sick headache coming on at periods of from a few weeks to two or three months, lasting two or three days, accompanied with nausea, and occasionally with vomiting. In these cases after using the emetic to relieve the present attack, take the Cathartic Syrup next following:

4. CATHARTIC SYRUP.—Best senna leaf 1 oz.; jalap ¼ oz.; butternut, the inner bark of the root, dried and bruised, 2 oz.; peppermint leaf ¼ oz.; fennel seed ¼ oz.; alcohol ½ pt.; water 1½ pts.; sugar 2 lbs.; put all into the spirit and water, except the sugar, and let it stand 2 weeks, then strain, pressing out from the dregs, adding the sugar and simmering a few minutes only, to form the syrup. If it should cause griping in any case, increase the fennel seed and peppermint leaf. DOSE—One tablespoon, once a day, or less often if the bowels become too loose, up to the next period when the headache might have been expected, and it will not be forthcoming.

This is a mild purgative, and especially pleasant. Most persons, after a trial of it, will adopt it for their general cathartic, and especially for children. Increase or lessen the dose, according to the effect desired.

FEMALES in a weak and debilitated condition, often have a headache which is purely sympathetic; this they will distinguish by their general weakness, irregularities, and light-headedness, often amounting to real pain; in such cases take the following:

5. HEADACHE DROPS.—Castor, gentian, and valerian roots. bruised, ¼ oz.; laudanum 1 oz.; sulphuric ether 1½ oz.; alcohol ½ pt.; water ½ pt.; put all into a bottle and let stand about 10 days. DOSE—A tea-spoon as often as required, or 2 or 3 times daily.

6. TINCTURE OF BLOOD-ROOT.—Made by putting 1 oz. of the dried, bruised root, to 1 pt. of gin, and taking 1 tea-spoon, before eating, every morning, and only eating a reasonable amount of easily digested food:

Has worked wonders in cases where headaches had been of very long standing. And it might not be amiss to say that the majority of headaches are found amongst those who are disposed to Dyspepsia, by long continued over-eating, then reducing the gastric juice by over-drinking, even of water, tea or coffee.

A Niles paper gives one which is easily tried It is as follows :

7. "CHARCOAL, A CURE FOR SICK HEADACHE.—It is stated that two tea-spoons of finely powdered charcoal, drank in half a tumbler of water, will, in less than 15 minutes, give relief to the sick headache, when caused, as in most cases it is, by superabundance of acid on the stomach. We have tried this remedy time and again, and its efficacy in every instance has been signally satisfactory."

When headache has been brought on by eating too freely of boiled beef, cabbage, &c., or any other indigestible din- ner, one cup of "good tea," at tea time, eating only a slice of dry bread, will often allay the nervousness, quiet the head, and aid in getting to sleep. The "Good Samaritan" applied to the head is also good.

DELIRIUM TREMENS.—To OBTAIN SLEEP.—Give an emetic of ipecacuanha, then give 15 to 18 grs. of the same, every 2 hours, using the shower bath, and giving all the beef-tea the patient desires.

The jail physician of Chicago reports thirty-six favorable cases treated as above. In Boston, at the "House of Cor- rection," the danger arising from the sudden loss of their accustomed stimulus, according to Puritanic economy, is overcome by administering, freely, a strong decoction of wormwood.

2. STIMULATING ANODYNE.—Sulphate of quinine 12 grs. sulphate of morphine 1 gr.; mix, and divide into 6 powders Dose—One powder every hour.

Prof. King, of Cincinnati, O., says that from two to four powders of the above anodyne, will nearly every time pro- duce sleep in this whisky delirum.

TYPHUS FEVER.—To PREVENT INFECTION.—Take nitre, (salt petre,) pulverized, ¼ oz. ; oil of vitriol ¼ oz. ; put the nitre into a tea-cup and set it on a red hot shovel, adding the vitriol one-sixth at a time, stirring it with a pipe stem; avoiding the fumes as they rise from the cup ; no danger, however, in breath- ing the air of the room.

The above amount is sufficient for a room twelve by six teen feet, and less or more according to the size of other rooms. Dr. J. C. Smith, of London, is said to have re-

:eived from Parliament £5000 for making this recipe public

2. To purify the air from noxious effluvia in sick rooms, not of a contagious character, simply slice three or four onions, place them on a plate upon the floor, changing them three or four times in the twenty-four hours.

3. DISINFECTANT, FOR ROOMS, MEAT, AND FISH.—Common salt ½ a tea-cup; sulphuric acid 2 or 3 oz.; put about ½ oz. of of the acid upon the salt at a time, every 15 minutes, stirring, until all put on :

Which will purify a large room ; and for meat or fish, hang them up in a box having a cover to it, and thus confine the gas, and tainted articles of food will soon be purified, by the same operation. And notwithstanding so much was paid for the " Smith Disinfectant," the above will be found equally good.

4. COFFEE, dried and pulverized, then a little of it sprinkled upon a hot shovel, will, in a very few minutes, clear a room of all impure effluvia, and especially of an animal character.

5. CHLORIDE OF LIME—Half a saucer of it, moistened with an equal mixture of good vinegar and water, a few drops at a time only, will purify a sick-room in a few min utes.

SWEATING PREPARATIONS.—SWEATING DROPS.—Ipecacuanha, saffron, Virginia snake root, and camphor gum, each 2 ozs.; opium ½ oz.; alcohol 2 qts. Let stand 2 weeks, shaking occasionally. DOSE—A tea-spoon in a cup of hot pennyroyal, spearmint, or catnip tea, every half hour, until perspiration is induced ; then once an hour, for a few hours.

It is excellent in colds, fevers, pleurisy, inflammation of the lungs, &c. It is good to soak the feet in hot water at the same time.

2. SWEATING WITH BURNING ALCOHOL.—Pour alcohol into a saucer, to about half fill it; place this under a chair; strip the person, to be sweated, of all clothing, and place him in the chair, putting a comforter over him, also ; now light a match and throw into the saucer of alcohol, which sets it on fire, and by the time the alcohol is burned out he will be in a profuse perspiration, if not, put in half as much more of alcohol and fire it again, which will accomplish the object; then rise up and draw the comforter around you, and get into bed, following up with hot teas and sweating drops, as in the first above.

This last plan of sweating is also good in recent colds, pleurisy, inflammation of the lungs, and all other inflammatory diseases, either in recent attacks, or of long standing complaints. See the closing remarks after the treatment of 'Pleurisy," also " Ginger Wine."

IMPERIAL DROP,—FOR GRAVEL AND KIDNEY COMPLAINTS.—Take saltpetre 1 oz. ; putting it into an iron mortar, dropping in a live coal with it, which sets it on fire; stir it around until it all melts down into the solid form, blow out the coals, and pulverize it ; then take an equal amount of bi-carbonate of potassia, or saleratus, and dissolve both in soft water 2 ozs. DOSE—from 20 to 30 drops, morning and evening, in a swallow of tea made from flax seed, or a solution of gum arabic.

In connection with the drops, let the patient take from a table-spoon to two or three table-spoons of onion juice— that is, all the stomach will bear—eating all the raw onions he can, and continue it until free of the complaint. I have seen gravel the size of a common quill, crooked, and one and one-fourth inches in length, which a lady passed from the bladder, and smaller bits almost innumerable, by the simple use of onion juice alone.

The onion juice, (red onions are said to be the best,) has, and may be injected through a catheter into the bladder ; have no fears to do this, for I know a physician of forty years' practice who has done it five times with success—a physician, however, would have to be called to introduce the catheter.

2. In what is termed " Fits of the gravel," that is, where small gravel has become packed in the ureter, (tube which leads from the kidney to the bladder,) causing excruciating pain in that region, a pill of opium must be given, varying in size from one to three grains, according to the pain, strength, and age of the patient.

3. A strong decoction made by using a large handful of smart weed, adding a gill of gin, and a gill each of horse mint and onion juices, and taking all in 12 hours, has been known to discharge gravel in large quantities.—*Philadelphia Eclectic Journal.*

The surest sign of gravel is the dark appearance of the urine, as if mixed with coffee grounds, and a dull pain in the region of the kidney—if only inflamation, the darkness will not appear. See the closing remarks upon Gout.

CAMPHOR ICE.—FOR CHAPPED HANDS OR LIPS.—Spermaceti tallow 1½ ozs.; oil of sweet almonds 4 tea-spoons; gum camphor ¼ oz.; made fine. Set on the stove until dissolved, constantly stirring. Do not use only just sufficient heat to melt them.

Whilst warm, pour into moulds if desired to sell, then paper and put up in tin foil. If for your own use, put up in a tight box. Apply to the chaps or cracks two or three times daily, especially at bed time.

BURNS.—SALVE FOR BURNS, FROST-BITES, CRACKED NIP-PLES, &c.—Equal parts of turpentine, sweet oil, and beeswax; melt the oil and wax together, and when a little cool, add the turpentine, and stir until cold, which keeps them evenly mixed.

Apply by spreading upon thin cloth—linen is the best. I used this salve upon one of my own children, only a year and a half old, which had pulled a cup of hot coffee upon itself, beginning on the eye lid and extending down the face, neck and breast, also over the shoulder, and in two places across the arm, the skin coming off with the clothes; in fifteen minutes from the application of the salve, the child was asleep, and it never cried again from the burn, and not a particle of scar left.

It is good for chaps on hands or lips, or for any other sore. If put on burns before blistering has taken place, they will not blister. And if applied to sore or cracked *nipples* every time after the child nurses, it soon cures them also. For nipples, simply rubbing it on is sufficient. I find it valuable also for pimples, and common healing purposes; and I almost regret to add any other preparations for the same purposes, for fear that some will neglect this; but as there may be cases where some of the following can be made when the above cannot, I give a few others known to be valuable. The first one is from Dr. Downer, of Dixboro, within six miles of our city; he used it in a case where a boy fell backwards into a tub of hot water, scalding the whole buttock, thighs, and privates, making a bad scald in a bad place, but he succeeded in bringing him successfully through, and from its containing opium, it might be prefer-able to the first in deep and very extensive burns, but in that case the opium might be added to the first. It is as follows:

2. DR. DOWNER'S SALVE FOR BURNS.—Beeswax 4 ozs.; opium ¼ oz.; sugar of lead 1 oz.; melt the beeswax, and rub the lead

up in the wax, then the opium; and finally add about a gill of sweet oil, or sufficient to make a salve of proper consistence.

Spread lightly on cloth—no pain, he says, will be felt under its use. He highly recommends it for the pain and inflamation of Piles, also.

3. POULTICE FOR BURNS AND FROZEN FLESH.—A. Bronson, of Meadville, Pa., says, from 15 years' experience, that Indian meal poultices covered with young hyson tea, moistened with hot water, and laid over burns or frozen parts, as hot as can be borne, will relieve the pain in 5 minutes, and that blisters, if they have not, will not arise, and that one poultice is usually sufficient.

4. SALVE FOR BURNS.—Beeswax, Burgundy pitch, white pine pitch, and rosin, of each ¼ lb.; mutton tallow ¼ lb.; goose oil 1 gill; tar ½ gill, mixed and melted together, and used as other salves.

This was used successfully on a very bad case, burned all over the face, neck, breast, bowels, &c., soothing and quieting pain, giving rest and sleep directly.

5. GARDEN AND KITCHEN SALVE FOR BURNS AND FROST BITES.—Liveforever and sweet clover leaves, camomile and sweet elder, the inner bark, a handful of each; simmer them in fresh butter and mutton tallow, of each ¼ lb.; when crisped, strain out and add 2 or 3 ozs. of beeswax to form a salve. Spread very thin on thin cloth.

Mrs. Miller, of Macon, Mich., cured a bad case with this, burned by the clothes taking fire, nearly destroying the whole surface. She speaks of it in equal praise for cuts and frost-bites. See the Green Ointment also for Chilblains.

6. The white of an egg beat up, then beat for a long time with a table-spoon of lard, until a little water separates from them, I have found good for burns.

7. The white oxide of bismuth, rubbed up in a little lard, is also a good application in burns.

8. Glycerine and tannin, equal weights, rubbed together into an ointment, is very highly recommended for sore or cracked nipples. See Dr. Raymond's statement in connection with the treatment of Piles.

ITCHING FEET FROM FROST BITES,--To CURE.— Take hydrochloric acid 1 oz.; rain water 7 ozs.; wash the feet with it 2 or 3 times daily, or wet the socks with the preparation, until relieved.

A gentleman whose feet had been frozen, in the Alps, eight years before, and another man's had been frozen two years before, on the Sierra-Nevada mountains, were effectually cured by its use.

CHILBLAINS,—To Cure.—Published by Order of the Government of Wirtemburg.—Mutton tallow and lard, of each ¾ lb.; melt in an iron vessel and add hydrated oxyde of iron 2 oz.; stirring continually with an iron spoon, until the mass is of an uniform black color; then let it cool and add Venice-turpentine 2 oz.: and Armenian bole 1 oz.: oil of bargamot 1 dr.; rub up the bole with a little olive oil before putting it in.

Apply several times daily by putting it upon lint or linen —heals the worst cases in a few days

Chilblains arise from a severe cold to the part, causing inflammation. often ulcerating, making deep, and very troublesome. long continued sores.

FELONS,—If Recent, to Cure in Six Hours.—Venice turpentine 1 oz., and put into it half a tea-spoon of water, and stir with a rough stick until the mass looks like candied honey, then spread a good coat on a cloth and wrap around the finger. If the case is only recent, it will remove the pain in 6 hours

2 A poke root poultice on a felon cures by absorption, unless matter is already formed; if it is, it soon brings it to a head, and thus saves much pain and suffering.

3 Blue flag and hellebore roots, equal parts, boiled in milk and water, then soak the felon in it for twenty minutes, as hot as can be borne, and bind the roots on the parts for one hour, has cured many felons, when commenced in time.

4 A poultice of clay, from an old log house, made and kept wet with spirits of camphor, is also good.

5. Felon Ointment.—Take sweet oil ½ pt., and stew a 3 cent plug of tobacco in it until the tobacco is crisped; then squeeze it out and add red lead 1 oz., and boil until black; when a little cool, add pulverized camphor gum 1 oz.

Mrs Jordan, of Clyde, O., paid ten dollars for this recipe, and has cured many bad felons, as well as fellows, with it. Bad fellows because they did not pay her. Certainly, this is a rational use of tobacco.

6. Felon Salve.—A salve made by burning one tablespoon of copperas, then pulverizing it and mixing with the yolk of an egg, is said to relieve the pain, and cure the felon

in twenty-four hours; then heal with cream two parts, and soft soap one part. Apply the healing salve daily after soaking the part in warm water.

DEAFNESS.—IF RECENT, TO CURE—IF NOT, TO RELIEVE.— Hen's oil 1 gill; and a single handful of the sweet clover raised in gardens; stew it in the oil until the juice is all out, strain it and bottle for use.

Where deafness is recent, it will be cured by putting three or four drops daily into the ear, but if of long standing, much relief will be obtained if continued a sufficient length of time.

2. Much has been said in France about sulphuric ether, first tried by Madam Cleret, of Paris; and, although she lost her reason by the elation of feeling brought on, no doubt, by the honor given her for the discovery, yet the continued trial of the article does not give the satisfaction which had been hoped for, from its first success.

WARTS AND CORNS.—TO CURE IN TEN MINUTES.—Take a small piece of potash and let it stand in the open air until it slacks, then thicken it to a paste with pulverized gum arabic, which prevents it from spreading where it is not wanted.

Pare off the seeds of the wart or the dead skin of the corn, and apply the paste, and let it remain on ten minutes; wash off, and soak the place in sharp vinegar or sweet oil, either of which will neutralize the alkali. Now do not jam nor squeeze out the wart or corn, like "street-corner pedlers," but leave them alone, and nature will remove them without danger of taking cold, as would be if a sore is made by pinching them out. Corns are caused by pressure; in most cases removing the pressure cures the corn. Nine of every ten corns can be cured by using twice, daily, upon it, any good liniment, and wearing loose shoes or boots. See Good Samaritan.

2. CURE FOR CORNS.—If a cripple will take a lemon, cut off a piece, then nick it so as to let in the toe with the corn, the pulp next the corn—tie this on at night, so that it cannot move—he will find next morning that, with a blunt knife, the corn will come away to a great extent. Two or three applications of this will make a " poor cripple" happy for life.—*London Field.*

DR. CHASE'S RECIPES.

3. ACETIC ACID, touched to hard or soft corns, night and morning, for one week, will cure them. So will the Samaritan liniment, which see.

4. DR. HARIMAN'S INNOCENT AND SURE CURE FOR CORNS, WARTS AND CHILBLAINS.—Nitric and muriatic acids, blue vitriol, and salts of tartar, of each 1 oz.; add the blue vitriol, pulverized, to either of the acids, and in the same way add the salts of tartar; when done foaming, add the other acid, and in a few days it will be fit for use.

DIRECTIONS.—For frosted feet, rub them with a swab or brush, wet with this solution very lightly, every part that is red and dry; in a day or two, if not cured, apply again as before. For corns, apply in like manner, scraping off dead skin before using. For warts, wet once a week until they disappear, which will be soon, for it is a certain cure in all the above cases, and very cheap. So says the Doctor, of Anderson, Ind.

5. A gentleman in Ohio offers to pay ten dollars a-piece for all corns not cured in three days by binding a bit of cotton batting upon it, and wetting it three times a day with spirits of turpentine.

6. I am assured by a gentleman of Syracuse, N. Y., that a plaster of the "Green Mountain Salve," put upon a corn, will completely cure it by the time it naturally comes off.

LINIMENTS.—GOOD SAMARITAN—IMPROVED.—Take 98 per cent. alcohol 2 qts., and add to it the following articles: Oils of sassafras, hemlock, spirits of turpentine, tinctures of cayenne, catechu, guaicaci, (guac,) and laudanum, of each 1 oz.; tincture of myrrh 4 ozs.; oil of origanum 2 ozs.; oil of wintergreen ¼ oz.; gum camphor 2 ozs.; and chloroform 1½ ozs.

I have used the above liniment over five years, and cannot speak too highly of its value; I have cured myself of two severe attacks of rheumatism with it, the first in the knee and the last in the shoulder, three years after; my wife has cured two corns on the toes with it, by wetting them twice daily for a few days; and it is hard to think of anything which it has not cured, such as sprains, bruises, cuts, jams, rheumatism, weak back, reducing swellings, curing leg-ache in children from over-playing, for horse-flesh, &c., &c. But you will allow me one remark about liniments—they ought in all cases to be put on and rubbed in from twenty to thirty minutes, and laying the hand on the part until it burns from its effects, instead of one or two minutes, as is the usual custom; and if made by the quart, you can use them freely, as the cost is not more than about one-eighth as much as to purchase the two shilling bottles. Wetting flannel with the liniment, and binding on, is a good manner of application. Dr. Hale, of this city, has adopted this liniment for general use; but for headache and neuralgia, he takes eight ounces of it and adds an ounce of chloroform, and half an ounce of oil of wintergreen, rubbing upon the head, holding to the nostrils, &c. The full precription will usually cost about two dollars.

2. LINIMENT FOR OLD SORES.—Alcohol 1 qt.; aqua ammonia 4 ozs.; oil of origanum 2 ozs.; camphor gum 2 ozs.; opium 2 ozs.; gum myrrh 2 ozs.; common salt 2 table-spoons. Mix, and shake occasionally for a week.

This was presented for insertion by H. Loomis, of Edwardsburg, Mich., hoping it might do many others as much good as it had done himself and neighbors. He showed me scars of an old sore on his leg which he had cured with it, after years of suffering; and also called up a young man whose father he had cured of a similar sore, years before, which had never broken out again; he used it twice daily. His leg became sore after a protracted fever. I have great confidence in it. He uses it also for cuts, bruises, horse-flesh, inflammatory rheumatism, &c., &c.

3. DR. RAYMOND'S LINIMENT.—Alcohol 1 qt.; oils of origanum 2 ozs., and wormwood 1 oz.; with camphor gum 2 ozs.; spirits of turpentine 2 ozs.; and tincture of cantharides 1 oz. Mixed, and used as other liniments.

Dr. D. W. Raymond, of Conneaut, O., thinks that the last is the best liniment in the world.

4. GERMAN RHEUMATIC FLUID.—Oils of hemlock and cedar, of each ½ oz.; oils of origanum and sassafras, each 1 oz.; aqua ammonia 1 oz.; capsicum, pulverized, 1 oz.; spirits of turpentine and gum camphor, each ½ oz.; put all into a quart bottle and fill with 95 per cent. alcohol.

The Germans speak equally in praise of this fluid, as a liniment, as Dr. Raymond does of his, besides they say it is very valuable for cholic in man or horse. DOSE.—For cholic. for man, half a tea-spoon; for a horse, one-half to one ounce in a little warm water, every fifteen minutes, until relieved.

A gentleman purchased a horse for seventy-five dollars, which had been strained in one of the fetlocks, worth before the strain one hundred and twenty-five dollars. He cured him with this liniment, and sold him for the original value. He cured his wife also of neuralgia, with the same, since I have published this recipe. Judge ye of its value.

5. COOK'S ELECTRO-MAGNETIC LINIMENT.—Best alcohol 1 gal.; oil of amber 8 ozs.; gum camphor 8 ozs.; castile soap, shaved fine, 2 ozs.; beef's gall 4 ozs.; ammonia 3 F.'s strong, 12 ozs.; mix, and shake occasionally for 12 hours, and it is fit for use.

This will be found a strong and valuable liniment, and also cheap. It may be used in swellings, strains, &c., and rubbed upon the throat, breast, and lungs, in asthma, sore throat, &c.

6. LINIMENT FOR SPINAL AFFECTIONS.—Take a pt. bottle and put into it oil of origanum, wormwood, spirits of turpentine, and gum camphor, of each 1 oz., and fill it with best alcohol.

Mr. Barr, a gentleman with whom I have been acquainted for some four years, has been troubled with spinal weakness and pains, and he finds great relief from the use of this liniment; and his daughter took it internally for a cough also, with success.

7. GREAT LONDON LINIMENT.—Take chloroform, olive oil, and aqua ammonia, of each, 1 oz.; acetate of morphia, 10 grs. Mix, and use as other liniments. Very valuable.

8. GUM LINIMENT.—Take gum myrrh, gum camphor, and gum opium, of each, ¼ oz.; cayenne pepper ¼ oz.; alcohol 1 pt.; mix.

This liniment is ready for use in three or four days, and is very highly recommended by E. Burrows, of Matamora Lapeer Co., Mich. He prefers rum, if a good article can be got, in place of the alcohol. This would be excellent in cholic, or diarrhea also.

9. PATENT LINIMENT.—In order that those who purchase the patent liniments may know what they are buying, I give a formula, from which over twelve-thousand dollars worth of liniment was sold in two years' time, but one of the partners going out of the firm, and into the livery-business, gave me the plan as follows:

Take whisky 15 gals.; and put into it 2 lbs. of capsicum, pulverized, let stand 10 days and percolate, or draw off the whisky, free of the sediment; in the mean time take 1 gal. of spirits of turpertine and put into it oils of origanum, horse-mint, sassafras, hemlock, 6 ozs. each; add gum camphor 2 lbs. Mix and it ready to sell, for the purpose of gulling those who suppose everybody to be *honest* because they are *themselves* so.

But that no loss may arise from the space this liniment recipe occupies here, I will tell you how to make a good liniment, by using a part of that with the following:

Take of the patent liniment 8 ozs.; sweet oil and oils of origanum, sassafras and aqua ammonia, of each 2 ozs., and mix, shaking well as used, and this mixture will make a splendid horse liniment, with which you can easily blister, by bandaging the part, if desired, and wetting the bandage with it.

The first would cost less than $1.00 per gallon, whilst the retail price, two shillings per bottle, makes it over $2.00 per quart. See where your money goes.

10. LOBELIA AND CAYENNE LINIMENT.—Take a quart bottle and put into it ½ oz. of cayenne, pulverized, then put in 2 ozs. of lobelia herb, and fill up the bottle with whisky; in two weeks it is ready for use, and applicable for cuts, bruises, strains, sprains, &c.; and it will heal cork cuts in the feet of oxen or horses, without stopping them from labor, and with but very little soreness, by applying 2 or 3 times daily.

I know a gentleman who had a gash cut in his scalp, four inches in length, and to the scull in depth, by a falling limb, which by the use of this liniment only, as strange as it may appear, it healed without pain or soreness. But some may object to it as a whisky liniment. I admit it to be such, but by knowing how to make it yourselves, you get it for a whisky price, and if it be not found as good as one-half of the two-shilling-a-bottle liniments, then you may tell me that I do not know when I have a good thing.

11. LINIMENT—SAID TO BE ST. JOHN'S.—For 70 doz. bottles, take spirits of turpentine and seneca oils, of each, 4 gals.; linseed or sweet oil, 2 gals.; oils of origanum, hemlock, juniper, amber, and laudanum, of each, 3 qts.; spirits of ammonia 1 qt.; tincture of arnica 2 gals.; camphor gum 1 lb. Put all into a keg and shake well; when you wish to fill into small bottles, shake it well and draw into a convenient bottle or pitcher to pour from; and shake it well every time you fill 5 bottles; and shake the bottle whenever you use the liniment; thus it might be called *Shaking* Liniment. No matter what you call it, however, it is a good one.

I obtained the recipe of a young gentleman who worked in Mr. St. John's store over a year, yet much care was taken to prevent the knowledge of its exact composition from being found out by assistants; it is a well known fact, however, that an observing mind can learn much, although not expressed in words. Perhaps he will blame me for publishing information gained in that way, but I obtain knowledge for the benefit of the people; and as I have called on the Doctor two different times, to sell my work, but could not succeed, I do not feel under any special obligations to him, and if I did, I go in for the greatest good to the greatest number Were it not so, I should not publish *much* that is contained in this work, for there are many persons who have and are making fortunes out of single recipes, now published for the benefit of the world.

Because I could not sell my Recipes to I. L. St. John, a Druggist of Tiffin, O., however, is not saying that I do not sell them to Druggists generally, as I do. In Aurora, Ill., I sold to six, and in Pomeroy, O., to seven, every one in either place, which is not common. They are, however, not only anxious to obtain information generally, but also willing to impart it to others; and how Mr. St. John should have obtained as good recipes as the ones here attributed to him, without sometime having bought, is a little surprising; for, as a general rule, those who put out "Patent Medicines," are not themselves the originators of the recipes; even Dr. Jayne is reported, I know not how truly, to have picked up the recipe, in an out-house, for his celebrated Alterative. I say, then, am I not justified in publishing these recipes? Nay, more! am I not honorable in thus benefiting the people? I rest the matter with them; always willing to abide their decision.

Persons only wishing to put up for their own use, will take one-seventieth of the various amounts, which will be about as follows:

Turpentine and seneca oils, of each 7¼ ozs.; sweet oil and tincture of arnica, of each 3¾ ozs.; oils of origanum, hemlock, juniper, amber, and laudanum, of each 1¼ ozs.; spirits of ammonia ¼ oz.; and gum camphor ¼ oz.; which makes a little less than 1 qt., there being 64 qts., besides the gum camphor, in the whole amount.

This calculation will be sufficiently near for all practical purposes.

I have sold the condition powder and liniment, out of the

drug store, made by the Doctor, which has always given good satisfaction. And I think any one who tries both will be as well pleased with those made from these recipes as with that which is sent out from Tiffin, and make it for one-fourth the cost of the other.

COD LIVER OIL—Made Palatable and more Digesti-ble.—To each bottle, add fine table salt 1 oz. Mix well.

By this very simple plan cod liver oil has its peculiar un-pleasantness overcome, as well as made far more easy for the stomach to dispose of. But even with this improvement, I do not consider a table-spoon of it equal, for consumption, to a glass of rich, sweet cream, with a tea-spoon of best brandy in it, to be drank at each meal.

CONSUMPTIVES.—Syrup Very Successful.—Take tam-arack bark, without rossing, (the moss may be brushed off,) 1 peck; spikenard root ½ lb.; dandelion root ¼ lb.; hops 2 ozs. Boil these sufficiently to get the strength, in 2 or 3 gals. of water, strain and boil down to 1 gal.; when blood warm add 3 lbs. of honey and 3 pts. of best brandy; bottle, and keep in a cool place. Dose—A wine-glass or a little less, as the stomach will bear, 3 or 4 times daily, before meals and at bed time.

Consumption may justly be called the King of diseases, but he has, many times, been obliged to haul down his col-ors, and give place to health, and consequent happiness, when he came in contact with the above syrup. It does not, how-ever, contain any of the articles usually put into syrups for this disease—this of itself ought to obtain for it a considera-tion. I have been told, and that by a professional man, that there was not an article in it of any value for consumption. I have acknowledged it does not contain any articles com-monly used for that disease; but allow me to ask if they cure the disease in one case out of a hundred? The answer is, No. I am now using this on a case within a few miles of the city, who had called one of our Professors. He promised benefit, and did benefit about one week; subsequently, two other physicians were also called without any lasting benefit. He had not cut his wood for nearly a year, nor done other labor to any extent; he has now taken our syrup nearly three months; he was weak, spare in flesh, and coughed very much, with cold feet and surface; he is now stout, fleshy, and scarcely any cough; surface and feet warm. What

more could be asked ? Yet he is very careless, for I called
on him on a cold, snowy day lately, and he was in the woods,
for wood. Do I need better proof of its value ? No one
would expect sickness of the stomach to arise from its use,
from the articles of which it is composed, but the first dose
usually makes the person rather sick at the stomach, and
sometimes vomits, but don't fear to continue its use. I had
rather trust to tamarack-bark tea than three-fourths of the
consumptive syrups of the day. Let every one who is afflicted with cough, be careful to avoid exposure as much as possible. Remember, with this *syrup*, or *disease*, as long as
there is life, there is hope.

But it would be deceptive and wicked to hold out to all
consumptives the idea that they could be cured—*facts*
speak like this, although I have never seen it in print, nor
heard the remark, but my own observation says that nine
of every ten *hereditary* consumptives, will, in the end, die
of the disease, while an equal number of those whose disease is brought on by colds being neglected, or from neglect
of acute inflammations, &c., may be cured. Then those
who know their parents or others in their family to have
gone with this disease, need hardly expect a cure, notwithstanding much benefit may be derived from *care*, with the
above treatment, good diet, and out-of-door exercise, while
those whose systems are not tainted from parents may expect a permanent cure.

I shall now throw in a few thoughts of my own, and from
the experience of many others in the profession, which I
hope may benefit all, needing light on the subject.

First, then—Do not go South, to smother and die ; but
go North, for cool, fresh air, hunt, fish, and eat freely of
the roasted game ; cast away care, after having trusted all in
Christ, that it may be well, living or dying. Take a healthy,
faithful friend with you, to lean upon when needed, in your
rambles. So shall it be well with many who would otherwise sink to the consumptive's grave. Have your potatoes
with you, and roast them in the embers ; your corn meal
also, which you will mix with cold water, having a little salt
in it, and bake on a board before the fire, and then say you
cannot make out a good-flavored meal, and a healthy one
also, from your roast *venison*, or broiled *fish*, with *roast pota-*

toes and *johnny*-cake, I will then acknowledge that you are indeed far gone on the consumptive's track, and *especially* if you have been wandering over hills and through the valleys of our northern country in pursuit of the game of which you are about to partake.

SECONDLY—Do not leave home after having tried everything else in vain, and just ready to wrap the mantle of the grave around you; then you need all the care of many friends, and a quiet place to die; but strike out the first thing when you become certain that permanent disease has fastened upon the lungs; then you may not only reasonably expect a cure, but be almost certain. Have the means with you to avoid getting wet by rains; but often wash and rub the whole surface, wearing flannel next the skin, and clothe yourself according to the weather and sex; for there is no reason why females should not pursue about the same course They can dress *a la Bloomer*, and with their father, husband, brother, or other *known* friend, derive the same benefit from out-door exercise, like field or forest rambles, botanical huntings, geological surveys, or whatever sports or realities may give just the amount of exercise not to *fatigue* the invalid

For females who have families and cannot leave them, gardening will be the best substitute for the travel, or of all the employments which can be engaged in.

LASTLY—Those who are already far down the consumptive track and confined at home, will derive much benefit by using, at each meal, half a pint of rich, fresh cream. In *all* cases it is ahead of Cod-Liver Oil, with *none* of its disagreeableness. And if it can be borne, a tea, to a table-spoon of the best brandy may be added.

Much is being said, now-a-days, about the necessity of constant inflation of the lungs by long-drawn breaths, holding the breath, also, as long as possible, when thus fully inflated; but, for those whose lungs are extensively diseased, it is not only useless, but very dangerous, from the liability to burst blood-vessels in the lungs, causing hemorrhage, if not instant death. In the commencement of the disease, however, or for those in health, the practice is decidedly good.

2. Half a pint of new milk, with a wine-glass of expressed

juice of green hoarhound, each morning for a month, is said to have worked wonders in relieving the soreness of the lungs, and giving tone to the general health in this disease.

3. CHLORATE OF POTASH, FOR CONSUMPTION —A gentleman of Iowa read a paper about a year ago before the "American Medical Association," upon the subject of Chlorate of Potash in Consumption, giving the history of a few cases only. For the want of a more extended trial of it, the Association thought best not to publish his paper but referred it back to him, and to the consideration of the other members for further test.

Amongst those members is Dr. A. B. Palmer, of this city one of the Vice-Presidents of the Association, and Professor of "Practice, Materia Medica," &c., in the University of Michigan, at Ann Arbor—by the way, a gentleman and a scholar. Having had much experience in practice, he saw fit to give it a trial. He has used it in about thirty cases, and with a single exception with marked success; and in that case there was at first much improvement, but the patient was a German who does not understand our language very well, and from this fact when he found that it caused a heat or burning sensation in the stomach instead of going to the Professor and having the quantity lessened, he abandoned it altogether. But through Prof. Palmer's kindness I have been permitted to refer to other cases where a very marked amelioration has taken place. One of these, a married lady, although her lungs were full of tubercles, with much coughing, soreness of the lungs, with sharp pains upon full breaths being taken, &c., finds her cough loose, soreness all gone, and that full breaths can be taken without pain, (or stitching, as commonly called,) and fully believes that if she could have had this prescription early in the disease, she would now have been well, yet derives much relief from its use. Another lady has been using it only a few months, and finds that her symptoms are all very much relieved, and she has gained seventeen pounds in flesh.

The Professor assures me that in the first few cases where he prescribed the chlorate, the benefits were so marked, it was really astonishing; which, of course, caused him to go on in its use, until, as before remarked, about thirty cases have been more or less benefitted by its use, under his care.

His method of giving it is to put about a tea-spoon of the chlorate into a glass of water, which is to be drank a little at a time, in from six to twenty-four hours, with other appropriate treatment.

If in any case the chlorate should cause a heat or burning sensation at the stomach, lessen the quantity; and unless this does occur, no apprehensions need be felt in using it It improves the general symptoms, lessening the pulse, &c., whilst the Cod-Liver Oil has never done anything more than to benefit merely as food; and from its very disgusting smell and taste, and the almost impossibility of keeping it upon the stomach, I greatly prefer the fresh sweet cream mentioned above, or the fat meat, as mentioned below.

The hyper-phosphites have been extensively used, but Prof. Palmer tells me that in Paris and other parts of Europe. where he traveled during the past summer, that not one well authenticated case of cure by them can be produced. Bet he feels much encouraged to hope that the chlorate will prove itself worthy of great confidence.

The above was written one year ago; and the reports coming in since then, both in America and from Europe, more than confirms the *expected* benefits and hoped-for advantages from the use of the *chlorate* in this disease.

4. REMARKS ON THE USE OF FAT MEATS—PREVENTIVE OF CONSUMPTION.—There is so much said against the use of fat meats, and especially pork, as an article of diet, that I cannot better close my remarks upon this subject than by giving the opposite opinions of those in high places, corroborated also by my own experience.

Dr. Dixon, of the Scalpel, some time ago, assumed the position that "the use of oils would diminish the victims of consumption nine-tenths, and that that was the whole secret of the use of Cod-Liver Oil, to take the place of fat meats."

Dr. Hooker's observations on the use of fat meats, connected with consumption, are as follows:

" FIRST—Of all persons between the ages of 15 and 22 years, more than one-fifth eat no fat meat. SECOND—Of persons at the age of 45, all, excepting less than 1 in 50, habitually use fat meat. THIRD—Of persons who, between the ages of 15 and 22, avoid fat meat, a few acquire an appetite for it, and live to a good old age, while the greater portion die with phthesis (consumption,) before 35. FOURTH—Of persons dying with phthesis between the ages of 12 and 45, nine-tenths, at least, have never used fat meats."

"Most individuals who avoid fat meat, also use little butter or oily gravies, though many compensate for this want in part, at least, by a free use of those articles, and also milk, eggs, and various saccharine substances. But they constitute an imperfect substitute for fat meat, without which, sooner or later, the body is almost sure to show the effects of deficient calorification."

A lady-lecturer recently said in this city, in one of her lectures—"Set a piece of *pork* before a lady : oh, horrible! the dirty, nasty, filthy stuff; give us *chicken*—clean, nice chicken." Now this lady, certainly, was no farmer's wife or she would have observed that the habits of chickens are ten times more filthy than that of the hog, if it be possible; for even the hog's leavings and droppings are carefully overhauled by them, and much of it appropriated to "Ladies' meat." But their filthiness is no argument in either case; for nature's strainer, (the stomach,) throws off all impurities. Why do so many young *ladies*, young *clergymen*, and *students* die of consumption? Simply because *chicken* or other *lean* meats, hot biscuit, &c., without exercise, make up the sums of their diet; when, if they would eat fat meats, with bread not less than one day old, scrub floors, saw wood, or other arm exercise, according to sex, an hour at each end of each day, they might be spared for years—perhaps to long lives of usefulness, to their families, congregations, or the world.

5. So far as *pork* is concerned as food, the following rule may be safely followed : If it agrees with the stomach, which is known by its digesting without "Risings," as it is called, its use may be continued, but if it rises, lessen the quantity, and if it still rises, abandon its use altogether; but † digests better with me than mutton, or *chicken*, and I have been trying them for nearly *fifty* years. The same rule is good for all articles of food. As to exercise, for men who are not regular laborers, wood-sawing is the best, next, horseback riding, then walking; for women, hoeing in the garden or field, next sweeping, dusting, &c., then horseback riding, walking, &c.

6. But I have recently seen a piece going the rounds of the papers as the best cure for consumption in the world, which contains so much good sense that I will close my remarks on the subject by giving it a quotation, and let every one judge for themselves, which to try, if they see fit to give either a trial. It is represented as coming from an *exchange* only, but from its style of remark, I think it must have started from Hall's Journal of Health :

" Eat all that the appetite requires of the most nourishing food, such as fresh beef, lamb, oysters, raw eggs, fruit, vegetables, and 3 times a day take a glass of egg-nog, made as rich as the patient can bear. Avoid all other alcoholic drinks. Bathe twice a week in water made agreably warm, and in a warm room; after bathing rub the body and limbs with sweet cream or sweet oil. Exercise daily in the open air; walking is the best. Stand erect, exercise the arms and lungs freely, keep the mind cheerful; take freely of the best cough syrup, and consumption will be a stranger to your household.

" For making the best cough syrup, take 1 oz. of thoroughwort; 1 oz. of slippery elm; 1 oz. of stick licorice, and 1 oz. of flax seed; simmer together in 1 qt. of water until the strength is entirely extracted. Strain carefully, add 1 pt. of best molasses and ½ lb. of loaf sugar; simmer them all well together, and when cold bottle tight. This is the cheapest, best, and safest medicine now or ever in use."

" A few doses of one table-spoon at a time will alleviate the most distressing cough of the lungs, soothes and allays irritation, and if continued, subdues any tendency to consumption; breaks up entirely the whooping cough, and no better remedy can be found for croup, asthma, bronchitis, and all affections of the lungs and throat. Thousands of precious lives may be saved every year by this cheap and simple remedy, as well as thousands of dollars which would otherwise be spent in the purchase of nostrums which are both useless and dangerous."—*Exchange.* For egg-nog see " Stimulant in Low Fevers."

OINTMENTS.—For Old Sores.—Red precipitate ½ oz; sugar of lead ½ oz.; burnt alum 1 oz.; white vitriol ¼ oz, or a littl less; all to be very finely pulverized; have mutton tallow made warm ¼ lb.; stir all in, and stir until cool.

Mr. Brownell, of Dowagiac, Mich., thinks there is no ointment equal to this for fever or any other old sores, from actual trial, as much so as Mr. Loomis does of his Liniment No. 2.

2. JUDKINS' OINTMENT.—This ointment has been long celebrated through Ohio and the Eastern States. It was invented and put up by an old Doctor of that name, whose family took to the profession of medicine as naturally as ducks to water. I obtained it of one of the sons, who is practicing at Malaga, Ohio, from whom I also obtained Landolfi's and his own method of curing cancer, (see those recipes,) and he always uses this ointment to heal cancers and all other sores :

Linseed-oil 1 pt.; sweet oil 1 oz.; and boil them in a kettle on coals for nearly 4 hours, as warm as you can ; then have pulverized and mixed, borax ¼ oz.; red lead 4 ozs., and sugar of lead 1½ ozs.; remove the kettle from the fire and thicken in the powder; continue the stirring until cooled to blood heat, then stir in 1 oz. of spirits of turpentine; and now take out a little, letting it get cold, and if not then sufficiently thick to spread upon thin, soft linen, as a salve, you will boil again until this point is reached.

He says, and I have no doubt of it, that it is good for all kinds of wounds, bruises, sores, burns, white swellings, rheumatisms, ulcers, sore breasts, and even where there are wounds on the inside, it has been used with advantage, by applying a plaster over the part.

3. SISSON's OINTMENT.—Best brandy ½ pt.; turpentine 1 gill ; camphor gum 1 oz.; beef's gall ½ pt.; (beef's gall bottled with ¼ alcohol will keep nice for future use,) neats-foot oil 1 pt. Mix.

This ointment, or properly liniment, is probably not equaled for reducing swellings which arise from bad bruises, or swellings of long standing ; rub it in for quite a length of time, then wet a flannel in it and wrap around the parts.

4. GREEN OINTMENT.—White pine turpentine and lard ¼ lb. each ; honey and bees-wax ¼ lb. each ; melt all together and stir in ½ oz. of *very* finely pulverized verdigris.

In deep wounds and old sores this works admirably, it keeps out proud flesh and heals beyond all calculation, keeping up a healthy discharge. It was used on a horse, which had run upon a fence stake, the stake entering under the shoulder-blade and penetrating eighteen inches alongside of the ribs ; the ointment was introduced by stiffening linen cloth with warm beeswax, and rolling it up into what is called a *tent*, then smearing the ointment upon the tent, and pushing it to the bottom of the wound, which kept the outside from healing until it healed from the bottom, and thus saved the horse, which everybody said must die; and of course everybody always knows. The man owning the horse was thrown from his buggy whilst the horse was running and had a leg broken; the horse was well before the man. Hiram Sisson, an old farrier and farmer, of Crown Point, Essex Co., N. Y., has used this and the one bearing his name, No. 3, several years, and speaks of them in the highest terms. Mr. Wykoff, a few miles north of this city, has used this green ointment for several years, curing a deep cut in the thigh of a friend in a few days with it, which induced him to pay ten dollars to an English lady for the recipe; since then he cured a bad case of chilblains, with it, upon a German boy who had not worn boot or shoe for three years, on their account. I have now known it for two years, curing cuts on horses' feet, from stepping over corn stubble in spring ploughing, by only a few applications. It is worth more than the cost of this book to any family who has not got it.

This, mixed with equal parts of the "Magnetic," No. 11, and the world cannot beat it for general use.

5. GREEN OINTMENT —Honey and bees-wax, each ½ lb.; spirits of turpentine 1 oz.; wintergreen oil and laudanum, each 2 ozs.; verdigris, finely pulverized, ¼ oz.; lard 1½ lbs; mix by a stove fire, in a copper kettle, heating slowly.

I have given this green ointment, varying somewhat from the first, obtained of a gentleman at Jamestown, N. Y., who was selling it in large quantities, as he uses the spirits of turpentine instead of the white pine, for that frequently is hard to get, and by some this will be preferred, for the flesh of a few persons will inflame under the free use of verdigris, and it will be seen that this last recipe has not near as much of it in as the first.

6. DR. KITTREDGE'S CELEBRATED OINTMENT,—FOR "PIMPLED-FACE," "PRAIRIE-ITCH, &c.—Take a pint bottle and put into it nitric acid 1 oz.; quicksilver 1 oz., and let stand until the silver is cut; then melt lard ½ lb. in an earthen bowl and mix all together, and stir with a wooden spatula until cold.

Old Dr. Kittredge is an Allopathic Physician, but his ointment has been known, over the whole State, as death to the "Michigan or Prairie Itch," and the Doctor recommends it for Cancerous, Scrofulous, and Syphilitic Ulcers, also Salt-rheum, Ring-worms, " Pimpled Face," Chronic Inflammation of the eyelids, &c. APPLICATION.—For cutaneous erup-tions, scratch off the scab, warm the cerate, rub in thorough-ly once a day ; for running ulcers, spread a thin plaster, and not change oftener than once in thirty-six or forty-eight hours.

7. MEAD'S SALT-RHEUM OINTMENT.—Aquafortis 1 oz. ; quick-silver 1 oz. ; good hard soap dissolved so as to mix readily 1 oz. ; prepared chalk 1 oz., mixed with 1 lb of lard ; incorporate the above by putting the aquafortis and quicksilver into an earthen vessel, and when done effervescing, mix with the other ingredi-ents, putting the chalk in last, and add a little spirits of turpen-tine, say ½ a table-spoon.

Mr. Mead is a resident of this city, advanced in age, over ninety years, and great confidence may be placed in this re-cipe. He sent it for insertion in the seventh edition of this work, and many have tried it with satisfaction. He first proved it on himself, after suffering with Salt-rheum for ten years ; at first it came back after two years ; he then cured it again, and now has been free from it about fourteen years. His only object in presenting me the recipe was to do good to his fellow-creatures. Some physicians think that if nitric acid one ounce and three drachms, was put upon the quick-silver, and cut or dissolved by gentle heat, that it would be a better way to prepare it ; but I never wish to change when an article works as well as this does.

8. Dr. Gibson, of Jamestown, Pa., says he has never failed in curing salt-rheum or leprosy, (meaning very bad skin dis-cases) with the following :

First, wash the part with Castile soap and water, dry with a soft cloth, then wet the parts erupted with the tincture of iodine, and after this gets dry, anoint with citron ointment. When the eruption exists about parts not covered with clothing, use the following wash alternately with the tincture : Corrosive subli-mate 1 dr.; sugar of lead 3 ozs.; white vitriol 2 scruples; sal-ammoniac 3 drs.; common salt 2 drs.; soft water 1 pt.; mix.

He had a case—a young gentleman who was engaged to be married, but the lady would not marry him until cured from the fact that a sore of a leprous or obstinate character surrounded his head where the hat came in contact with it. But patience and *nine* months perseverance removed the scab from his *crown*, and *crowned* him with a help-meet

Let me here say, that in any disease of long standing, use some of the alterative medicines to cleanse the blood, while using the outward applications. The "Cathartic Alterative" is especially adapted to these skin diseases, and should be continued some time, even if you are not anxious to get married. The Citron Ointment is kept by nearly all Druggists.

9. White lead in sweet oil, used as an ointment, cured a lady in Lafayette, Ind., of a bad case of Salt-Rheum.

10. ITCH OINTMENT.—Unsalted butter 1 lb.; Burgundy pitch 2 oz.; spirits of turpentine 2 ozs.; red-precipitate, pulverized, 1¼ ozs.; melt the pitch and add the butter, stirring well together; then remove from the fire, and when a little cool add the spirits of turpentine, and lastly the precipitate, and stir until cold.

This will cure all cases of psora, usually called "The Itch," and many other skin eruptions, as pimples, blotches, &c.

Dr. Beach thinks the animal which infests the skin, in real itch, is the result of the disease, whilst most authors think it the cause.

11. MAGNETIC OINTMENT.—SAID TO BE TRASK'S.—Lard, raisins, cut in pieces, and fine-cut tobacco, equal weights; simmer well together, then strain and press out all from the dregs.

The above is an excellent ointment, and looks like its namesake, and its action is really magnetic. Mix this in equal parts with the first Green Ointment No. 4, and it will make a good application in Piles, Salt-Rheum, and all cutaneous or skin diseases, as well as cuts, bruises, &c. If used in Salt-Rheum, some of the alterative remedies must be taken at the same time, and long continued.

12. STRAMONIUM OINTMENT.—The probability is, that for general use, no ointment will be found superior to this, when properly made. It is kept by most Druggists, but it is not half as good, generally, as if made by the following directions. I give large proportions, from the fact that it will be used in large quantities. Stramonium is known by the names of "Jimpson," "Stink-Weed," "Thorn-Apple," &c., from its thorny burr.

Pick about a bushel of the leaves, while yet green, having a suitable iron kettle placed over a slow fire; put in a few of the leaves and mash them as you keep adding until you get

5—COPY RIGHT SECURED.

them all mashed into a pulpy mass, then put in lard 5 lbs., and stew to a crisp; then strain and box for use. Those who live in towns and prefer to make it with less trouble, will purchase 1 dr. of the soft extract, kept by druggists, rubbing it with a little water until it is of such a consistence as to allow it to be rubbed into an ointment with lard 1 oz. This will be better than the sale ointment, but not as good as the "Home Made," above.

It is anodyne, (relieves pain,) in burns, scalds, old irritable ulcers, skin diseases, painful hemorrhoids, (Piles,) and is discutient, (driving away swellings,) and very strengthening to broken limbs, *i. e.*, after the bones are healed to rub over the limb freely, and thoroughly; it reduces the swelling and gives tone to the muscles, tendons, &c.

We have recently known two cases of fracture, one a compound fracture of the ancle, the other of the wrist, both in persons well advanced in life; in both cases strength returned very slow, but with double speed by the free application of this ointment; and in the first case it undoubtedly prevented mortification. It is valuable, also, in painful or swelled rheumatism. Or, perhaps what would be preferable, n such cases, is a tincture made of the seeds from the horny-burr, two ounces, to alcohol and water, of each, a half-pint. If it is not found ahead of the "Tincture of Arnica," I will give you my head for a "Foot-Ball." In applying it, wet cloths or brown paper, and bind upon the parts, keeping them well wet. To make this tincture. see "Tinctures."

13. TOAD OINTMENT.—For sprains, strains, lame-back, rheumatism, caked breasts, caked udders, &c., &c.

Good sized live toads, 4 in number; put into boiling water and cook very soft; then take them out and boil the water down to ¼ pt., and add fresh churned, unsalted butter 1 lb. and simmer together; at the last add tincture of arnica 2 ozs.

This was obtained from an old Physician, who thought more of it than of any other prescription in his possession. Some persons might think it hard on toads, but you could not kill them quicker in any other way.

JAUNDICE.—DR. PEABODY'S CURE.—IN ITS WORST FORMS. —Red iodide of mercury 7 grs.; iodide of potassium 9 grs.; aqua dis. (distilled water,) 1 oz.; mix. Commence by giving 6 drops 3 or 4 times a day, increasing 1 drop a day until 12 or 15 drops are given at a dose. Give in a little water immediately after meals. If it causes a griping sensation in the bowels, and fullness in the head when you get up to 12 or 15 drops, go back to 6 drops, and up again as before.

In two very bad cases of jaundice, I have known the above to be entirely successful.

I am aware that many persons will not use any preparation containing mercury in any of its forms, while there are many others who would use them for that very reason; my object is to benefit *all*, without strengthening the *prejudices* of *any*; for this reason I give you the following:

2. DRINK FOR JAUNDICE.—Tie up soot and saffron, equal parts, in a cloth to the size of half of a hen's egg, let it lie in a glass of water over night; in the morning put the yolk of an egg, beaten, into this water, and drink it. Do this 3 mornings, skipping 3, until 9 doses have been taken.

I am assured that it has proved successful in many bad cases. See also Soot Coffee, No. 12, amongst the Ague remedies.

PILES.—SUCCESSFUL REMEDIES.—INTERNAL REMEDY.— Cream of tartar, jalap pulverized, senna, and flowers of sulphur 1 oz. each; nitrate of potash, (saltpetre,) ½ oz.; golden seal 1 oz.; thoroughly pulverize all together, in a mortar, and give a tea-spoon three times every day, or the dose may be varied to suit the condition of the patient, taking more or less to suit circumstances, keeping the bowels in a solvent state.

EXTERNAL APPLICATION.—Inner bark of the white oak tree, boil and strain, and boil again until you obtain ½ pt. of the extract, very thick; then add ½ pt. of the oil of the oldest and strongest bacon you can procure; simmer together until a union takes place when cold. Then apply by the finger up the rectum every night until well. Be very strict to abstain from strong and stimulating diet. The above is a sure cure for blind or bleeding piles, in all cases, sooner or later.

Dr. Hariman, of Andersontown, Ind., has been very successful with this plan of treating Piles; and since I obtained the plan, now two years, I have had one opportunity of proving its efficiency, upon a gentleman who had been laid up for days, and sometimes weeks, with the complaint; by a few applications of the external remedy he has been enabled to keep directly along with his labor.

2. PILE CERATE.—Carbonate of lead ½ oz.; sulphate of morphia 15 grs.; stramonium ointment 1 oz.; olive oil 20 drops. Mix, and apply 3 times a day, or as occasion and pain may require

This cerate has been highly celebrated as a remedy in Piles. It will relieve the pain most assuredly. Piles have been cured with lamp oil applied to the parts two or three times a day. Even tallow, or any simple ointment, is good for dry Piles, that is, for pain in those parts, coming on often in the dead of night, without apparent cause.

3. FOR EXTERNAL PILES,—The following is very highly spoken of: Take oyster shells, wash and burn them, then finely pulverize and rub up with fresh lard; annoint with this, and take internally sulphur one ounce, mixed with three ounces of pulverized rosin; take night and morning what will lay on a five cent piece. Take every day for the first week, then every three or four days, until well, continuing the ointment.

4. MRS. MOREHEAD,—Of Danville, Ind., cured herself of Piles by simply sitting in a hip-bath of warm water, every time the pains would come on, after stools, or any other time, remaining in the bath until the pains left her. Her husband cured himself by sitting in cold water, and using upon the parts an ointment made by stewing celendine in fresh lard. I give these various plans, so that if one fails, a remedy may certainly be found amongst the many given.

5. G. P. ROGERS, of Ironton, O., has known cases cured by using the following ointment: Powdered opium and powdered rosin, one ounce each, mixed with one ounce of tallow, and anoint as required.

6. DR. D. W. RAYMOND, of Conneaut, O., says: Equal weights of glycerine and tannin will cure Piles, by anointing with it, and that very speedily; also cures sore or cracked nipples in twenty-four hours, and is remarkably good for any excoriation, or sore, of the skin. I know that simple tallow introduced into the rectum is exceedingly beneficial in Piles, which satisfies me that any preparation containing oil or any kind of grease, is good.

7. I have found in the scrap of an old newspaper, the following, and it is so easily tried, and speaks with so much certainty, and is so simple, that I give it an insertion:

"SIMPLE CURE FOR PILES.—Mix one table-spoon of sulphur with half a pint of milk, to be taken every day until favorable symptoms appear, and then occasionally, as the case may require. The above is a cheap, simple, and most infallible cure for that most painful and unpleasant disorder. It has been used with complete success in old and inveterate cases where individuals had spent scores of dollars in medical advice. It is equally useful as a preventive. It will injure none, and only requires a trial."

8. PASCHAL MASON, living near this city, cured a Southern lady, visiting in the neighborhood, who was confined to the bed with them, by making a strong tea of the wild swamp-currant root, drinking occasionally for a few days only.

9. JIMPSON LEAVES and parsely, a handful of each, stewed in lard, one pound, and used as an ointment, has cured many cases.

ANODYNES—HOFFMAN'S ANODYNE, OR GOLDEN TINCTURE. —Sulphuric ether 2 ozs.; alcohol 4 ozs.; and etherial oil ¼ dr.; mix. DOSE—From half to two tea-spoons, (¼ dr. to 2 drs.) according to the urgency or pain for which it is given.

It is given in a little sweetened water, and much preferred by the Germans to laudanum, especially where laudanum causes sickness of the stomach. · It makes an excellent local application in neuralgia and other painful affections, being second cousin to the Magnetic Tooth Cordial and Paralytic Liniment.

2. LAUDANUM.—Best Turkey opium 1 oz., slice, and pour upon it boiling water 1 gill, and work it in a bowl or mortar until it is dissolved; then pour it into the bottle, and with alcohol of 76 per cent proof ½ pt., rinse the dish, adding the alcohol to the preparation, shaking well, and in 24 hours it will be ready for use. DOSE—From 10 to 30 drops for adults, according to the strength of the patient, or severity of the pain.

Thirty drops of this laudanum will be equal to one grain of opium. And this is a much better way to prepare it than putting the opium into alcohol, or any other spirits alone, for in that case much of the opium does not dissolve. See the remarks occuring after Godfrey's Cordial.

3. PAREGORIC.—Best opium ¼ dr., dissolve it in about 2 tablespoons of boiling water; then add benzoic acid ½ dr.; oil of anise ½ a fluid dr.; clarified honey 1 oz.; camphor gum 1 scruple; alcohol, 76 per cent, 11 fluid ozs.; distilled water 4½ fluid ozs.; macerate, (keep warm,) for two weeks. DOSE—For children, 5 to 20 drops, adults, 1 to 2 tea-spoons.

Used as an anodyne and antispasmodic, allays cough, relieves nausea and slight pains in the stomach and bowels, checks diarrhea, and procures sleep. Used principally for children. See the remarks after No. 5, below.

4. BATEMAN'S PECTORAL DROPS.—Opium in powder, catechu in powder, camphor gum, red saunders, rasped, of each ¼ oz.; oil of anise 1 dr.; dilute alcohol, (alcohol of 76 per cent, and water in equal proportions,) 1 gal. Keep warm for 2 weeks.

The opium strength of this is about equal to paregoric, and it is used for similar purposes, and doses. See the remarks below.

5. GODFREY'S CORDIAL.—Dissolve pure carbonate of potassa 1 oz. in water 5 qts., and add nice golden syrup or best molasses 3 qts., and heat until they begin to simmer; take off the scum, and add laudanum 9 ozs., and oil of sassafras 1 dr. Mix well. Used similar to the two last.

REMARKS.—It is a well known fact that much injury is done to children by the use of anodynes, such as the above, and "Mrs. Winslow's Soothing Syrup," which is now taking the place, to a great extent, in towns of the foregoing, for I noticed a short time ago eighty-seven empty bottles with Mrs. Winslow's label upon them, sitting on a counter of one of our drug stores, which led me to ask if they put up her syrup. The answer was no, a *lady* in this city has fed that much to *one* child within the past *eighteen* months.

The question might be asked, why do you tell people how to make *any* of these anodynes? Because they are good in proper cases, when properly used, and to give a place for these remarks; for those who are evil disposed will find a way to accomplish their designs, whilst the well disposed will, or can, act only from knowledge, and if they do not know the evils arising from the constant use of anodynes on children, are as liable to do evil as the evil disposed.

Then let it be remembered that the constant use of opium in any of its preparations on children, or adults, disturbs the nervous system, and establishes a nervous necessity for its continuation. Then use them only in severe pain, or extreme nervousness, laying them by again as soon as possible under the circumstances of the case. Of course we do not give a receipe for the Soothing Syrup spoken of, as its exact composition has not yet come out to the public; but that its soothing properties are owing to opium, there is not the least doubt. See " Carminatives," which are preferable to opiates, especially for children.

RHEUMATISM'S—INFLAMMATORY RHEUMATISM—BILL WRIGHT'S, AND OTHER CURES.—Sulphur and salt-petre, of each 1 oz.; gum guaiac ½ oz.; colchicum root, or seed, and nutmegs, of each ¼ oz.; all to be pulverized and mixed with simple syrup or molasses 2 oz. DOSE—One tea-spoon every 2 hours until it moves the bowels rather freely; then 3 or 4 times daily until cured.

Mr. Wright, of the Niagara Hotel, Toledo, O., has several times proved this to be an excellent medicine, and since I obtained it I found a man at Marshall, Mich., one Saturday evening, with his feet and legs so swollen with this disease, that he could but just crawl with two crutches. I filled this prescription and gave him a tea-spoon of it every two hours, until it moved his bowels, then every four hours, and on Monday noon he could walk quite comfortably without cane or crutch, the medicine costing only twenty cents.

2. RHEUMATIC ALTERATIVE.—In Rheumatism of long standing, the following preparation has often proved very valuable :

Colchicum seed, and black cohosh root, of each ¼ oz., the root to be bruised; best rye whisky 1 pt.; put together and let stand 3 or 4 days. DOSE—From one tea-spoon to a table-spoon 3 times daily, before meals.

The action will be to loosen the bowels, or cause a little sickness at the stomach ; and the dose may be modified not to cause too great an effect upon the patient either way, but increasing the dose if necessary until one of these specific actions is felt, and lessening it if the action is too great in any case.

3. RHEUMATIC LINIMENT.—Olive oil, spirits of camphor, and chloroform, of each 2 ozs.; sassafras oil 1 tea-spoon. First add the oil of sassafras to the olive oil, then the spirits of camphor, and shake well before putting in the chloroform, shaking when used, keeping it corked, as the chloroform evaporates very fast if left open. Apply 3 or 4 times daily, rubbing it well, and always towards the body.

I had a brother-in-law cured of a very bad case of inflammatory, or swelling rheumatism, by the use of this liniment—accomplished in about four days, without other treatment

He paid five dollars for the recipe after the cure. But I would recommend the use of this in connection with "Bill Wright's Cure," above, feeling perfectly assured that no attack will stand before the internal and external combination.

4. J. B. HITCHCOX, Ypsilanti, Mich., uses spirits of turpentine 1 pt.; tar 2 tea-spoons; oil of vitriol 1 tea-spoon, mixing in a mug; then sets them on fire, letting it burn 15 minutes, and bottle for use.

He bathes the parts freely twice daily with this preparation, then binds on the mashed tory-weed, as mentioned under the head of "Reducing Swellings," and gives a little spirits of turpentine internally.

5. ALVAH RAYMOND—Takes Rum 1 pt.; neats-foot oil ½ pt., or if the joint is stiff, skunk's oil instead of the other; spirits of turpentine 1 gill, and simmers them together, and bottle for use, rubbing it in thoroughly 3 times daily.

He also directs to soak the feet in hot water, scraping the bottoms of the feet with an old knife; then he has poke root roasted and mashed, mixing with it tar and sulphur to form drafts for the feet. With this method of treatment he assures me he has been very successful for 30 years. And it bears so strong a resemblance to Dr. Kittredge's preparation, next following, for stiffened joints in rheumatism, that it gives me double confidence in them both.

6. DR. KITTREDGE'S REMEDY FOR RHEUMATISM AND STIFF JOINTS.—Strong camphor spirits 1 pt.; neats-foot, coon, bear, or skunk's oil 1 pt.; spirits of turpentine ½ pt. Shake the bottle when used, and apply 3 times daily, by pouring on a little at a time and rubbing in all you can for 20 to 30 minutes.

The old Doctor recommends this as a sure cure for chronic rheumatism, sprains, stiff-joints where they have not formed an anchylosis, that is, if the bones have not actually grown together; and as remarked in connection with his ointment, No. 6, he has been a very celebrated Physician for many years; but like many *other* men with superior minds, oh! how fallen. Rum, and its advocates, have got a most fearful account to balance.

7. FRENCH AND OTHER REMEDIES FOR CHRONIC RHEUMATISM.—Dr. Bonnet, of Graulbet, France, states in a letter to the Abeille Medicale, that he "has been long in the habit of prescribing:

"The essential *oil* of turpentine for frictions against rheumatism. And that he has used it himself with perfect success, having almost instantaneously got rid of rheumatic pains in both knees and in the left shoulder."

He was led to make the prescription from having used the *oil* of turpentine to wash coal-tar and other sticking mixtures from his hands. After having washed his hands in soap and water, and drying them, a pricking sensation like an electric spark upon the knuckles from a machine, lasting about two hours, was always experienced, and it is to this exciting action that he attributes its efficacy. It may be used twice or thrice daily.

8. Chronic rheumatism has been cured in twenty-four hours, after two years' suffering, by using alcohol, spirits of turpentine, sweet spirits of nitre, and oil of juniper, equal parts of each; mix; rub well into the parts, and take ten drops at bed time in water.

9. BITTERS FOR CHRONIC RHEUMATISM.—Prickly-ash berries, spikenard root, yellow poplar and dog-wood barks, of each ¼ lb.; all pulverized and put into a gallon jug, and fill it up with brandy. DOSE—A wine-glass of it is to be taken 3 times daily before meals.

A baker of Lafayette, Ind., was cured by the use of this amount, of a very bad case of this disease of long standing.

10. DAVID MOWRY, of Greenville, Ohio, says yellow poplar, dog-wood, prickly-ash, wild cherry and white-ash barks of the trees, equal quantities of each, a good large handful, boiled in 2 gals. of water, to 1, and add 1 gal. of good old rye, will, if taken freely 3 times daily, cure the worst inflammatory rheumatism in the world.

There is no question but what both of these preparations, and the next also, are good, if made sufficiently strong with the barks. But I should consider them much more applicable in chronic cases, or rheumatism of long standing; and in these cases very applicable indeed, and I am well satisfied that no one will take them for the spirits.

11. CHRONIC RHEUMATISM, has been cured by taking the bark of a bearing crab-apple tree, and putting a sufficient amount of it into whisky to make it *very* strong, then taking a wine-glass three times daily, until a gallon was used.

12. GREEN BAY INDIAN'S REMEDY FOR RHEUMATISM.—Wahoo, bark of the root, 1 oz.; blood root 1 oz.; black cohosh root 2 ozs.;

swamp hellebore ¼ oz.; prickly ash, bark or berries 1 oz.; poke root, cut fine, 1 oz.; rye whisky 1 qt.; let stand a few days before using. DOSE—One tea-spoon every 3 or 4 hours increasing the dose to 2 or 3 tea-spoons, as the stomach will bear.

Soak the feet well and go to bed, covering up warm, and taking the "Sweating Drops" between each dose, as there directed, for three or four hours, and repeat the sweating every day until the disease surrenders to the treatment. If at any time the head feels too full, or the stomach sickens too much, drop down to the first dose of a tea-spoon, or even less, if necessary.

This prescription is from Jacob S. Cornelius, an Indian of Green Bay, who was very successful in Illinois, with it, in this disease.

13. I know an old physician who assures me that he has cured cases where all other remedies failed, with saltpetre, beginning with twenty grains, and doubling the dose every three or four hours, until it reached half an ounce, in a very robust and plethoric patient; but this dose would be too large to venture upon by persons not of a plethoric habit. But as it is mostly prescribed, by putting a table-spoon to a pint of whisky, then a tea-spoon for a dose; you might as well expect to dip the Atlantic into the Pacific with a tea-spoon, as to cure rheumatism in that slow way. It may be taken in quantities from half an ounce to an ounce and a half in the twenty-four hours, being largely diluted with water. If pain should come on in the stomach, under its use, stop it at once, and give large quantities of mucilaginous drinks, such as slippery-elm water, gum-arabic water, flax-seed tea, &c.

14. NEW REMEDY.—Kerosene oil 3 ozs.; skunk's oil 1 oz.; mix, and shake when applied. Put it on quite freely, and heat it in by the stove, or by means of a hot shovel.

A firm of grocers, Slawson & Geer, of this city, have been using this mixture during the past winter upon their own persons, and have recommended to many others amongst them, one of the Clergymen, and also the President of the University, and so far as they know, it has proved very successful, relieving the pain directly.

15. One of our physicians in the city has used a preparation very nearly resembling the above, but varying sufficient to

satisfy myself that any other animal oil will do as well as that from the highly-flavored one, above mentioned.

He used kerosene oil 2 ozs.; neats-foot oil 1 oz., oil of origanum ½ oz.; mixed and shaken as used.

The smell of the kerosene is not very pleasant, but if a pair of ankles and feet, badly swollen, so much so that you could not walk on them for months, could be cured in two or three weeks, as it was in this case, it might be well to put up with its disagreeable smell. Rub and heat it in thoroughly twice daily.

ASTHMA—REMEDIES.—Elecampane, angelica, comfrey, and spikenard roots, with hoarhound tops, of each 1 oz.; bruise and steep in honey 1 pt. DOSE—A table-spoon, taken hot every few minutes, until relief is obtained, then several times daily until a cure is effected.

It cured a young lady, near the " Falls of the Ohio," whom the doctors said it was wicked to disturb ; " let her *die* in peace," was their advice to the parents. An old lady, instead, let her *live* in peace. It will be found very excellent in any cough; even low consumptives will find great relief from its use.

2. Dr. J. K. Finley, of Pittsburg, cured a lady with whom I afterwards became acquainted, and from the completeness of the cure, I was induced to write to the doctor and obtain the prescription. It is as follows :

Oil of tar 1 dr.; tincture of veratrum viride 2 drs.; simple syrup 2 drs.; mix. DOSE—For adults 15 drops 3 or 4 times daily.

I have very great confidence in this prescription.

3. A lady at Yellow Springs, O., tells me that she cured herself of Asthma, by using, for her common drink, a tea made of the leaves of common chestnut, which had fallen from the tree in autmn; sweeten well, and continue its use for 2 or 3 months.

She used it for a month at first, and it returned, when she continued its use for two months; and ten years have elapsed without its return. It is certainly safe as well as simple, and of easy trial.

Lobelia is considered by some a specific in asthma, but the prejudice against it is so great I forbear speaking further of it; but :

4. Iodide of potasium has cured a bad case of asthma, by

taking 5 gr. doses, 3 times daily. Take ⅛ oz. and put it into a vial and add 32 tea-spoons of water—then 1 tea-spoon of it will contain the 5 grs., which put into ½ gill more of water, and drink before meals.

COMPOSITION POWDER—Thompsons.—"Bayberry bark 2 lbs.; hemlock bark 1 lb.; ginger root 1 lb.; cayenne pepper 2 ozs.; cloves 2 ozs.; all finely pulverized and well mixed. Dose—One-half of a tea-spoon of it, and a spoon of sugar; put them into a tea-cup and pour it half full of boiling water; let it stand a few minutes and fill the cup with milk, and drink freely If no milk is to be obtained, fill up the cup with hot water.

"This, in the first stages and less violent attacks of disease is a valuable medicine, and may be safely employed in all cases. It is good in relax, pain in the stomach and bowels, and to remove all obstructions caused by cold. A few doses, the patient being in bed with a steaming stone at the feet, or having soaked the feet fifteen or twenty minutes in hot water, drinking freely of the tea at the same time, will cure a bad cold, and often throw off disease in its first stages." I use it, taking, or giving, lobelia emetics as mentioned under the head of "Eclectic Emetics." I use it also, as a :

2. Dyspeptic Tea.—Where an attack has been brought on by over-indulgence at an extra rich meal, you will find immediate and generally perfect relief by having a cup of this tea made; and drinking about one-half of it fifteen minutes before meals, and the balance just as you sit down to the meal, not taking any other fluid at all until after digestion is over, following up the same plan for a few days or weeks, as may be necessary. It stimulates the stomach to action, causing dijestion and absorption, preventing also the accumulation of gas, which is the cause of eructations of wind from the stomach, commonly called belching, and gives tone to the whole system.

A cup of this tea taken when going out into extreme cold, will be found a better warmer than the whisky or any other ardent spirit, which so many resort to upon such occasions; and, what is best of all, it will be found :

3. A Perfect Cure for Drunkenness.—Let those who are accustomed to the excessive use of ardent spirits, and who wish to stop the practice, I say, let such have a cup of this tea made, as above directed, and drink a part of

ft immediately on rising in the morning, and the balance
just before meal time, keeping entirely away from the
places of temptation, they will find a warm, healthy glow
spreading from the stomach over the whole system, with a
desire for food, instead of "rot-gut." Follow this up faithfully two or three times daily, or whenever the *craving* begins,
for the accustomed stimulus, for a few days or *weeks*, if
necessary, and it will be found that the cayenne, which is
the purest stimulant in the whole Materia Medica, with its
assistant, the bayberry, which stimulate without an after
prostration, have gradually *supplied and satisfied* the previous false appetite or cravings of the stomach; whilst the
combination has *toned* up the stomach together with the
whole system, AND AGAIN YOU FIND YOURSELF A MAN.
But remember, oh, remember! *your only safety is in keeping entirely away from places where intoxicating spirits are
kept or sold!*

A *burned* child will not play with fire. I would to God
that a burned *man* was equally wise. For not *one* in a *thousand* can resist the solicitation of enemies, (called friends,)
to take a glass, just *one*, and that one glass acts like *fresh
coals* upon *extinguished* brands, and the fire goes ahead again
with a hundred fold more energy than if thrown upon wood
which had never been charred; hence, the propriety of the
sentence "plucked as a brand from the everlasting burn-
ings,"—for if *re-kindled* there is but little prospect of another
extinguishment of the raging fire. Dr. Thompson, notwithstanding all that has been said against him, has done more
good than any other medical man that ever lived; for he set
the people to studying for themselves.

STIMULANT—IN LOW FEVERS, AND AFTER UTERINE HEM-
ORRHAGES.—MISTURA SPIRITUS VINI GALLICI.—Best brandy,
and cinnamon water, of each 4 fluid ozs.; the yolks of 2 eggs,
well beaten; loaf sugar ½ oz.; oil of cinnamon 2 drops; mix.
DOSE—From ½ to 1 (fluid) oz.; as often as required. This makes
both eat and drink. Of course, any other flavoring oils can be
used, if preferred, in place of the cinnamon.

This mixture is an imitation of the well-known compound
termed "egg-flip." It is an exceedingly valuable stimulant
and restorative, and is employed in the latter stages of low
fevers, and in extreme exhaustion from uterine hemorrhages

It may be used in place of the "egg-nog" spoken of in the treatment of consumption, No. 6.

ALTERATIVES.—SYRUP OR BLOOD PURIFIER.—Honduras sarsaparilla 12 ozs.; guaiacum shavings 6 ozs.; winter green leaf 4 ozs.; sassafras-root bark 4 ozs.; elder flowers 4 ozs.; yellow dock 3 ozs.; burdock-root 4 ozs.; dandelion-root 6 ozs.; bitter-sweet-root 2 ozs.; all bruised. Place these ingredients in a suitable vessel and add alcohol 1 pt., with water sufficient to cover handsomely, set them in a moderately warm place for 3 or 4 days, pour off 1 pt. of the tincture and set it aside until you add water to the ingredients and boil to obtain the strength, pour off and add more water and boil again, then boil the two waters down to 1 qt.; strain, and add the liquor first poured off, and add 2½ lbs. crushed or coffee sugar, and simmer to form a syrup; when cool, bottle and seal up for use, DOSE—One to 2 table-spoons, according to the age and strength of the patient, ½ hour before meals and at bed time.

This, or any other alterative, when given, should be followed up for weeks or months, according to the disease for which it is prescribed, as scrofula, and for every disease depending upon an impure condition of the blood. It ought to be used in sore eyes of long standing, old ulcers, salt-rheum, &c. I would not give this for Jayne's Alterative, nor Swain's, Townsend's or Ayer's Sarsaparillas, because I know it is good, and we also know what it is made of.

2. ALTERATIVE, VERY STRONG.—Poke, mandrake, yellow dock, sassafras, blue flag, roots, and bark of the roots, guaiac wood raspings, and sweet elder flowers, of each 4 ozs.; caraway seed 3 ozs.; bruise the roots, and put to the whole, alcohol 1 qt., and water to cover all handsomely; let stand 3 or 4 days in a warm place as the last recipe above, making every way the same except to pour off 1 qt., instead of 1 pt., as in the first, of spirit; then boil the waters to 1 qt., adding 4 lbs. of sugar with the qt. of spirit tincture. The dose being only 1 table-spoon 4 times daily as above.

But if that amount should make the bowels too loose, reduce the quantity; and if that amount does not act upon the bowels at all, increase the dose to keep the bowels solvent. This may be used in the most inveterate diseases of long standing, syphilis not excepted.

3. ALTERATIVE CATHARTIC—POWDER.—Rochelle salts 5 ozs.; cream of tartar 2 ozs.; sulphur 1 oz.; (epsom salts may be used, but are not quite as good,) place the salts in a dripping-pan and set in the stove oven until all the water of crystalization is dried out; then place all in a mortar and rub finely and thoroughly

togethei. DOSE—Mix up a few spoons of the powder with mo
.asses; then take a tea-spoon every 3 or 4 hours until a free
cathartic action is kept up for 24 to 36 hours; then take once oi
twice daily only, to act on the blood, increasing once in 10 dayi
to get up the cathartic action, as at first.

This alterative is especially valuable in any disease of
the skin, as itch, pimples, salt-rheum, and any other erup-
tions where an outward application is being made, or is about
to be made, also valuable in sore eyes.

4. ALTERATIVE, TONIC, AND CATHARTIC BITTERS.—Best rye
whisky, and water, of each, 1 qt.; best unground Peruvian bark,
colombo root, and prickly-ash berries, of each, 2 ozs.; prickly-
ash, black cherry, and poplar barks, of each, 1 oz.; poke-root,
mandrake-root, and cloves, of each, ½ oz.; all to be the dry articles, and all to be pulverized before putting into the spirits;
shake every day for a week, by which time it will be ready for
use.   DOSE—One to 2 table-spoons at morning and evening
meals.

Although this alterative is mentioned last in the list, yet
it is not least in value.   I first made this prescription for my
own use, feeling that I needed something of just such a
nature, and it worked so admirably that I gave it to others.
It has given such entire satisfaction, that I am now at the
tenth edition, giving it a place to do a greater good than if
kept from the world.

If, in any case, it causes any griping sensations, or too
great action upon the bowels, lessen the dose, and if neither
of these actions are felt, increase the dose, or take it three
times daily.   I think any of the fruit wines will do in
place of the spirits and water, by adding alcohol one-half
pint.

It will be found very valuable in all cases of weakness
from general debility, and especially so when the liver is
inactive, known by constant costiveness.

After using out the spirits, it may be filled again in the
same way.   It will be found very valuable in ague, and after
all fevers, preventing relapse, and strengthening up the general system.

DIURETICS—PILL, DROPS, DECOCTION, &c.—Solidified copaiba 2 parts; alcoholic extract of cubebs 1 part; formed into
pills with a little oil of juniper.   DOSE—One or 2 pills 3 or 4
times daily.   Druggists can obtain them of Tilden & Co., New
York.

This pill has been found very valuable in affections of the kidneys, bladder, and urethra, as inflammation from gravel, gonorrhea, gleet, whites, lucorrhea, common inflammations, &c. For giving them a sugar coat, see that heading, if desired.

2. DIURETIC DROPS.—Oil of cubebs ½ oz.; sweet spirits of nitre ½ oz.; balsam of copaiba 1 oz.; Harlem Oil 1 bottle; oil of lavender 20 drops; spirits of turpentine 20 drops; mix. DOSE—Ten to 25 drops, as the stomach will bear, 3 times daily.

It may be used in any of the above diseases with great satisfaction.

3. DIURETIC DECOCTION.—Queen of the meadow, dwarf-elder, yellow dock and poke-roots, of each 1 oz.; dandelion, burdock, American Sarsaparilla, and blue flag roots, of each ½ oz.; grind or pound all up, and thoroughly mix. DOSE—Take up a pinch with the ends of the fingers and thumb of one hand, say ½ to ½ oz., and pour upon it 1 pt. of boiling water, steeping awhile; when cool, take a swallow or two sufficiently often to use up the pt. in the course of the day.

Follow this plan two or three days, or as may be necessary, resuming the course once in ten or twelve days. It may be used in all obstructions of the kidneys, where the urine is high colored or scanty.

4. DIURETIC TINCTURE.—Green or growing spearmint mashed, put into a bottle and covered with gin, is an excellent diuretic.

5. DIURETIC FOR CHILDREN.—Spirits of nitre—a few drops in a little spearmint tea—is all sufficient. For very young children pumpkin seed, or watermelon seed tea is perhaps the best.

DROPSY.—SYRUP AND PILLS.—Queen of the meadow root dwarf-elder flowers, berries, or inner bark, juniper berries, horseradish root, pod milkweed or silkweed, often called, root of each 4 ozs.; prickly-ash bark or berries, mandrake-root, bittersweet bark of the root, of each 2 ozs.; white mustard seed 1 oz. · holland gin 1 pt.

Pour boiling water upon all, except the gin, and keep hot for twelve hours; then boil and pour off twice, and boil down to three quarts and strain, adding three pounds of sugar, and lastly the gin. DOSE—Take all the stomach will bear, four times daily, say a wine-glass or more. This will be used in connection with the following :

2. DROPSY PILLS.—Jalap 50 grs.; gamboge 30 grs.; podophyllin 20 grs.; elaterium 12 grs.; aloes 30 grs.; cayenne 30 grs.; castile soap shaved, dried and pulverized, 20 grs.; croton oil 90

irops; powder all finely, and mix thoroughly; then form into pill mass by using a thick mucilage made of equal parts of gum arabic and tragacanth, and divide into 3 gr. pills. DOSE—One pill every 2 days for the first week, then every 3 or 4 days until the water is evacuated by the combined aid of the pill with the above syrup.

In this disease the work must be very thorough, and I am inclined to think that if our directions are followed, that whoever find themselves under the operations of the medicine will consider the work to be about as thorough as we expect. Some sickness of the stomach may be expected under the operation of the pill, but never mind it, go ahead and four or five days will satisfy most persons of the value of the treatment; for you may expect to see the greatest evacuations, front and rear, that you ever have witnessed. If the patient should become weak and exhausted under the continued treatment, slack up a little and throw in beef tea, wine, &c., with rich nourishing diet, and no danger need be apprehended. The above pill will be found very valuable in bilious colic, and other cases hard to operate upon. They have operated in fifteen minutes, but not usually so quick, of course; but it will generally be found best not to venture over one pill at a dose; two have been taken, however but they made a scattering among the *waste* paper, causing *fourteen* evacuations, having to call for the second "chamber" the first fire. Some have called them the "Irish Pill," from their resemblance to the Irish girl with her brush and scrub-broom. They make clean work.

IRRITATING PLASTER.—EXTENSIVELY USED BY ECLECTICS.—Tar 1 lb.; burgundy pitch ¼ oz.; white pine turpentine ⅜ oz.; rosin 2 ozs. Boil the tar, rosin and gum together a short time, remove from the fire, and stir in finely pulverized mandrake root, blood root, poke root, and Indian turnip, of each 1 oz.

This plaster is used extensively in all cases where counter irritation or revulsives are indicated; as in chronic affections of the liver and lungs, or diseased joints, &c. It is applied by spreading it on cloth and over the seat of pain, renewing it every day, wiping off any matter which may be on it, and also wiping the sore produced by it with a dry cloth, until relief is obtained, or as long as the patient can bear it. Always avoid wetting the sore, as it will cause inflammation, and you will be obliged to heal it up immedi-

ately, instead of which the design is to keep a running sore
as long as may be necessary, using at the same time constitutional remedies as the case may require.

INFLAMMATION,—OF THE LIVER.—Inflammation
of the liver, or as it is generally called, " Liver complaint,"
is of two forms, acute and chronic. The acute form is
known by a sense of weight and pain in the right side, under the short ribs, and often in that shoulder, or between
the shoulders, pale or yellow appearance, often great depres-
sion of spirits, not much appetite, costiveness, high colored
urine, &c., and often with fever, and sometimes with pain
similar to that of pleurisy, difficult breathing, dry cough,
and sometimes sickness, with vomiting.

In the chronic, or long standing complaint, in addition to
the above, there is generally flatulence, with pain in the
stomach, foul breath and mouth, coated tongue, indigestion,
eyes yellow, stools clay colored, with great weakness and slow
emaciation, frequently going on to ulceration, giving symptoms as mentioned under the head of " Ointment for Ulcerated Liver," &c.

In the acute form you will pursue the same course as
mentioned under the head of "Pleurisy," besides taking
either of the Liver Pills or Liver Drops mentioned below, in
full cathartic doses, until relieved ; but in the chronic form,
the Pills, in connection with the " Ointment," or " Irritating Plaster," will be found all sufficient, unless Jaundice
has already set in ; then look to the directions under that
disease.

2. ECLECTIC LIVER PILL.—Podophyllin 10 grs. ; leptandrin
20 grs.; sanguinarin* 10 grs. ; extract of dandelion 20 grs.;
formed into 20 pills, by being moistened a little with some essential oil, as cinnamon or peppermint, &c. DOSE—In chronic
diseases of the liver, take 1 pill at night, for several days, or 2
may be taken at first to move the bowels; then 1 daily.

In connection with the pill, wear the " Irritating Plaster,"
over the region of the liver, washing the whole body daily,
by means of towels, and rubbing dry, being careful not to
wet the sore caused by the plaster ; as an active cathartic

*NOTE.—These articles are kept by Eclectic Physicians, and are beginning to
be kept by Druggists generally.

from two to three pills may be taken in all cases where calomel or blue pills are considered applicable by " Old School Physicians."

3. LIVER PILL IMPROVED.—Leptandrin 40 grs.; podophyllin and cayenne, 30 grs. each; sanguinarin, iridin and ipecac 15 grs. each; see that all are pulverized and well mixed; then form into pill-mass by using ½ dr. of the soft extract of mandrake and a few drops of anise oil, then roll out into 3 grain pills.

DOSE—Two pills taken at bed time will generally operate by morning; but there are those that will require three, whilst one pill every night on retiring, will be found the best corrective of the liver of anything now in use, for common cases; but in very bad cases where the pill does not arouse the liver to action, take the following:

4. LIVER DROPS FOR OBSTINATE CASES.—Tinctures of mandrake and blue flag roots, of each 1 oz.; and of culvers root 2 ozs. DOSE—For adults, 1 tea-spoon every 3 to 5 hours, increasing the dose gradually until you reach two or three tea-spoons, if the mouth does not become sore and the stomach not sickened nor the bowels moved too freely.

These drops are especially applicable in liver and spleen enlargements, and cases of very long standing disease of these organs; and in such cases it may be well to use externally, over the liver and spleen, especialy if there is believed to be ulceration, the following:

5. OINTMENT FOR ULCERATED LIVER, AGUE CAKE, &C.—Take a good handful of smartweed, wormwood, and the bark of sumac root; boil all together to get the strength, then strain and boil down carefully to about ½ pt., adding lard ¼ lb., and simmering together; when nearly cool add a tea-spoon of spirits of turpentine.

Apply at night, by rubbing it over the liver or other organ which may have pain or disease located upon it, heating it in well by the stove or by a heated iron, putting it on, rubbing, and heating it in three or four times each application.

I obtained this prescription from the Rev. Mr. Fraser, of this city, whose nephew was so afflicted with ulceration of the liver that a council of Doctors said he must die; the pain was situated just under the short ribs of the right side, completely bowing him together, like the one of old who could " in no wise lift up herself." He had had a sister,

who died some years before ; but at this juncture of the case
the invalid dreamed of meeting her, and she gave him this
prescription, which he told his mother in the morning ; and
she would not rest until it was tried, and it entirely cured
the patient. The Elder tells me he has given it to a great
many persons, for pains of internal organs, ague cakes, &c.,
and that it has given great satisfaction—a perfect cure. The
two first named articles I know to be good for what they are
here recommended, but they are generally used by boiling
and laying the herbs over the affected parts, or by steaming
the parts over the herbs. I see no reason why spirits from
the other world should not be permitted to communicate
with the spirits of friends here; but that they are so permitted, to communicate in such a way as to be understood
by us frail mortals, I never did, nor do I now believe, neither
do I believe this to be the *first* dream of this character which
was proved valuable. There are many things of a similar
character in the history of a number of individuals in the
range of my acquaintance, more singular and more unac-
countable than the above, which would be very interesting
to relate, but the nature of this work does not admit. If
this shall benefit any, I shall be satisfied.

PILLS—NERVOUS PILL.—Alcoholic extract of the Ignatia
Amara, (St. Ignatius bean) 30 grs. ; powdered gum arabic 10 grs.
Make into 40 pills.
Dose—One pill to be taken an hour after breakfast, and one
an hour before retiring at night. Half a pill is enough for young,
or very old or very delicate persons. The pills may be easily
cut if laid on a damp cloth for a few moments.

These pills will be found applicable in bad Dyspepsia,
nervous headache, sleeplessness, palpitation of the heart, con-
fusion of thought, determination of blood to the head, failure of memory, and all other forms of general nervous debility, no matter of how long standing. Where a prominent
advantage is discovered in two weeks from the commencement of the medicine, one a day will suffice until all are
taken.

The extract is made by pulverizing the seed or bean, and
putting it into alcohol from ten to fourteen days, then evap-
orating to the consistence for working into pill mass with the
powdered gum.

This is the prescription of the Rev. John M. Dagnal, the 'Retired Physician," brought out in 1854, and to my attention, and that of the medical class, by Prof. Palmer, in the University of Michigan, in the winter of '56-7. He said when this prescription first came out he was practicing in Chicago, and many persons sent for the pills, and derived much benefit from their use, at first, but soon after they seemed to lose their efficacy, and he presumed the reason to be that the demand was so great that something else was substituted in place of the extract. This being the case, druggists ought to prepare the extract themselves, so as to furnish patients with the genuine article for home use. It is undoubtedly a splendid prescription, if put up with fidelity

2. PILLS—To SUGAR COAT.—Pills to be sugar-coated must be very dry, otherwise they will shrink away from the coating and leave it a shell, easily crushed off. When they are dry, you will :

Take starch, gum arabic, and white sugar, equal parts, rubbing them very fine in a marble mortar, and if damp, they must be dried before rubbing together; then put the powder into a suitable pan, or box, for shaking; now put a few pills into a small tin box having a cover, and pour on to them just a little simple syrup, shaking well to moisten the surface only, then throw into the box of powder and keep in motion until completely coated, dry, and smooth.

If you are not very careful you will get too much syrup upon the pills; if you do, put in more and be quick about it to prevent moistening the pill too much, getting them into the powder as soon as possible.

3. ANODYNE PILLS.—Morphine 9 grs.; extract of stramonium and hyosciamus, of each 18 grs; form into pill-mass by using solution of gum arabic and tragacanth, quite thick. Divide into 40 pills. DOSE—In case of severe pain or nervousness, 1 pill taken at bed time will be found to give a quiet night of rest.

The advantage of this pill over those depending entirely upon opium or morphine for their anodyne properties, is, that they may be taken without fear of constipation.

CROUP—SIMPLE, BUT EFFECTUAL REMEDY.—This disease is attended with inflammation of the windpipe, spasms of the muscles of the throat, occasioning a peculiar sound, hard to be described, but when once heard by a mother, never to be forgotten; cough, difficult respiration, and fever. The phlegm or mucous often filling, or very much obstructing the throat, and finally forming a false membrane which cuts off all possibility of breathing.

The first thing to be done is to get hot water ready as soon as possible, having *always* on hand a bottle of emetic tincture, composed of equal parts of the tinctures of lobelia and blood-root. DOSE—According to the age of the child; if 2 years old, about 1 tea-spoon every 10 to 15 minutes until free vomiting takes place; if 5 years old 2 tea-spoons, and increasing in proportion to age to 1 table-spoon for a child of 10 years, decreasing for very young children, say of 4 to 8 months, only 8 to 12 drops. Place the feet as soon as possible into hot water, and keep them there until vomiting takes place, laying cloths wrung out of hot water upon the breast and throat, changing sufficiently often to keep them hot. The next morning give sufficient of the "Vegetable Physic" to move the bowels rather freely. The emetic tincture should be given in some warm tea.

Repeat the emetic as often as the returning symptoms demand it, which usually occur the following night, repeating the cathartic every second or third day, and I will guarantee success if commenced in any kind of reasonable time; but usually no repetition will be needed if parents keep the preparation in the house so as to begin with the beginning of the disease.

2. DUTCH REMEDY.—Goose oil, and urine, equal quantities. DOSE—From a tea to a table-spoon of the mixture, according to the age of the child. Repeat the dose every 15 minutes, if the first does not vomit in that time.

This remedy will be found valuable in mild cases, and where the first is not at hand; and I know it to have saved a child when one of their best Doctors said it must die; but bear in mind he had not used our first prescription; yet an old Dutch woman came in at the *eleventh* hour, from the next door neighbors' wash-tub, and raised the child with what she called "p—s and goose grease." I have used it with success.

3. CROUP OINTMENT.—Take mutton suet and nice lard, of each ½ lb.; spermaceti tallow ¼ oz.; melt them together and add ¼ pt. of the best vinegar, and simmer until the vinegar is nearly evaporated, skimming well, and constantly stirring, until it begins to granulate; then add oils of amber and spruce, and pulverized sugar of lead, of each ¼ oz.; now remove from the fire and stir it until cool. DOSE—For a child of 2 years old, give

from ¼ to 1 tea-spoon every ½ hour, until relief is obtained, or until vomiting takes place; at the same time rubbing it upon the chest, and over the throat and lungs, freely.

Dr. ——, of Finley, O., says, from his experience, he knows it will cure as often as quinine will break up the ague.

HYDROPHOBIA AND SNAKE BITES—To Pre-vent, and Cure.—A. Hubbard, of Boone Co., Ill., in a letter to the St. Louis Republican, says : " Eighteen years ago my brother and myself were bitten by a mad-dog. A sheep was also bitten at the same time. Among the many cures offered for the little boys, (we were then ten or twelve years old,) a friend suggested the following which he said would cure the bite of a rattlesnake :

"Take the root of the common upland ash, commonly called black ash, peel off the bark, boil it to a strong decoction, and of this, drink freely. Whilst my father was preparing the above, the sheep spoken of began to be afflicted with hydrophobia. When it had become so fatigued from its distracted state as to be no longer able to stand, my father drenched it with a pint of the ash root ooze, hoping to ascertain whether he could depend upon it as a cure for his sons. Four hours after the drench had been given, to the astonishment of all, the animal got up and went quietly with the flock to graze. My brother and myself continued to take the medicine for 8 or 10 days, 1 gill 3 times daily. No effects of the dread poison were ever discovered on either of us. It has been used very successfully in snake bites, to my knowledge."

There is no doubt in the author's mind but what this gen-tleman has made a mistake in the kind of ash meant, as the upland ash is white-ash, from which flooring is made, having a thick, rough outside bark, whilst the black has a smooth bark, and grows in low, wet land, and is the same from which the flour barrel hoop is extensively manufactured. It is the upland white-ash that is to be used ; it is known, as he says, to cure rattlesnake bites, and a gentleman of this place has tried it with success in rheumatism, boiled very strong and taken in half gill doses. May vomit and purge if taken too freely. Yet a moderate action, either up or down, will not be amiss. I have cured a case of rheumatism, in a boy twelve or fourteen years of age, with the above, since it came to my knowledge.

2. SAXON REMEDY.—Gastell, a Saxon forester, now of the venerable age of eighty two, unwilling to take to the grave with him a secret of so much importance, has made public in the *Leipsic Journal* the means which he has used fifty years, and wherewith he affirms, he has rescued many human beings and cattle from the fearful death of Hydrophobia.

Take immediately after the bite, warm vinegar or tepid water, wash the wound clean therewith, and dry it; then pour upon the wound a few drops of hydrochloric acid, because mineral acids destroy the poison of the saliva.

3. GRECIAN REMEDY.—Eat the green shoots of asparagus raw; sleep and perspiration will be induced, and the disease can be thus cured in any stage of canine madness.

A writer in the *Providence Journal*, says a man in Athens, Greece, was cured of Hydrophobia by this remedy, even after the paroxysms had commenced.

4. QUAKER REMEDY—FIFTY YEARS SUCCESSFUL.— Jacob Ely, a good old honest Quaker merchant, of Lloydsville, O., gave me the following plan which his father had used since 1806 with success, to his knowledge, both on persons and domestic animals; and the New York Tribune has recently published something of the same character.

The dried root of elecampane, pulverize it and measure out 9 heaping table-spoons, and mix it with 2 or 3 tea-spoons of pulverized gum arabic; then divide into 9 equal portions. When a person is bitten by a rabid animal, take one of these portions and steep it in 1 pt. of new milk, until nearly half the quantity of milk is evaporated; then strain, and drink it in the morning, fasting for 4 or 5 hours after. The same dose is to be repeated 3 mornings in succession, then skip 3, and so on until the 9 doses are taken.

The patient must avoid getting wet, or the heat of the sun, and abstain from high seasoned diet, or hard exercise, and, if costive, take a dose of salts. The above quantity is for an adult—children will take less according to age. The *Tribune's* publication is as follows :

5. TRIBUNE'S CURE FOR HYDROPHOBIA.—The following was sent to the N. Y. *Tribune*, by J. W. Woolston, of Philadelphia :

" RECIPE.—First dose, 1 oz. of elecampane root, boiled in 1 pt. of milk until reduced to ½ pt. Second dose, (to be taken two days after the first,) 1½ ozs. of elecampane root, boiled in 1 pt of milk, same as the first. Third dose, same as the second, (to be taken two days after,)—in all, three doses."

If there is any virtue in the elecampane, at all, the preference, of course, is to be given to the Quaker's plan, which gives nine instead of three doses. But it substantiates Mr Ely's plan, as it comes from the place of his father's former residence. Consequently it would seem to strengthen confidence in the first.

6. SNAKE BITES.—In case of being bitten by any of the poisonous snakes, the best plan is to wash off the place *immediately*, then if the position of the wound is such that you can get the *mouth* to the spot, *suck* out all the poison in that way, or if any other person is present, whose mouth is not sore, no danger need be apprehended.

For all the poison may be upon the outside, and washed off, yet most likely penetrates more or less into the wound, if a snake bite, as the arrangement of their teeth is such that the poison comes out *near* the point and when in the wound, thus you see the propriety of sucking it out. Or :

7. Spirits of ammonia, a small vial of it, can be carried in the pocket, and if bitten, sharpen a little piece of wood to a small point, dipping this stick into the ammonia, and then penetrating the wound with it. A piece of lunar caustic can be carried in the pocket, and sharpened, if needed, and used the same as the stick and ammonia—and one of the celebrated English farriers has reported that this caustic, used freely on the bite of the *mad dog*, destroys the poison ; but to insure even a reasonable hope of success, it must be used *immediately*. This holds good in any of the sucking or caustic applications.

All persons working on or near marshes, or wherever the massasauger is known to inhabit, should always have one of these caustics with them.

8. But when a person is bitten in the absence of all these caustics, and not being able to reach the spot to suck out the poison, he must drink whisky enough to get as drunk as a fool, or his whole dependence must be upon the ash, asparagus, or elecampane.

The *National Intelligencer*, a year or two since, published a recipe for the cure of the rattlesnake bite, which it claimed was infallible, it having been tried in a number of cases, and always with success. It was nothing more nor less than the use of whisky as above recommended, and it is but justice to say that a daughter of Wm. Reed, of the town of Pittsfield, in this county, who was bitten on the arm some three years ago, was cured by drinking whisky until drunkenness and stupor were produced, and she has never felt any inconvenience from the bite since, which goes to show that the bite of the *Devil's tea* is worse than the bite of a rattlesnake.

9. I know an old physician who was called to a boy bitten by a rattlesnake, and in the absence of all other remedies, he cured him upon the principle that, " The hair of the *dog* will cure his bite," taking a piece of the snake about two inches long, splitting it on the back, and binding it upon the bite. It cleansed the wound very white, and no bad effects were seen from it.

10. SALERATUS, moistened and bound upon the bite; then dissolve more, and keep the parts wet with it for a few hours has cured many massasauger-bites, as also bee-stings.

11. SNAKE BITTEN CATTLE.—REMEDY.—Cattle or hor ses are usually bitten in the feet. When this is the case, all that is necessary to do is to drive them into a mud-hole and keep them there for a few hours ; if upon the nose, bind the mud upon the place in such a manner as not to interfere with their breathing. And I am perfectly satisfied that soft clay mud would be an excellent application to snake bites on persons, for I know it to draw out the poisoning from ivy, and have been assured that it has done the same for snake bites, of persons as well as for cattle.

EYE PREPARATIONS—EYE WATER.—Table salt and white vitriol, of each, 1 table-spoon; heat them upon copper or earth en until dry; the heating drives off the acrid or biting water-called the water of crystalization, making them much milder in, their action; now add them to soft water ½ pt.; putting in white sugar 1 table-spoon; blue vitriol a piece the size of a common pea. If it should prove too strong in any case, add a little more soft water to a vial of it. Apply it to the eyes 3 or 4 times daily

If the eyes are *very* sore, or if the soreness has been of *long* standing, take the " Alterative Syrup," or the " Ca thartic Alterative," continuing them for several weeks accord ing to the necessities of the case. I find it an excellent plan, in using any preparation for sore or weak eyes, to apply it again about twenty minutes from the first applica

tion. More than double speed is made by this repetition.
For inflammation of any part of the body, apply this by
wetting cloths. Even for sores about the ears and groins of
babes, reduce it, and three or four applications will cure
them. I have also found it valuable for horses, as a wash,
when they get the eye injured by straws, or otherwise, which
causes the eye to water, or matterate, using it freely.

The use of this eye water enabled me to lay by the spec-
tacles after four years' wearing, and I have since studied
medicine and graduated as a physician, without resorting
again to their use, by the occasional application of the eye
water. But I need not have resorted to the use of the eye
water again, had I not done in study, as I do in all things
else, that is, when I have anything to do, I do it with all
my might. I read steadily, day by day, sixteen hours—
more than five other students, read altogether, who roomed
at the same house. Yet this counted in the end; for when
the class began to inquire and look around, near the end of
the term, for one to deliver the *Valedictory*, on their behalf,
which is the custom in the Eclectic Medical Institute, I received that, the first honor of the class. I do not mention
this to boast, by no means, but to show the necessity, as well
as the advantages, of hard study, especially to those who
begin their studies late in life, and are obliged to pay their
way with their own hands, and support a family also. This
was my case exactly. In the commencement of my medical studies, I worked all day, reading half of the night,
copying off the *latin terms*, with their significations, on a slip
of paper, which I carried in my pocket during the next day,
looking at two or three of the terms at a time, through the
day, until all were committed. And thus I accomplished,
no more than what any other man may do, if he goes at it
with a will, and does as I did; and that some one may be
stimulated to this course is the only object of this recital.
See "Advice to Young Men."

2. D. Raymond, of Grass Lake, Mich., who obtained
the above prescription of me, adds to each ounce of water
used, one grain of morphine, and he tells me he has great
success with it; the addition of the morphine making it
nearly resemble the celebrated prescription used by the English surgeons in India, which is as follows :

3. INDIA PRESCRIPTION FOR SORE EYES.—Sulphate of zinc 2 grs.; tincture of opium, (laudanum) 1 dr.; rose water 2 ozs.; mix. Put a drop or two in the eye 2 or 3 times daily.

4. AN EYE DOCTOR, of Xenia, O., makes a great use of the ollowing:

Sulphate of zinc, acetate of lead, and rock salt, of each ½ oz., loaf sugar 1 oz.; soft water 12 ozs.; mix without heat, and use as other eye waters.

5. DR. COOK, of Ashtabula, Ohio, makes and sells large quantities, under the head of "Cook's Eye Water." It is as. follows:

Sulphate of zinc 1 oz.; sugar of lead ½ oz.; precipitated carbonate of iron ½ oz.; salt, and sugar, of each 1 table spoon; the whites of 2 eggs; soft water 32 ozs.; mix the whites of the eggs, zinc, salt, lead, sugar, and iron well together, then add the water.

6. FOR EXCESSIVE INFLAMMATION OF THE EYES.—Poultice by boiling a handful of hops in water, putting in from ½ to 1 dr. of opium, while boiling; when still warm, lay the hops over the eyes and keep them wet with the water 'n which they were boiled.

A lady who had been blistered and starved, according to the old plan, in this disease, was soon cured by this poultic ing and washing the eyes often with the hop-water contain ing the opium, with generous diet, &c., contrary to the ex- pectations of friends, and the predictions of enemies, to the plan.

7. IF sore eyes shed much water, put a little of the oxide of zinc into a vial of water, and use it rather freely—it will soon cure that difficulty.

8. COPPERAS and water has cured sore eyes of long stand ing and used quite strong, it makes an excellent application in erysipelas.

9. GARDEN RHUBARB.—The juice of the root applied to the eye, has cured bad cases.

10. BOIL an egg, remove the yolk, and have ready equal parts of sulphate of zinc and loaf sugar, pulverized; fill the place occupied by the yolk, and squeeze out the oil through a linen cloth, while hot, and apply as needed. If too strong, add a little rain water.

I sold a book to a Mrs. Johnson, in Wayne county, Mich who had used this preparation very successfully for several years, and had I not have already had it in my book, I could not have purchased it of her for less than five dollars and she regretted very much that I was taking from her a source of profit by selling the books in her neighborhood containing the recipe.

11. SAILOR'S EYE PREPARATION.—Burn alum, and mix it with the white of eggs and put between two cloths and lay it upon the eyes; taking salts and cream of tartar, equal parts, to cleanse the blood.

This was given to me, and very highly recommended, by an old Scotch sailor, with whom I have had much enjoyment, talking over the sufferings of the sea, he having used it many times in places where nothing else could be obtained.

12. FATHER PINKNEY'S PREPARATION FOR VERY BAD SORE EYES.—Castile soap, scraped fine, and half the quantity of very finely pulverized chalk; wet them up to a paste with strong juice of tobacco; when desired to apply to the eye, drop two or three drops of brandy into the box of paste; then take out a bit of it where the brandy was dropped, equal in size to the fourth of a grain of wheat, to the diseased eye; wet it on a bit of glass, and put it into the eye with a camel's hair pencil.

Apply it twice daily at first, and from that to only once in two days, for from one to two weeks, will, and has cured wretched bad cases, so says old Father Pinkney, of Wayne Co., Mich., who has used it over fifty years, he being over ninety years of age. His only object in giving it an insertion here is to do good to his fellow creatures; and also for animals, it being equally applicable to horses or cattle.

13. INDIAN EYE WATER.—Soft water 1 pt.; gum arabic 1 oz; white vitriol 1 oz.; fine salt ½ tea-spoon; put all into a bottle and shake until dissolved. Put into the eye just as you retire to bed.

I paid Mrs. Pinny, south of Ypsilanti, Mich., fifty cents for this prescription. She would not, however, let her own family know its composition. Her husband had removed films from horses' eyes with it, and cured Mr. Chidister, a merchant of Ypsilanti, by only two applications, as the saying is, after he had "Tried everything else." It came from an old Indian, but my knowledge of the articles would lead me to say for common, at least, it would require to be reduced one-half.

14. TOBACCO EYE WATER.—Fine cut tobacco the size of a

common hickory nut; sugar of lead equal in bulk; rain water 2 ozs.; opium the size of a pea. Reduce it with more water if necessary.

15. VERDIGRIS AND HONEY, have cured inflamed eyes, by using just sufficient verdigris to color the water a grass color, then making it one-third honey. It is also said to prevent scars by using upon burns.

16. RAW POTATO POULTICE, for inflamed eyes, is one of the very best applications in recent cases, scraping fine and applying frequently.

17. SLIPPERY-ELM POULTICES, are also an excellent application, used as above.

18. FILMS—To REMOVE FROM THE EYE.—Wintergreen leaf, bruised, and stewed in a suitable quantity of hens' oil to make the oil strong of the wintergreen—strain and apply daily.

The above cured a boy of this city, and I am satisfied that the hens' oil has cured recent cases, without the wintergreen, but with it, it has cured beasts also. For cases of a year or two's standing, however, it is best to use the following:

19. LIME water 1 pt.; finely pulverized verdigris ½ oz.; set on embers for 1 hour; then strain and bottle tight. Touch the film over the pupil, or on the speck, 2 or 3 times daily, by putting the point of a small camel's hair pencil into the preparation, then to the eye, holding away the lids for a short time by placing the thumb and finger upon them for that purpose.

It will be found necessary to persevere for two or three months with this application, and also to use one of the " Alteratives," to cleanse the blood. This course, pursued for three months, gave sight to a young lady who had not seen light for two years, which Doctors could not do, nor were willing for others to do.

20. EYE SALVE.—Take white precipitate 1 tea-spoon and rub it into a salve with 3 tea-spoons of fresh lard, and applied upon the outside of the lid of the worst chronic, (long continued), sore eyes, has cured them when they were so bad that even the eyelashes, (cilia), had fallen out, from the disease.

A Physician was cured with this eye salve when he could not cure himself. If red precipitate will cure the itch, why should not the white cure disease of the eye.

21. SORE EYES—To REMOVE THE GRANULATIONS.—Crystalized nitrate of silver 2 grs.; morphia 1 gr.; blue vitriol 1 gr.; salammoniac 1 gr.; pulverize each one separately, and mix. Ap-

ply once daily, by putting a small bit of the mixture upon a piece of glass, moistening it with a little water, and putting into the eye by means of a small camel's hair pencil.

22. ANOTHER METHOD—Is to take a stick of tag-alder about 2 feet long, boring a hole nearly through the middle of the stick, crosswise, filling it with salt, and plugging it up; then put one end into the fire and char it nearly to the salt, then the other end the same way; and finally pulverizing and applying the salt, the same as the above, once daily only.

In either case after the granulations (little lumps) are removed from the eye, or eyes, finish the cure by using any of the foregoing eye waters which you may choose; all the time using some of the alteratives for cleansing the blood.

FEVER SORES—PLASTER, SALVES, &c.—BLACK SALVE. —Sweet oil, linseed oil, and red lead pulverized, of each 1 oz. (or in these proportions). Put all into an iron dish over a moderate fire, stirring constantly, until you can draw your finger over a drop of it on a board when a little cool, without sticking. Spread on cloth and apply as other salves.

My brother, J. M. Chase, of Caneadea, N. Y. says he has used this salve about fifteen years, and knows it to be one of the best in the world for all kinds of old sores, as ulcers, fever sores, and all inflamed parts, cleaning and taking out redness or inflammation, causing a white healthy appearance in a short time, and a certain preventive of mortification &c., &c., as well as to prevent soreness in more recent cuts and bruises, also; and from my own knowledge of a salve which is very similar, I have introduced it into this work, feeling assured that whoever may have occasion to try it, will not regret the space it occupies, especially after reading the following : A gentleman said to me during the past summer, " I will give you one of the most valuable salves in the world, for I cured a man's hand, with it, which was so swollen that it looked more like a ham than a hand ; and two Doctors said it must be cut off, also ulcerated." When he told me how it was made, I opened my book to the above salve, which was precisely the same as the one he used.

2. RED SALVE.—Some prefer to prepare the salve as follows :

Red lead 1 lb.; bees-wax and rosin, of each 2 ozs. ; linseed and sweet oils, of each 3 table-spoons ; spirits of turpentine 1 tea-spoon ; melt all, except the first and last, together, then stir in the lead and stir until cool, adding the turpentine.

Used upon fever, and all other sores of an inflammatory character; at the same time taking the following pill to purify the blood :

3. MANDRAKE root, dried and pulverized, ¼ oz.; blood root, in the same way, ¼ oz.; form into pills with extract of dandelion. DOSE—Three pills may be taken at bed time, for 2 or 3 days, then add another pill, and at the end of a week take any cathartic you choose; then take iodide of potash 10 grs., and put it into a vial with 1 oz. of water, and take 20 to 30 drops of it in a little more water, instead of the mandrake pill, for 3 or 4 days; then that pill again, as at first.

By the time you have gone around three or four times, the blood will be pretty thoroughly cleansed—do not be afraid of the mandrake pill, as it will not act as a cathartic. but simply work upon the blood—if it does, reduce the number. You will be pleased with this method of purifi cation

4. INDIAN CURE.—G. A. Patterson, of Ashtabula, O., was cured by an Indian physician, in Cleveland, of one of the worst fever sores almost ever known. The muscles of his leg were so contracted that no use could be made of his leg in getting about. Four months, and the following treat ment, did the work :

A syrup of Wahoo (Euonymus Atropurpureus)—and here let me say that the Wahoo is the great Indian remedy for purifying the blood—was made by boiling very strong, then molasses and rum added to make it palatable and keep it from souring; this was used sufficient to keep the bowels solvent, sometimes chew- ing the bark of the root from which the syrup is made, prefer- ring it a part of the time to the syrup. The sore was dressed with the following salve: Rosin 1 lb.; mutton tallow 1 lb.; bees- wax 1 lb.; linseed oil 1 pt.; ambrosial (highly flavored) soap 1¼ ozs.; to make it, mix in an iron kettle and simmer 2 hours, stir- ring all the time. Spread on cloth, and apply as needed. The contracted muscles were anointed with skunk's oil only.

Mr. Patterson also extols it very highly for all common purposes. And as I have a few other recipes for fever sores which have been so highly recommended by those who have used them, I cannot omit their insertion, and I would espe- cially recommend the next one following, called :

5. KITRIDGE'S SALVE.—Bitter-sweet and sweet elder roots, of each 1½ lbs.; hop vines and leaves, and garden plantain, top and root, of each ¼ lb.; tobacco 1 three-cent plug. Boil all in rain water to get out the strength; then put the herbs in a thick cloth

and press out the juice, and boil down carefully to ¼ pt.; then add unsalted butter 1 lb.; bees-wax and rosin, of each 1 oz., and simmer over a slow fire until the water is all out.

I obtained the above from S. B. Newton, a farmer Doctor near Mooreville, Mich., who had cured fever sores, with it, of thirty-five years' standing; used it also on swellings in every case, once upon a boy who had an eye kicked out and swelled very bad; he keeps it in his stable all the time for wounds of horses and cattle, in castration, &c., &c. I know it must be a very valuable salve.

6. FEVER SORE POULTICE.—Sassafras, bark of the root, drie and pulverized very fine; make a bread and milk poultice quite thin, and stir in of the above powder to make it of proper con sistence, applying 3 times in the 24 hours for 3 weeks; then heal with a salve made by thickening honey to a salve with whea, flour.

If there are loose bones it will be quite sore while they are working out, but persevere. A case was cured by it of twelve years' standing; the same man cured eight other cases, never having a failure, and it has proved successful on an abscess of the loins also.

7. YEAST POULTICE.—Fresh yeast, the thick part, thickened with flour and applied to fever sores has proved very valuable, continuing it for several weeks, touching any points, which does not heal readily, with finely pulverized verdigris rubbed up with a little lard; then putting the poultice directly over the whole again.

This heals, leaving the parts white and natural, instead of dark, as I have seen many cases which had been cured.

8. SALVE FOR FEVER SORES, ABSCESSES, BROKEN BREASTS, &c.—Thoroughly steep tobacco ½ oz., in soft water 1 pt., strain-ing out from the tobacco and boiling down to 1 gill; then have melted, lard, rosin, and bees-wax, of each ½ oz. simmering to a thick salve, then stirring in 1 gill of old rum, and, if necessary, continuing the simmering a little longer. To be used as other salves.

9. OINTMENT.—Sweet clover (grown in gardens) stewed in lard; then add bees-wax and white pine turpentine, equal parts, to form an ointment, is highly recommended.

10. SALVE FOR FEVER SORES, CUTS, &c.—Spirits of turpentine and honey, of each ½ pt., simmered over a slow fire until they unite by stirring; then set aside to cool until you can put in the yolk of an egg without its being cooked by the heat; stir it in and return it to the fire, adding camphor gum ¼ oz., simmer and stir until well mixed.

By putting in the egg when cool, it combines with the other, but if put in while the salve is hot it cooks, but does not combine. This is very highly recommended, as above indicated.

11. WILLIAM HOWELL, a farmer living about six miles from Jackson, Mich., says he had a fever sore on his shin for twenty years, sometimes laying him up for months, and at one time preparations were made to cut off the limb, bu an old man, in New Jersey, told him to:

Scrape a fresh turnip and apply it every 4 hours, night and day, until healed, which cured him.

And he feels assured, from using it in other cases, that all will be pleased with it who have any occasion for its use Apply it oftener if it becomes too offensive.

SALVES.—GREEN MOUNTAIN SALVE.—Rosin 5 lbs.; Burgundy pitch, bees-wax, and mutton tallow, of each ¼ lb.; oil of hemlock, balsam of fir, oil of origanum, oil of red cedar, and Venice turpentine, of each 1 oz.; oil of wormwood ½ oz.; verdigris, very finely pulverized, 1 oz.; melt the first articles together and add the oils, having rubbed the verdigris up with a little of the oils, and put it in with the other articles, stirring well; then pour into cold water and work as wax until cool enough to roll.

This salve has no equal for rheumatic pains, or weakness in the side, back, shoulders, or any place where pain may locate itself. Where the skin is broken, as in ulcers, and bruises, I use it without the verdigris, making a white salve, even superior to "Peleg White's old salve." It is valuable in Dyspepsia, to put a plaster of the green salve over the stomach, and wear it as long as it will stay on, upon the back also, or any place where pain or weakness may locate. In cuts, bruises, abrasions, &c., spread the white salve upon cloth and apply it as a sticking plaster until well; for rheumatism or weakness, spread the green salve upon soft leather and apply, letting it remain on as long as it will stay. For corns, spread the green salve upon cloth and put upon the corn, letting it remain until cured. It has cured them.

A gentleman near Lancaster, O., obtained one of my books having this recipe in it, and one year afterwards he told me he had sold over four-thousand rolls of the salve, curing an old lady of rheumatism in six weeks, who had

been confined to her bed for seven weeks, covering all the
the large joints with the salve, without other treatment.
For rolling out salves, see the cut below.

2. CONKLIN'S CELEBRATED SALVE.—Rosin 4 lbs.; bees-wax,
burgundy pitch, white pine turpentine, and mutton tallow, each
¼ lb.; camphor gum and balsam of fir, of each ¼ oz.; sweet oil
¼ oz.; and alcohol ½ pt. Melt, mix, roll out, and use as other
salves. Wonders have been done with it.

3. BALM OF GILEAD SALVE.—Mutton tallow ¼ lb.; balm of
gilead buds 2 ozs.; white pine gum 1 oz.; red precipitate ¼ oz.;
hard soap ½ oz.; white sugar 1 table-spoon. Stew the buds in
the tallow until the strength is obtained, and press out or strain,
scrape the soap and add it with the other articles to the tallow,
using sufficient unsalted butter or sweet oil to bring it to a proper
consistence to spread easily upon cloth. When nearly cool, stir
in the red precipitate, mixing thoroughly.

This may be more appropriately called an ointment. It
is used for cuts, scalds, bruises, &c., and for burns by spreading very thin—if sores get proud flesh in them, sprinkle a
little burned alum on the salve before applying it. It has
been in use in this county about forty years, with the greatest success.

4. ADHESIVE PLASTER, OR SALVE, FOR DEEP WOUNDS, CUTS,
&c., IN PLACE OF STITCHES.—White rosin 7 ozs.; bees-wax and
mutton tallow, of each ½ oz.; melt all together, then pour into
cold water and work as wax until thoroughly mixed, then roll
out into suitable sticks for use.

It may be spread upon firm cloth and cut into narrow
strips. In case of deep wounds, or cuts, it will be found to
firmly hold them together, by first pressing one end of a
strip upon one side of the wound until it adheres, then draw
the edges of the wound closely together, and press down
the other end of the strip until it adheres also. The strips
should reach three or four inches upon each side of the cut,
and run in different directions across each other, to draw
every part of the wound firmly in contact It will crack
easily after being spread until applied to the warm flesh, ye
if made any softer it cannot be be depended upon for an
length of time, but as it is, it has been worn as a strengthening plaster, and remained on over a year.

5. PELEG WHITE'S OLD SALVE.—This, formerly celebrated, salve was composed of only three very simple articles

Our "Green Mountain Salve" is far ahead of it, yet for the satisfaction of its old friends I give you its composition :

Rosin 3 lbs. ; mutton tallow and beeswax, of each ¼ lb. ; melt ed together and poured into cold water, then puiled, and worked as shoe-makers wax.

It was recommended for old sores, cuts, bruises, rheu r atic-plasters, &c., &c.

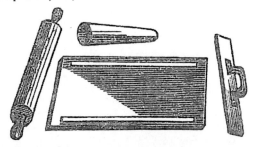

APPARATUS FOR MAKING SALVES AND LOZENGES

The above cut represents a board prepared with strips upon it of the desired thickness for the diameter of the rolls of salve, also a piece of board with a handle, with which to roll the salve when properly cooled for that purpose. The salve is laid between the strips, which are generally one inch thick, then, with the handle piece, roll it until that board comes down upon the strips which makes the rolls all of one size, use a little tallow to prevent sticking to the boards or hands ; then cut off the desired length and put a label upon them, to prevent them sticking to each other.

A roller, and tin-cutter, is also represented in the same cut, with which, and another board, having thin strips upon it to correspond with the thickness of lozenges required, you can roll the mass down until the roller touches the strips ; and thus you can get them as well as the salve, of uniform thickness ; then cut out with the cutter, laying them upon paper until dry.

VERMIFUGES.—SANTONIN LOZENGES.—Santonin 60 grs. ; pulverized sugar 5 ozs. ; mucilage of gum tragacanth sufficient to make into a thick paste, worked carefully together. that the santonin shall be evenly mixed throughout the whole mass·

then, if not in too great a hurry, cover up the mortar in which you have rubbed them, and let stand from 12 to 24 hours to temper; at which time they will roll out better than if done immediately; divide into 120 lozenges. See apparatus, above, for rolling, and cutting out. DOSE—For a child 1 year old, 1 lozenge, night and morning; of 2 years, 2 lozenges; of 4 years, 3; of 8 years, 4; of 10 years or more 5 to 7 lozenges; in all cases, to be taken twice daily, and continuing until the worms start on a voyage of discovery.

A gentleman came into the drug store one morning, with the remark, " Do you know what your lozenges have been doing?" As though they had killed some one, the answer was, no, is there anything wrong; he held up both hands together, scoop shovel style, saying, " They fetched away the worms by the double handful." It is needless to attempt to give the symptoms by which the presence of worms might be distinguished; for the symptoms of nearly every other disease is, sometimes, manifested by their presence. But if the belly be quite hard and unusually large, with a peculiar and disagreeable breath, in the morning, foul or furred tongue, upper lip swollen, itching of the nose and anus, milky white urine, bowels sometimes obstinately costive, then as obstinately loose, with a craving appetite, then loathing food at times; rest assured that worm medicine will not be amiss, whether the person be child, or adult. It would be well to take a mild cathartic after four to six days use of the lozenges, unless the worms have passed off sufficiently free before that time, to show their general destruction. Very high praise has also been given to the following :

2. VERMIFUGE OIL—PROF. FREEMAN'S.—In the May number of the *Eclectic Medical Journal* of Cincinnati, O., I find so valuable a vermifuge from Prof. Z. Freeman, that I must be excused for its insertion, as the articles can always be obtained, whilst in some places you might not be able to get the santonin called for in the lozenges. His remarks following the recipe will make all needed explanations, and give confidence in the treatment.

The explanations in brackets are my own, according to the custom through the whole work.

" Take oil of chenopodii, ½ oz. (oil of worm-seed,); oil of terebinth, 2 drs. (oil of turpentine,); oil of ricini, 1½ ozs. (castor oil,); fluid extract of spigelia, ½ oz. (pink) hydrastin 10 grs.; syrup of menth. pip. ½ oz. (syrup of peppermint.) DOSE—To a child 10 years of age, a tea-spoon 3 times a day, 1 hour before each meal; if it purges too freely, give it less often.

"This is an excellent vermifuge, tonic, and cathartic, and has never failed (as well as I can judge,) to eradicate worms, if any were present, when administered for that purpose I have given no other vermifuge for the last five years, and often one tea-spoon has brought away from three to twenty of the lumbrica. Only a few days ago I prescribed one fluid drachm of it, (about one tea-spoon,) and caused the expulsion of sixty lumbricoids, and one fluid drachm, taken a few days afterwards, by the same child, brought away forty more, some of them six inches in length. Where no worms are present, it answers the purpose of a tonic, correcting the condition of the mucus membrane of the stomach and bowels, improving the appetite and digestion, and operating as a mild cathartic."

3. WORM TEA.—Carolina pink-root, senna leaf, manna, and American worm-seed, of each ¼ oz.; bruise and pour on boiling water 1 pt., and steep without boiling. Sweeten well, add half as much milk. DOSE—A child of five years, may take 1 gill 3 times daily, before meals, or sufficient to move the bowels rather freely.

If this does not carry off any worms, wait one day and repeat the operation; but if the bowels do not move by the first day's work, increase the dose and continue to give it until that end is attained before stopping the medicine. This plan will be found an improvement upon the old where the lozenges or oil cannot be obtained, as above.

4. WORM CAKE—ENGLISH REMEDY.—Wheat flour and jalap, of each ¼ lb.; calomel, grain-tin, and ginger, of each 1 oz. Mix thoroughly and wet up as dough, to a proper consistence to roll out; then roll out as lozenge cakes, to three-sixteenths of an inch in thickness; then cut out ¾ inch square and dry them. DOSE—For a child from 1 to 2 years, ¾ of a cake; 4 to 5 years, 1 cake; from 5 to 7 years, 1¼ cakes; from 7 to 10, 1½; from 10 to 12, 1¾; from 12 to 14, 2; from 14 to 17, 2½; from 17 to 20 years, and all above that age, 2½ cakes, but all men above that age 3 cakes.

"Children may eat them, or they can be shaved off very fine and mixed in a little treacle, honey, or preserves. If after taking the first dose, they do not work as you desire,

increase the dose a little. The patient to take the medicine twice a week—Sundays and Wednesdays. To be taken in the morning, fasting, and to be worked off with a little warm tea, water gruel, or warm broth. N. B.—Milk must not be used in working them off, and be careful of catching cold.--
Snodlin, Printer, Oakham, Eng."

I obtained the above of an English family who praised it very highly as a cathartic for common purposes, as well as for worms. And all who are willing to take *calomel*, I have no doubt will be pleased with its operations.

TAPE-WORM.—SIMPLE, BUT EFFECTUAL REMEDY. --This, very annoying and distressing, worm has been removed by taking two ounce doses of common pumpkin-seeds, pulverized, and repeated every four or five hours, for four or five days; spirits of turpentine, also in doses of one-half to two ounces, with castor oil, have proved very effectual; the root of the male fern, valerian, bark of the pomegranate root, &c., have been used with success. But my chief object in speaking upon this subject, is to give the successes of Drs. Beach, of New York, and Dowler, of Beardstown, Ill., from their singularity and perfect eradication of the worm, in both cases: The first is from "Beach's American Practice, and Family Physician," a large work, of three volumes, costing Twenty Dollars, consequently not generally circulated; whilst the latter is taken from the "Eclectic Medical and College Journal," of Cincinnati, and therefore only taken by physicians of that school. The last was first published by the "New Orleans Medical and Surgical Journal." First then, Dr. Beach says:

"The symptoms of a tape-worm, as related to me by Miss Dumouline, who had suffered with it for twenty-five years, are in substance as follows: It commenced at the age of ten, and afflicted her to the age of thirty-five. The worm often made her distressingly sick at the stomach; she would sometimes vomit blood and be taken suddenly ill, and occasionally while walking. It caused symptoms of many other diseases, great wasting of the flesh, &c. Her appetite was very capricious, being at times good, and then poor for months, during which time her symptoms were much aggravated; sickness, vomiting, great pain in the chest, stomach and side, motion in the stomach, and also in the bowels, with pain, a sense of fullness or swelling, and beating or throbbing in the same, dizziness, heaviness of the eyes;—and she was altogether so miserable that she feared it would destroy her. When she laced or wore anything tight, it produced great distress. The worm appeared to rise up in her throat and sicken her. Her general health was very bad. At intervals, generally some time after taking medicine pieces of the worm would pass from the bowels,—often as many as forty during the day, all alive, and would swim in water.

"TREATMENT.—Miss Dumonine stated that she had employed twenty physicians, at different periods, and taken a hundred different kinds of medicine without expelling the worm. She had taken spirits of turpentine, but could not retain it upon the stomach. Under these circumstances I commenced my treatment. Cowage stripped from the pod, a small tea-spoon three times a day, to be taken, fasting, in a little arrow-root jelly; then occasionally a purgative of mandrake. In connection with this, I directed her to eat freely of garlic, and common fine salt. I gave these under the belief that each article possessed vermifuge properties, without ever having administered them for the tape-worm. After having taken them for some time, all her unfavorable symptoms ceased, and subsequently the remaining portion of the worm passed lifeless from her—an unprecedented circumstance.

"She immediately recovered, and has since retained her health, and there is no evidence that there is any remaining The patient stated that the worm which passed from her during the time she was afflicted with it, would fill a peck measure, and reach one mile in length. Her relief and gratitude may be better imagined than described. I have a portion of this worm in my possession. When once the tapeworm begins to pass the bowels, care must be taken not to break it off, for it will then grow again—it has this peculiar property."

2. SECONDLY, Dr. Dowler says: "The subject of this notice is a daughter of Mr. E. Fish, of Beardstown, Ill., about six years old. The only point of special interest in the case consists in the efficiency of the remedy—to me wholly new, and accidentally brought to my notice—which was used in its treatment.

"I was treating a brother of this patient; a part of my

prescription for whom was, as a drink, the mucilage of elm bark, made by putting pieces of the solid bark into water. The girl was seen to be frequently eating portions of the bark during the day; the next morning after which, upon my visiting the boy, the mother, with much anxiety, showed me a vessel containing something that had that morning passed the girl's bowels, with bits of the elm bark, enveloped in mucilage, which, upon examination, proved to be about three feet of tape-worm. As I supposed the passage of the worm was accidental, and had occurred from the looseness caused by the bark, I proceeded to prescribe what I supposed a much more potent anthelmintic, a large dose of turpentine and castor oil. The turpentine and oil were given several times during the three consecutive days, causing pretty active purging, but with no appearance of any portions of the worm. The girl being slender, and of irritable temperment, I was forced to desist from further active medications; and partly to allay irritation of the bowels, and partly to test the influence of the bark on the worm, I directed that she should resume the use of the bark as before, by chewing and swallowing in moderate quantities.

" On visiting her the succeeding morning, I was shown portions of the worm, mostly in separate joints, that had been passed over night. Feeling now some confidence in the *anthelmintic* powers of the elm bark, I directed the continued use of it, in the solid form, as before, while there should be any portions of worm passing. In my daily calls for some days, I had the satisfaction to learn that portions of the worm continued to pass, from day to day, and sometimes several times a day.

" I now ceased to vist my little patient, intending only an occasional visit; but my confidence in the efficacy of the *elm bark* being so well established, I advised its use to be continued for even two or three days after any portions of the worm should be seen in the evacuations. The portions of the worm expelled—even the separate joints—were alive showing more or less motion; a sense of their presence in the rectum, from their action, seemed to urge the patient to go to stool for their removal.

" Having given direction for the links or joints to be counted, care was taken to do so, by the mother; and from

my notes of the case, I find that during about seven weeks
of the intervening time, there had been expelled, by estimate, (taking the average lengths of the joints,) about *forty-
five feet* of worm.   At this time there had been no portions
of the worm passed for two weeks, during which time the
use of the bark had been omitted.   The head of the
worm, with about fifteen inches of the body attached, had
been expelled !   But thinking that all portions of the worm
or worms might not have been removed, I advised that the
patient should resume the use of the bark.   Very soon the
next day, after doing so, further portions commenced com
ing away, among them one about *six feet* long, tapering to
a thread-like termination.

" The next time I took notes of the case, my estimate of
the entire length of the worm that had been expelled, foot-
ed up *one hundred and thirty-five feet*, whether one or
more worms, I am unable to say, as in the portions I saw,
there were a head and tail, of what I supposed one worm.
Since the last estimate, there have been joints occasionally
evacuated

" This patient, when first treated, was thin in flesh—had
been growing so for some two years—attended with the
usual nervous symptoms, starting out of sleep, variable appetite, etc., but with no great departure from good health.

" As to the influence of this very bland agent in the dis
lodgment of the tape-worm, in this case, I think there can
be no doubt, whatever may be the *theory* of its action. '
*   *   *   *   *   *   *   *   *

" The passage of portions of the worm, so promptly, on
the use of the bark, and the ceasing to do so on the discon
tinuance of its use—even while active purgative anthelmin-
tics were used—leave no room to doubt its effectiveness in
at least this case, as a worm-expelling agent.

" It seems probable that the bark, with its thick mucilage so interposes between the animal and the inner surface
of the bowels, as to prevent its lateral grasp on their surface
in consequence of which it is compelled to yield to the forces
naturally operating, and is carried out with the discharges.
But as my object was simply to state the *practical facts* in
this case, I will offer no further reflections.

COUGHS.—COUGH LOZENGES.—Powdered epecacuanha 25

grs.; kermes mineral 50 grs.; sulphate of morphia 8 grs.; powdered white sugar, gum arabic, and extract of licorice, of each 1¼ ozs.; oil of anise 20 drops; syrup of tolu sufficient to work into mass form; roll out and cut into 160 lozenges. Dose—One lozenge 3 times daily.—*Parish's Pharmacy.*

The above is the prescription of the "regulars," but there are those, perhaps who would prefer the more rational prescription of the "irregulars," next following; and there are those who would prefer the "Cough Candy" in place of either of the lozenges. By the insertion of the variety, all can please themselves.

2. Cough Lozenges.—Another valuable lozenge is made as follows: Extract of blood-root, licorice, and black cohosh, of each ¼ oz.; tinctures of ipecac and lobelia, with laudanum, of each ¼ oz.; cayenne, powdered, 10 grs.; pulverized gum arabic and starch, of each ¾ oz.; mix all together, and add pulverized sugar 3 ozs. If this should be too dry to roll into lozenges, add a thick solution of gum arabic to give it that consistence; and if it should be yet too moist, at any time, add more sugar. Divide into 320 lozenges. Dose—One, 3 to 6 times daily, as needed.

3. Pulmonic Wafers.—Pulverized sugar 7 ozs.; tincture of ipecac 3 drs.; tincture of blood-root and syrup of tolu, of each 2 drs.; tincture of thoroughwort ½ oz.; morphine 1¼ grs. Dissolve the morphine in water ¼ tea-spoon, having put in sulphuric acid 2 drops; now mix all, and add mucilage of comfrey root or gum arabic, to form a suitable paste to roll and cut into common sized wafers or lozenges. Directions.—Allow 1 to dissolve in the mouth for a dose, or dissolve 6 in 3 table-spoons of warm water, and take ¼ of a spoon 6 times daily, or oftener if need be.

4. Coughs from Recent Colds — Remedy.—Linseed-oil, honey, and Jamaica rum, equal parts of each; to be shaken when used.

This has given very general satisfaction in recent coughs, but the following will probably give the most general satisfaction:

5. Cough Mixture for Recent Colds.—Tincture of blood-root, syrups of ipecac and squills, tincture of balsam of tolu, and paregoric, equal parts of each. Dose.—Half of a tea-spoon whenever the cough is severe. It is a very valuable medicine.

6. Cough Candy.—Tincture of squills 2 ozs.; camphorated tincture of opium, and tincture of tolu, of each ¼ oz.; wine of ipecac ¼ oz.; oils of gaultheria 4 drops, sassafras 3 drops, and of anise-seed oil 2 drops. The above mixture is to be put into 5

lbs. of candy which is just ready to take from the fire, continuing tne boiling a little longer, so as to form into sticks.—*Parish's Pharmacy.*

Druggists will get confectioners to make this for a trifle on the pound over common candies, they, of course, furnishing their own compound.

7. Cough Syrup.—Wahoo, bark of the root, and elecampane root, of each 2 ozs.; spikenard root, and tamarack bark (unrossed, but the moss may be brushed off,) of each 4 ozs.; mandrake root ½ oz.; blood-root ¼ oz.; mix alcohol 1 pt., with sufficient water to cover all, handsomely, and let stand 2 or 3 days; then pour off 1 qt., putting on water and boiling twice, straining the two waters and boiling down to 3 pts.; when cool add 3 lbs. of honey, and alcoholic fluid poured off, with tincture of wine of ipecac 1½ ozs.; if the cough should be very tight, double the ipecac; and wash the feet daily in warm water, rubbing them thoroughly with a coarse towel, and, twice a week, extending the washing and rubbing to the whole body. Dose.—One tablespoon 3 to 5 times daily.

If the cough is very troublesome when you lie down at night or on waking in the morning, put tar and spirits of nitre, of each one tea-spoon into a four ounce vial of water, shaking well; then at these times just sip about a tea-spoon from the bottle without shaking, which will allay the tickling sensation, causing the cough.

I have cured a young lady, during the past winter, with the above syrup, whose cough had been pretty constant for over two years; her friends hardly expected it ever to be any better, but it was only necessary to make the above amount of syrup twice to perform the cure.

8. Cough Tincture.—Tinctures of blood-root and balsam of tolu, of each four ounces; tinctures of lobelia and digitalis, of each two ounces; tincture of opium (laudanum) one ounce; tincture of oil of anise (oil of anise one-half tea-spoon in an ounce of alcohol,) one ounce. Mix. Dose. —About one-half tea-spoon three times daily, in the same amount of honey, increasing to a tea-spoon if needed to loosen and lessen the cough. It has raised cases which doctors said must die, causing the patient to raise matter resembling the death-smell, awful indeed. It will cure cough, not by stopping it, but by loosening it, assisting the lungs and throat to throw off the offending matter, which causes the cough, and thus *scientifically* making the cure

perfect; while most of the cough remedies kept for sale, stop the cough by their anodyne and constringing effects, retaining the mucus and all offending matters in the blood, causing *permanent* disease of the lungs.

But, notwithstanding the known value of this " Cough Tincture," where the tamarack and other ingredients can be obtained, I must give my preference to the " Cough Syrup," No. 7.

9. COUGH PILL.—Extract of hyoscyamus, balm of gilead buds, with pulverized ipecac, or lobelia, and balsam of fir, of each ¼ oz.; oil of anise a few drops to form into common sized pills. DOSE—One or 2 pills 3 or 4 times daily.

Dr. Beach says he endeavored for more than twenty-five years to obtain a medicine to fulfill the indications which are effected in this cough pill, particularly for ordinary colds and coughs; and this admirably answers the intention, excelling all others. It allays the irritation of the mucus membrane, the bronchial tubes, and the lungs, and will be found exceedingly valuable in deep-seated coughs and all diseases of the chest. The bad effects of opium (so much used in coughs) are in this pill entirely obviated, and it is altogether better than the Cough Drops, which I now dispense with.—*Beach's American Practice.*

WHOOPING COUGH—SYRUP.—Onions and garlics, sliced, of each 1 gill; sweet oil 1 gill; stew them in the oil, in a covered dish, to obtain the juices; then strain and add honey 1 gill; paregoric and spirits of camphor, of each ½ oz.; bottle and cork tight for use. DOSE—For a child of 2 or 3 years, 1 tea-spoon 3 or 4 times daily, or whenever the cough is troublesome, increasing or lessening, according to age.

This is a granny's prescription, but I care not from what source I derive information, if it gives the satisfaction that this has done, upon experiment. This lady has raised a large family of her own children, and grand children in abundance. We have tried it with three of our children also, and prescribed it in many other cases with satisfaction, for over seven years. It is excellent also in common colds attended with much cough. This is from experience, too, whom I have found a very competent teacher.

It is said that an European physician has discovered that the dangerous symptoms of whooping cough are due to suppressed cutaneous eruptions, and that an external irritant or artificial rash, is a sure remedy. See "Small Pox."

2. DAILEY'S WHOOPING COUGH SYRUP.—Take the strongest West India rum, 1 pt.; anise oil 2 ozs.; honey 1 pt.; lemon juice 4 ozs.; mix. DOSE—For adults 1 table-spoon 3 or 4 times a day,—children, 1 tea-spoon, with as much sugar and water.

He says that he has successfully treated more than one hundred cases with this syrup.

3. SORENESS OR HOARSENESS FROM COUGHS.—REMEDY. · Spikenard root, bruised and steeped in a tea-pot, by using half water and half spirits; then inhaling the steam, when not too hot, by breathing through the spout, will relieve the soreness and hoarseness of the lungs, or throat, arising from much coughing.

IN-GROWING TOE NAIL—To CURE.—We take the following remedy for a very common and very painful affliction, from the *Boston Medical and Surgical Journal:*

"The patient on whom I first tried this plan was a young lady who had been unable to put on a shoe for several months, and decidedly the worst I have ever seen. The edge of the nail was deeply undermined, the granulations formed a high ridge, partly covered with the skin ; and pus constantly oozed from the root of the nail, The whole toe was swollen and extremely painful and tender. My mode of proceeding was this :

" I put a very small piece of tallow in a spoon, and heated it until it became very hot, and poured it on the granulations. The effect was almost magical. Pain and tenderness were at once relieved, and in a few days the granulations were all gone, the diseased parts dry and destitute of all feeling, and the edge of the nail exposed so as to admit of being pared away without any inconvenience. The cure was complete, and the trouble never returned.

" I have tried the plan repeatedly since, with the same satisfactory results. The operation causes but little pain, if the tallow is properly heated. A repetition in some cases might be necessary, although I have never met with a case that did not yield to one application." It has now been proven, in many other cases, to be effectual, accomplishing in one minute, without pain, all that can be effected by the painful application of nitrate of silver for several weeks."

OILS—BRITISH OIL.—Linseed and turpentine oils, of each 3 ozs.; oils of amber and juniper, of each 4 ozs.; Barbadoes tar 3 ozs.; seneca oil 1 oz.; Mix.

This is an old prescription, but it is worth the whole cost of this book to any one needing an application for cuts, bruises, swellings, and sores of almost every description, on persons, horses, or cattle; so is the following, also:

2. BALM OF GILEAD OIL.—Balm of Gilead buds any quantity; place them in a suitable dish for stewing, and pour upon them sufficient sweet oil to just cover them; stew thoroughly and press out all of the oil from the buds, and bottle for use.

It will be found very valuable as a healing oil, or lard can be used in place of the oil, making an excellent ointment for cuts, bruises, &c.

3. HARLEM OIL, OR WELCH MEDICAMENTUM.—Sublimed or flowers of sulphur and oil of amber, of each 2 oz.; linseed oil 1 lb.; spirits of turpentine sufficient to reduce all to the consistence of thin molasses. Boil the sulphur in the linseed oil until it is dissolved, then add the oil of amber and turpentine. DOSE—From 15 to 25 drops, morning and evening.

Amongst the Welch and Germans it is extensively used for strengthening the stomach, kidneys, liver and lungs, asthma, shortness of breath, cough, inward or outward sores, dropsy, worms, gravel, fevers palpitation of the heart, giddiness, head-ache, &c., &c., by taking it internally, and for ulcers, malignant sores, cankers, &c., anointing externally, and wetting linen with it and applying to burns. In fact, if one-half that is said of its value is true, no other medicine need ever be made. It has this much in its favor, however,—probably no other medicine now in use, has been in use half so long,—over 160 years. The dose for a child is one drop for each year of its age.

4. OIL OF SPIKE.—The genuine oil of spike is made from the *lavendula spica* (broad leaved lavender,) but the *commercial* oil of spike is made by taking the rock oil, and adding 2 ozs. of spirits of turpentine to each pint.

The rock oil which is obtained in Ohio, near Warren, is thicker and better than any other which I have ever used.

5. BLACK OILS.—Best alcohol, tincture of arnica, British oil, and oil of tar, of each 2 ozs., and *slowly* add sulphuric acid ½ oz.

These black oils are getting into extensive use, as a liniment, and are indeed valuable, especially in cases attended with much inflammation.

6. ANOTHER METHOD—Is to take sulphuric acid 2 ozs.; nitric acid 1 oz.; quicksilver ¼ oz.; put them together in a quart bot-

tle, or an open crock until dissolved; then slowly add olive oil and spirits of turpentine, of each ½ pt., putting in the oil first. Let the work be done out of doors to avoid the fumes arising from the mixture; when all is done, bottle and put in all the cotton cloths it will dissolve, when it is fit for use.

The mixture becomes quite hot, although no heat is used in making it, from setting free what is called latent, or insensible heat, by their combining togetner. Rev. Mr. Way, of Plymouth, Mich., cured himself of sore throat by taking a few drops of this black oil upon sugar, letting it slowly dissolve upon the tongue, each evening after preaching, also wetting cloths and binding upon the neck. It will be necessary to avoid getting it upon cotton or linen which you would not wish to show a stain. A colt which had a fistulous opening between the hind legs, from a snag, as supposed, which reduced him so that he had to be lifted up, when down, was cured by injecting twice only, of this oil to fill the diseased place. Also a very bad fever sore, upon the leg, ah! Excuse me, upon the *limb* of a young lady, which baffled the scientific skill of the town in which she lived. In case they bite too much in any of their applications, wet a piece of brown paper in water and lay it over the parts.

OPODELDOC—LIQUID.—Best brandy 1 qt.; warm it and add gum camphor 1 oz.; salammoniac and oil of wormwood, of each ¼ oz.; oils of origanum and rosemary, of each ½ oz.; when the oils are dissolved by the aid of the heat, add soft soap 6 oz.

Its uses are too well known to need further description.

DIARRHEAS—CORDIAL.—The best rhubarb root, pulverized, 1 oz.; peppermint leaf 1 oz.; capsicum ½ oz.; cover with boiling water and steep thoroughly, strain, and add bi-carbonate of potash and essence of cinnamon, of each ½ oz.; with brandy (or good whisky) equal in amount to the whole, and loaf sugar 4 oz. DOSE—For an adult 1 to 2 table-spoons; for a child 1 to 2 tea-spoons, from 3 to 6 times per day, until relief is obtained.

This preparation has been my dependence, in my travels and in my family for several years, and it has never failed us; but in extremely bad cases it might be well to use, after each passage, the following:

2. INJECTION FOR CHRONIC DIARRHEA.—New milk, with thick mucilage of slippery elm, of each 1 pt.; sweet oil 1 gill; molasses ½ pt.; salt 1 oz.; laudanum 1 dr. Mix, and inject what the bowels will retain.

Very many children, as well as grown persons die, annually, of this disease, who might be saved by a proper use of the above injection and cordial. The injection should never be neglected, if there is the least danger apprehended.

Although I believe these would not fail in one case out of one hundred, yet I have some other prescriptions which are so highly spoken of, I will give a few more. The first from Mr. Hendee, of Warsaw, Indiana, for curing Diarrhea, or Bloody Flux, as follows :

3. DIARRHEA TINCTURE.—Compound tincture of myrrh 6 ozs.; tincture of rhubard, and spirits of lavender, of each 5 ozs.; tincture of opium 3 ozs.; oils of anise and cinnamon, with gum camphor and tartaric acid, of each ¼ oz. Mix. DOSE—One tea-spoon in ½ a tea-cup of warm water sweetened with loaf sugar; repeat after each passage.

He says he has cured many cases after given up by phycians. It must be a decidedly good preparation. Or, again :

4. DIARRHEA DROPS.—Tincture of rhubarb, and compound spirits of lavender, of each 4 ozs.; laudanum 2 ozs.; cinnamon oil 2 drops. Mix. DOSE—One tea-spoon every 3 or 4 hours, according to the severity of the case.

This speaks from ten years successful experience.

5. DIARRHEA SYRUP—FOR CASES BROUGHT ON BY LONG-CONTINUED USE OF CALOMEL.—Boxwood, black cherry and prickly ash barks, with dandelion root, of each 2 ozs ; butternut bark 1 oz.; boil thoroughly, strain and boil down to 1 qt.; then add loaf sugar 2 lbs., and alcohol 1 gill, or brandy ½ pt. DOSE—A wine-glass from 3 to 5 times daily, according to circumstances.

This regulates the bowels and tones up the system at the same time, no matter whether loose or costive. In one case of costiveness it brought a man around all right who had been sowed up tight for twelve days. On the other hand, it has regulated the system after months of calomel-Diarrhea.

6. WINTERGREEN BERRIES have been found a valuable corrector of Diarrhea brought on by the long-continued use of calomel in cases of fever, eating a quart of them in 3 days time.

The gentleman of whom I obtained this item tells me that wintergreen essence has done the same thing, when the berries could not be obtained. In the first place, " everything else," as the saying is, had been tried in vain, and the man's wife, in coming across the woods, found these berries and picked some, which when the husband saw, he craved, and would not rest without them, and, notwithstanding the fears of friends, they cured him.   Many valuable discoveries are made in a similar manner.

7. DRIED WHORTLEBERRIES, steeped, and the juice drank freely, has cured Diarrhea and Bloody Flux, both in children and adults.

8. DIARRHEA AND CANKER TEA.—Pulverized hemlock bark, (it is generally kept by Druggists,) 1 table-spoon, steeped in half a tea-cup of water.

For young children, in Diarrhea, or Canker, or when they are combined, feed a tea-spoon of it, or less, according to the child's age, two or three times daily, until cured.   To overcome costiveness, which may arise from its use, scorch fresh butter, and give it in place of oil, and in quantities corresponding with oil.   Children have been saved with three cents worth of this bark which " Alopath" said must die.   If good for children, it is good for adults, by simply increasing the dose.

9. Sumac bobs, steeped and sweetened with loaf sugar, has been found very valuable for Diarrhea; adding in very severe cases, alum pulverized, a rounding tea-spoon, to 1 pt. of the strong tea.   DOSE—A tea, to a table-spoon, according to the age of the child, and the severity of the case.

It saved the life of a child when two M. D.'s (Mule Drivers,) said it could not be saved.

CHOLERA TINCTURE.—Select the thinest cinnamon bark, cloves, gum gauiac, all pulverized, of each 1 oz.; very best brandy 1 qt.   Mix, and shake occasionally for a week or two. DOSE—A tea-spoon to a table-spoon for an adult, according to the condition and robustness or strength of the system.   It may be repeated at intervals of 1 to 4 hours, if necessary, or much more often, according to the condition of the bowels.

This I have from an old railroad-boss who used it with his men during the last Cholera in Ohio, and never lost a man, whilst other jobbers left the road, or lost their men in abund ance, thinking the above too simple to be of any value.

2. ISTHMUS CHOLERA TINCTURE.—Tincture of rhubarb, cayenne, opium, and spirits of camphor, with essence of pepper mint, equal parts of each, and each as strong as can be made DOSE—From 5 to 30 drops, or even to 60, and repeat until relief is obtained, every 5 to 30 minutes.

C. H. Cuyler, who was detained upon the Isthmus during the cholera period, was saved by this prescription, as also many others.

3 CHOLERA PREVENTIVE.—Hoffman's anodyne and essence of peppermint, of each 2 ozs.; tincture of ginger 1 oz.; laudanum, spirits of camphor, and tincture of cayenne, of each ¼ oz.; mix. DOSE.—For an adult, from a tea to a table-spoon, according o symptoms.

4. CHOLERA CORDIAL.—Chloroform, spirits of camphor, laudanum and aromatic spirits of ammonia, of each 1 dr.; cinnamon water 2 ozs.; mix. DOSE.—From 1 tea to a table-spoon, to be well shaken, and taken with sweetened water.

5. GERMAN CHOLERA TINCTURE.—Sulphuric ether 2 ozs.; and put into it castor and gentian, of each ¼ oz.; opium and agaric, each 1 dr.; gum camphor ½ oz.; let them stand 2 days, then add alcohol 1 qt., and let stand 14 days, when it is ready for use. DOSE.—One tea-spoon every 15 or 20 minutes, according to the urgency of the case.

I obtained this prescription of a German at Lawrenceburgh, Ind., who had done very much good with it during the last cholera period in that place.

6. EGYPTIAN CURE FOR CHOLERA.—Best Jamaica ginger root, bruised, 1 oz.; cayenne 2 tea-spoons; boil all in 1 qt. of water to ½ pt., and add loaf sugar to form a thick syrup. DOSE.—One table-spoon every 15 minutes, until vomiting and purging ceases, then follow up with a blackberry tea.

The foregoing was obtained of a physician who practiced in Egypt, (not the Illinois Egypt,) during the great devastation of the cholera there, with which he saved many lives.

7. INDIA PRESCRIPTION FOR CHOLERA.—First dissolve gum camphor ¼ oz. in 1½ ozs. of alcohol—second, give a tea-spoon of spirits of hartshorn in a wine glass of water, and follow it every 5 minutes with 15 drops of the camphor, in a tea-spoon of water, for 3 doses, then wait 15 minutes, and commence again as before, and continue the camphor for 30 minutes, unless there is returning heat. Should this be the case, give one more dose and the cure is effected; let them perspire freely, (which the medicine is designed to cause,) as upon this the life depends, but add no additional clothing.

Lady Ponsonby, who had spent several years in India, and had proved the efficacy of the foregoing, returned to Dublin in 1832, and published it in the *Dublin Mail*, for the benefit of her countrymen, declaring that she never knew it to fail.

I would say, be very sure you have the cholera, as the tea-spoon of hartshorn would be a double dose for ordinary cases of disease.

8. NATURE'S CHOLERA MEDICINE.—Laudanum, spirits of cam-phor, and tincture of rhubarb, equal parts of each. DOSE—One table-spoon every 15 to 30 minutes until relieved.

In attacks of cholera, the patient usually feels a general uneasiness and heat about the stomach, increasing to actual distress and great anxiety, finally sickness, with vomiting and purging, surface constringed, the whole powers of the system concentrated upon the internal organs, involving the nervous system, bringing on spasms, and in the end, death. Now, whatever will allay this uneasiness, drive to the sur-face, correct the discharges, and soothe the nerves, cures the disease. The laudanum does the first and the last, the camphor drives to the surface, and the rhubarb corrects the alimentary canal; and if accompanied with the hot bath, frictions, &c., is doubly sure. And to show what may be done with impunity in extreme cases, let me say that Merritt Blakeley, living near Flat Rock, Mich., came home from Detroit, during the last cholera season, having the cholera in its last stage, that is, with the vomiting, purging and spasms; the foregoing medicine being in the house, the wife, in her hurry and excitement, in place of two-thirds of a table-spoon, she read two-thirds of a tea-cup; and gave it accordingly, and saved his life; whilst if taken in the spoon doses, at this stage of the disease, he would most undoubtedly never have rallied from the collapse into which he was fast sinking; yet in the commencement they would have been as effectual; so, *mistake*, would be generally ac-credited for saving the patient, I say *Providence* did the work.

Five to 10 drops would be a dose for a child of 2 to 5 years, and in this dose it saved a child of 2½ years in a bad case of bloody flux.

If any one is permitted to die with all these prescription before them, it must be because a proper attention is not given; for God most undoubtedly works through the use of means, and is best pleased to see his children *wear* out, rather than *break* by collision of machinery on the way.

CHOLIC AND CHOLERA MORBUS.—TREATMENT

—Cholera morbus arises from a diseased condition of the bile, often brought on by over-indulgence with vegetables, especially unripe fruits; usually commencing with sickness and pain at the stomach, followed by the most excruciating pain and griping of the bowels, succeeded by vomiting and purging, which soon prostrate the patient. The person finds himself unavoidably drawn into a coil by the contraction of the muscles of the abdomen and extremities. Thirst very great, evacuations first tinged with bile, and finally, nearly all, very bilious.

TREATMENT.—The difficulty arises from the acidity of the bile: then take saleratus, peppermint leaf, and rhubarb root pulverized, of each a rounding tea-spoon, put into a cup, which you can cover, and pour upon them, boiling water ½ pt.; when nearly cold add a table-spoon of alcohol, or twice as much brandy or other spirits. Dose—Two to 3 table-spoons every 20 to 30 minutes, as often and as long as the vomiting and painful purgations continue. If there should be long continued pain about the naval, use the "Injection" as mentioned under that head, in connection with the above treatment, and you will have nothing to fear. If the first dose or two should be vomited repeat it immediately, until retained.

The above preparation ought to be made by every family, and kept on hand, by bottling; for diseases of this character are as liable to come on in the night as at any other time; then much time must be lost in making fires, or getting the articles together with which to make it.

2. COMMON CHOLIC.—There is a kind of cholic which some persons are afflicted with, from their youth up, not attended with vomiting or purging. I was afflicted with it, from my earliest recollection until I was over twenty years of age, sometimes two or three times, yearly.

In one of these fits, about that age, a neighbor woman came in, and as soon as she found out what was the matter with me, she went out and pulled up a bunch of blue vervain, knocked the dirt from the roots, then cut them off and put a good handful of them into a basin, and poured boiling water upon them, and steeped for a short time, poured out a saucer of the tea and gave me to drink, asking no questions, but simply saying, "If you will drink this tea every day for a month, you will never have cholic again as long as you live." I drank it, and in 15 minutes I was perfectly happy; the transition from extreme pain to immediate and perfect relief, is too great to allow one to find words adequate to describe the difference.

I continued its use as directed, and have not had a cholic pain since, nearly thirty years. I have told it to others, with the same result. It also forms a good tonic in agues, and after fevers, &c.

CARMINATIVES.—For the more common pains of the stomach, arising from accumulating gas, in adults or child ren, the following preparation will be found very valuable, and much better than the plan of resorting to any of the opium mixtures for a constant practice, as many unwisely, or wickedly, do. See the remarks after "Godfrey's Cordial," and through this subject.

Compound spirits of lavender, spirits of camphor, and tincture of ginger, of each 1 oz.; sulphuric ether and tincture of cayenne, of each ½ oz. Mix and keep tightly corked. Dose—For an adult, one tea-spoon every 15 minutes, until relieved; for a child of 2 years, 5 drops; and more or less, according to age and the severity of the pain.

2. CARMINATIVE FOR CHILDREN.—Angelica and white roots, of each 4 oz.; valerian and sculcap roots, with poppy heads, of each 2 ozs.; sweet-flag root ¼ oz.; anise, dill, and fennel seed, with catmint leaves and flowers, motherwort and mace, of each 1 oz.; castor and cochineal, of each ½ oz; camphor gum 2 scruples, benzoic acid (called flower of benzoin) ¼ oz.; alcohol and water, of each 1 qt., or rum, or brandy 2 qts.; loaf or crushed sugar 1 lb. Pulverize all of the herbs and roots, moderately fine, and place in a suitable sized bottle, adding the spirits, or alcohol and water, and keep warm for a week, shaking once or twice every day; then filter or strain, and add the camphor and benzoin, shaking well; now dissolve the sugar in another quart of water, by heat, and add to the spirit tincture, and all is complete. Dose.—For a very young child, from 3 to 5 drops; if 1 year old, about 10 drops, and from that up to 1 teaspoon if 2 to 5 years old, &c. For adults, from 1 to 4 tea-spoons, according to the severity of the pain—to be taken in a cup of catmint or catnip tea for adults, and in a spoon of the same for children. It may be repeated every 2 to 6 hours, as needed.

USES.—It eases pain, creates a moderate appetite and perspiration, and produces refreshing sleep; is also excellent for removing flatulency or wind cholic, and valuable in hysteria and other nervous affections, female debility, &c, in place of the opium anodynes.

SEIDLITZ POWDERS—GENUINE.—Rochelle salts 2 drs.; bi-carbonate of soda 2 scruples; put these into a blue paper, and put tartaric acid 35 grs. into a white paper. To use, put each

Into different tumblers; fill $\frac{1}{2}$ with water and put a little loaf sugar in with the acid, then pour together and drink.

This makes a very pleasant cathartic, and ought to be used more generally than it is, in place of more severe medicines. Families can buy 3 ozs. of the Rochelle-salts, and 1 oz. of the bi-carbonate of soda, and mix evenly together, using about 2 tea-spoons for 1 glass, and have the tartaric acid by itself, and use a little over $\frac{1}{2}$ a tea-spoon of it for the other glass, with a table-spoon of sugar, all well dissolved, then pour together and drink while effervescing; and they will find this to do just as well as to have them weighed out and put up in papers, which, cost three times as much, and do no better. Try it, as a child will take it with pleasure, as a nice beverage, and ask for more.

A lady once lost her life, thinking to have a little sport, by drinking one glass of this preparation, following it directly with the other; the large amount of gas, disengaged, ruptured the stomach immediately.

DIPTHERIA—Dr. PHINNEY'S REMEDY, OF BOSTON —Dr. Phinney, of Boston, furnishes the *Journal* of that city with a recipe for diptheria, which has recently been re-published by the *Detroit Daily Advertiser*, containing so much sound sense, and so decidedly the best thing that I have ever seen recommended for it, that I cannot forbear giving it an insertion, and also recommend it as the dependence in that disease.

He says "the remedy on which I chiefly depend is the Actea Racemosa, or black snake-root, which is used both locally as a gargle and taken internally.

As a gargle, 1 tea-spoon of the *tincture* is added to 2 table-spoons of water, and gargled *every hour* for *twenty-four* hours, or till the progress of the disease is arrested; after which the intervals may be extended to an hour and a half, or more, as the symptoms may justify. In connection with the use of the gargle, or separately, the adult patient should take internally to the amount of two or three tea-spoons of the tincture in the course of twenty-four hours.

"In addition to the foregoing, give 10 drops of the muriated tincture of iron 3 times in the 24 hours, and a powder from 3 to 5 grains of the chlorate of potash in the intervals.

" Under this treatment a very decided improvement takes place within the first twenty-four hours, the ash colored nembrane disappears usually within two days, and the patient overcomes the malignant tendency of the disease.

"The foregoing doses are for adults; for children they should of course be diminished according to age, &c. It will be observed that great importance is attached to the frequent use of the gargle—that is, *every hour*—in order to overcome the morbific tendency of disease by a constantly counteracting impression. In order to guard against a relapse, an occasional use of the remedies should be continued for several days after the removal of the membrane and subsidence of unpleasant symptoms. To complete the cure, a generous diet and other restoratives may be used as the intelligent practitioner shall direct."

CATHARTICS.—VEGETABLE PHYSIC.—Jalap and peppermint leaf, of each 1 oz.; senna 2 ozs.; pulverize all very finely, and sift through gauze, bottle it and keep corked. DOSE—Put a rounding tea-spoon of the powder and a heaping tea-spoon of sugar into a cup, and pour 3 or 4 spoons of boiling water upon them; when cool stir it up and drink all. The best time for taking it is in the morning, not taking breakfast, but drinking freely of corn-meal gruel. If it does not operate in 3 hours, repeat half the dose until a free operation is obtained.

Dr. Beach first brought this preparation, nearly in its present proportions, to the notice of the Eclectic practitioners who have found it worthy of very great confidence, and applicable in all cases where a general cathartic action is required. It may be made into syrup or pills, if preferred.

2. INDIAN CATHARTIC PILLS.--Aloes and gamboge, of each 1 oz.; mandrake and blood-root, with gum myrrh, of each ¼ oz.; gum camphor and cayenne, of each 1¼ drs.; ginger 4 ozs.; all finely pulverized and thoroughly mixed, with thick mucilage (made by putting a little water upon equal quantities of gum arabic and gum tragacanth,) into pill mass; then formed into common sized pills. DOSE—Two to 4 pills, according to the obustness of the patient.

Families should always have some of these cathartics, as well as other remedies, in the house, to be prepared for accident, providence, or emergence, whichever you please to call it. They may be sugar-coated, as directed under that head, if desired.

TOOTHACHE AND NEURALGIA REMEDIES.—MAGNETIC TOOTH CORDIAL AND PAIN KILLER.—Best alcohol 1 oz. laudanum ¼ oz.; chloroform, liquid measure, ½ oz.; gum cam

phor ½ oz.; oil of cloves ½ dr.; sulphuric ether ¼ oz.; and oil of
lavender 1 dr. If there is a nerve exposed this will quiet it.
Apply with lint. Rub also on the gums and upon the face
against the tooth, freely.

" The raging toothache why endure, when there is found a perfect cure,
Which saves the tooth and stops the pain, and gives the sufferer ease again."

In the case of an ulcerated tooth at Georgetown, Ohio,
Mr. Jenkins, the proprietor of the " Jenkins' House," had
been suffering for eight days, and I relieved him by bathing
the face with this preparation, using a sponge, for two or
three minutes only, taking a tea-spoon or two into the mouth,
for a minute or two, as it had broken upon the inside. The
operation of the cordial was really *magical*, according to
old notions of cure.

I offered to sell a grocer a book, at Lawrenceburgh, Ind.
He read until he saw the " Magnetic Tooth Cordial" men-
mentioned, then he says, "If you will cure *my* toothache, I
will buy one." I applied the cordial, it being late Saturday
evening, and on Monday morning he was the first man on
hand for his book.

The Sheriff of Wayne Co., Ind., at Centerville, had been
suffering three days of *neuralgia*, and I gave him such decided relief in one evening, with this cordial, that he gave
me a three-dollar piece, with the remark, " Take whatever
you please."

In passing from Conneatville, Pa., upon a canal boat, the
cook, (who was wife of one of the steersmen,) was taken,
after supper, with severe pain in the stomach. There being no peppermint on board, and as strange as it may appear,
no spirits of any kind whatever; I was applied to as a physician to contrive something for her relief; I ran my mind
over the articles I had with me, and could not hit upon any
other so likely to benefit as the " Tooth Cordial," arguing
in my mind that if good for pain where it could be applied
to the spot externally, I could apply it to the point of pain
internally in this case, (the stomach,) as well. I gave her a
tea-spoon of it in water, and waited five minutes without
relief, but concluding to go " whole hog or none," I repeated the dose, and inside of the next five minutes she was
perfectly cured. Her husband, the other steersman also,
and one of the drivers, bought each a book, and the next
week, in Erie, one of her neighbors bought another, upon

her recommendation; since which myself and agents have freely used it, and recommend it for similar conditions with equal success.

The cases are too numerous to mention more. I mention these to give confidence to purchasers, that all, who need it, will not fail to give it a trial. It is good for any local pain, wherever it can be applied. Pain will not long exist under its use.

2. HOMEOPATHIC TOOTH CORDIAL.—Alcohol ½ pt.; tincture of arnica and chloroform, of each 1 oz.; oil of cloves ½ oz. Mix and apply as the other.

There are many persons who would prefer this last to the foregoing, from the presence of arnica; and it is especially valuable as a liniment for bruises involving effusion of blood under the skin.

3. NEURALGIA—INTERNAL REMEDY.—Sal-ammoniac ½ dr., dissolve in water 1 oz. DOSE—One table-spoon every 3 minutes, for 20 minutes, at the end of which time, if not before. the pain will have disappeared.

The foregoing is from a gentleman who had been long afflicted with the disease, who found no success with any other remedy. Instead of common water, the "Camphor Water" or "Mint Water" might by some be preferred. The ammonia is a very diffusable stimulant, quickly extending to the whole system, especially tending to the surface.

4. KING OF OILS, FOR NEURALGIA AND RHEUMATISM.—Burning fluid 1 pt.; oils of cedar, hemlock, sassafras, and origanum, of each 2 ozs.; carbonate of ammonia, pulverized, 1 oz.; mix. DIRECTIONS.—Apply freely to the nerve and gums, around the tooth; and to the face, in neuralgic pains, by wetting brown paper and laying on the parts, not too long, for fear of blistering,—to the nerves of teeth by lint.

A blacksmith, of Sturgis, Mich., cured himself and others, with this, of neuralgia, after physicians could give no relief.

5. SEVERAL years ago, I was stopping for a number of weeks at a hotel near Detroit; whilst there, toothache was once made the subject of conversation, at which time the landlady, a Mrs. Wood, said she had been driven by it, to an extreme measure—no less than boiling wormwood herb in alcohol and taking a table-spoon of it into the mouth.

boiling hot, immediately closing the mouth, turning the head in such a way as to bring the alcohol into contact with all of the teeth, then spitting it out and taking the second immediately, in the same way, having the boiling kept up by sitting the tin containing it upon a shovel of hot coals, bringing it near the mouth. She said she never had toothache after it, nor did it injure the mouth in the least, but, for the moment, she thought her head had collapsed, or the heavens and earth come together. And although the lady's appearance and deportment was such as to gain general esteem, I dared not try it or recommend it to others. But during the last season I found a gentleman who had tried the same thing, in the same way, except he took four spoons in his mouth at a time, and did not observe to keep his mouth closed to prevent the contact of the air with the alcohol, the result of which was a scalded mouth, yet a perfect cure of the pain and no recurrence of it for twelve years up to the time of conversation. And I do not now give the plan expecting it to become a general favorite, but more to show the severity of the pain, forcing patients to such extreme remedies. It would not be applicable only in cases where the pain was confined entirely to the teeth.

6. HORSE-RADISH ROOT, bruised and bound upon the face, or other parts where pain is located, has been found very valuable for their relief. And I think it better than the leaf for drafts to the feet, or other parts.

7. TEETH—EXTRACTING WITH LITTLE OR NO PAIN.—Dr. Dunlap, a dentist of Chillicothe, O., while filling a tooth for me, called my attention to the following recipe, given by a dental publication, to prevent pain in extracting teeth. He had used it. It will be found valuable for all who must have teeth extracted, for the feeling is sufficiently unpleasant even when all is done that can be for its relief.

TINCTURE of aconite, chloroform, and alcolol of each 1 oz., morphine 6 grs. Mix. MANNER OF APPLICATION.—Moisten two pledgets of cotton with the liquid and apply to the gums on each side of the tooth to be extracted, holding them to their place with pliers or some other convenient instrument for 5 to 15 minutes rubbing the gum freely inside and out.

My wife has had six teeth taken at a sitting, b'it the last
two she wished to have out, she could not mak; up her
mind to the work until I promised her it should not hurt
in the extraction, which I accomplished by accompanying
her to Dr. Porter's dental office, of this city, and adminis
tering chloroform in the usual way, just to the point of
nervous stimulation, or until its effects were felt over the
whole system, at which time the teeth were taken, not
causing pain, she says, equal to toothache for one minute
Not the slightest inconvenience was experienced from the
effects of the chloroform. I consider this plan, and so
does Dr. Porter, far preferable to administering it until
entire stupefaction, by which many valuable lives have
been lost.

8. DENTRIFICE WHICH REMOVES TARTAREOUS ADHESIONS,
ARRESTS DECAY, AND INDUCES A HEALTHY ACTION OF THE
GUMS.—Dissolve 1 oz. of borax in 1½ pints of boiling water, and
when a little cool, add 1 tea-spoon of the tincture of myrrh and
1 table-spoon of the spirits of camphor, and bottle for use. DI-
RECTIONS.—At bedtime, wash out the mouth with water; using
a badger's hair brush (bristle brushes tear the gums and should
never be used); then take a table-spoon of the dentrifice with as
much warm water, and rub the teeth and gums well, each night
until the end is attained.

9. TOOTH-WASH—TO REMOVE BLACKNESS.—Pure muriatic
acid 1 oz.; water 1 oz.; honey 2 ozs.; mix. Take a tooth brush
and wet it freely with this preparation, and briskly rub the black
teeth, and in a moment's time they will be perfectly white; then
immediately wash out the mouth with water, that the acid may
not act upon the *enamel* of the teeth.

It need not be used often, say once in three or four
months, as the teeth become black again, washing out
quickly every time. Without the washing after its use it
would injure the teeth, with it, it never will. This blackness
is hard to remove, even with the brush and tooth powder.

10. DR. THOMPSON, of Evansville, Ind., gives the above
n twenty drop doses, three times daily, for laryngitis or bronchitis, taken in a little water, throwing it back past the
teeth.

11. TOOTH POWDER—EXCELLENT.—Take any quantity of
finely pulverized chalk, and twice as much finely pulverized
charcoal; make very fine; then add a very little suds made
with Castile soap, and sufficient spirits of camphor to wet all to

a thick paste. Apply with the finger, rubbing thoroughly, and it will whiten the teeth better than any tooth powder you can buy.

I noticed the past season, a piece going the rounds of the papers, "That charcoal ought not to be used on the teeth." I will only add that a daughter of mine has used this powder over six years, and her teeth are very white, and no damage to the enamel, as yet. *Six years* would show up the evil, if *death was in the pot.* Coal from basswood or other soft wood is the easiest pulverized.

ESSENCES.—Druggists' rules for making essences is to use one ounce of oil to one quart of alcohol, but many of them do not use more than half of that amount, whilst most of the peddlars do not have them made of over one-fourth that strength. I would hardly set them away if presented I have always made them as follows :

Peppermint oil 1 oz. ; best alcohol 1 pt. And the same amount of any other oil for any other essences which you desire to make. DOSE—A dose of this strength of essence will be only from 10 to 30 drops.

With most essences a man can drink a whole bottle without danger, or benefit. Peppermint is colored with tincture of tumeric, cinnamon with tincture of red sandal or sanders wood, and wintergreen with tincture of kino. There is no color, however, for essences, so natural as to put the green leaf of which the oil is made into the jar of essence, and let it remain over night, or about twelve hours ; then pour off, or filter if for sale. But if families are making for their own use they need not bother to color them at all. But many believe if they are high colored they are necessarily strong, but it has no effect upon the strength whatever, unless colored with the leaf or bark, as here recommended. Cinnamon bark does in place of the leaf. See "Extracts."

TINCTURES.—In making any of the tinctures in common use, or in making any of the medicines called for in this work, or in works generally, it is not only expected, but absolutely necessary, that the roots, leaves, barks, &c., should be dry, unless otherwise directed ; then :

Take the root, herb, bark, leaf or gum called for, 2 ozs. ; and bruise it, then pour boiling water ¼ pt., upon it, and when cold add best alcohol ¼ pt., keeping warm for from 4 to 6 days, or letting it stand 10 or 12 days without warmth, shaking once or twice daily; then filter or strain; or it may stand upon the dregs and be carefully poured off as needed.

With any person of common judgment, the foregoing directions are just as good as to take up forty times as much space by saying—take lobelia, herb and seed, 2 ozs.; alcohol ½ pt.; boiling water ½ pt.,—then do the same thing over and over again, with every tincture which may be called for; or at least those who cannot go ahead with the foregoing instructions, are not fit to handle medicines, at all; so I leave the subject with those for whom the given information is sufficient.

In making compound tinctures, you can combine the simple tinctures, or make them by putting the different articles into a bottle together, then use the alcohol and water it would require if you was making each tincture separately.

TETTER, RINGWORM, AND BARBER'S ITCH—To CURE.—Take the best Cuba cigars, smoke one a sufficient length of time to accumulate ¼ or ½ inch of ashes upon the end of the cigar; now wet the whole surface of the sore with the saliva from the mouth, then rub the ashes from the end of the cigar thoroughly into, and all over the sore; do this three times a day, and inside of a week all will be smooth and well.

I speak from extensive experience; half of one cigar cured myself when a barber would not undertake to shave me   It is equally successful in tetters on other parts of the body, hands, &c

Tobacco is very valuable in its place (medicine)— like spirits, however, it makes *slaves* of its devotees.

2. NARROW LEAVED (yellow) dock root, sliced and soaked in good vinegar, used as a wash, is highly recommended as a cure for tetter, or ring-worm.

BALSAMS.—DR. R. W. HUTCHINS' INDIAN HEALING, FORMERLY, PECKHAM'S COUGH BALSAM.—Clear, pale rosin 3 lbs., and melt it, adding spirits of turpentine 1 qt.; balsam of tolu 1 oz; balsam of fir 4 ozs.; oil of hemlock, origanum, with Venice turpentine, of each 1 oz.; strained honey 4 ozs.; mix well, and bottle. DOSE—Six to 12 drops; for a child of six, 3 to 5 drops. on a little sugar. The dose can be varied according to the ability of the stomach to bear it, and the necessity of the case.

It is a valuable preparation for coughs, internal pains, or strains, and works benignly upon the kidneys.

2. DOCTOR MITCHEL'S BALSAM, FOR CUTS, BRUISES, &c.—Fenugreek seed, and gum myrrh, of each 1 oz.; sassafras root-bark, a good handful; alcohol 1 qt. Put all into a bottle, and keep warm for 5 days.

Dr. Mitchel, of Pa., during his life, made great use of this balsam, for cuts, bruises, abrasions, &c., and it will be found valuable for such purposes.

ARTIFICIAL SKIN—FOR BURNS, BRUISES, ABRASIONS, &c. PROOF AGAINST WATER.—Take gun cotton and Venice turpentine, equal parts of each, and dissolve them in 20 times as much sulphuric ether, dissolving the cotton first, then adding the turpentine; keep it corked tightly.

The object of the turpentine is to prevent pressure or pinching caused by evaporation of the ether when applied to a bruised surface. Water does not affect it, hence its value for cracked nipples, chapped hands, surface bruises, etc., etc.

DISCUTIENTS—TO SCATTER SWELLINGS.—Tobacco and cicuta (water hemlock) leaves, of each 2 ozs.; stramonium, (jimpsom) and solanum nigrum (garden night shade, sometimes erroneously called *deadly* night shade,) the leaves, and yellow dock root, of each 4 ozs.; bitter-sweet, bark of the root, 3 ozs. Extract the strength by boiling with water, pressing out, and re-boiling, straining and carefully boiling down to the consistence of an ointment, then add lard 18 ozs., and simmer together.

It will be used for stiff joints, sprains, bruises attended with swelling when the skin is unbroken, for cancerous lumps, scrofulous swellings, white swellings, rheumatic swellings, &c. It is one of the best discutients, or scatterers in use, keeping cancers back, often for months.

SMALL POX—TO PREVENT PITTING THE FACE.—A great discovery is reported to have recently been made by a Surgeon of the English army in China, to prevent pitting or marking the face. The mode of treatment is as follows:

When, in small pox, the preceding fever is at its height, and just before the eruption appears, the chest is thoroughly rubbed with Croton Oil and Tartaremetic Ointment. This causes the whole of the eruption to appear on that part of the body to the relief of the rest. It also secures a full and complete eruption, and thus prevents the disease from attacking the internal organs. This is said to be now the established mode of treatment in the English army in China, by general orders, and is regarded as perfectly effectual.

It is a well known fact, that disease is most likely to make its attack upon the weakest parts, and especially upon places in the system which have been recently weakened by previous disease; hence, if an eruption (disease) is caused by the application of croton oil mixed with a little of the Tartaremetic Ointment, there is every reason to believe that the eruption, in Small Pox, will locate upon that part instead of the face. The application should be made upon the breast, fore part of the thighs, &c., not to interfere with the posture upon the bed.

It has been suggested that a similar application will relieve whooping-cough, by drawing the irritation from the lungs; if so, why will it not help to keep measles to the surface, especially when they have a tendency to the internal organs, called, striking in. It is worth a trial, in any of these cases. See "Causes of Inflammation," under the head of "Inflammation."

2. COMMON SWELLINGS, TO REDUCE.—Tory-weed pounded so as to mash it thoroughly and bound upon any common swelling, will very soon reduce the parts to their natural size.

This weed may be known from its annoyance to sheep raisers, as it furnishes a small burr having a dent on one side of it. There are two species of it, but the burr of the other kind has no dent—is round. It will be found very valuable in rheumatisms attended with swellings.

WENS—To CURE.—Dissolve copperas in water to make it very strong; now take a pin, needle, or sharp knife and prick, or cut the wen in about a dozen places, just sufficient to cause it to bleed; then wet it thoroughly with the copperas water, once daily.

This, followed for four weeks, cured a man residing within four miles of this city, who had six or eight of them, some of them on the head as large as a hen's egg. The preparation is also valuable, as a wash, in erysipelas.

BLEEDINGS—INTERNAL AND EXTERNAL—STYPTIC BALSAM—For internal hemorrhage, or bleeding from the lungs, stomach, nose, and in excessive menstruation or bleeding from the womb, is made as follows:

Put sulphuric acid 2½ drs. by weight, in a Wedgewood mortar and slowly add *oil* of turpentine 1 fluid dr., stirring it constantly with the pestle, then add slowly again, alcohol 1 fluid dr., and continue to stir as long as any fumes arise from the mixture, then bottle in glass, ground stoppered, bottles. It should be a clear red color, like dark blood, but if made of poor materials it will be a pale, dirty red, and unfit for use. Dose—To be given by putting 40 drops into a tea-cup and rubbing it thoroughly with a tea-spoon of brown sugar, and then stir in water until the cup is nearly full, and drink immediately—repeat every hour for 3 or 4 hours, but its use should be discontinued as soon as no more fresh blood appears. Age does not injure it, but a skim forms on the top which is to be broken through, using the medicine below it.

This preparation was used for thirty years, with uniform success, by Dr. Jas. Warren, before he gave it to the public; since then, Dr. King, of Cincinnati, author of the Eclectic Dispensatory, has spread it, through that work, and many lives have been saved by it. It acts by lessening the force of the circulation (sedative power,) as also by its astringent effects in contact with the bleeding vessels. And the probability is that no known remedy can be as safely depended upon for more speedy relief, or certainty of cure, especially for the lungs, stomach, or nose; but for bleedings from the womb, or excessive menstruation, I feel to give preference to Prof. Platt's treatment as shown in the recipe for "Uterine Hemorrhages." No relaxation from business need be required, unless the loss of blood makes it necessary, nor other treatment, except if blood has been swallowed, or if the bleeding is from the stomach, it would be well to give a mild cathartic. Bleeding from the stomach will be distinguished from bleeding from the lungs by a sense of weight, or pain, and unaccompanied by cough, and discharged by vomiting, and in larger quantities at a time than from the lungs. The blood will be darker also, and often mixed with particles of food.

Exercise in the open air is preferable to inactivity; and if any symptoms of returning hemorrhage show themselves, begin with the remedy without loss of time, and a reasonable hope of cure may be expected.

2. EXTERNAL STYPTIC REMEDIES.—Take a glazed earthern vessel that will stand heat and put into it water 2½ pts.; tincture of benzoin 2 ozs.; alum ¼ lb., and boil for 6 hours, replacing the water which evaporates in boiling, by pouring in boiling water so as not to stop the boiling process, constantly stirring. At the end of the 6 hours it is to be filtered or carefully strained and bottled, also in glass stoppered bottles. APPLICATION—Wet lint

and lay upon the wound, binding with bandages to prevent the thickened blood (coagula) from being removed from the mouths of the vessels, keeping them in place for 24 to 48 hours will be sufficient.

If any doubt is felt about this remedy, pour a few drops of it into a vessel containing human blood—the larger the quantity of the *styptic*, the thicker will be the blood mass, until it becomes black and thick. Pagliari was the first to introduce this preparation to public notice.—*Eclectic Dispensatory.*

3. STYPTIC TINCTURE—EXTERNAL APPLICATION.—Best brandy 2 ozs.; finely scraped Castile soap 2 drs.; potash 1 dr.; mix all, and shake well when applied. Apply warm by putting lint upon the cut, wet with the mixture.

I have never had occasion to try either of the preparations, but if I do, it will be the "Balsam," or "External Styptic" first, and if they should fail I would try the "Tincture," for I feel that it must stop blood, but I also am certain that it would make a sore, aside from the cut; yet, better have a sore than lose life, of course. These remedies are such, that a physician might pass a lifetime without occasion to use, but none the less important to know.

BRONCHOCELE—ENLARGED NECK—TO CURE.—Iodide of potassium (often called hydriodate of potash,) 2 drs.; iodine 1 dr.; water 2 ½ ozs.; mix and shake a few minutes and pour a little into a vial for internal use. DOSE—Five to 10 drops before each meal, to be taken in a little water. EXTERNAL APPLICATION.—With a feather wet the enlarged neck, from the other bottle, night and morning, until well.

It will cause the scarf skin to peel off several times before the cure is perfect, leaving it tender, but do not omit the application more than one day at most, and you may rest assured of a cure, if a cure can be performed by any means whatever; many cures have been performed by it, and there is no medicine yet discovered which has proved one-hundreth part as successful.

2. BUT if you are willing to be longer in performing the cure, to avoid the soreness, dissolve the same articles in alcohol 1 pt., and use the same way, as above described, (*i. e.*) both internal and external.

PAIN KILLER—SAID TO BE PERRY DAVIS'.—Alcohol 1 qt.; gum guaiac 1 oz.; gums myrrh and camphor, and cayenne pulverized, of each ¼ oz. Mix. Shake occasionally for a week or

10 days and filter or let settle for use. Apply freely to surface pains, or it may be taken in tea-spoon doses for internal pains, and repeat according to necessities.

If any one can tell it from its namesake, by its looks or actions, we will then acknowledge that the old minister, from whom it was obtained, was greatly deceived, although he was perfectly familiar for a long time with Mr. Davis, and his mode of preparing the pain-killer.

POISONS—ANTIDOTE.—When it becomes known that a *poison* has been swallowed, stir salt and ground mustard, of each a heaping tea-spoon, into a glass of water, and have it drank *immediately*. It is the *quickest* emetic known.

It should vomit in one minute. Then give the whites of two or three eggs in a cup or two of the strongest coffee. If no coffee, swallow the egg in sweet-cream, and if no cream sweet-milk, if neither, down with the egg.

I have used the mustard, with success, in the case of my own child, which had swallowed a " Quarter" beyond the reach of the finger, but remaining in the throat, which, to all appearances, would have soon suffocated him. I first took " granny's plan" of turning the head down and patting on the back; failing in this, I mixed a heaping tea-spoon of mustard in sufficient water to admit its being swallowed readily; and in a minute we had the quarter, dinner, and all; without it, we should have had no child.

I knew the mustard to work well once upon about twenty men in a boat-yard, on Belle River, Newport, Mich. I had been furnishing them with "Switchel" at twenty cents per bucket, made by putting about a pound of sugar, a quart of vinegar, and two or three table-spoons of ginger to the bucket of water, with a lump of ice. An old man, also in the grocery business, offered to give it to them at eighteen pence per bucket, but, by some mistake, he put in mustard instead of ginger. They had a general vomit, which made them think that Cholera had come with the horrors of " Thirty-Two," but as the downward effects were not experienced, it passed off with great amusement, safely establishing my custom at the twenty cents per bucket.

INFLAMMATORY DISEASES—DESCRIPTION.—Before I attempt to speak of the inflammation of particular organs, I shall make a few remarks upon the subject in gen

eral, which will throw out the necessary light for those not
already informed ; and I should be glad to extend my treatment to all of the particular organs of the body, but the
limits of the work only allows me to speak of Pleurisy, Inflammation of the Lungs, &c.; yet, *Eclectic* ideas of inflammation are such, that if we can, successfully, treat inflammation in one part of the system, (body,) we can, with but
little modification, succeed with it in all of its forms : And
my general remarks shall be of such a nature as to enable
any judicious person to, successfully, combat with inflammations in every part of the system. Then :

FIRST.—Inflammation is, generally, attended with *pain,*
increased heat, redness, ar d *swelling.* Some, or all of these
signs *always* accompanyii g it, according to the *structure* of
the organ affected.

SECOND.—The more loose the structure of the organ,
the less severe will be the pain ; and the *character* of the
structure also modifies the character of the *pain.* In *mucous*
membranes, it is burning or stinging. In *serous* membrane?
it is lancinating, and most usually very sharp and cutting
In *fibrous* structures, it is dull, aching, and gnawing. In
nervous structures, it is quick, jumping, and most usually
excruciatingly severe ; and in nearly all structures more or
less soreness is soon present.

THIRD.—To make the foregoing information of value,
it becomes necessary to *know* the structure of the various
parts of the system. Although the ultimate portions of
muscle or flesh, as usually called, is fibrous, yet, there is a
loose cellular structure blended with it, which fills up and
rounds the form to its graceful beauty—hence, here, we
have more swelling, and less severity of pain. With the
rose, or red of the lips, commences the *mucous* membrane.
which forms the lining coat of the mouth, stomach, &c.,
through the whole alimentary canal, also lining the urethra,
bladder, ureters, vagina, womb, fallopian tubes, &c., hence
the heat always felt in inflammation of these organs The
whole internal surface of the cavity of the body is lined by
a *serous* membrane, which is also reflected or folded upon
the lungs—here called *pleura,* (the side,) hence pleurisy,
(inflammation of the pleura or side,) and also folded upon

the upper side of the diaphragm; the diaphragm forming a partition between the upper and lower portions of the cavity of the body, the upper portion containing the lungs, heart, large blood vessels, &c., called the *chest*, more commonly the breast—the lower portion containing the stomach, liver, kidneys, intestines, bladder, &c., called the *abdomen* —more commonly the bowels. The sides of the abdomen are covered with a continuation of this *serous* membrane, which is also reflected upon the lower side of the diaphragm, liver, stomach, small and large intestines, bladder, &c.,— here called *peritoneum*, (to extend around) in all places it secretes (furnishes) a moistening fluid enabling one organ of the body to move upon itself or other organs without friction. This serous membrane is thin, but very firm, hence the sharpness of the pain when it is inflamed, as it cannot yield to the pressure of the accumulating blood.

FOURTH.--The ligaments or bands which bind the different parts of the body together at the joints, and the gracefully contracted ends of the muscles (called tendons) which pass the joint, attaching themselves to the next bone above, or below, and the wristlet-like bands which are clasped around the joints through which these tendons play, as over a pully, when the joint is bent, are all of a *fibrous* construction, hence the grinding or gnawing pains of rheumatism (inflammations), and injuries of, or near joints; and it also accounts for that kind of pain in the latter stages of intestinal inflammations, as the stomach, intestines, &c., are composed of three coats, the external, serous,—middle fibrous, internal, mucous; and when inflammation of the external, or internal; coats are *long* continued, it generally involves the middle—fibrous layer.

FIFTH.—The greatest portion of the substance of the lungs is of *fibrous* tissue, consequently, dull or obtuse pain only, is experienced when inflamed.

LASTLY.—The nervous system, although of a *fibrous* character is so indescribably fine in its *structure*, that, like the telegraph wire, as soon as touched, it answers with a bound, to the call—quick as thought, whether pain or pleasure, jumping, bounding, it goes to the grand citadel (the brain) which overlooks the welfare of the whole temple.

In general, the intensity of the pain attending inflammations will surely indicate the violence of the febrile (sympathetic) reaction; for instance, in inflammation of the bronchial tubes, the pain is not very severe, consequently not much fever, (reaction); but in inflammation of the pleura (pleurisy) the pain is very severe, conse quently the febrile reaction exceedingly great.

CAUSES OF INFLAMMATION.—In health, the *blood* carried evenly, in proportion to the size of the blood vessels, to every part of the body. And the vessels (arteries and veins) are proportioned in size to the necessity of the system for vitality, nutrition, and reparation. Whatever it may be that causes the blood to *recede* from the surface, or any considerable portion of it, will cause inflammation of the weakest portion of the system; and whatever will draw the blood unduly to any part of the system, will cause inflammation of that part,—for instance, cold drives the blood from the surface, consequently, if sufficiently long continued, the internal organ least able to bear the accumulation of blood upon it will be excited to inflammation—a blow upon any part, if sufficiently severe, will cause inflammation of the injured part. Also mustard poultices, drafts to the feet, &c., hence the propriety of their proper use to draw the blood away from internal organs which are inflamed. A check of perspiration is, especially, liable to excite inflammation. and that in proportion to the degree of heat producing the perspiration and the length of time which the person may be exposed to the cold. The object of knowing the cause of disease is to avoid suffering from disease, by keeping clear of its cause; or thereby to know what remedy to apply for its cure or relief.

There is a class of persons who claim that *causes* will have their legitimate *effects, physical* or *moral;* physicians *know* that it is absurd physically; that is, when philosophically and scientifically combated with,—for instance, a person is exposed to cold; the blood is driven in upon the internal organs, and the one which is the least able to bear the pressure gives way before the invading enemy, and an inflammation is the result; which, if left to itself, will terminate in death; but heat and moisture are applied to the constringed urface—the blood is brought back and 'held there, and a cure is speedily effected—the natural or physical *effect* of the cause is *obviated* or avoided.

Then why should it be thought impossible with God that a *moral* remedy should be provided against moral evils? Thanks be to God, it has been provided to the *willing* and *obedient*, through our Lord Jesus Christ, but *only* to the willing and obedient, morally as well as physically, for if a person *will not* permit a proper course to be pursued to overcome tne consequences arising to his body from cold, he *must* suffer, not only the inflammation to go on, but also guilt ot mind for neglecting his known duty. The same is true in either point of view, only it looks so curious that there should be those who can reason of physical things, but utterly refuse to give up their moral blindness; the consequences be upon their own heads.

Just in proportion to the susceptibility of an organ to take on diseased action, is the danger of exposure; for example if a person has had a previous attack of pleurisy, or inflammation of the lungs, those organs, or the one which has been diseased, will be almost certain to be *again* prostrated, usually called *relapse;* which is in most cases, *ten times* more severe than the first attack; then be *very* careful about exposures when just getting better from these, or other disease.

Inflammation terminates by *resolution, effusion, suppuration, or mortification.* By *resolution,* is meant that the parts return to their *natural* condition; by *effusion,* that *blood* may be thrown out from the soft parts, or from *mucous membranes,*—that *lymph,* or *serum,* a colorless part of the blood may be thrown out by *serous* membranes, which often form adhesions, preventing the after motions of the affected parts—and here what wisdom is brought to light, in the fact that whatever is thrown out from the *mucus* surface never, or at least *very* seldom adhere, or grow up; if it did, any part of the alimentary canal from the mouth to the stomach, and so on through the intestines, would be constantly adhering; so, also of the lungs; for these various organs are more frequently affected by inflammations than any other parts of the body—by *suppuration,* when *abscesses* are formed containing pus (matter,) or this may take place upon the surface, when it is usually called canker, or corroding ulcers, cancers, &c.; by *gangrene,* (mortification,) when death of the parts take place; in this case, if the part is sufficiently extensive, or if it is an internal part, death of the whole body, if not relieved, is the result.

The methods of inflammatory termination is believed to result from the grade of inflammation—for instance, at the circumference of a boil, the inflammation is weak, *serum* is thrown out; near the centre, where the inflammation is a little higher, *lymph* is poured out and adhesion takes place; —next *pus*—at the centre, *mortifiction* and consequent sloughing takes place.

In *boils*, the tendency is to suppuration; in *carbuncles*, the tendency is to mortification; but in rheumatism, mumps, &c., there is a strong tendency to resolution; and it is often very difficult to avoid these natural terminations.

The five different tissues of the body also modify the inflammation according to the tissue inflamed, viz: the *cellular* (fleshy) tissue, is characterized by great swelling, throbbing pain, and by its suppurating in cavities—not spreading all over that tissue. Inflammation of the *serous* tissue, has sharp lancinating pain, scarcely any swelling, but much reaction (fever), throws out lymph, and is very liable to form adhesion—not likely to terminate in mortification, except in peritonitis (inflammation of the lining membrane of the abdominal cavity), which sometimes terminates thus in a few hours, showing the necessity of immediate action. Inflammation of the *mucous* tissue, is characterized by burning heat, or stinging pain (hence the heat of the stomach, bowels, &c.)—without swelling, not much febrile reaction, and never terminates in resolution (health) without a copious discharge of mucus, as from the nose and lungs, in colds, catarrhs, coughs, &c. Inflammation of the *dermoid* (skin) tissue, as in erysipelas, is characterized by burning pain—spreads irregularly over the suaface, forming blisters containing a yellowish serum, but never forms adhesions, nor suppurates in cavities, but upon the surface. Inflammation of the *fibrous* tissue, or rheumatic inflammation, is characterized by severe aching or gnawing pain—is not liable to terminate in suppuration nor mortification—nearly always throwing out a gelatinous serum, often causing stiff joints, or depositing earthy matter, as in gout—is peculiarly liable to change its place, being very dangerous if it change any of the vital organs, as the brain, heart, stomach, &c., a a in the acute form the febrile reaction is usually quite severe. *Internal* inflammation will be known by the constant pain of the inflamed part, by the presence of fever, which does not generally attend a spasmodic or nervous pain, and by the position chosen by the patient, to avoid pressure upon the afflicted organs.

Inflammation is known under two heads, *acute* and *chronic*. The first is generally rapid and violent in its course and characteristics. The last is usually the result of the first, —is more slow and less dangerous in its consequences.

TREATMENT.—Sound philosophy (Eclecticism) teaches, that if cold has driven the blood (consequently the heat) from the surface, heat will draw it back; and thus relieve the internal engorgements (over-full organs) and if held there, sufficiently long, entirely cure the difficulty (inflammation), upon the same ground, if a person is cold, warm him; if wet and cold, warm and dry him; if hot, cool him; if dry and hot, wet and cool him—equalize the circulation and pain or disease cannot exist.

The foregoing remarks must suffice for general directions; but the following special application to *pleurisy* and *inflammation of the lungs* shall be sufficiently explicit to enable all to make their *general* applications.

2. PLEURISY.—Pleurisy is an inflammation of the *serous* membrane inveloping (covering) the lungs, which is also reflected (folded) upon the parieties (sides or walls) of the chest, (but I trust all will make themselves familiar with the description of "Inflammation in General," before they proceed with the study of pleurisy,) attended with sharp lancinating pain in the side, difficult breathing, fever, with a quick, full, and hard pulse, usually commencing with a chill. In many cases the inflammation, consequently the pain, is confined to one point, most commonly about the short ribs; but often gradually extends towards the shoulder and forward part of the breast; the pain increasing, and often becoming very violent. It may not, but usually, is attended with cough, and the expectoration is seldom mixed with blood, or very free, but rather of a glairy or mucous character. As the disease advances, the pain is compared to a stab with a sharp instrument, full breathing

not being indulged, from its increasing the difficulty; the cough also aggravates the pain; great prostration of strength, the countenance expressing anxiety and suffering. The breathing is short, hurried, and catching, to avoid increase of pain; in some cases, the cough is only slight. It may be complicated with inflammation of the lungs, or bronchial tubes, and if so complicated, the expectoration will be mixed or streaked with blood. Yet it makes but very little difference, as the treatment is nearly the same—with the exception of expectorants, quite the same; although expectorants are not *amiss* in pleurisy, but absolutely *neces sary* in inflammation of the lungs. Even Mackintosh, of the "Regulars," says: "It must be recollected that pneu- monia" (inflammation of the lungs) "and pleuritis" (pleu- risy) "Frequently co-exist" (exist together); "But neither is that circumstance of much consequence, being both inflammatory diseases, and requiring the same general remedies." But there I stop with him, for I cannot go the bleeding, calomel, and antimony. I have quoted his words to satisfy the people that the "Regulars" acknowledge the necessity of a similar treatment in all inflammatory diseases, the *difference* between the two branches of the profession, existing only in the *remedies* used.

CAUSES OF PLEURISY.—Cold, long applied, constringes (makes smaller) the capillaries (hair-like blood-vessels) which cover as a net-work the whole surface, impairing the circulation, driving the blood internally, causing congestion (an unnatural accumulation of blood) upon the pleura, hence pleurisy. Exposures to rains, especially cold rains, cold, wet feet, recession (striking in) of measles, scarlet fever, rheumatism, &c., often cause inflammation of this char- acter.

INDICATIONS.—Relax the whole surface, which removes the obstructions—restore, and maintain, an equal circulation, and the work is accomplished. The temperature of the surface and extremities is much diminished, showing that the blood has receded (gone) to the internal, diseased. or- gans, the temperature of which is much increased; for with the blood goes the vitality (heat) of the body. This condi- tion of the system clearly indicates the treatment, viz: the application of heat to the surface in such a way as to be ut le to keep it there until nature is again capable of carrying on her own work, in her own way.

TREATMENT.—It has been found that the quickest and least troublesome way in which heat could be applied to the whole surface, is by means of burning alcohol, formerly called a "Rum sweat," because rum was stronger than at present, and more plenty than alcohol; but now alcohol is the most plenty, and much the strongest and cheapest. It should always be in the house (the 98 per cent.) ready for use as described under the head of " Sweating with Burning Alcohol," (which see), or if it is day time, and fires are burning, you can give the vapor-bath-sweat, by placing a pan, half or two-thirds full of hot water, under the chair, having a comforter around you; then putting into it occasionally a hot stone or brick, until a free perspiration is produced and held for from 15 to 30 minutes, according to the severity of the case; and if this is commenced as soon as the attack is fairly settled upon the patient, in not more than one case out of ten will it be necessary to do anything more; but if fairly established, or if of a day or two's standing, then, at the same time you are administering the *sweat,* place the patient's feet in water as hot as it can be borne; have also a strong tea made of equal parts of pleurisy-root and catnip, (this root is also called white root—Doctors call it asclepias tuberosa)—into a saucer of this hot tea put 2 tea-spoons of the " Sweating Drops," drinking all at one time, repeating the dose every hour for 5 or 6 hours, using only 1 tea-spoon of the drops at other times, except the first, giving the tea freely once or twice between doses. As soon as the sweating is over, place the patient comfortably in bed so as to keep up the perspiration from 6 to 12 hours, or until the pain and uneasiness yield to the treatment. If necessary, after the patient takes the bed, place bottles of hot water to the feet and along the sides, or hot bricks, or stones wrapped with flannel wet with vinegar, to help keep up the perspiration. Mustard may also be placed over the seat of pain, and upon the feet also rubbing the arms and legs with dry flannel, which very much aids the process when the attack is severe. If the pain *continues* severe, and perspiration is hard to maintain, steep cayenne, or common red peppers in spirits and rub the whole surface with it, well and long, and I will assure the blood to come out soon and see what is going on externally. Keep the patient well covered all the time, and avoid drafts cf cold air. As the painful symptoms begin to subside, the doses of medicine may be lessened, and the time between doses lengthened, until the disease is fairly under control; then administer a dose of the "Vegetable Physic," or some other cathartic, if preferred, or if that is not at hand, this course may be repeated or modified to meet returning or changing symptoms.

Wetting the surface daily, with alcohol and water, equal parts, will be found an excellent assistant in treating any disease, especially, internal inflammations, as Pleurisy, Inflammation of the Lungs, Consumption, Bronchits, &c., &c.

The pleurisy root is almost a specific in pleurisy or in flammation of the lungs; no other known root or herb is equal to it for producing and keeping up perspiration (drug gists usually keep it,) but if it cannot be got, pennyroyal, sage, &c., or one of the mints, must be used in its place. The only objection to the foregoing treatment is this, the Doctors say:

> Heigh! I guess he wasn't very sick;
> For see! he's round in "double quick";
> But alopath holds 'em for weeks, six or seven,
> When bleeding, calomel, and antimony are given.

To illustrate: I awoke one night with severe pain in the left side (I had been exposed to cold during the afternoon,) could not move or draw a full breath without very much increasing the difficulty; the night was cold and fires all down; I studied my symptoms for a few minutes, and also reflected upon the length of time which must elapse, if I waited for fires to be built; then awoke my wife, saying do not be frightened, I have an attack of Pleurisy; you will get me a comforter, saucer, and the alcohol, and return to bed without disturbing any one; with persuasion, or almost compulsion, she did so; for she desired to build a fire and make a more thorough work of it; but I had made up my mind and resolved to carry out the experiment upon myself, and now had the only chance. I arose and poured the saucer nearly full of alcohol, and set it on fire; wrapping the comforter around me, I sat down upon the chair, over it, and continued to sit until the alcohol was all burned out, and I in a most profuse perspiration; the pain and diffi cult breathing having nearly all subsided; I then returned to bed, the perspiration continuing for some considerable longer, by retaining the comforter around me to avoid checking it as I returned to bed, during which time I again fell asleep. When I awoke in the morning I could just realize a little pain, or rather uneasiness, upon taking a full breath, but did nothing more, being very careful about exposure however, through the day; but at bed time I took another alcohol sweat, and that was the last of the pleurisy.

Again: Mr. ——, a medical student rooming in the same house where I lived, awoke in the night, attacked with pleurisy, the same as myself, after exposure; but as he was attending the lectures of alopathic professors. of course, he must have one of them to attend him; one was called, three pints of blood were taken, calomel and antimony were freely given; and in about three or four days the disease gave way to time, or the treatment; but a calomel-Diarrhea set in, and came very near terminating his life, and kept him from college and his studies over six weeks; and he said if he was ever calomelized again, he would prosecute the doer to the end of his life; but he graduated in that school of medicine, and no doubt is now expecting to go and do the same thing. Choose ye your *servant*. Shall he be reason, with common-sense results, or shall he be silver-slippered fashion. with his health-destroying policy? It need not be argued that these were not parallel cases, for I had the pleurisy when young, and was treated in the fashionable style, and was constantly liable to, and had frequent attacks of it during my earlier life.

In chronic cases, which sometimes occur, and frequently under other treatment, it will be necessary, not only to use the foregoing treatment, but to add to it an emetic about once a week, alternating with the sweating process, with much external friction, occasionally, with the pepper and spirits to hold the blood to the surface.

Since the first publication of the foregoing, I have seen a statement going the rounds of the "Papers," that a bad case of burning had taken place in N. Y., by the alcohol process of sweating, calling it *new;* but it has been in use more than *forty* years; I have used it, I speak safely, more than a *hundred* times, and never before heard of its injuring any one; but still it is possible that some accident may have occurred in its use, or that some one has undertaken it who was not capable of prescribing; but if *calomel* could claim *one* year's use under its most accomplished prescribers with only one case of *injury*, I would say, let it be continued, but in place of one, it is *hundreds;* farther comment is unnecessary.

But, those who prefer, or from the absence of alcohol, or other necessities, can take "grandmother's plan," *i. e.*, place the feet into hot water, and drink freely of pennyroyal, sage, or other hot teas, for fifteen to twenty minutes; then get into bed, continuing the teas for a short time, remaining in bed for a few hours; which, if commenced soon after the attack of colds, or even more severe diseases, will, in nine out of ten cases, not only relieve, but prevent days, perhaps weeks, of inconvenience and suffering.

Where there are complications with the substance of the lungs, you will find explanations under the next head.

3. INFLAMMATION OF THE LUNGS—Is usually, by phy-sicians, called Pneumonia, from the Greek, *Pneumon*, the Lungs. It may involve the whole lung, on one or both sides, but is more generally confined to one side, and to the lower portion, than to the whole lung.

CAUSES.—Exposure to cold, wet, cold feet, drafts of air, especially if in a perspiration, recession of eruptive diseases, &c., and consequently more liable to come on in the winter, or cold wet changes of spring, than at any other time; and upon those whose lungs are debilitated by previous attacks, or are predisposed to, or actuallysuffering under disease.

SYMPTOMS.—Inflammation of the Lungs, like other dis-eases of an inflammatory character, nearly always commen-ces with a chill, soon followed by fever, more or less violent, according to which, the severity of the case may be some-what predetermined, unless of a congestive character; in which case, instead of a hot and fevered surface, there will be a cold, clammy feel to the hand, as well as unpleasant to the patient. There will be difficulty in taking full breaths, as well as an increased number of breaths to the minute, which in healthy persons is generally about twenty. Dull pain, with a tightness of the chest, short and perpetual hack-ing cough, scanty expectoration, which is tough, and sticks to the vessel used as a spittoon, and is more or less streaked with blood, or more like iron-rust in color, and may have so much blood in it as to make it a brighter red. The pulse is variable, so much so that but little confidence can be placed in it. The tongue soon becomes dry and dark; but a dry and glossy tongue, with early delirium, are considered dan-gerous symptoms, that is, under "Old School treatment." But with our rational treatment we very seldom have a fatal termination, yet it is occasional, and really wonderful that it is not more frequent, when we take into account the neglect of some physicians and imprudence of many patients.

INDICATIONS.—As the blood has receded from the surface and centered upon the lungs; the indications are to return it to its original vessels, by judiciously applying heat and moisture, which is sure to relax their constringed condition, instead of cutting a hole and letting it run *out* (bleeding), which prostrates the patient and retards his recovery.

TREATMENT.—The treatment of Inflammation of the Lungs in recent cases, will be, at first, the same as for "Pleurisy," that is, to produce free perspiration—soak the feet in hot water while administering the "Alcohol Sweat," or Vapor Bath, as there directed, with the white-root tea and "Sweating Drops," for several hours, with bottles of hot water or hot bricks to the feet and sides, mustard-drafts to the feet also, as they can be borne; and after 6 or 8 hours, the "Vegetable," or other cathartic should be administered, and great care not to expose the patient to drafts of air during its operation, especially if in perspiration. If this course is faithfully persevered in, it will call the blood to the surface—prevent congestion of the lungs (unnatural accumulation of blood)—lessen the fever—ease the pain and aid expectoration. But if the expectoration becomes difficult, and the disease should not seem to yield in from 8 to 12 hours at farthest, or by the time the cathartic has freely operated, then, or soon after, give the "Eclectic," or "Lobelia-seed Emetic," as directed under that head; and if called to a case which is already confirmed, it is best to *begin* with the emetic, then follow up as above directed in recent cases. An expectorant, in confirmed (established) cases will be needed—let it be composed of tincture of lobelia 1 oz.; tincture of ipecac ½ oz.; tincture of blood-root ¼ oz.; simple syrup or molasses 2 ozs.; mix. DOSE—One teaspoon every 2 hours, alternately with the white-root tea and "Sweating Drops," except the first dose may be 2 tea-spoons. The case must then be watched carefully; and any part or all of the treatment may be repeated, lessened, increased, or modified, to suit returning or remaining symptoms.

Persons having this book in the house, and being governed by it, having also the leading medicines on hand; and commencing with this disease, or inflammation of any other organs, modifying the treatment by common sense, according to the remarks on "General Inflammation," will not have to repeat the course in one case out of ten.

In inflammations of the *stomach*, known by heat, according to the *degree* of the inflammation, drinks of slippery-elm water, or mucilage of gum arabic, &c., may be freely taken; and in inflammation of other organs, other modifications will be required; as for Dysentery, which is an in-

flammation of the large intestines, the "Injection" must be
freely used, as also the perspiring processes, in all cases.

In chronic inflammation, the emetic should be given once a
week; and some other time during the week, the sweating
should be gone through also, with dry frictions to the whole
surface, by means of a coarse towel, for fifteen to twenty minutes each time, twice daily; and if the feet are habitually cold,
wash them in cold water and wipe them dry, at bed time, then
rub them with a coarse cloth or the dry hand until they are
perfectly warm and comfortable; and it may be expected that
these long standing cases will soon yield to this *rational*
course.

FEMALE DEBILITY AND IRREGULARITIES.—It is a self evident fact that the finer the work, and the more complicated a
piece of machinery, the more liable is it to become deranged,
or out of order; and the more skillful must be the mechanic
who undertakes to make any necessary repairs.

Upon this consideration I argue that the system of the
female is the finer and more complicated, having to perform a
double work, (child-bearing,) yet confined to the same or less
dimensions than the male. And to perform this *double* function of sustaining her own life, and giving life to her species,
it becomes necessary in the wisdom of God to give her such
a peculiar formation, that between the ages of fifteen and
forty-five, or the *child-bearing period*, she should have a sanguineous, monthly flow, called by various names, as, monthly
periods, menstruation, menses, catamenia, courses, &c., &c.

Why it should have been so arranged, or necessary, none
can tell. We are left to deal with the simple fact; and it
would be just as wise in us to say that it was *not* so, as to say
there was no one who *planned* it, because we cannot see and
fully understand the reason why it is so. This flow varies in
amount from one to three, four, or five ounces, lasting from
three to four or five days only, when usual health is enjoyed.
And as this book will fall into the hands of very many families who will have no other medical work for reference upon
this subject, it will not be amiss for me to give the necessary
instructions here, that all may be able to qualify themselves
to meet the exigencies (demand) of all cases. A day or two
previous to the commencement of these periods, for the first
time, an uneasiness often amounting to pain, in the parts, is
felt, with sense of heaviness also in the womb—lying in the
lower part of the abdomen.

Some females are very nervous at these periods, others
have a flushed face accompanied with dizziness and headache
sickness at the stomach, &c. In young girls these new feelings produce uneasiness, for want of knowledge as to their
cause and result, and should lead them to seek maternal

advice and counsel, unless they have some book of this kind which explains the whole matter. And it would certainly be advisable, in all cases, for girls to not only seek such advice from the mother, or lady with whom they may be living, but be guided by it also. And although, with many girls, there may be uneasiness in the mammæ, often amounting to real pain, yet, no real danger need be apprehended; for these unpleasant sensations will continue, and increase in severity, until in healthy young females there will be what is knows as a "*show*," which will afford immediate relief, not from the quantity of the flow, at the first few periods, but from the fact that the organs peculiar to the female have accomplished their mysterious work. Ordinarily these periods begin at about fifteen years of age, some earlier or later even as much as a year and sometimes more. With girls who take an active part in the labors of the house, freely romping, playing, &c., their health and strength becoming fully developed thereby, these periods come on a little earlier, and are more healthy and regular.

Allow me here to give a word of caution about taking cold at this period. It is very dangerous. I knew a young girl, who had not been instructed by her mother upon this subject, to be so afraid of being found with this show upon her apparel which she did not know the meaning of, that she went to a brook and washed herself and clothes—took cold, and immediately became *insane*—remaining so as long as I knew her. Any mother who so neglects her duty to her child, in not explaining these things, nor by putting a work of this kind into her hands, runs the risk of injury to her daughter that may never be remedied, even with the best treatment, after the harm is done.

After this flow takes place, the unpleasant feelings usually subside, and the health again becomes good for the month, when all of the foregoing sensations recur again, with a larger flow and longer continued, recurring every four weeks, and is then called menses &c., &c.

This function of the female system, from the fineness and complication of the structures, is very liable to become deranged in various ways.

It may be partially suppressed or entirely stopped, called, *amenorrhea*,—it may become painful or imperfect, *dysmenorrhea*,—it may be very free or excessive, *menorrhagia*, (like hemorrhage, for the treatment of which see recipe for Uterine Hemorrhage in another part of the book),—or, it may be irregular in its recurrence and duration, or a continual glairy flow which indicates an inflammation of the parts, *leucorrhea*.

But as this monthly flow is absolutely necessary to health, between these periods of life, say *fifteen to forty-five*—its suppression,—painfulness—excessiveness, or irregularity, will soon produce general debility.

CAUSES.—The female organism is such that what affects the general system of the male, much more frequently affects the organs *peculiar* to her system only. No reason can be given for it except the wisdom of the Creator, and the necessities of her construction. But this *debility* and *irregularity* are so interwoven together that what causes one must necessarily affect the other.

In the good old *grandmother-days*, when girls helped with the work of the household, warm but loose clothing, plain food, good thick-soled shoes, and absence of novels, to excite the passions, &c., such a thing as a feeble, debilitated woman or girl was seldom known; but now, sedentary habits, stimulating food, every conceivable unphysiological style of dress, paper-soled shoes, checking perspiration, excitable reading, repeated colds by exposure going to and from parties, thinly clad, standing by the gate talking with supposed friends (real enemies) when they ought to be by the fire or in bed, all tend to general debility; and the real wonder is that there is not more debility than there is.

SYMPTOMS.—The very word *debility*, shows plainly the leading symptom, weakness. She appears pale, especially about the lips, nose, &c., with a bluish circle about the eyes, which appear rather sunken, she feels dull, languid, and drowsy, stomach out of order, nausea, often with fluttering about the heart; the nervous system sometimes becoming so much involved as to bring on fits of despondency leading many to commit suicide. The feet and limbs frequently become swollen, restless in sleep, often craving unnatural food, as clay, soft stones, &c. There may also be a sensation of bearing down, or even *falling* of the womb, as it is called, (prolapsus uteri) which is much the most common among the married. The bowels are usually costive, often griping pains which cause much suffering. Pains in the head and back also; but instead of being looked upon as unfavorable, they rather show that nature is trying to accomplish her work, and needs the assistance of *rational* remedies.

It is not to be supposed that every patient will experience all of these symptoms, at one time, or all of the time; but they commence as pointed out, and if allowed to go on without proper correction, they will increase in severity until they may be all experienced in a greater or less degree.

INDICATIONS.—The symptoms indicate (point out) the treatment, that is, if there is debility, tonics are required; paleness shows that the blood has become deficient in iron; and the

softness of the flesh indicates that a more nutritious diet is
needed. The dullness and drowsy languidness indicate the
necessity of out-door, active exercise. Travel, or, agreeable
home company, to ramble over hill and dale, resting as often
and as long as may be necessary, not to tire, but sufficient to
create an appetite and aid digestion—using, once a week, any
gentle cathartic to move the bowels once or twice only at
each time, with the "*Tonic Wine Tincture*," given in another
part of this work, or the *iron* and *ginger*, given below, as
deemed best or most convenient to obtain.

In cases of *inflammation* of these organs, known by a glairy
flow, cooling and astringent injections are called for, both as an
act of cleanliness, as also of cure. In cases where the womb has
fallen—settled low in the pelvis—the necessity is shown for a
pessary support, until the general treatment relieves the difficulty. Costiveness, points out laxatives, whilst nature's ef-
forts, shown by pains in the head, back, &c., call for the whole
general remedies above pointed out; and which shall be a little more particularized in the following:

TREATMENT.—For the weakness and general debility of the
patient, let the "Tonic Wine Tincture" be freely taken in
connection with iron to strengthen and invigorate the system;
beth-root, (often called birth-root, Indian balm, ground lily,
&c.,) the root, is the part used, Solomon's seal and columbo.
spikenard, comfrey, gentian, the roots, with camomile flowers,
of each 1 oz.; with a little white-oak bark, may be added to
the *wine tincture* to adapt it to these particular cases, taking
a wine-glass, if it can be borne, from 3 to 5 times daily. Domestic wine can be used in place of the Port, in making the
tonic wine tincture.

1. A very good way to take iron, is to go to a blacksmith
and have him take a piece of nail-rod, a foot or two in length,
and heat it, letting it cool in the cinders of the forge, which
softens it; then have him file it all up for you, saving the
filings on a piece of paper, with which filings, mix as much
ground ginger, rubbing them thoroughly together. Dose—
Half of a tea-spoon three times daily, in a little honey or molasses. The natural action of the iron upon the system will
be to make the stools dark, or nearly black, so do not be fearful about that condition; for, without it, we should not be
sure of the desired action of the iron. Let the use of the iron
be kept up for two or three months at least, or until health is
obtained.

In places where it may be difficult to get the iron filings,
given in No. 1., the sweet liquor of the protoxide of iron, kept
by druggists, the technical name of which is *Liq. Ferri Protox-
idi Dulc.*, may be used in place of that, a dose of which will

oe about one teaspoon 3 times daily, just after meals. I have prescribed this preparation with very great success, continuing its use, in one very bad case, nearly a year.

With the above treatment, let there be a warm bath taken, once a week, putting into the water a quart or two of weak-lye, made by putting a fire-shovel or two of wood ashes into the water and stirring up well, and let stand a while, then pour off into the bathing water. Castile-soap will do about as well, but common soap is not as good. Wash well, and wipe off the water from the body, then with a dry coarse towel, have some one to rub the whole body and limbs briskly unti the surface glows with warmth and comfort.

For diet, moderate quantities of broiled pork, broiled beef, baked beef or mutton, wild game &c., baked or broiled, with bread baked, at least, the day before, roast or baked potatoes, with but little butter, unless very nice, or just made, then, not very freely. This treatment, and diet, will soon overcome the softness of the flesh, and give strength for the necessary exercise, which will remove the dullness and drowsy, languid feelings. The exercise may be labor about the house, but better to be out of doors, as gardening, romping, swinging, singing and riding, or running, when it can be borne, with agreeable company, travel, &c. The following pill will be found a gentle and excellent cathartic, or laxative:

2. FEMALE LAXATIVE PILL.—Aloes, macrotin, and cream of tartar, of each 2 drs.; podophylin and ground ginger, 1 dr. each; make into common sized pills by using oil of peppermint 15 to 20 drops and thick solution of gum Arabic mucilage. DOSE—One pill at bed time, or two if found necessary, and sufficiently often to keep the bowels just in a solvent condition, but not less often than once a week.

If the aloes should not agree with any, they may use the following:

3. FEMALE LAXATIVE AND ANODYNE PILL.—Macrotin and rhubarb, of each 10 grs.; extract of hyoscyamus, 10 grs; Castile-soap, 40 grs.; scrape the soap and mix well together, forming into common sized pills with gum solution as in the above recipe. DOSE—One pill, as the other, or sufficiently often to keep the bowels solvent, but not too loose. The hyoscyamus tends to quiet the nerves without constipating the bowels.

Some females are always troubled with pains, to a greater or less degree, in the commencement of these periods, and some through the whole period. The following pill will be found very soothing and quieting to the nervous system of all such persons.

4. PILL FOR PAINFUL MENSTRUATION—ANODYNE—Extract of stramonium and sulphate of quinine, of each 16 grs.; macrotin * 8 grs.; morphine, 1 gr.; make into 8 pills. DOSE —One pill, repeating once or twice only, 40 minutes to an hour apart, if the pain does not subside. If the pain subsides, there is no need of repeating the dose. The advantage of this pill is that costiveness is not increased, and pain *must* subside under its use.

5. TEA—INJECTION FOR LEUCORRHEA.—In cases of leucorrhea which continue any length of time, the following decoction, will be found very valuable as an injection:

The inner bark of the common hemlock tree, and the leaves and bark of the witch-hazel, sometimes called spotted-alder, an ounce of each, will make a quart of the decoction, a little of which, with a female syringe, should be injected, morning and evening, while in a recumbent position.

If the case does not yield to the above in a few days then use a little of the following, in the same way:

6. INJECTION FOR LEUCORRHEA.—White vitriol and sugar of lead, of each 10 grs.; common salt, loaf sugar and pulverized alum, of each 5 grs.; soft water, 1 pt. Simmer all over a slow fire for ten or fifteen minutes, when cool strain' and bottle, keeping well corked. When desired to use, pour out about half as much as needed and put an equal amount of soft water with it, and inject, as of the above. It may be reduced with more soft water if there should be sufficient inflammation to cause much uneasiness. A little uneasines is expected, however, and necessary.

7. In cases of permanent falling of the womb, a good pessary may be made of a piece of fine, firm sponge, cut to a proper size to admit, when damp, of being placed in the *vagina* to hold the womb to its place. The sponge should have a stout piece of small cord sewed two or three times through its center, and left of sufficient length to aid in its removal, morning and evening, for the purpose of cleansing it, using the necessary injections, &c. After having injected either No. 5 or 6 of the above, as thought preferable, the sponge having been thoroughly washed and pressed dry, it will be again introduced sufficiently high to hold the womb in place. Remembering, however, in almost all of these cases of falling of the womb, that the patient will find it necessary to keep the bed until well, or very much relieved.

One thing is very evident in these cases of debility; the blood is deficient in iron; consequently that article should en-

---

* NOTE.—Macrotin, Podophylin, &c., are kept by all Eclectic Physicians and should be kept by all druggists.

ter largely into any medicine intended for its relief; and in *most* cases the iron-filings and ginger, or the sweet liquor, will be found, continued for two or three months, all the medicine required; and the iron must not be omitted in any case whatever. Iron is the *main-spoke* in these female-wheels, and very valuable in general debility of males as well as females.

For real hemorrhage, which may be known by the coagulation (clotting) of the blood, as the menstrual flow does not coagulate, see "Uterine Hemorrhage," or the "Styptic Balsam," but for profuse or long continued flowing or wasting, use the following:

8. POWDER FOR EXCESSIVE FLOODING.—Gums kino and catechu, of each 1 dr.; sugar of lead and alum, of each 1-2 dr.; pulverize all and thoroughly mix, then divide into 7 to 10 grain powders. DOSE—One every 2 to 3 hours until checked, then less often, merely to control the flow.

If any female, into whose hands this book shall come, will carefully study and use the foregoing rational remarks and prescriptions, and is not an hundred times better pleased with the results than she would have been by calling half of the physicians of the day, I should be very much disappointed, and I would be sure that the remedies did not have their common effects, which, I feel, will not be the case from the great good they have already done, many times; besides they save the delicacy of exposures, in many instances; and they will always save the delicacy of conversing with and explaining their various feelings and conditions, to one of the opposite sex. So highly important is this fact—that the information should become general—every girl, old or young, ought to be furnished with "Dr. Chase's Recipes," and also receive all the additional instruction that a mother's *experience* can give her.

TANNER'S, SHOE, AND HARNESS MAKER'S DEPARTMENT.

COLORS—BEST COLOR FOR BOOT, SHOE, AND HARNESS EDGE, AND INK WHICH CANNOT FREEZE.—Alcohol 1 pt.; tincture of iron 1½ oz.; extract of logwood 1 oz.; nutgalls, pulverized, 1 oz.; soft water ½ pt.; mix. Or:

2. TAKE alcohol 1 pt.; extract of logwood and tincture of iron, of each 1 oz.; nutgalls, pulverized, 1 oz.; and sweet oil ½ oz.; mix.

I have found shoemakers using these colors, each thinking he had the best color in the world. The sweet oil is believed to prevent the hot iron from sticking, and to make a better polish.

The first one makes a very passable ink for *winter* use, by carrying a quick hand to prevent it from spreading in the paper, from the presence of the alcohol, which, of course, is what prevents it from freezing, and that is the only argument in favor of it as an ink for writing purposes.

3. CHEAP COLOR FOR THE EDGE.—Soft water 1 gal.; extract of logwod 1 oz.; and boil them until the extract is dissolved, then remove from the fire and add copperas 2 ozs.; bi-chromate of potash and gum arabic, of each ½ oz.; all to be pulverized.

This makes a cheap and good color for shoe or harness edge, but for cobbling or for new work, upon which you do not wish to use the " hot kit," but finish with heel-ball, you will find that if, as you pour this out into the bottle to use, you put a table-spoon of lamp-black to each pint of it it will make a blacker and nicer finish. It makes a good color for cheap work, but for fine work, nothing will supercede the first colors given. This also makes a very good ink for *writing* purposes, if kept corked to avoid evaporation, which makes it gummy or sticky. See also "Grain Side Blacking."

4. SIZING FOR BOOTS AND SHOES, IN TREEING-OUT.—Take water 1 qt., and dissolve in it, by heat, isinglass 1 oz., adding more water to make up for evaporation; when dissolved, add starch 6 oz.; extract of logwood, bees-wax, and tallow, of each 2 oz.; and continue the heat until all is melted and well mixed. Rub the starch up first, by pouring on sufficient boiling water for that purpose.

(215)

It makes boots and shoes soft and pliable, applying it when treeing-out, and is especially nice to clean up work which has stood long on the shelves.

5. WATER-PROOF OIL-PASTE BLACKING.—Take camphene 1 pt., and put into it all the India-rubber it will dissolve; when dissolved, add currier's oil 1 pt.; tallow 6 lbs.; lamp-black 2 ozs. mix thoroughly by heat.

This is a nice thing for old harness or carriage tops, as well as for boots and shoes. Or you can dissolve the rubber in tne oil by setting them in rather a hot place for a day or two; and save the expense of camphene, as that is of no use only as a solvent to the rubber. There are those, however, who do not like to use the *rubber*, thinking it rots the leather; then use the following:

6. WATER-PROOF PASTE WITHOUT RUBBER.—Take tallow 1 lb.; bees-wax ¼ lb.; castor or neats-foot oil ¼ pt.; and lamp-black ¼ oz.; mix by heat. Or:

7. NEAT'S-FOOT OIL, brought to a proper consistene with a little bees-wax and tallow; colored with lamp-black, will be found proof against snow or water.

8. SOME, however, may prefer the following manner of preserving their boots and shoes, from a correspondent of the *Mechanics' Gazette ;* but if they do the boots must be made large, from the fact that the preparation has a tendency to shrink the leather. He says: " I have had only three pair of boots for the last six years, (no shoes) and I think I shall not require any more the next six years to come. The reason is, that I treat them in the following manner :

" I put 1 lb. of tallow and ½ pound of rosin in a pot on the fire; when melted and mixed, I warm the boots and apply the hot stuff with a painter's brush until neither the *sole nor the upper* will soak in any more. If it is desired that the boots should immediately take a polish, dissolve 1 oz. of wax in spirits of turpentine, to which add a tea-spoon of lamp-black A day after the boots have been treated with the tallow and rosin, rub over them this wax in turpentine, but not before the fire.

" Thus the exterior will have a coat of wax alone, and will shine like a mirror. Tallow or any other grease becomes rancid, and rots the stitching as well as the leather, but the rosin gives it that antiseptic quality which preserves the whole. Boots and shoes should be made so large as to admit of wearing cork soles.   Cork is so bad a conductor of heat, that with it in the boots, the feet are always warm on the coldest stone floor."

9. BLACK VARNISH FOR EDGE.—Take 98 per cent alcohol 1 pt.; shellac 3 ozs.; rosin 2 ozs.; pine turpentine 1 oz.; lamp-black ¼ oz.; mix, and when the gums are all cut, it is ready to use; but bear in mind that low proof alcohol will not cut gums properly, for any varnish.

This, applied to a boot or shoe edge, with a brush, gives it the shining gloss resembling much of the Eastern work. It is also applicable to wood or cloth requiring a gloss, after having been painted.

10. VARNISH FOR HARNESS, THE BEST IN USE.—Take 98 per cent alcohol 1 gal.; white pine turpentine 1¼ lbs.; gum shellac 1¼ lbs.; Venice turpentine 1 gill.   Let these stand in a jug in the sun or by a stove until the gums are dissolved, then add sweet oil 1 gill, and lamp-black 2 ozs., rub the lamp-black first with a little of the varnish.

This varnish is better than the old style, from the fact that it's polish is as good, and it does not crack when the harness is twisted or knocked about.

If you wish a varnish for *fair* leather, make it as the above, in a clean jug, but use no lamp-black.   The pine turpentine and sweet oil make it pliable, yet not sticky.

TANNING, BLACKING, AND FINISHING.—PROCESS FOR CALF, KIP, AND HARNESS, IN FROM SIX TO THIRTY DAYS.—For a 12 lb. calf skin, take terra-japonica 3 lbs.; common salt 2 lbs.; alum 1 lb.; put these into a copper kettle with sufficient water to dissolve the whole by boiling.

The skin, or skins, will first be limed, haired, and treated in every way as for the old process; then it will be put into a vessel with sufficient water to cover it, at which time you will put in one pint of the composition, stirring it well; adding the same amount each night and morning for three days, when you will add the whole; handling two or three times daily all the time tanning; you can continue to use the tanning liquid by adding half the quantity each time, of new liquor, and by keeping these proportions for any amount, and if you desire to give the leather the appearance of bark color, you will put in one pound of Sicily sumac.

Kip skins will require about twenty days, light horse hides for harness, thirty days, to make good leather, while calf skins will only require from six to ten days at most. The japonica is put up in large cakes of about one hundred and fifty pounds, and sells, in common times, at about four cents per pound, in New York

BYRON ROSE, a tanner, of Madison, O., says that one quart of oil of vitriol to fifty sides of leather, with the japonica and alum, as above, leaving out the salt, will very much improve it; the acid opens the pores, quickening the process without injury to the leather.

2. CANADIAN PROCESS.—The Canadians make four liquors in using the japonica:

The FIRST liquor is made by dissolving, for 20 sides of upper, 15 lbs. of terra japonica in sufficient water to cover the upper, being tanned. The SECOND liquor contains the same amount of japonica, and 8 lbs. of saltpetre also. The THIRD contains 20 lbs. of japonica, and 4½ lbs. of alum. The FOURTH liquor contains only 15 lbs. of japonica, and 1½ lbs. of sulphuric acid; and the leather remains 4 days in each liquor for upper; and for sole, the quantities and time are both doubled. They count 50 calf skins in place of 20 sides of upper, but let them lie in each liquor only 3 days.

3. DEER SKINS—TANNING AND BUFFING FOR GLOVES.—For each, skin, take a bucket of water, and put into it 1 qt. of lime; let the skin or skins lay in from 3 to 4 days; then rinse in clean water, hair, and grain; then soak them in cold water to get out the glue; now scour or pound in good soap suds, for half an hour; after which take white vitriol, alum, and salt, 1 tablespoon of each to a skin; these will be dissolved in sufficient water to cover the skin and remain in it for 24 hours; wring out as dry as convenient; and spread on with a brush ½ pt. of currier's oil, and hang in the sun about 2 days; after which you will scour out the oil with soap suds, and hang out again until perfectly dry; then pull and work them until they are soft; and if a reasonable time does not make them soft, scour out in suds again as before, until complete. The oil may be saved by pouring or taking it from the top of the suds, if left standing a short time. The buff color is given by spreading yellow ochre evenly over the surface of the skin, when finished, rubbing it in well with a brush.

The foregoing plan was pursued for a number of years by a brother of mine, and I have worn the gloves and know the value of the recipe; but there are plans of using acid, and if the quantity is not too great, there is no reason in the world why it may not be used; the only caution necessary is to see that the strength of acid does not kill the nature of

the leather; in proper quantities it *tans* only, instead of destroying the fiber. I will give a couple of the most valuable
methods.

4 TANNING WITH ACID.—After having removed the hair,
scouring, soaking, and pounding in the suds, &c., as in the last
recipe, in place of the white vitriol, alum, and salt, as there
mentioned, take oil of vitriol, (sulphuric acid) and water, equal
parts of each, and thoroughly wet the flesh-side of the skin
with it, by means of a sponge or cloth upon a stick; then
foldi g up the skin, letting it lie for 20 minutes only, having
cadyn a solution of sal-soda and water, say one lb. to a bucke
of water, and soak the skin or skins in that for 2 hours, whet
you will wash in clean water and apply a little dry salt, lettinn
lie in the salt over night, or that length of time; then removg
the flesh with a blunt knife, or, if doing business on a large
scale, by means of the regular beam and flesh-knife; when drye
or nearly so, soften by pulling and rubbing with the hands,
and also with a piece of pumice-stone. This, of course, is the
quickest way of tanning, and by only wetting the skins with,
the acid and soaking out in twenty minutes, they are noe
rotted

5. ANOTHER METHOD.—Oil of vitriol $\frac{1}{4}$ oz.; salt 1 teacupof
milk sufficient to handsomely cover the skin, not exceeding 3
qts.; warm the milk, then add the salt and vitriol; stir the
skin in the liquid 40 minutes, keeping it warm; then dry and-
work it as directed in No. 4.

6 TANNING SHEEP-SKINS, APPLICABLE FOR MITTENS
DOOR-MATS, ROBES, &c.—For mats, take two long-wooled
skins, make a strong suds, using hot water; when it is cold
wash the skins in it, carefully squeezing them between the
hands to get the dirt out of the wool; then wash the soap.
out with clean cold water. Now dissolve alum and salt, of
each half a pound, with a little hot water, which put into a
tub of cold water sufficient to cover the skins, and let them
soak in it over night, or twelve hours, then hang over a pole
to drain. When they are well drained, spread or stretch
carefully on a board to dry. They need not be tacked if
you will draw them out, several times with the hand, while
drying. When yet a little damp, have one ounce, each,
of saltpetre and alum, pulverized, and sprinkle on the flesh-
side of each skin, rubbing in well; then lay the flesh-sides
together and hang in the shade for two or three days, turn
ing the under skin uppermost every day, until perfectly dry
Then scrape the flesh-side with a blunt knife, to remove any
remaining scraps of flesh, trim off projecting points, and rub

the flesh-side with pumice or rotten stone, and with the hands; they will be very white and beautiful, suitable for a foot-mat, also nice in a sleigh or wagon of a cold day. They also make good robes, in place of the buffalo, if colored, and sewed together. And lamb-skins, (or sheep-skins, if the wool is trimmed off evenly to about one-half or three fourths of an inch in length) make most beautiful and warm mittens for ladies, or gentlemen.

7. TANNING FUR AND OTHER SKINS—FIFTY DOLLAR RECIPE.—FIRST,—Remove the legs and other useless parts, and soak the skin soft; then remove the fleshy substances and soak in warm water for an hour; now:

Take for each skin, borax, saltpetre, and glauber-salts, of each ¼ oz., and dissolve or wet with soft water sufficient to allow it to be spread on the flesh-side of the skin.

Put it on with a brush, thickest in the centre or thickest part of the skin, and double the skin together, flesh-side in, keeping it in a *cool* place for twenty-four hours, not allow ing it to freeze, however.

SECOND,—Wash the skin clean, and then :
Take sal-soda 1 oz.; borax ¼ oz.; refined soap 2 ozs.; (Col gate's white soap is recommended as the best, but our "White Hard Soap" is the same quality,); melt them slowly together, being careful not to allow them to boil, and apply the mixture to the flesh-side as at first—roll up again and keep in a *warm* place for 24 hours.

THIRD.—Wash the skin clean, as above, and have salera-tus two ounces, dissolved in hot rain water sufficient to well saturate the skin, then :

Take alum 4 ozs.; salt 8 ozs.; and dissolve also in hot rain water; when sufficiently cool to allow the handling of it without scalding, put in the skin for 12 hours; then wring out the water and hang up, for 12 hours more, to dry. Repeat this last soaking and drying from 2 to 4 times, according to the desired softness of the skin when finished.

LASTLY,—Finish by pulling, working, &c., and finally by rubbing with a piece of pumice-stone and fine sand-paper.

This works admirably on sheep-skins as well as on fur-skins, dog, cat, or wolf-skins also, making a durable leather well adapted to washing.

A man in our county paid fiifty dollars for this recipe, and oas made his money out of it many times. It is very valuable.

8. TANNING DEER AND WOODCHUCK-SKINS FOR WHIPS, STRINGS, &c.—Prepare the skin according to the last recipe, then:

Take oil of vitriol 1 oz.; salt 1 pt.; milk 3 qts.; mix.

Now dip the skin in warm rain water having sufficient saleratus in it to make it rather strong, or as in the THIRD head of last recipe, and work and squeeze it well for a few minutes, then wring dry as convenient and put it into the vitriol mixture for fifty minutes, stirring all the time; now wring out and soak awhile; and finally dry and work until soft.

9. GRAIN-SIDE BLACKING, FOR TEN CENTS A BARREL.—Take a barrel and put into it quite a quantity of old iron, cast or wrought, then fill nearly full of soft water, and add 1 pt. of oil of vitrol; stir it up well, and in a month or two you have just as good blacking for the grain-side, as could be made by using vinegar in place of water.

This makes good blacking for boot, shoe, or harness edge, also. The acid used is so trifling that no injury will arise to the leather.

Tanners will, of course, first apply the urine before applying the blacking, saving from ten to twenty dollars yearly, in this way, instead of the old plan of using vinegar.

10. FRENCH FINISH, FOR LEATHER.—Take a common wooden pail of scraps, (the legs and pates of calf-skins are the best) and put a handful each, of salt and pulverized alum amongst them and let them stand three days; then boil them until you get a thick paste; in using you will warm it; in the first application, put a little tallow with it, and for the second, a little soft soap, and use it in the regular way of finishing, and your leather will be soft and pliable, like the French calf-skin.

I have no doubt that this would make a good preparation for shoemakers to use in treeing-out, leaving a soft pliableness, not otherwise obtained.

11. FRENCH PATENT LEATHER.—The process which has been so successfully adopted by the French artisans in glazing leather, so as to give it the repute for superior quality and beauty which it now universally sustains, is as follows:

Work into the skin with appropriate tools three or four suc cessive coatings of drying varnish, made by boiling linseed-oil with white-lead and litharge, in the proportion of one pound of each of the latter to a gallon of the former, and adding a por- tion of chalk or ochre—each coating being thoroughly dried be- fore the application of the next. Ivory black is then substituted for the chalk or ochre, the varnish thinned with spirits of tur- pentine, and five additional applications made in the same man- ner as before, except that it is put on thin and not worked in. The leather is rubbed down with pumice-stone, in powder, and then placed in a room at 90 degs., out of the way of dust. The last varnish is prepared by boiling ¼ lb. of asphaltum with 10 lbs. of the drying oil used in the first step of the process, and then stirring in 5 lbs. of copal varnish and 10 lbs. of turpentine.

It must have a month's age before it is fit for use, in order to exhibit its true characteristics.—*U. S. Gazette.*

PAINTER'S DEPARTMENT.

DRYING OILS—To Prepare for Carriage, Wagon, and Floor Painting.—Take linseed oil 1 gal., and add gum shellac 2 lbs.; litharge ¼ lb.; red-lead ¼ lb.; umber 1 oz. Boil slowly, 2 or 3 hours, until the gums are dissolved.

Grind your paints in this (any color) and reduce with turpentine. Yellow ochre is used for floor painting. This dries quick and wears exceedingly well.

2. Drying Oil, Equal to the Patent Dryers.—Linseed-oil 2 gals., and add litharge, red-lead, and umber, of each 4 ozs., and sugar of lead and sulphate of zinc, of each 2 ozs.

Boil until it will scorch a feather. Use this, or either of the others, in quantity to suit the object of the work being done.

3. Japan Dryer of the Best Quality.—Take linseed-oil 1 gal., and put into it gum shellac ¼ lb.; litharge and burned Tur- key umber, of each ¼ lb.; red-lead ¼ lb., and sugar of lead 6 ozs. Boil in the oil until all are dissolved, which will require about 4 hours; remove from the fire, and add spirits of turpentine 1 gal., and it is done.

While in Princeton, Ind., after selling one of my books to T. & J. T. Ewing, extensive carriage manufacturers of that place, I obtained the foregoing recipe. It was published in a work printed in Columbus, O., devoted to the art of painting, From this fact, and also that the gentlemen from whom I obtained it, had tested it and were using it, I have not myself tried it, but know, from the nature of the articles used, that nothing better will be required.

4. ANOTHER.—Another dryer is made by taking linseed oil 5 gals., and adding red-lead and litharge, of each 3½ lbs.; raw umber 1¼ lbs.; sugar of lead and sulphate of zinc, of each ¼ lb.; pulverize all the articles together, and boil in the oil until dissolved; when a little cool, add turpentine, 5 gals., or to make it of a proper consistence.

The gentleman of whom I obtained this recipe paid ten dollars for it. He was using it successfully, and said he used two or three drops of it to a quart of varnish also, and especially when the varnish did not dry readily.

OIL—PAINT—To REDUCE WITH WATER.—Take gum shel lac 1 lb.; sal-soda ½ lb.; water 3 pts.; put all into a suitable kettle and boil, stirring till all is dissolved. If it does not all dissolve, add a little more sal-soda; this, when cool, can be bottled for use. If it smells bad when opened it does not hurt it.

DIRECTIONS FOR USING.—Mix up two quarts of oil paint as usual, except no turpentine is to be used—any color desired. Now put one pint of the gum shellac mixture with the oil paint when it becomes thick, and may be reduced with water to a proper consistence to lay on with a brush. Two coats will be required, and with the second coat sand may be applied if desired. I used this upon a picket-fence with white-lead and yellow ochre for the body and a little lamp-black to give it a dark shade, putting on sand with the second coat. It is still firm and good, the work being done nearly four years ago.

The sand was applied with a tub-like box, with many small holes to allow the even spreading of the sand, as with a pepper-box. I do not regret using this kind of paint, nor the sanding, as it adds much to the durability of any outdoor painting. But a better plan of sanding is represented in the "Painter's Sanding Apparatus" below.

2 ANOTHER METHOD.—Take soft water 1 gal., and dissolve in it, pearlash 3 ozs.; bring to a boil, and slowly add shellac 1 lb.; when cold it is ready to be added to oil-paint, in equal proportions. The expense of these is only one-third of oil-paint.

Some persons may think it bad policy to learn painters to reduce oil-paint with water, but I think every man should be told of the plan, who is going to have a job of work done, and if he makes up his mind to try any thing of the kind, it is then his own business; and I am perfectly sincere in recommending it, for if there was any great fault in it four years would show it.

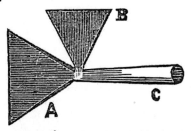

PAINTER'S SANDING APPARATUS.

3. It is made of tin; the tube C, enters upon the nozzle of a small bellows; the sand is put into the funnel B, which stands perpendicular upon the apparatus when the broad mouth-piece A, is held level in using. The funnel discharges the sand, just before the nozzle of the bellows; and by working the bellows the sand is blown evenly upon the freshly put on paint, through the mouth-piece A, the escape orifice not being over the sixteenth part of an inch in depth, and may be made two and a half or three inches wide.

Many persons like the plan of sanding generally, after painting; but from the fact that when it is desired to renew the paint, brushes cannot last long upon the sand, I think it only proper to sand fences or fronts, where boys' *knives* would be too freely used.

PAINT SKINS—To Save and Reduce to Oil.—Dissolve sal-soda ¼ lb., in rain-water 1 gal.

The skins that dry upon the top of paint, which has been left standing for any length of time, may be made fit for use again by covering them with the sal-soda-water and soaking them therein for a couple of days; then heat them, adding oil to reduce the mixture to a proper consistence for painting, and straining. Painters who are doing extensive business will save many dollars yearly by this simple process.

NEW TIN ROOFS—VALUABLE PROCESS FOR PAINT-ING.—Scrape off the rosin as clean as possible and sweep the roof; now:

Dissolve sufficient sal-soda in a bucket of water to make it quite strong; wash the roof thoroughly with the soda-water and let it remain until it is washed off by the rains, or after a few hours, washing off with clean water, rinsing well.

When dry give it one coat of pure Venetian-red, mixed with one-third boiled, and two-thirds raw linseed-oil; the second coat may be any color desired. The soda-water dissolves the rosin remaining after scraping; destroys the greasy nature of the solder, and of the new tin, so that there will be sufficient "Grip" for the paint to adhere firmly. The pure Venetian-red is one of the most durable paints for metallic-roofs, but is often rejected on account of its color. The above mode of painting will set aside this difficulty.

2. FIRE-PROOF PAINT—FOR ROOFS, &c.—Slack stone-lime by putting it into a tub, to be covered, to keep in the steam. When slacked, pass the powder through a fine sieve; and to each 6 qts. of it add, 1 qt. of rock-salt, and water 1 gal.; then boil and skim clean. To each 5 gals. of this add, pulverized alum 1 lb. pulverized copperas ¼ lb.; and still slowly add powdered potash ¼ lb.; then fine sand or hickory ashes 4 lbs.

Now add any desired color, and apply with a brush—looks better than paint, and is as durable as slate. It stops small leaks in roofs, prevents moss, and makes it incombustible · and renders brick impervious to wet.—*Maine Farmer*.

3. WATER-PROOF, OIL-RUBBER PAINT.—Dissolve about 5 lbs. of India rubber in 1 gal. of boiled linseed-oil, by boiling. If this is too thick, reduce with boiled-oil; if too thin, use more rubber.

Especially applicable to cloth, but valuable for any other material.

FROSTING GLASS.—The frosty appearance of glass, which we often see, where it is desired to keep out the sun, or " Man's observing eye," is done by using a paint composed as follows :

Sugar of lead well ground in oil, applied as other paint; then pounced, while fresh, with a wad of batting held between the thumb and finger.

After which it is allowed to partially dry; then with a straight-edge laid upon the sash, you run along by the side of it, a stick sharpened to the width of line you wish to appear in the diamonds, figures, or squares, into which you choose to lay it off; most frequently, however, straight lines are made an inch or more from the sash, according to the size of light, then the centre of the light made into diamonds.

ORIENTAL—CRYSTAL PAINTING.—The colors used are Prussian-blue, crimson, white, and yellow-lakes, Rosseau, white-zinc, and No. 40 carmine. Druggists keep them, in small tubes. They must be mixed with Demar-varnish, rubbing with a table-knife or spatula upon glass.

DIRECTIONS FOR MAKING VARIOUS SHADES, OR COMPOUND COLORS.—Proportion them about as follows—for green 1-5 blue, 4-5 yellow—purple, 1-6 blue, 5-6 crimson—orange, ¼ crimson, ¾ yellow—wine-color, 1-12 blue, 11-12 crimson—pink, add a little crimson to white-zinc—brown, mix a dark purple and add yellow according to the shade desired—black, add crimson to dark green until the shade suits you—to make the compound colors lighter, add the lightest color in it, and make darker by using more of the darkest color in the compound. For backgrounds—white, white-zinc, or pink white with turpentine and boiled inseed-oil and Demar-varnish—black, lamp-black, with asphaltum-varnish and boiled linseed-oil and turpentine in equal quantities—flesh-color, white-zinc with a small portion of crimson and chrome-yellow to suit. For sketching out the figures on the ground-work, use a little lamp-black with asphaltum-varnish, turpentine and boiled linseed-oil to make it flow freely.

DIRECTIONS FOR PAINTING.—Make your glass perfectly clean, and place it over the picture you wish to copy; then with the sketching preparation, trace on the glass all the lines connected with the figures of the picture which you are copying, being careful to sketch vines very distinct; when the sketching is done and dry, proceed to lay on the background inside of the sketched lines until all the sketching is closed; and when the background is dry, proceed to put on the colors, commencing with green, if any in the figures, ending with yellow. When the colors are all laid, put the background upon the balance of the glass; and when all is dry have tin foil crumpled very much in your hand, and then partly straightened out, and lay it over the figure and keep it in its place by pasting paper over it in such a manner that it cannot slip away, letting the paper cover the whole back of the glass, or a wood-back can be

placed behind the glass, and all is complete, and will look
well or ill, according to the practice and taste of the painter.

2. FANCY GREEN.—Unscorched, pulverized coffee, put
into the white of an egg will, in twenty-four hours, produce
a very beautiful green for fancy painting—proof of poison,
in unbrowned coffee.

SKETCHING PAPER—To PREPARE.—Bleached linseed-oil,
turpentine and baisam of fir, equal parts of each; mix.

Have a frame of a little less size than the paper to be
prepared, and apply paste or thick gum solution to one side
and the outer edge of it; wet the paper in clean water and
lay it upon the frame and press it down upon the pasted
side of the frame, and turn the outer part of the paper over
the outside of the frame upon the paste there, which holds
it firm; and when it becomes dry it is tight like a drum-
head; whilst in this condition, with a brush saturate it with
the above mixture; three or four coats will be needed, giving each one time to dry before applying the next. Only
sufficient is needed to make it transparent, so that when you
wish to sketch a rose, or other flower or leaf, from nature,
the paper can be placed upon it like the glass in the "Oriental Painting"; then trace the lines and finish it up in the
same way also, as there described; or that you may see
through it in taking perspective views of distant scenery.

DOOR PLATES—To MAKE.—Cut your glass the right size,
and make it perfectly clean with alcohol or soap; then cut a
strip of tin-foil sufficiently long and wide for the name, and with
a piece of ivory or other burnisher rub it lengthwise to make it
smooth; now wet the glass with the tongue, (as saliva is the best
sticking substance,) or if the glass is very large, use a weak solution of gum arabic, or the white of an egg in half a pint of
water and lay on the foil, rubbing it down to the glass with a bit
of cloth, then also with the burnisher; the more it is burnished
the better will it look; now mark the width on the foil which is
to be the hight of the letter, and put on a straight-edge and hold
it firmly to the foil, and with a sharp knife cut the foil and take
off the superfluous edges; then either lay out the letters on the
back of the foil, (so they shall read correctly on the front) by
your own judgment or by means of pattern-letters, which can be
purchased for that purpose; cut with the knife, carefully holding down the pattern or straight-edge, whichever you use; then
rub down the edge of all the letters with the back of the knife,
or edge of the burnisher, which prevents the black paint or
japan which you next put over the back of the plate, from get-

ting unde: the foil; having put a line above and one below the
name, or a border around the whole plate or not, as you oargain
for the job. The japan is made by dissolving asphaltum in just
enough turpentine to cut it (see "Asphaltum Varnish"); apply
with a brush as other paint over the back of the letters and over
the glass, forming a background. This is used on the iron frame
of the plate also, putting it on when the plate is a little hot, and
as soon as it cools it is dry. A little lamp-black may be rubbed
into it if you desire it any blacker than it is without it.

If you choose, you can remove every other foil letter,
after the japan is dry, and paint in its place, red, blue, or
other colored letters, to make a greater variety out of which
for your customers to choose, as the one they desire you to
follow in getting up their plate. Tin foil being thicker
than silver or gold foil, will not show the paint through it
in little spots as they do; but if these foils are desired to
be used, you can put on two thicknesses by proceeding as
follows, which prevents the paint from showing through
them : Lay on the first coat of these foils the same as directed for the tin-foil, and smooth it down by rubbing on
the front of the glass; then breathe on it until a dampness
is caused ; now put on the second and burnish well, having
paper over it ; but instead of the knife to cut around your
pattern or straight-edge, take a sharp needle, using the point,
make lines through the leaf around the pattern letter or
straight-edge ; then with a bit of Jewelers' wood, or other
hard wood, made to a narrow and sharp point, remove all
up to the lines, both in and around the letters, as these
foils have not the substance to peel off as the tin-foil, japan-
ning over them the same as the other letters. Paper letters
can be cut out of advertisements and put on by wetting the
glass the same as for the foil, jappanning over them, and
when dry, removing them and painting the places out of
which they came with various colors as desired, as the japan
will not peel, but makes a sharp and distinct edge ; and
these painted letters look well, in this way ; and by taking
advantage of printed letters, saves the skill and time necessary to form them.

To illustrate ; in the name given below, A may be gold
foil ; W will be blue; C, red ; H, black ; A, gold-foil ; S,
blue ; E, red ; M, black ; and again D, gold-foil, which any
one can see makes a more showy plate than if all were of
one foil, or one color.

Set your glass in the frame with putty and put a thin coat of putty over the whole plate, as the plaster of Paris filling which is generally used soon eats out the japan or paint, and spoils the job. Persons with any ingenuity can very soon make a nice plate if they will pay attention to the above rules, as well as to pay five dollars for instructions, as a little practice must be had to become perfect, even if you do pay five dollars for an hour or two's telling and showing. Shellac varnish colored with lamp-black is good in place of the japan. See "Varnish—Transparent, for Wood."

ETCHING AND GRINDING UPON GLASS—For Signs, or Side Lights.—Take the "Asphaltum Varnish," and with a small pencil lay out the name or design, not putting the varnish upon the letters, but around it, leaving the space which the letters of the sign are to occupy, free and clear, as seen in the following door plate, represented in the wood cut, and by the way, a very nice style of letter for that purpose also, we think:

The varnish is to cover the black surface in the sign or name. The white line around the outside represents a border which improves the appearance of the plate; when the varnish is dry have some melted bees-wax and as it begins to cool, with a knife take some of it up and scrape it off upon the edge of the glass, being etched, so as to form a wall to hold the acid upon the glass while etching; now lay the glass flat and pour a little fluoric acid on to the name, letter, or design thus prepared, and let it remain on for one hour, not allowing the glass to be touched or moved for that time; then pour off the acid into your bottle, and it can be used again. The asphalt prevents the acid from eating or etching only the letter, and the wax wall prevents the acid from flowing off and being wasted. When you pour off the acid wash the glass with a little water, scrape off the wax, and remove the asphalt with a little turpentine, and all is done.

The above directions are for plain glass; but if you desire, you can gild the letter which is etched (eat out,) or you can gild all except the letter, if desired, as described in the recipe for "Door Plates," or you can grind the surface of the glass as described under the head of "Glass-grinding for Signs, Shades," &c. This applies equally well to "flashed," or what is called "stained glass," worked in the same way as above, putting the design or letters upon the stained side, which eats away the color and leaves the design clean and white ; or you can etch only a part of the way through the stain, which shows up the letter or flower lighter in color than the rest of the glass, which makes it look very beautiful for side-lights in halls, lamps, druggists' windows, &c.

There are two kinds of colored glass—one is called "Pot metal," the other "Flashed." The pot-metal glass is made by mixing the stain or coloring with the melted glass, while making, and consequently is alike all the way through.— The stained glass is made by applying the color to one side of the glass after it is made, then applying sufficient heat to allow it to take hold of the glass only—the color is all on one side ; this is the kind desired.

If it is desired to etch upon druggists' or other jars, it can be done by preparing the name to be put on, with the varnish and wax ; then have a lead box without top or bottom ; in shape on the lower edge to fit the shape of the jar, and press this down upon the wax to make it tight; then pour your acid into the box which keeps it in its place the same as the wax does on a flat surface. Ornaments or flourishes can be put on as well as letters.

The old plan was to cover the whole surface with wax, then remove it from the letter, which was very slow and troublesome, and if a bit of wax remained upon the bottle, the acid could not cut where the wax remained, then to hold the glass over the fumes of the acid, instead of putting the acid upon the glass.

2. GLASS-GRINDING FOR SINGS, SHADES, &c.—After you have etched a name or other design upon uncolored glass, and wish to have it show off to a better advantage by permitting the light to pass only through the letters, you can do so by :

Taking a piece of flat brass sufficiently large not to dip into the letters, but pass over them when gliding upon the surface of the glass ; then with flour of emery, and keeping it wet, you can grind the whole surface, very quickly, to look like the ground glass globes, often seen upon lamps, except the letter which is eaten below the general surface.

Whole fights of glass can be ground in this way instead of frosting, or the frosting can be done here in place of the grinding, if preferred.

3. FLUORIC ACID, TO MAKE FOR ETCHING PURPOSES.—You can make your own fluoric (sometimes called hydro-fluoric) acid, by getting the fluor or Derbyshire spar, pulverizing it and putting all of it into sulphuric acid which the acid will cut or dissolve.

Druggists through the country do not keep this acid generally, but they can get it in the principal cities and furnish it for about seventy-five cents per ounce, and that ounce will do at least fifty dollars worth of work. It is put up in gutta percha-bottles, or lead-bottles, and must be kept in them when not in use, having corks of the same material. Glass, of course, will not hold it, as it dissolves the glass, otherwise it would not etch upon it.

PORCELAIN FINISH—VERY HARD AND WHITE, FOR PARLORS.—To prepare the wood for the finish, if it be pine, give one or two coats of the "Varnish--Transparent for Wood," which prevents the pitch from oozing out causing the finish to turn yellow; next, give the room, at least, four coats of pure zinc, which may be ground in only sufficient oil to enable it to grind properly, then mix to a proper consistence with turpentine or naptha. Give each coat time to dry. When it is dry and hard, sandpaper it to a perfectly smooth surface when it is ready to receive the finish, which consists of two coats of French zinc ground in, and thinned with Demar-varnish, until it works properly under the brush.

Mr. Miles, of this city, one of our scientific painters, has been sufficiently kind to furnish me this recipe prepared expressly for this work, therefore, the most implicit confidence may be placed in it, yet any one can judge for themselves, from the nature of the articles used, that it must be white and hard. He goes on to say that if the French-zinc in varnish cannot be procured, the varnish may be whitened with zinc ground in oil as a very good substitute, being careful not to use too much, in which case it will diminish the gloss, and be more liable to turn yellow. A little turpentine or naptha may be added, if too thick to work well, but in no instance should oil be used to thin the paint.

This finish, if properly applied, is very beautiful, and although purely white, may be kept clean more easily than other kinds of painting by simply using a dusting brush; or if soiled, a sponge wet in cold soft water without soap, is the better way.

N. B.—Not a particle of white-lead should be used where this finish is to be applied, either in the priming, or any subsequent coats, or a brush used that has been in lead without being thoroughly cleansed, as a yellow hue will soon present itself, which is caused by a chemical change taking place between the lead and zinc

PAINTERS' ECONOMY IN MAKING COLORS.—PRUSSIAN BLUE.—1st. Take nitric acid, any quantity, and as much iron shavings from the lathe as the acid will dissolve; heat the iron as hot as can be handled with the hand ; then add it to the acid in small quantities as long as the acid will dissolve it, then slowly add double the quantity of soft water that there was of acid, and put in iron again as long as the acid will dissolve it 2nd. Take Prussiate of potash, dissolve it in hot water to make a strong solution, and make sufficient of it with the first to give the depth of tint desired, and the blue is made.   Or :

2. ANOTHER METHOD.—A very passable Prussian-blue is made by taking sulphate of iron (copperas) and Prussiate of potash, equal parts of each, and dissolving each separately in water, then mixing the two waters.

3. CHROME YELLOW.—1st.   Take sugar of lead and Paris-white, of each 5 lbs.; dissolve them in hot water.   2nd.   Take bi-chromate of potash 6½ ozs., and dissolve it in hot water also, each article to be dissolved separately, then mix all together, putting in the bi-chromate last.   Let stand 24 hours.

4. CHROME GREEN.—Take Paris-white 6½ lbs.; sugar of lead, and blue vitriol, of each 3½ lbs.; alum 10½ ozs.; best soft Prussian blue and chrome yellow, of each 3¼ lbs.   Mix thoroughly while in fine powder, and add water 1 gal., stirring well and let stand 3 or 4 hours.

5. GREEN, DURABLE AND CHEAP.—Take spruce yellow and color it with a solution of chrome yellow and Prussian-blue, until you give it the shade you wish.

6. PARIS GREEN.—Take unslacked lime of the best quality, slack it with hot water ; then take the finest part of the powder and add alum water, as strong as can be made, sufficient to form a thick paste, then color it with bi-chromate of potash and sulphate of copper, until the color suits your fancy.   N. B.—The sulphate of copper gives the color a blue tinge—the bi-chromate of potash a yellow.   Observe this and you will never fail.

7. ANOTHER METHOD.—Blue vitriol 5 lbs.; sugar of lead 6¼ lbs.; arsenic 2½ lbs.; bi-chromate of potash 1⅓ ozs.; mix them thoroughly in fine powder, and add water 8 pts., mixing well again and let stand 3 or 4 hours.

8. PEA BROWN.—1st. Take sulphate of copper, any quantity and dissolve it in hot water. 2nd. Take prussiate of potash, dissolve it in hot water to make a strong solution; mix of the two solutions, as in the blue, and the color is made.

9. ROSE PINK.—Brazil wood 1 lb., and boil it for 2 hours, having 1 gal. of water at the end; then strain it and boil alum 1 lb. in the same water until dissolved; when sufficiently cool to admit the hand, add muriate of tin ¼ oz. Now have Paris-white 12½ lbs., moisten up to a salvy consistence, and when the first is cool stir them thoroughly together. Let stand 24 hours.

When any of the above mixtures have stood as mentioned, in their respective recipes, all that is necessary is to drain off the water by placing the preparations into muslin bags for that purpose, and then exposing the mixture to the air, to dry for use.

Glass, stone, or wood vessels only should be used, as the acids soon work upon iron, tin, copper, &c., giving you a tinge not desired in the color, and always observe that if water is to be mixed with strong acids, it must be added slowly, especially if in light vials, or you will break the vessel by means of the great heat which is set free by the combination Painters can use their own judgment about making these colors; but if they do not do it for profit there will be pleasure in testing them, even in vials-full only, as the chemical action is just as fine in small as in large quantities.

BLACKSMITHS' DEPARTMENT.

FILES AND RASPS—TO RE-CUT BY A CHEMICAL PROCESS. Dissolve saleratus 4 ozs., to water 1 qt., sufficient to cover the files, and boil them in it for half an hour; then take out, wash and dry them; now stand them in a jar, filling it up with rain-water and sulphuric acid, in the proportion of water 1 qt., to acid 4 ozs.

If the files are coarse, they will need to remain in about twelve hours; but for fine files, six to eight hours will be all-sufficient. When you take them out, wash them clean, dry quickly, and put a little sweet oil upon them, to prevent rust.

This plan is applicable to blacksmiths, gun-smiths, tinners, copper-smiths, machinists, &c., &c. Copper and tin workers will only require a short time to take the articlea out of their files, as the soft metals with which they become filled, are soon dissolved, leaving the files about as good as new. For blacksmiths and saw-mill men, it will require the full time.

They may be re-cut two or three times, making in all more service than it took to wear out the file at first.

The preparation can be kept and used as long as you see action take place upon putting the files into it. Keep it covered when not in use.

If persons, when filing, would lift up the file, in carrying back, there would be no necessity of a re-cutting, but in *drawing* it back they soon turn a wire-edge, which the acid removes. It also thins the tooth. Many persons have doubted this fact; but I know that the common three-square file, (used for sharpening saws,) when worn out and thrown by, for a year or two, may be again used with nearly the same advantage as a new one. The philosophy of it is this —the action of the atmosphere acts upon the same principle of the acid, corrodes (eats off) the surface, giving a-new, a square, cutting edge. Try it, all ye doubtful; I have tried both, and know their value. Boiling in the saleratus-water removes grease, and allows the acid to act upon the steel.

VARNISHES—To Prevent Rust on Iron or Steel.—Tallow 2 ozs.; rosin 1 oz.; melt and strain while hot.

Apply a light coat of this, and you can lay away any artı cles not in constant use, for any length of time, such as knives and forks, or mechanics' tools which are being laid by, or much exposed. But for axes or other new tools, which are exposed to the air before sold, you will find the following varnish preferable :

2. Transparent, for Tools, Plows, &c.—Best alcohol 1 gal.; gum sandarach 2 lbs.; gum mastic ¼ lb. Place all in a tin can which admits of being corked; cork it tight, and shake it frequently, occasionally placing the can in hot water. When dissolved, it is ready to use.

This makes a very nice varnish for new tools which are exposed to dampness ; the air, even, will soon (more or less) tarnish new work.

3. Seek-No-Farther, for Iron or Steel.—Take best or pal

varnish, and add sufficient olive oil to make it feel a little greasy; then add nearly as much spirits of turpentine as there is of varnish, and you will probably *seek no farther.*

4. TRANSPARENT BLUE, FOR STEEL PLOWS.—Take Demar varnish ½ gal.; finely ground Prussian-blue ¼ oz; mix thoroughly.

For ground steel-plows, or other ground steel, one or two coats of this will be found sufficient to give a nice blue appearance, like highly-tempered steel; some may wish a little more blue; if so, add the Prussian-blue to your liking. Copal varnish is not so transparent as the Demar, but if you will have a *cheap* varnish, use No. 4.

6. BLACK, HAVING A POLISH, FOR IRON—Pulverized gum asphaltum 2 lbs.; gum benzoin ¼ lb.; spirits of turpentine 1 gal. 𝑜 make quick, keep in a warm place and shake often; shade to suit with finely ground ivory black.

Apply with a brush. And it ought to be used on iron exposed to the weather as well as on inside work desiring a nice appearance or polish. Or:

7. VARNISH FOR IRON.—Asphaltum 8 lbs.; melt it in an iron kettle, slowly adding boiled linseed-oil 5 gals.; litharge 1 lb.; and sulphate of zinc ¼ lb.; continuing to boil for 3 hours; then add dark gum amber 1¼ lbs., and continue to boil 2 hours longer When cool reduce to a proper consistence, to apply with a brush, with spirits of turpentine.

8. I WISH here, also, to state a fact which will benefit those wishing to secure vines or limbs of trees to the side of a white house, with nails, and do not wish to see a streak of rust down the white paint, as follows:

Make a hole, in which to start the nail, putting a little strip of zinc into the hole, and drive the nail in contact with the zinc.

The electrical action of the two metals, in contact, prevent rust, proven by over eight years trial.

WELDING—CAST STEEL WITHOUT BORAX.—Copperas 2 ozs.; saltpetre 1 oz.; common salt 6 ozs.; black oxyde of manganese 1 oz.; Prussiate of potash 1 oz.; all pulverized and mixed with nice welding sand 3 lbs., and use it the same as you would sand.

Higher tempered steel can be used with this better than with borax, as it welds at a lower heat—such as pitchfork tines, toe-corks, &c. The pieces should be held together while heating. I have found some blacksmiths using it without the manganese; but from what I know of the purifying properties of that article upon iron, I am sure it must be preferable with it, as that is the principal purifyer in the next recipe.

POOR IRON,—To IMPROVE.—Black oxide of manganese 1 part; copperas and common salt 4 parts each; dissolve in soft water and boil until dry; when cool pulverize and mix quite freely with nice welding sand.

When you have poor iron which you cannot afford to throw away, heat it and roll it in this mixture, working for a time, re-heating, &c., will soon free it from all impurities, which is the cause of its rottenness. By this process you can make good horse-nails, even out of only common iron.

WRITING UPON IRON OR STEEL, SILVER OR GOLD, NOT TO COST THE TENTH PART OF A CENT PER LETTER.—Muriatic acid 1 oz.; nitric acid ½ oz. Mix, when it is ready for use.

DIRECTIONS—Cover the place you wish to mark, or write upon, with melted bees-wax; when cold, write the name plain with a file point or an instrument made for the purpose, carrying it through the wax and cleaning the wax all out of the letter; then apply the mixed acids with a feather, carefully filling each letter; let it remain from one to ten minutes, according to the appearance desired; then put on some water, which dilutes the acids and stops the process. Either of the acids, alone, would cut iron or steel, but it requires the mixture to take hold of gold or silver. After you wash off the acids it is best to apply a little oil

MILL-PICKS,—To TEMPER.—To 6 qts. of soft water, put in pulverized corrosive sublimate 1 oz., and 2 hands of common salt; when dissolved it is ready for use. The first gives toughness to the steel, whilst the latter gives the hardness. I have found those who think it better to add sal-ammoniac, pulverized, 2 ozs., to the above.

DIRECTIONNS.—Heat the picks to only a cherry red and plunge them in and do not draw any temper. In working mill-picks, be very careful not to over-heat them, but work them at as low a heat as possible. The reason why so many fail in making good picks, is that they don't work them at as low heat as they should. With care upon that point, and the above fluid, no trouble will be experienced, even on the best diamond burrs. Be sure to keep the preparation covered when not in use, as it is poison. Pigs or dogs might drink of it, if left uncovered. This is the mixture which has gained me the name of having the best preparation in use for mill-picks, and the certificates on this subject, but as I have some others which are very highly spoken of, I give you a few others.

2. AN English Miller, after buying my book, gave me the following recipe, for which he paid ten dollars. He had used it all his life, or from the time he began business for himself, (about thirty years,) and he would use no other.

Salt ¼ tea-cup; saltpetre ½ oz.; alum, pulverized, 1 tea-spoon; soft water 1 gal.; never heating over a cherry red, nor drawing any temper.

3. SALT PETRE, sal-ammoniac, and alum, of each 2 ozs.; salt 1¼ lbs.; water 3 gals.; and draw no temper.

There must be something in this last, as the next one I obtained at least five hundred miles from where I did this, and both from men who knew their value, and yet they resemble each other near enough to be called "The twins."

4. MILL-PICKS AND SAW GUMMERS, TO TEMPER.—Saltpetre and alum, each 2 ozs.; sal-ammoniac ½ oz.; salt 1¼ lbs.; soft water 3 gals. Heat to a cherry-red and plunge them in, and draw no temper.

The steel must never be heat above a cherry-red, and in working and drawing the picks there ought to be quite an amount of light water-hammering, even after the steel is quite cool. Once more and I am done: yet it may be possible that the last, in this case, may be the best; read it.

5. MILL-PICK-TEMPERING AS DONE BY CHURCH, OF ANN ARBOR. Water 3 gals.; salt 2 qts.; sal-ammoniac and saltpetre, of each 2 ozs.; ashes from white-ash bark 1 shovel, which causes the picks to scale clean and white as silver.

I obtained this recipe of a blacksmith who paid young Mr. Church five dollars for it, he coming into the shop and showing him how to work the picks, as also the composition—his instructions were, not to hammer too cold, to avoid flaws; not to heat too high, which opens the pores of the steel, nor to heat more than one or two inches of the pick when tempering The gentleman says, if care is taken in heating and working, that no other tempering liquid will equal it, yet he spoiled the first batch by over heating, even after Mr. Church had taken all pains to show him. They (the Messrs. Church) have picks sent to them, for tempering, from Illinois and even Wisconsin

BUTCHER-KNIVES—Spring-Temper and Beautiful Edge.—In forging out the knife as you get it near to its proper thickness, be very careful not to heat it too high, and to water-hammer as for mill picks; when about to temper, heat only to a cherry-red and hold it in such a way that you can hold it plumb as you put it into the water which prevents it from springing—put it plumb into the water and it will come out straight.

Take it from the water to the fire and pass it through the blaze until a little hot; then rub a candle over t upon both sides and back to the fire, passing it backward and forward, in the blaze, turning it over often to keep the heat even over the whole surface, until the tallow passes off as though it went into the steel; then take out and rub the candle over it again (on both sides each time) and back to the fire, passing it as before, until it starts into a blaze, with a snap, being careful that the heat is even over the whole length and width of the tool, then rub the tallow over it again and back, for 3 times, quickly as it burns off; and lastly rub the tallow over it again and push it into the dust of the forge, letting it remain until cold.

If these directions are followed with dexterity you will have the temper alike from edge to back; and the edge will be the best you ever saw, as Davy Crockett used to say "It will jump higher, dive deeper," shave more hogs, bend farther without breaking, and give better satisfaction than all other knives put together.

It works equally well on drawing-knives and other thin tools; and for trap-springs which are to be set on dry ground; but if set in water, "pop goes the weasel" the first time the trap is sprung; but the following is the plan for tempering springs for general trapping.

2. TRAP SPRINGS—To Temper.—For tempering cast-steel trap-springs, all that is necessary is to heat them in the dark just that you may see it is read, then cool them in lukewarm water. This is a short recipe, but it makes long-lasting springs.

The reason why darkness is required to temper springs is that a lower degree of heat can be seen in the night than by day-light; and the low heat and warm water give the desired temper.

SILVER PLATING—For Carriage Work,—First, let the
parts which are to receive the plate be filed very smooth; then
apply over the surface the muriate of zinc, which is made by
dissolving zinc in muriatic acid; now hold this part over a dish
containing hot soft-solder, (pewter solder is probably the softest)
and with a swab apply the solder to the part, to which it adheres; brush off all superfluous solder, so as to leave the surface
smooth; you will now take No. 2 fair, silver plate, of the right
size to cover the surface of the part prepared with solder, and
lay the plate upon it, and rub it down smooth with a cloth which
is moistened with oil, then, with a soldering-iron, pass slowly
over all the surface of the plate, which melts the solder under-
neath it, and causes the plate to adhere as firmly as the solder
does to the iron; then polish the surface, finishing with buck-
skin.

The soldering-irons must be tinned, and also kept very
smooth, and used at about the same heat as for soldering
tin.

IRON—To Prevent Welding.—Where it is desired to weld
two bars of iron together, for making axletrees or other purposes, through which you wish to have a bolt-hole, without punch-
ing out a piece of the iron, you will take a piece of wet pasteboard, the width of the bar and the length you desire not to
weld, and place it between the two pieces of iron, and hold them
firmly upon the pasteboard while taking the heat, and the iron
will weld up to the pasteboard, but not where it is; then open
the hole, with swedge and punch, to the desired size.

In this way blacksmith's tongs may be relaid, without the
trouble of cutting the joints apart and making a new jaw.
Simply fit two pieces of iron, the thickness you wish to add
to the jaw of the tongs, have them of the right length and
width also, then take them both between the jaws and heat
them so you can pound them together, that they will fit
closely for a weld; now put a piece of the wet pasteboard
between the pieces which you are to weld, having the
handles of the tongs stand sufficiently apart that you may
put on a link or ring to hold all firmly; then put into the
fire, and take a good welding heat; and yet they do not
weld where the paper was between them; if they stick a
little at the end, just put them on the swedge and give them
a little tap with the hammer, and they will fly right apart
as nice as new. I am told that the dust from the ground
or floor of the blacksmith-shop is as good as the pasteboard,
yet I have not seen that tried; but I know there is no mis-

take in the other; and yet I have found one blacksmith who declared he would not believe it could be done, even if he saw it.

CAST-IRON—To Case-Harden.—Cast-iron may be case-hardened by heating to a red heat, and then rolling it in a composition composed of equal parts of Prussiate of potash, sal-ammoniac, and saltpetre, all pulverized and thoroughly mixed; then plunged, while yet hot, into a bath containing 2 ozs. of the Prussiate, and 4 ozs. of the sal-ammoniac to each gal. of cold water.—*Scientific Artisan.*

2. CAST-IRON—THE HARDEST, TO SOFTEN FOR DRILLING.— Heat to a cherry red, having it lie level in the fire, then with a pair of cold tongs put on a piece of brimstone, a little less in size than you wish the hole to be when drilled, and it softens entirely through the piece; let it lie in the fire until a little cool, when it is ready to drill.

Sleigh-shoes have been drilled, by this plan, in five minutes, after a man had spent half a day in drilling one-fourth of an inch into it. It is applicable to any article which can be heat without injury.

WROUGHT-IRON—To Case-Harden.—To case-harden wrought-iron, take the Prussiate of potash, finely pulverized, and roll the article in it, if its shape admits of it, if not, sprinkle the powder upon it freely, while the iron is hot.

This is applicable to iron-axletrees, by heating the axle-tree and rolling the bottom of it in the powder, spread out for that purpose, turning it up quickly and pouring cold water upon it, getting it into the tub of cold water as quick as possible. They will wear for years, without showing wear.

2. WELDING A SMALL PIECE OF IRON UPON A LARGE ONE, WITH ONLY A LIGHT HEAT.—It is often desirable to weld a small bit of iron upon a large bar, when the large piece must be heated equally hot as the small one. To save this :

Take borax 1 lb.; red oxide of iron 1 to 2 ozs.; melt them together in a crucible; and when cold, pulverize it and keep the powder dry for use.

When you want to perform the operation, just bring the large piece to a white heat, having a good welding heat upon the small slip; take the large one from the fire, and sprinkle some of the powder upon the place, and bring the other upon it, applying the hammer smartly, and the weld will be as good as could be made with the *greater heat* without the powder.

BRONZING—For Iron or Wood.—First, make a black paint; then put in a little chrome-yellow, only sufficient to give it a dark-green shade; apply a coat of this to the article to be bronzed; when dry, give it a coat of varnish; and when the varnish is a little dry, dust on bronze by dipping a piece of velvet into the bronze and shaking it upon the varnish; then give it another coat of varnish, and when dry, all is complete.

Cast-iron bells, which are now being extensively introduced to the farming community, will be much improved in their appearance by this bronzing, and also protected from rust, without injury to its sound. Iron fences around yards, porches, verandas, &c., will be much improved by it. It may also be applied to wood, if desired.

TRUSS SPRINGS.—Directions for Blacksmiths to Make—Better than the Patent Trusses.—After having tried the various kinds of trusses, over two years, having to wear one upon each side, I gave them all up as worse than useless.

I then went to a blacksmith and had springs made, bending them as represented in the cut.

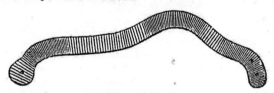

TRUSS SPRING.

Then they were bent to suit the shape of the body, and to press upon the body only sufficient, after the pads are put on, to hold back that which would otherwise protrude. The pad upon the back end of the spring I make of sole-leather, covered with cotton or linen cloth, having stuffed in a little batting to make it rest as easy as possible. The front pad I make by having a piece of wood turned the shape and size of a small hen's egg, sawing it through the center lengthwise, putting two screws into it through the holes represented in the end of the spring for that purpose. The back pad is secured by one screw only. The spring is oiled, then covered with sheep skin, to prevent rusting. Then it is secured around the body with a leather strap and buckle, or with a piece of cloth sewed into a string of suitable width to sit easy where it bears upon the hip, in passing to tie upon the other end of the spring, just back of the front pad. The bend which is given the spring, before it is bent to the shape of the body, gives it room to rise when the leg is raised, without lifting the pad from its position, saving the necessity of another strap to pass around *under* the thigh, as with the patent truss, which is very annoying to the wearer. Make the springs of spring-steel, about ½ or ⅝ of an inch in width, and about 1-16 in thickness, and of sufficient length to have a bearing just short of the spine.

I now speak from *eight* years personal experience, which ought to be a sufficient length of time for an experiment to be well established.

------------◆-◆------------

TINNER'S DEPARTMENT.

BLACK VARNISH—For Coal Buckets.—Asphaltum 1 lb.; lamp-black ¼ lb.; rosin ¼ lb.; spirits of turpentine 1 qt.

Dissolve the asphaltum and rosin in the turpentine; then rub up the lamp-black with linseed-oil, only sufficient to form a paste, and mix with the others. Apply with a brush.

JAPAN FLOW FOR TIN—All Colors.—Gum sandarach 1 lb.; balsam of fir, balsam of tolu, and acetate of lead, of each 2 ozs.; linseed-oil ½ pt.; spirits of turpentine 2 qts.

Put all into a suitable kettle, except the turpentine, over a slow fire, at first, then raise to a higher heat until all are melted; now take from the fire, and when a little cool, stir in the spirits of turpentine and strain through a fine cloth. This is transparent; but by the following modifications any or all the various colors are made from it.

2. Black.—Prussian blue ¼ oz.; asphaltum 2 ozs.; spirits of turpentine ½ pt.

Melt the asphaltum in the turpentine; rub up the blue with a little of it, mix well and strain; then add the whole to one pint of the *first*, above.

3. Blue.—Indigo and Prussian blue, both finely pulverized, of each ¼ oz.; spirits of turpentine 1 pt. Mix well and strain.

Add of this to one pint of the *first* until the color suits.

4. RED.—Take spirits of turpentine ½ pt.; add cochineal ½ oz.
.et stand 15 hours, and strain.

Add of this to the *first* to suit the fancy.

5 YELLOW.—Take 1 oz. of pulverized root of curcuma and stir of it into 1 pt. of the *first*, until the color pleases you, let stand a few hours and strain.

6. GREEN.—Mix equal parts of the blue and yellow together then mix with the *first* until it suits the fancy.

7. ORANGE.—Mix a little of the red with more of the yellow and then with the *first* as heretofore, until pleased.

8. PINK.—Mix a little of the blue to more in quantity of the red, and then with the *first* until suited.

In this simple and philosophical way you get all the various colors. Apply with a brush.

GOLD LACQUER FOR TIN.—TRANSPARENT, ALL COLORS.—Alcohol in a flask ½ pt.; add gum shellac 1 oz.; turmeric ½ oz.; red-sanders ¼ oz. Set the flask in a warm place, shake frequently for 12 hours or more, then strain off the liquor, rinse the bottle and return it, corking tightly for use.

When this varnish is used, it must be applied to the work freely and flowing, or, if the work admits of it, it may be dipped into the varnish, and laid on the top of the stove to dry, which it will do very quickly; and they must not be rubbed or brushed while drying; or the article may be hot when applied. One or more coats may be laid on, as the color is required more or less light or deep. This is applied to lanterns, &c. If any of it should become thick from evaporation, at any time, thin it with alcohol. And by the following modifications, all the various colors are obtained.

2. ROSE COLOR.—Proceed as above, substituting ¼ oz. of finely ground, best lake, in place of the turmeric.

3. BLUE.—The blue is made by substituting pulverized Prussian blue ½ oz. in place of the turmeric.

4. PURPLE.—Add a little of the blue to the *first*.

5. GREEN.—Add a little of the rose-color to the *first*.

Here again philosophy gives a variety of shades with only a slight change of materials or combinations.

LACQUER FOR BRASS.—TRANSPARENT.—Turmeric root, ground fine, 1 oz.; best dragon's blood ½ dr.; put into alcohol 1 pt.; place in a moderate heat, shake well for several days. It must be strained through a linen cloth and put back into the bottle, and add powdered gum shellac 3 ozs.; then keep as before in a warm place for several days, frequently shaken; then again strained, bottled and corked tight.

Lacquer is put upon metal for improving its appearance and preserving its polish. It is applied with a brush when the metal is warm, otherwise it will not spread evenly.

IRON—To Tin for Soldering or Other Purposes.—Take any quantity of muriatic acid and dissolve all the zinc in it that it will cut; then dilute it with one-fourth as much soft water as of acid, and it is ready for use.

This rubbed upon iron, no matter how rusty, cleanses it and leaves some of the zinc upon the surface, so that solder readily adheres to it, or copper as mentioned below for coppering iron or steel.

2. Iron, Iron Wire, or Steel, to Copper the Surface.—Rain water 3 lbs.; sulphate of copper 1 lb. Dissolve.

Have the article perfectly clean; then wash it with this solution and it immediately exhibits a copper surface.

Lettering on polished steel is done in this way; flowering or ornamenting can also be done in the same way Sometimes dilute muriatic acid is used to clean the surface; the surface must be clean by filing, rubbing, or acid; then cleaned by wiping off.

COPPER—To Tin for Stew-Dishes or Other Purposes.—Wash the surface of the article to be tinned, with sulphuric acid; and rub the surface well, so as to have it smooth and free of blackness caused by the acid; then sprinkle calcined and finely pulverized sal-ammoniac upon the surface, holding it over a fire where it will become sufficiently hot to melt a bar of solder which is to be rubbed over the surface; if a stew-dish put the solder into it and swab it about when melted.

You will wipe off any surplus solder, and also for the purpose of smoothing the surface, by means of a tow or cotton swab, tied or tacked to a rod. In this way any dish or copper article may be nicely tinned.

BOX-METAL—To Make for Machinery.—Copper 4 parts; lead 1 part—zinc is sometimes substituted for the lead—either makes a durable box for journals.

Printer's worn out type, in place of the lead, makes an improvement.

SOLDERS—For Brazing.—Copper 3 parts; zinc 2 parts or sheet brass 3 parts; zinc 1 part.

2. Solder for Lead.—Take tin 1 part; lead 2 parts.

3. Solder for Tin.—Lead 10 parts; tin 7 parts

4. SOLDER FOR BRITANNIA.—Bismuth ½ of one part; tin 1 part, lead 1 part.

BRITANNIA—To USE OLD, INSTEAD OF BLOCK TIN, IN SOL-DER.—Take old Britannia and melt it; and while hot sprinkle sulphur over it and stir for a short time.

This burns out the other articles in it, and leaves the black tin, which may now be used for making solder as good as new tin.

TIN—To PEARL, OR CRYSTALIZE.—Sulphuric acid 4 ozs.; soft water 2 to 3 ozs., according to strength of acid.; salt 1 oz.; mix.

Heat the tin quite hot over a stove or heater; then with a sponge wet with the mixture, washing off directly with clean water. Dry the tin; then varnish it with Demar-varnish.

This brings out the crystalline nature of the tin. Used in making water-coolers, spit-toons, &c.

2. TINNING FLUX—IMPROVED.—It has been customary for tinners to use the muriate of zinc only; but if you take 1 lb. of muriatic acid and put in all the zinc it will cut; then put in 1 oz. of sal-ammoniac, you will have no more trouble with old dirty or greasy seams.

Sometimes I think it is still improved by adding to it an equal amount of soft water.

3. LIQUID GLUE, FOR LABELING UPON TIN.—Boiling water one quart; borax, pulverized, two ounces; put in the borax; then add gum shellac four ounces, and boil until dissolved.

Labels put upon tin with common glue or common paste will not stick long. But this preparation obviates the diffi-culty entirely.

SCOURING LIQUID—FOR BRASS, DOOR-KNOBS, &c.—Oil of vitrol 1 oz.; sweet oil ½ gill; pulverized rotton stone 1 gill; rain-water 1½ pts.; mix all, and shake as used.

Apply with a rag, and polish with buck-skin or old wool-en. This makes as good a preparation as can be purchased, and for less than half the money. It does not give a coat-ing, but is simply a scourer and polisher. The following gives it a silver coating:

SILVERING POWDER—FOR COPPER OR WORN PLATED GOODS.—Nitrate of silver and common salt, of each 30 grs.; cream of tartar 3½ drs.; pulverize finely, mix thoroughly and bottle for use.

When desired to re-silver a worn spoon or other article, first clean them with the "Scouring Liquid"; then moisten a little of the powder and rub it on thoroughly with a piece of buck-skin. For Jewelry, see "Jewelry Department."

OIL CANS—Size of Sheet, for from 1 to 100 Gallons.—

For 1	gallon,	7 by 20 inches	25 gallons,	30 by 56 inches,
3½	"	10 by 28 "	40 "	36 by 63 "
5	"	12 by 40 "	50 "	40 by 70 "
6	"	14 by 40 "	75 "	40 by 84 "
10	"	20 by 42 "	100 "	40 by 98 "
15	"	30 by 42 "		

This includes all the laps, seams, &c., which will be found sufficiently correct for all practical purposes.

- - - - -

GUNSMITHING DEPARTMENT.

GUN-BARRELS—Browning Process—Spirits of nitre 1 lb.; alcohol 1 lb.; corrosive sublimate 1 oz.; mix in a bottle and keep corked for use.

DIRECTIONS.—Plug both ends of the barrel, and let the plugs stick out three or four inches, to handle by, and also to prevent the fluid from entering the barrel, causing it to rust; polish the barrel perfectly; then rub it well with quick-lime by means of a cloth, which removes oil or grease; now apply the browning fluid with a clean white cloth, apply one coat and set in a warm, dark place, until a red rust is formed over the whole surface, which will require, in warm weather, from ten to twelve hours, and in cold weather, from fifteen to twenty hours, or until the rust becomes red; then card it down with a gun-maker's card and rub off with a clean cloth; repeat the process until the color suits, as each coat gives a darker shade.

2. QUICKER AND LESS LABORIOUS PROCESS.—While in Evansville, Ind., I sold one of my books to C. Keller, a man who carries on gunsmithing, extensively. He gave me the following; which he was using, and says it makes a dark brown, with but little labor compared with the first.

Soft water 1 qt., and dissolve in it blue vitriol 2 ozs.; corrosive sublimate 1 oz.; and add 1 oz. of spirits of nitre. Have the barrel bright and put on one coat of the mixture; and in 1 hour after, put on another, and let the barrel stand 12 hours; then oil it and rub it with a cloth, of course having the ends of the bar rel tightly plugged, as in the first case.

But Mr. Sutherland, the gunsmith of this city, says the brown from this recipe will soon rub off; none being permanent unless carded down properly, as directed with the first recipe, that mixture being also superior.

3. BROWNING FOR TWIST BARRELS.—Take spirits of nitre ¼ oz.; tincture of steel ½ oz.; (if the tincture of steel cannot be obtained, the unmedicated tincture of iron may be used, but it is not so good) black brimstone ¼ oz.; blue vitriol ½ oz.; corrosive sublimate ¼ oz.; nitric acid 1 dr. or 60 drops; copperas ¼ oz.; mix with 1¼ pts. of rain water, keep corked, also, as the other, and the process of applying is also the same.

You will understand this is not to make an *imitation* of twist barrels, but to be used upon the real twist barrels, which brings out the twist so as to show; but if you use the first upon the real twist barrels, it will make the whole surface brown like the common barrel.

CASE-HARDENING—FOR LOCK-WORK.—Take old boots and shoes and lay them on a fire, and burn them until charred; now put them into a clean kettle and pulverize them coarsely, while hot; be careful not to get any wood coals mixed with them.

DIRECTIONS.—Take the pulverized leather and place in a sheet-iron box, placing the articles to be hardened in the centre of the box, or amongst the pulverized leather, and cover with a sheet-iron cover; or make the box so as to shut up; now blow up a fire of *very dry* charcoal; the coarser the charcoal the better; then open the fire and place the closed box in the centre, cover it up and let stand from forty to sixty minutes, not blowing; but if the coals burn off and leave the box exposed, you will put on more; at the expiration of the time, take the box and pour its contents into clean, moderately cool or cold water—never use warm water; these articles will now be found very hard, and will easily break; so you will draw the temper to suit.

BROKEN SAWS—TO MEND PERMANENTLY.—Pure silver 19 parts; pure copper 1 part; pure brass 2 parts; all are to be filed into powder and intimately mixed. If the saw is not recently broken, apply the tinning preparation of the next recipe.

Place the saw level upon the anvil the broken edges in close contact, and hold them so; now put a small line of the mixture along the seam, covering it with a larger bulk of powdered charcoal; now, with a spirit-lamp and a jewelers' blow-pipe, hold the coal-dust in place, and blow sufficient to melt the solder mixture; then with a hammer set the joint smooth, if not already so, and file away any superfluous solder; and you will be surprised at its strength. The heat upon a saw does not injure its temper as it does other tools, from the fact that the temper is rolled in, in place of by heat and water.

TINNING—Superior to the Old Process.—Take first, the same as the old way; that is, muriatic acid 1 pt., and as much pure block or sheet zinc as it will cut, in an open dish, a bowl, or something of that character, as much heat is set free and bottles are often broken by it; now take sal-ammoniac 4 ozs.; pulverize it and add to the other, and boil 10 minutes in a copper kettle—bear in mind, only copper is to be used to boil in.

You will find this will cause the solder to flow right along without difficulty. Keep corked tight when not in use.

VARNISH AND POLISH FOR STOCKS—German.—Gum shellac 10 ozs.; gum sandarach 1 oz.; Venice turpentine 1 drachm; alcohol 95 to 98 proof 1 gal.; shake the jug occasionally for a day or two, and it is ready for use.

After using a few coats of this, you can have a German polish, by simply leaving out 8 ozs. of the shellac; and a coat or two of the polish makes an improvement on the varnish, and does not require the rubbing, that it would if the full amount of shellac was used, in the last coat or two. It is recommended also to put upon cuts, sores, &c., burns excepted.

JEWELERS' DEPARTMENT.

GALVANIZING—Without a Battery.—Dissolve cyanuret of potassium 1 oz., in pure rain or snow water 1 pt., to which add a 1 dr. bottle of the chloride of gold, and it is ready to use. Scour the article to be plated, from all dirt and grease, with whiting, chalk, or rotten stone, pulverized, and put in alcohol;

using a good brush—or the "Polishing Compound," No. 3; if there are cracks, it may be necessary to put the article in a solution of caustic potash—at all events, every particle of grease and dirt must be removed; then suspend the article to be plated in the cyanuret of gold solution, with a small strip of zinc cut about the width of a common knitting-needle, hooking the top over a stick which will reach across the top of the jar holding the solution.

Every five to ten minutes, the article should be taken out and brushed over with the scouring preparation; or on smooth surfaces it may be rinsed off and wiped with a piece of cotton cloth, and return until the coating is sufficiently heavy to suit.

When the plating fluid is not in use, bottle it, keeping it corked, and it is always ready for use, bearing in mind that it is as poison as arsenic, and must be put high, out of the way of children, and labeled—*Poison*, although you will have no fears in using it; yet accidents might arise, if its nature were not known. The zinc strip, as far as it reaches into the fluid, will need to be rubbed occasionally, until it is bright.

2. GALVANIZING WITH A SHILLING BATTERY.—I have found some persons who thought it much better to use a simple battery, made by taking a piece of copper rod about three-eighths of an inch in thickness, and about eighteen or twenty inches long, and bend it, as seen in the accompanying cut:

SHILLING BATTERY.

The rod should be about 4 or 5 inches in the circle or bend, then run parallel, having 5 strips of sheet zinc, an inch wide and 6 to 8 inches long, bent in their centre around the copper, with a rivet through them, close to the rod, as shown above; these strips of zinc are to be placed into tumblers, the rod resting on top of the tumblers, which are to be nearly filled with rain water; then pour into each tumbler a little oil of vitriol, until you see that it begins to work a little on the zinc.

The article to be plated is to be suspended upon the strip of zinc, as represented upon the long end of the rod, which is to be placed as before spoken of, in a jar containing the gold solution, instead of having it upon the stick spoken of when plating without the battery. And all the operations are the same as before described.

JEWELRY—CLEANING AND POLISHING COMPOUND.—Aqua ammonia 1 oz.; prepared chalk ¼ oz.; mix, and keep corked.

To use, for rings, or other smooth-surfaced jewelry, wet a bit of cloth with the compound, after having skaken it, and rub the article thoroughly; then polish by rubbing with a silk handkerchief or piece of soft buck-skin. For articles which are rough-surfaced, use a suitable brush. It is applicable for gold, silver, brass, britannia, plated goods, &c.

FARRIERS' DEPARTMENT.

CHOLIC—CURE FOR HORSES OR PERSONS.—Spirits of turpentine 3 ozs.; laudanum 1 oz.; mix, and give all for a dose, by putting it into a bottle with half pint of warm water, which prevents injury to the throat. If relief is not obtained in one hour, repeat the dose, adding half an ounce of the best powdered aloes, well dissolved together, and have no uneasiness about the result.

SYMPTOMS.—The horse often lies down, suddenly rising again, with a spring; strikes his belly with his hind feet, stamps with his fore feet, and refuses every kind of food, &c. I suppose there is no medicine in use, for cholic, either in man or horse, equal to this mixture.

For persons, a dose would be from 1 to 2 tea-spoons—*children or weak* persons, less, according to the urgency of the symptoms, to be taken in warm water or warm tea.

I have been familiar with it for about five years, and know that it has been successful in many cases—all where it has been used. Many think it the best cholic remedy in the world.

2. ANOTHER.—Laudanum ¼ oz.; sulphuric ether 1 oz. Mix, and for a horse, give all at a dose, in warm water as above. Dose for a person, as the first.

A Mr. Thorpe, of whom I obtained this recipe, tells me he has cured cholic in horses in every case with the firs dose, except one, and in that case by repeating the dose thirty minutes after the first. There is no question but what it is good, and some would prefer it to the turpentine I know it is valuable.

BOTS—SURE REMEDY —When a horse is attacked with bots, it may be known by the occasional nipping at their own sides, and by red pimples or projections on the inner surface of the upper lip, which may be seen plainly by turning up the lip.

FIRST, then, take new milk 2 qts.; molasses 1 qt.; and give the horse the whole amount. SECOND, 15 minutes afterwards give very warm sage tea 2 qts. LASTLY, 30 minutes after the tea, you will give of currier's oil 1 pt , (or enough to operate as physic.) Lard has been used, when the oil could not be obtained, with the same success.

The cure will be complete, as the milk and molasses cause the bots to let go their hold, the tea puckers them up, and the oil carries them entirely away. If you have any doubt, one trial will satisfy you perfectly. In places where the currier's oil cannot be obtained, substitute the lard, adding three or four ounces of salt with it; if no lard, dissolve a double handful of salt in warm water three pints, and give all.

RING-BONE AND SPAVINS—To CURE.—Egyptiacum and wine vinegar, of each 2 ozs.; water of pure ammonia, spirits of turpentine, and oil of origanum, of each 1 oz.; euphorbium and cantharides, of each ¼ oz.; glass made fine and sifted through gauze 1 dr.; put them in a bottle, and when used let them be well shaken. This is to be rubbed upon the bone enlargement with the hand or spatula, for half an hour each morning, for six or seven mornings in succession. Let the horse be so tied that he cannot get his mouth to the place for 3 or 4 hours, otherwise he will blister his mouth and blemish the part. Then let him run until the scab comes off of itself without scraping, which injures the roots of the hair. Then repeat as before, and follow up for 3 or 4 times blistering, and all bone enlargements will be re-absorbed, if not of more than a year or two's standing.

It is also good for callous sinews, and strains of long standing, spavins, big-head, &c., but if there are ring-bones or spavins of so long standing that this does not cause their cure, you will proceed as follows :

2. Add to the above compound, corrosive sublimate in powder ¼ oz.; oil of vitriol ¼ oz.; and common salt ¼ oz.; when it is again

ready.for use, always shaking well as you use either preparation.

Now clip the hair and prick the bone or callous part as full of holes as you can with a pegging-awl, which is just long enough to break through the callous part only. Or a better way to break up this bony substance is to have a handle like a pegging-awl handle, with three or four awls in it, then tap it in with a stick and give it a wrench at the same time, which does the hurting part with more speed. This done, bathe the part with vinegar, until the blood stops flowing; then apply the double compound as at first, for four or five mornings only, repeating again if necessary; and ninety-nine out of every hundred ring-bones or spavins will be cured; and most of them with only the first preparation. The Egyptiacum is made as follows:

3. Take verdigris and alum in powder, of each 1½ ozs.; blue vitriol, powdered, ¼ oz.; corrosive sublimate, in powder, ¼ oz.; vinegar 2¼ ozs.; honey ¼ lb.; boil over a slow fire until of a proper consistence. When used it must be stirred up well, as a sediment will deposit of some of the articles.

If the hair does not come out again after using the last blister, use the "Good Samaritan Liniment" freely, on the part; but the first will never disturb the growth of hair. It is best always to commence this kind of treatment early in the season, so as to effect a cure before cold weather comes on.

4. O. B. BANGS' CURE FOR RING-BONE AND SPAVIN.—Take of cantharides pulverized; British oil; oils of origanum and amber; and spirits of turpentine, of each 1 oz.; olive oil ½ oz.; oil of vitriol 3 drs.; put all, except the vitriol, into alcohol, stir the mixture, then slowly add the vitriol and continue to stir until the mixture is complete, which is known by its ceasing to smoke. Bottle for use.

DIRECTIONS.—Tie a piece of sponge upon a stick and rub the preparation by this means, upon the spavin or ring-bone as long as it is absorbed into the parts; twenty-four hours after, grease well with lard; and in twenty-four hours more, wash off well with soap-suds. Mr. Bangs lives at Napoleon, Mich., and has sold books for me nearly two years. He says one application will generally be sufficient for spavins, but may need two; ring-bones always require two or three applications, three or four days apart, which prevents the loss of hair; if not put on oftener than once in three or four days, the hair not coming out at all. Said to cure wind-galls, splints, &c. He obtained five dollars for curing a neighbor's horse of ring-bone, with this preparation; stopping all lameness, but not removing the lump.

5. In very bad cases of long standing, he thinks it preferable to first apply the following:

Take alcohol 1 pt.; sal ammoniac, corrosive sublimate, and oil of spike, of each 1 oz.; mix.

Apply, by washing off and using lard afterwards, as above directed, washing also forty-eight hours after; and when dry, apply the first liniment once or twice, according to directions. The object of this last is to open the pores of the skin, and soften the lump.

6. RING-BONE REMEDY.—Pulverized cantharides, oils of spike, origanum, amber, cedar, Barbadoes tar, and British oil, of each 2 ozs.; oil of wormwood 1 oz.; spirits of turpentine 4 ozs.; common potash ½ oz.; nitric acid 6 ozs.; and oil of vitriol (sulphuric acid) 4 ozs.; lard 3 lbs.

DIRECTIONS.—Melt the lard and slowly add the acids, stir well and add the others, stirring until cold. Clip off the hair and apply by rubbing and heating in; in about three days or when it is done running, wash off with suds and apply again. In old cases it may take three or four weeks, but in recent cases two or three applications have cured. It has cured long standing cases.

7. RAWSON'S RING-BONE AND SPAVIN CURE.—Venice turpentine and Spanish-flies, of each 2 ozs.; euphorbium and aqua ammonia, of each 1 oz.; red precipitate ½ oz.; corrosive sublimate ¼ oz.; lard 1¼ lbs. Pulverize all and put into the lard simmer slowly over coals, not scorch or burn, and pour off free of sediment.

DIRECTIONS.—For ring-bones, cut off the hair and rub the ointment well into the lumps once in forty-eight hours. For spavins, once in twenty-four hours for three mornings, has perfectly cured them. Wash well, each application, with suds, rubbing over the place with a smooth stick to sqcez out a thick yellow matter.

Mr. Rawson, of Rawsonville, Mich., has cured some exceedingly bad cases of ring-bones, one as thick as a man'. arm; and spavins as unpromising in size. If properly cooked it will foam like boiling sugar.

8. INDIAN METHOD.—Bind a toad upon it ; or two, if one does not cover it, and keep it on from 8 to 10 days.

An Indian cured a horse in this way, near St. Louis, for which he coveted, and recieved a rifle. The cure proved permanent.

9. BONE-SPAVINS—FRENCH PASTE—$300 RECIPE.—Corrosive sublimate, quicksilver, and iodine, of each 1 oz.; with lard only sufficient to form a paste.

DIRECTIONS.—Rub the quicksilver and iodine together, then adding the sublimate and finally the lard, rubbing thoroughly.

Shave off the hair the size of the bone enlargement; then grease all around it, but not where the hair is shaved off; this prevents the action of the medicine, only upon the spavin; now rub in as much of the paste as will lie on a three cent piece only, each morning for four mornings only; in from seven to eight days the whole spavin will come out; then wash out the wound with suds, soaking well, for an hour or two, which removes the poisonous effects of the medicine and facilitates the healing, which will be done by ny of the healing salves; but I would prefer the green ointment to any other in this case.

Mr. Andrews, late of Detroit, who during his life, knew a good horse, and also desired to know how to take good care of them, did not hesitate to pay three hundred dollars for this recipe after seeing what it would do; he removed a spavin from a mare's leg with it, and she afterwards won him more than the expense.

10. BONE-SPAVINS—NORWEGIAN CURE.—S. B. Marshall, the Champion Horse-Shoer, and Farrier, of White Pigeon, Mich., obtained this plan of an old Norwegian Farrier, and also his plan of curing poll-evil, which see, and assures me that he has been very successful with them. I obtained them of him for the purpose of publication, and sincerely think I can recommend them to all who need them :

Take dog's grease ½ pt.; best oil of origanum 1½ ozs ; pulverized cantharides ½ oz. Mix, and apply each morning, for three mornings; heating it in with a hot iron each time; then skip 3 mornings, and apply again, as before, until it has been applied 9 times; after which wait about 10 days, and if it is not all gone, go over again in the same way

He says it does not remove the hair, but that it cures the largest and worst cases. He gives a test for good oil of origanum, saying that much of it is reduced with turpentine; and if so reduced, that it will spread on the skin, like turpentine; but if good, that it does not spread on the skin, but stands, like other oil, where a drop is put on. I am not certain about the genuineness of this test; yet I find quite a difference in the spreading of the oils; for that which is known to contain turpentine spreads fast and freely; whilst that which is believed to be pure, spreads very slowly, yet does finally spread. The pure is of a dark wine color, whilst the poor is of a lighter shade, and somewhat cloudy.

11. SPAVIN LINIMENT.—Oils of spike, origanum, cedar, British and spirits of turpentine, of each 1 oz.; Spanish-flies, pulverized ¼ oz.

Apply once in six to nine days only—removes the lump of spavins, splints, curbs, &c., if of recent occurrence; and the man of whom I obtained it, says he has scattered poll-evils before breaking out, with cedar oil, alone.

12. ANOTHER.—Alcohol and spirits of turpentine, of each ½ pt.; gum camphor, laudanum, and oil of cedar, of each 1 oz.; oils of hemlock and rhodium and balsam of fir, of each ½ oz.; iodine 1 dr.; mix.

Apply night and morning, first washing clean and rubbing dry with a sponge; then rub the liniment into the spavin with the hand. It causes a gummy substance to ooze out, without injury to the hair—has cured ring-bones, also removing the lumps in recent cases. It cured the lameness in a case of three years standing.

13 SPLINT AND SPAVIN LINIMENT.—Take a large mouthed bottle and put into it oil of origanum 6 ozs.; gum camphor 2 ozs.; mercurial ointment 2 ozs.; iodine ointment 1 oz.; melt by putting the bottle into a kettle of hot water.

Apply it to bone-spavins or splints twice daily, for four or five days. The lameness will trouble you no more. I have had men cure their horses with this liniment and remark that this recipe alone was worth more than the price of the book.

14. BOG-SPAVIN AND WIND-GALL OINTMENT, ALSO GOOD FOR CURBS, SPLINTS, RING-BONES, AND BONE-SPAVIN.—Take pulverized cantharides 1 oz.; mercurial ointment 2 ozs.; tincture of

iodine 1½ ozs.; spirits of turpentine 2 ozs.; corrosive sublimate 1¼ drs.; lard 1 lb.

Mix well, and when desired to apply, first cut off the hair, wash well and anoint, rubbing it in with the hand or glove, if preferred. Two days after, grease the part with lard, and in two days more, wash off and apply the ointment again. Repeat the process every week, as long as necessary.

SWEENY—LINIMENT.—Alcohol and spirits of turpentine, of each 8 ozs.; camphor gum, pulverized cantharides, and capsicum, of each 1 oz.; oil of spike 3 ozs. Mix.

Perhaps the best plan is to tincture the capsicum first and use the tincture instead of the powder, by which means you are free of sediment; bathe this liniment in with a hot iron. The first case has yet to be found where it has not cured this disease when faithfully followed.

2. ANOTHER.—Sal-ammoniac 2 ozs.; corrosive sublimate 1 oz.; alcohol 1 qt.; water 1 qt., pulverize and mix.

This last has cured many cases of sweeny, and also kidney complaints, known by a weakness in the back, of horses or cattle. Bathe the loins with it; and give one to two table-spoons at a dose, daily.

POLL-EVIL AND FISTULA—POSITIVE CURE.—Common potash ¼ oz.; extract of belladona ½ dr.; gum arabic ¼ oz. Dissolve the gum in as little water as practicable; then having pulverized the potash, unless it is moist, mix the gum water with it and it will soon dissolve; then mix in the extract and it is ready to use; and it can be used without the belladona, but it is more painful without it, and does not have quite as good an effect.

DIRECTIONS.—The best plan to get this into the pipes is by means of a small syringe, after having cleansed the sore with soap-suds; repeat once in two days, until all the callous pipes and hard fibrous base around the poll-evil or fistula, is completely destroyed. Mr. Curtis, a merchant of Wheaton, Ill., cured a poll-evil with this preparation, by only a single application, as the mare estrayed and was not found for two months—then completely sound; but it will generally require two or three applications.

This will destroy corns and warts, by putting a little of it upon the wart or corn, letting it remain from five to ten minutes, then wash off and apply oil or vinegar, not squeezing them out, but letting nature remove them.

2. POTASH, TO MAKE.—If you cannot buy the potash, called for in the last recipe, you can make it by leaching best wood ashes and boiling down the lye to what is called black salts, and continuing the heat in a thick kettle until they are melted; the heat burns out the black impurities and leaves a whitish-gray substance, called potash.

This potash, pulverized and put into all the rat holes about the cellars, causes them to leave in double quick time, as mentioned in the "Rat Exterminator." The black salts will do about as well for rats, but is not quite so strong. They get their feet into it, which causes a biting worse than their own, and they leave without further ceremony.

Potash making in timbered lands is carried on very extensively; using the thick, heavy potash-kettle to boil and melt in; then dipping it out into three and five pail iron-kettles to cool.

3. POLL-EVIL AND FISTULA—NORWEGIAN CURE.—Cover the head and neck with two or three blankets; have a pan or kettle of the best warm cider vinegar; holding it under the blankets; then steam the parts by putting hot stones, brick, or iron, into the vinegar, and continue the operation until the horse sweat freely; doing this 3 mornings and skipping 3, until 9 steaming have been accomplished.

Mr. Marshall says, the pipes, by this time, will seem to have raised up and become loose, except the lower end, which holds upon the bone or tendons, like a sucker's mouth; the apparent rising being caused by the going down of the swelling in the parts; now tie a skein of silk around the pipes and pull them out; washing the parts with weak copperas water until the sore heals up and all is well. He told me that he cured, in this way, a horse which had interfered until a pipe had formed at the place of interference, upon the leg, that when drawn out was as long as his finger. See the " Norwegian Cure for Bone-Spavin."

4. ANOTHER.—Rock salt and blue vitriol, of each 1 oz., copperas ½ oz.; pulverize all finely and mix well.

Fill a goose-quill with the powder and push it to the bottom of the pipe, having a stick in the top of the quill, so that you can push the powder out of the quill, leaving it at the bottom of the pipe; repeat again in about four days, and in two or three days from that time you can take hold of the pipe and remove it. without trouble.

9

5. POLL-EVIL, TO SCATTER.—Take a quantity of mandrake root, mash, and boil it; strain and boil down until rather thick; then form an ointment by simmering it with sufficient lard for that purpose.

Anoint the swelling once a day, for several days, until well. It has cured them after they were broken out, by putting it into the pipes a few times, also anointing around the sore.

6. ANOTHER.—Poll-evils and Fistulas have been cured by pushing a piece of lunar caustic into the pipe, then filling the hole with currier's oil. Or:

7. ANOTHER.—Corrosive subli ate the size of a common bean, pulverized and wrapped in tissue paper, and pressed to the bottom of the pipes, leaving it in eight days, then take out, and applying the blue ointment, (kept by druggists,) has cured them. Or:

8. ANOTHER.—Arsenic, the size of a pea, treated in the same way, has cured the same disease. But if the Norwegian plan will work as recommended, it is certainly the best of all.

9. ANOTHER.—Oil of vitriol put into the pipes has cured many poll-evils.

I found one man, also, who had cured poll-evil by placing barrel of water about fifteen feet high, on a platform, upon two trees—administering a shower bath daily upon the sore; drawing the water by a faucet, through a dinner horn placed little end down; tying the horse so as to keep him in position until the water all runs out. Fifteen or twenty baths cured him, but it broke out again the next season, when a few more baths made a final cure.

LOOSENESS OR SCOURING IN HORSES OR CATTLE—IN USE OVER SEVENTY YEARS.—Tormentil root, powdered. Dose for a horse or cow 1 to 1½ oz. It may be stirred in 1 pt. of milk and given, or it may be steeped in 1¼ pts. of milk then given from 3 to 5 times daily until cured.

It has proved valuable also for persons. Dose for a person would be from one-half to one tea-spoon steeped in milk; but if used for persons I should recommend that half as much rhubarb be combined with it.

An English gentleman from whom it was obtained, had been familiar with its use nearly eighty years, and never knew a failure, if taken in any kind of seasonable time. The tormentil, or septfoil, is an European plant, and very astringent.

2 Beef bones for Scours.—Burn the bones thoroughly and pulverize finely; then give 1 table-spoon in some dry feed, 3 times daily, until checked.

This preparation has thirty years experience of an American gentleman, near Fentonville, Mich., to recommend it to general favor.

3. Scours and Pin-Worms of Horses and Cattle.—White ash bark burnt to ashes and made into rather a strong lye; then mix ¼ pt. of it with warm water 1 pt., and give all, 2 or 3 times daily.

Whenever it becomes certain that a horse or cow is troubled with pin-worms, by their passing from the bowels, it is best to administer the above, as they are believed to be the cause, generally, of scours, and this remedy carries off the worms, thus curing the inflammation by removing the cause.

HORSE OINTMENT—De Gray or Sloan's.—Rosin 4 ozs.; bees-wax 4 ozs.; lard 8 ozs.; honey 2 ozs. Melt these articles slowly, gently bringing to a boil; and as it begins to boil, remove from the fire and slowly add a little less than a pint of spirits of turpentine, stirring all the time this is being added, and stir until cool.

This is an extraordinary ointment for bruises, in flesh or hoof, broken knees, galled backs, bites, cracked heels, &c., &c.; or when a horse is gelded, to heal and keep away flies. It is excellent to take fire out of burns or scalds in human flesh also.

CONDITION POWDERS—Said to be St. John's.—Fenugreek, cream of tartar, gentian, sulphur, saltpetre rosin, black antimony, and ginger, equal quantities of each, say 1 oz.; all to be finely pulverized; cayenne, also fine, half the quantity of any one of the others, say ¼ oz. Mix thoroughly.

It is used in yellow water, hide-bound, coughs, colds, distemper, and all other diseases where condition powders are generally administered. They carry off gross humors and purify the blood. Dose—In ordinary cases give two tea spoons once a day, in feed. In extreme cases give it twice daily. If these do not give as good satisfaction as St. John's or any other condition powder that costs more than double what it does to make this, then I will acknowledge that travel and study are of no account in obtaining information.

2. CATHARTIC CONDITION POWDER.—Gamboge, alum, salt petre, rosin, copperas, ginger, aloes, gum-myrrh, salts, and salt, and if the horse is in a very low condition, put in wormwood, all the same quantities, viz., 1 oz. each. DOSE—One tabl'e spoon in bran twice daily; not giving any other grain for a few days; then once a day with oats and other good feed.

This last is more applicable for old worn-down horses which need cleaning out and starting again into new life; and in such cases, just the thing to be desired.

HORSE LINIMENTS—FOR STIFF-NECK FROM POLL-EVILS.—Alcohol one pint; oil of cedar, origanum, and gum-camphor, of each two ounces; oil of amber one ounce; use freely.

2. ENGLISH STABLE LINIMENT—VERY STRNG.—Oil of spike, aqua ammonia, and *oil* of turpentine, of each 2 ozs.; sweet oil and oil of amber, of each 1½ ozs.; oil of origanum 1 oz. Mix.

Call this good for any thing, and always keep it in the stable as a strong liniment; the Englishman's favorite for poll-evils, ring-bones, and all old lameness, inflammations, &c.; if much inflammation, however, it will fetch the hair, but not destroy it.

3. NERVE AND BONE LINIMENT.—Take beef's gall 1 qt.; alcohol 1 pt.; volatile liniment 1 lb.; spirits of turpentine 1 lb.; oil of origanum 4 ozs.; aqua ammonia 4 ozs.; tincture of cayenne ¼ pt.; oil of amber 3 ozs.; tincture of Spanish-flies 6 ozs.; mix.

Uses too well known to need description. This is more particularly applicable to horse flesh.

4. LINIMENT FOR ONE-SHILLING A QUART.—Best vinegar 2 qts.; saltpetre, pulverized ¼ lb.; mix and set in a warm place, until dissolved.

It will be found valuable for spavins, sprains strains, bruises, old swellings, &c.

BROKEN LIMBS—TREATMENT, INSTEAD OF INHUMANLY SHOOTING THE HORSE.—In the greater number of fractures it is only necessary to partially sling the horse by means of a broad piece of sail or other strong cloth, (as represented in the figure,) placed under the animal's belly, furnished with two breechings and two breast-girths, and by means of ropes and pulleys attached to a cross beam above, he is elevated or lowered, as may be required.

It would seldom be necessary to raise them entirely off of their feet, as they will be more quiet, generally, when

allowed to touch the ground or floor.   The head-stall should
be padded, and ropes reaching each way to the stall, as well
as forward.   Many horses will plunge about for a time, but
soon quiet down, with an occasional exception ; when they
become quiet, set the bone, splint it well. padding the splints
with batting, securing carefully, then keep wet with cold
water, as long as the least inflammation is present, using
light food, and a little water at a time, but may be given
often.

The use of the different buckles and straps will be easily
understood.

SUPPORTING APPARATUS IN LAMENESS OF HORSES.

If he is very restive, other ropes can be attached to the
corner rings, which are there for that purpose, and will
afford much additional relief to the horse.

I knew a horse's thigh to crumble upon the race-course,
without apparent cause, which lost him the stake he would
have easily won; he was hauled miles upon a sled, slung,
and cured by his humane owner.   Then let every fair
means be tried, before you consent to take the life, even of
a broken-legged horse.

WOUND BALSAM—For Horse or Human Flesh.—Gum benzoin, in powder, 6 ozs.; balsam of tolu, in powder, 3 ozs.; gum storax 2 ozs.; frankincense, in powder, 2 ozs.; gum myrrh, in powder, 2 ozs.; Socotorine aloes, in powder, 3 ozs.; alcohol 1 gal. Mix them all together and put them in a digester, and give them a gentle heat for three or four days; then strain.

A better medicine can hardly be found in the *Materia Medica* for healing fresh wounds in every part of the body, particularly those on the tendons or joints. It is frequently given internally along with other articles, to great advantage in all colds, flatulency, and in other debilities of the stomach and intestines. Every gentleman, or farmer, ought to keep this medicine ready prepared in his house, as a family medicine, for all cuts, or recent wounds, either among his cattle or any of his family. Thirty or forty drops, on a lump of sugar, may be taken at any time, for flatulency, or pain at the stomach; and in old age, where nature requires stimulation.—*Every Man His Own Farrier.*

GREASE-HEEL AND COMMON SCRATCHES.—To Cure. —Lye made from wood ashes, and boil white-oak bark in it until it is quite strong, both in lye and bark ooze; when it is cold, it is ready for use.

First wash off the horse's legs with dish-water or castile soap; and when dry, apply the ooze with a swab upon a stick which is sufficiently long to keep out of his reach, as he will tear around like a wild horse, but you must wet all well once a day, until you see the places are drying up. The grease-heel may be known from the common scratches by the deep cracks, which do not appear in the common kind. Of course this will fetch off the hair, but the disease has been known to fetch off the hoof; then to bring on the hair again, use salve made by stewing sweet elder bark in old bacon; then form the salve by adding a little rosin according to the amount of oil when stewed, about a quarter of a pound to each pound of oil.

2. Another.—Verdigris ½ oz.; whisky 1 pt., are highly recommended for grease-heel

3. Common Scratches.—Use sweet oil 6 oz.; borax 2 oz.; sugar of lead 2 oz.; mix, and apply twice daily, after washing off with dish-water, and giving time to allow the legs to dry.

These plans have been used for years, by Geo. Clemm, of Logansport, Indiana, and he assured me that the worst cases will be cured, of either disease, in a very few days

4. ANOTHER.—Copperas and chamber-lye are known to be good for common scratches, applied, as the last, after washing with dish-water and drying. This last can be tried first, as it is easily obtained, and if it does not succeed you will not fail with the other.

SADDLE AND HARNESS GALLS—BRUISES, ABRASIONS, &c.—REMEDY.—White lead and linseed oil mixed as for paint, is almost invaluable in abrasions, or galls from the saddle or collar, or from any other cause, it will speedily aid the part in healing.

Applied with a brush to the leg of a horse, the outer coating of hair and skin of which was torn off, caused it to heal and leave no scar. It is good for scratches and all sores upon horses, or other animals, and equally good for men. It forms an air-tight coating, and soothes pain. Every farmer should keep a pot and brush ready for use. White lead is the carbonate of the metal, and when pure is very white. That having a greyish tint is impure, being generally adulterated. For use as a paint, a lead color is produced by adding lamp-black, and a drab or stone color, by adding burned umber

In applying it for scratches, first wash them clean with soap and water, then apply. Some persons prefer lamp oil. If that is used, you will mix both together until the oil assumes a light straw color. When the horse comes in at night, his legs should be washed perfectly clean and rubbed perfectly dry. Then apply the mixture, rubbing it well to the skin. Two or three applications are sufficient to effect a perfect cure, no matter how bad the case may be.—*Correspondence of the Country Gentleman.*

To give confidence in this, I would say that a lady, at Lafayette, Ind., told me she cured herself of salt-rheum with white-lead and sweet oil only.

2. ANOTHER.—Alcohol and extract of lead, of each 2 ozs.; soft water 4 ozs.; spirits of sal-ammoniac 1 oz.; white copperas ½ oz. Mix all and shake as used.

"Knowlson's Complete Farrier" speaks very highly of this last preparation, which can be tried, should the first above fail.

3. SORES FROM CHAFING OF THE BITS.—Chloroform and sulphuric ether, equal parts of each. Keep closely corked.

Sponge off the mouth with water every time the bits are

taken out; then wet well with the mixture. It will also
be found valuable to remove soreness from any cause, on
man or horse.

4. ANOTHER.—White ashes and spirits of turpentine, of each
1½ table-spoons; black pepper, ground, 1 table-spoon; lard to
make 1 pt. of all, mix well and anoint.

HEAVES.—GREAT RELIEF—Heaves, the common name
for any difficulty in the breathing of a horse, is susceptible
of great alleviation by attention to the character and quan
tity of food to be eaten by the animal, as every one
knows.   If a horse suffering from this disease, is allowed to
distend his stomach at his pleasure, with dry food entirely,
and then to drink cold water, as much as he can hold, he is
nearly worthless.   But if his food be moistened, and he be
allowed to drink a moderate quantity only at a time, the
disease is much less troublesome.

A still farther alleviation may be obtained from the use of balsam of fir and balsam of copaiba 4 ozs. each; and mix with
calcined magnesia sufficiently thick to make it into balls; give
a middling sized ball, night and morning for a week or 10 days
This gives good satisfaction, and is extensively sold by Eberbach
& Co., druggists of this city.

2. ANOTHER.—An old Farrier assures me that lobelia
one tea-spoon, once a day, in his feed, for a week, and then
once a week; that you can hardly tell whether a horse ever
had the heaves or not.

3. ANOTHER.—H. Sisson, another Farrier, gives me a
cure which somewhat resembles the ball first given under
this head, and thus each one supports the other.

He takes calcined magnesia, balsam of fir, and balsam of
copaiba, of each 1 oz.; spirits of turpentine 2 ozs.; and puts
them all into 1 pt. of best cider vinegar, and gives for a dose 1
table-spoon in his feed, once a day, for a week; then every other
day for 2 or 3 months.

The horse will cough more at first, but looser and looser
until cured.   Wet his hay with brine, and also wet his
feed.

4. ANOTHER.—Mr Bangs, highly recommends the following:
Lobelia, wild turnip, elecampane and skunk cabbage, equal
parts of each. Make into balls of common size, and give one
for a dose, or make a tincture, by putting 4 ozs. of the mixture
into 2 qts. of spirits; and after a week put 2 table-spoons into
their feed, once a day for a month or two.

5. ANOTHER.—Oyster shells 1 peck; burn into lime and pulverize; mix a single handful of it with ½ gill of alcohol, then mix it with the oats each morning until all given.

This for bellows-heaves has done very much good. Horseradish grated and put in with the feed has benefited. Cabbage, as common feed, is good to relieve, or any juicy food, like pumpkins, &c., &c., will be found to relieve very much. Farmers who have their horses always at home, can keep them comfortable with some of the foregoing directions; but broken-winded horses might as well be knocked in the head as to attempt to travel with them, expecting any satisfaction to horse or driver.

6. ANOTHER.—A correspondent of the *Country Gentleman* says that "heaves may be greatly alleviated by feeding raw fat pork.

"Commence with a piece of pork, say a cubic inch, chopped very fine, and mixed with the wetted grain or cut feed, twice a day for two or three days. Then from day to day increase the quantity and cut less fine, until there is given with each feed such a slice as usually by a farmer's wife is cut for frying—nearly as large as your hand, cut into fifteen or twenty pieces.

"Continue this for two weeks, and the horse is capable of any ordinary work with out distress, and without showing the heaves. I have experience and observation for the past ten years as proof of the above."—[*J., of Burlington, Vt.*

DISTEMPER—To DISTINGUISH AND CURE.—If it is thought that a horse has the distemper, and you do not feel certain, wet up bran with rather strong weak lye—if not too strong they will eat it greedily; if they have the distemper, a free discharge from the nostrils and a consequent cure will be the result, if continued a few days; but if only a cold, with swellings of the glands, no change will be discovered.

SHOEING HORSES—FOR WINTER TRAVEL.—N. P. Willis, of the *Home Journal*, in one of his recent Idlewild letters, says:

"You have discovered, of course, that you cannot have uninterrupted winter riding with a horse shod in the ordinary way. The sharp points of the frozen mud will wound the frog of the foot; and with snow on the ground, the hollow hoof soon collects a hard ball, which makes the footing very insecure. But

these evils are remedied by a piece of sole leather nailed on under the shoe—a protection to the hoof which makes a surprising
difference in the confidence and sure-footedness of the animal's
step."

FOUNDER—Remedy.—Draw about 1 gal. of blood from the
neck; then drench the horse with linseed-oil 1 qt.; now rub the
fore legs, long and well, with water as hot as can be borne without scalding.

This remedy entirely cured a horse which had been
foundered on wheat, two days before the treatment began.

PHYSIC—Ball for Horses.—Barbadoes aloes from 4 to 5,
or 6 drs., (according to the size and strength of the horse); tar
trate of potassia 1 dr.; ginger and castile soap, of each 2 drs.; oil
of anise or peppermint 20 drops; pulverize, and make all into
one ball with thick gum solution.

Before giving a horse physic, he should be prepared for
it by feeding scalded bran, in place of oats, for two days at
least, giving also water which has the chill taken off, and
continue this feed and drink, during its operation. If it
should not operate in forty-eight hours, repeat half the dose.

2. Physic for Cattle.—For cattle, take *half* only of the
dose, above, for a horse, and add to it glauber salts 8 ozs.; dissolve all in gruel 1 qt., and give as a drench; for cattle are not
easily managed in giving balls, neither is their construction
adapted to dry medicine.

There is not the need of preparation for cattle, generally,
as for horses, from the fact of their not being kept up to
grain, if they are, however, let the same precautions be observed as in "Physic Ball for Horses."

HOOF-AIL IN SHEEP—Sure Remedy.—Muriatic acid and
butter of antimony, of each 2 oz.; white vitriol, pulverized, 1 oz.
Mix.

Directions.—Lift the foot and drop a little of it upon
the bottom. It will need to be applied only once or twice
a week—as often only as they limp, which shows that the
foot is becoming tender again. It kills the old hoof, and a
new one soon takes its place. Have no fears about the result; apply the medicine as often as indicated, and all is
safe.

It has proved valuable in growing off horse's hoofs, when
snagged, or contraction made it necessary.

EYE WATER—For Horses and Cattle.—Alcohol 1 table-
spoon; extract of lead 1 tea-spoon; rain water ½ pt.

Wash the eye freely, two or three times daily. But I prefer the "Eye Water" as prepared for persons; and allow me here to say that what is good for man, in the line of medicine, is good for a horse, by increasing the dose to correspond.

TAMING—Principles Applied to Wild and Vicious Horses.—I have thought, in closing up this Department, that I could not devote a page to a better purpose than to the so-called *secret* of taming. For it *is* a secret, but it lies in a different point from what is *generally* believed, which I will attempt to show.

Several persons are advertising books for taming wild horses, and other persons are going about teaching the art to classes in private. Probably the pupils get their money's worth. But, why do so many fail? *The whole secret lies in this, that many persons can never handle a horse, with all the instruction in the world—it is not in them.* They cannot establish a sympathy between themselves and the horse, and if they become horse *trainers*, they have only mistaken their calling, and the money they laid out is perhaps as cheap a way as they could be taught their mistake.

To be a *successful* horse trainer, he must have a *sympathy* with the horse, and a *personal* power of control. This reminds us of an old gentleman's remarks on the subject of sweeny. He said : " There were a great many recipes of penetrating oils, applications, etc., but the great secret was in *faith*," without which no person will persevere a sufficient length of time with either of them. This holds good in all diseases, as well as in handling or taming a horse.

The mystery or secret, then, is in *knowing* how, and having the *stamina* (power) to do it.

As for recipes, they consist in using the horse-castor or wart, which grows upon the inside of the leg, grated fine, oil of cumin, and oil of rhodium, kept separate in air-tight bottles ; these all possess peculiar properties for attracting and subduing animals.

" Rub a little oil of cumin upon your hand, and approach the horse in the field, on the windward side, so that he can smell the cumin. The horse will let you come up to him without trouble.

"Immediately rub your hand gently on the horse's nose, getting a little of the oil on it. You can then lead him any where. Give him a little of the castor on a piece of loaf-sugar, apple, or potato.

"Put eight drops of the oil of rhodium into a lady's thimble. Take the thimble between the thumb and middle finger of your right hand, with the fore-finger stopping the mouth of the thimble to prevent the oil from running out whilst you are opening the mouth of the horse.

"As soon as you have opened the horse's mouth, tip the thimble over upon his tongue, and he is your servant. He will follow you like a pet dog. Very doubtful.—AUTHOR.

"Ride fearless and promptly, with your knee pressed to the side of the horse, and your toes turned in and heels out; then you will always be on the alert for a shy or sheer from the horse, and he can never throw you.

"If you want to teach him to lie down, stand on his nigh or left side; have a couple of leather straps, about six feet long; string up his left leg with one of them around his neck; strap the other end of it over his shoulders; hold it in your hand, and when you are ready, tell him to lie down, at the same time gently, firmly, and steadily pulling on the strap, touching him lightly with a switch. The horse will immediately lie down. Do this a few times, and you can make him lie down without the straps.

"He is now your pupil and friend. You can teach him anything, only be kind to him—be gentle. Love him and he will love you. Feed him before you do yourself. Shelter him well, groom him yourself, keep him clean, and at night always give him a good bed."

It will be perceived, by reference to the following item from *Bell's Life*, that the secret for taming horses, by which Mr. Rarey has made himself so rich and famous, instead of being a divination of his own, was probably obtained by him through some accidental contact with an old volume, which had long disappeared from observation, and hardly held a place in public libraries:

A correspondent sends us the following: "In the Gentleman's Farriery, by Bartlett, (sixth edition) published in 1762, (one hundred years ago,) page 293, is the following: 'The method proposed by Dr. Bracken is to tie up one of the fore feet close, and to fasten a cord or small rope about the other fetlock, bringing the end of it over the horse's shoulders; then let him be hit or kicked with your foot behind that knee, at the same time pulling his nose down strongly to the manger You will bring him upon his knees, where he should be held till he is tired which cannot be long, but if he does not lie down soon, let him be thrust sideways against his quarters, to throw him over; by forcing him down several times in this way, you may teach him to lie down, at the same words you first used for that purpose." You will see that Mr. Rarey's system is exactly the same.

From the foregoing it will be seen that he *obtained* the knowledge, and naturally possessing the firmness, *fearless energy.* and *muscle* sufficient to back the whole, he has become *the horse tamer of the world.*

Without all these qualifications no one need undertake the business, no matter how often he pays five dollars for recipes or instructions.

<hr>

CABINET MAKERS' DEPARTMENT.

POLISH—For New Furniture.—Alcohol 98 per cent. 1 pt.; gums copal and shellac, of each 1 oz.; dragon's blood ½ oz. Mix and dissolve by setting in a warm place.

Apply with a sponge (it is best in the sun or a warm room) about three coats, one directly after the other as fast as dry, say fifteen to twenty minutes apart; then have a small bunch of cotton batting tied up in a piece of woolen; wet this in alcohol and rub over the surface well; now go over the surface with a piece of tallow, then dust on rotten stone from a woolen bag and rub it with, what is often called, the heel of the hand; now wipe it off with cotton cloth, and the more you rub with this last cloth, the better will be the polish.

Although this professes to be for new work, it does not hurt the looks of old, not the least bit; try it all who want their furniture to show a gloss and answer in place of looking-glasses.

If soldiers will try it on their gun-stocks, they will find it just the thing desired.

2. POLISH FOR REVIVING OLD FURNITURE, EQUAL TO THE "BROTHER JONATHAN."—Take alcohol 1½ ozs.; spirits of salts (muriatic acid) ½ oz.; linseed-oil 8 ozs.; best vinegar ½ pt.; and butter of antimony 1½ ozs.; mix, putting in the vinegar last.

It is an excellent reviver, making furniture look nearly equal to new, and really giving a polish to new work, always shaking it as used. But if you cannot get the butter of antimony, the following will be the next best thing:

3. POLISH FOR REMOVING STAINS, SPOTS, AND MILDEW, FROM FURNITURE.—Take of 98 per cent. alcohol ½ pt.; pulverized rosin and gum shellac, of each ⅞ oz. Let these cut in the alcohol; then add linseed-oil ½ pt.: shake well, and apply with a sponge, brush, or cotton flannel, or an old newspaper, rubbing it well after the application, which gives a nice polish.

These are just the thing for new furniture when sold and about to be taken out of the shop; removing the dust and giving the new appearance again.

4. JET, OR POLISH FOR WOOD OR LEATHER, BLACK, RED, OR BLUE.—Alcohol (98 per cent.) 1 pt.; sealing wax, the color desired, 3 sticks; dissolve by heat, and have it warm when applied. A sponge is the best to apply it with.

For black on leather it is best to apply copperas water first, to save extra coats; and paint wood the color desired also, for the same reason. On smooth surfaces, use the tallow and rotten stone as in the first polish. It may be applied to carriage-bodies, cartridge-boxes, dashes, fancy-baskets, straw-bonnets, straw-hats, &c.

FURNITURE—FINISHING WITH ONLY ONE COAT OF VARNISH, NOT USING GLUE, PASTE, OR SHELLAC.—Take boiled linseed-oil and give the furniture a coat with a brush; then immediately sprinkle dry whiting upon it and rub it in well with your hand, or a brush which is worn rather short and stiff, over all the surface—the whiting absorbs the oil; and the pores of the wood are thus filled with a perfect coat of putty, which will last for ages; and water will not spot it nor have any effect upon it.

For mouldings and deep creases in turned work, you can mix them quite thick, and apply them together, with the old brush, but on smooth surfaces, the hand and dry whiting are best. If black walnut is the wood to be finished, you will put a trifle of burned umber in the whiting,—if for cherry, a little Venetian-red; beech or maple will re quire less red. Only sufficient is to be used, in either case, to make the whiting the color of the wood, being finished. Bedstead-posts, banisters, or standards for bedsteads and all other turned articles can have the finish put on in the lathe, in double quick time; spreading a newspaper on the lathe to save the scattering whiting, applying it with the hand or hands, having an old cloth to rub off the loose whiting which does not enter the pores of the wood,—the same with smooth surfaces also.

This preparation is cheap; and it is a wonder that furniture men have not thought of it before. Three coats of varnish without it is not as level as one with it. From the fact that some of the varnish enters the pores of the wood and does not dry smooth; but with the pores filled with this preparation, of course, it must dry smooth and level, without rubbing down.

STAINS—MAHOGANY ON WALNUT, NATURAL AS NATURE.—Apply aquafortis by means of a rag tacked to a stick; for if you use a brush it will very soon destroy it. Set the furniture in the hot sun to heat in the aquafortis, if no sun, heat it in by a stove or fire.

It is better if heat in, but does quite well without heating. Finish up in every other way as usual.

This finish is applicable to fancy tables, stands, lounges, coffins, &c., and equally beautiful on knots and crotches, giving walnut the actual appearance of mahogany, and as it is *appearances* only that most people depend upon, why will not this do as well as to trasport timber from beyond the seas.

2. ROSE-WOOD STAIN, VERY BRIGHT SHADE—USED COLD.—Take alcohol 1 gal.; camwood 2 ozs.; let them stand in a warm place 24 hours; then add extract of logwood 3 ozs.; aquafortis 1 oz.; and when dissolved it is ready for use; it makes a very bright ground, like the most beautiful rose-wood—one, two or more coats, as you desire, over the whole surface.

This part makes the bright streaks or grains; the dark ones is made by applying, in waves, the following:

Take iron turnings or chippings, and put vinegar upon them; let it stand a few hours and it is ready to apply over the other, by means of a comb made for graining; or a comb made from thinnish India-rubber; the teeth should be rather good length; say half an inch, and cut close together or further apart, as desired; and with a little practice, excellent imitation will be made.

This, for chairs, looks very beautiful to apply the darkening mixture by means of a flat, thin-haired, brush, leaving only a little of the red color in sight; and if you want to make the cringles, as sometimes seen in rose-wood, it is done with a single tooth or pen, bearing on sometimes hard and then light, &c., &c. All can and must be got by practice.

The above stain is very bright. If, however, you wish a lower shade, use the next recipe.

3. ROSE-WOOD STAIN—LIGHT SHADE.—Take equal parts of logwood and redwood chips, and boil well in just sufficient water to make a strong stain; apply it to the furniture while hot, 1 or 2, or even 3 coats may be put on, one directly after the other, according to the depth of color desired.

For the dark lines, use the iron chippings as in the above recipe. Or, if a rose-pink is desired, use the following:

4. ROSE-PINK, STAIN AND VARNISH, ALSO USED TO IMITATE ROSE-WOOD.—Put an ounce of potash into a quart of water, with red sanders 1½ ozs.; extract the color from the wood and strain; then add gum shellac ¼ lbs.; dissolve it by a quick fire—used upon logwood stain for rose-wood imitation.

5. BLACK WALNUT STAIN.—Whenever persons are using walnut which has sap-edges, or if two pieces are being glued together which are different in shade, or when a poplar pannel, or other wood is desired to be used to imitate black walnut, you will find the following to give excellent satisfaction:

Spirits of turpentine 1 gal.; pulverized gum asphaltum 2 lbs. Put them into an iron kettle and place upon a stove, which prevents the possibility of fire getting at the turpentine; dissolve by heat, frequently stirring until dissolved. Put into a jug or can while hot.

When desired to use any of it, pour out and reduce with turpentine to the right shade for the work being stained. With a little practice you can make any shade desired. If used with a brush over a red stain, as mentioned in the rose-wood stain recipes, especially for chairs and bedsteads, it very nearly resembles that wood. Mixing a little varnish with the turpentine when reducing it, prevents it from spotting, and causes it to dry quicker. By rubbing a little lamp-black with it you can make it a perfect black, if desired.

6. CHERRY STAIN.—Take rain water 3 qts.; anotta 4 ozs.; boil in a copper kettle until the anotta is dissolved ; then put in a piece of potash the size of a common walnut, and keep it on the fire about half an hour longer, and it is ready for use. Bottle for keeping.

This makes poplar or other light-colored woods so near the color of cherry that it is hard to distinguish ; and even improves the appearance of light-colored cherry.

VARNISHES—BLACK, WITH ASPHALTUM.—Spirits of turpen tine 1 gal.; pulverized gum asphaltum 2¼ lbs.; dissolve by heat, over a stove fire.

It is applied to iron, frames of door plates, back-grounds in crystal painting, etching upon glass, and also for fence-wire, or screens which are to go into water above mills to turn leaves and drift-wood, &c.

2. PATENT VARNISH, FOR WOOD OR CANVASS.— Take spirits of turpentine 1 gal.; asphaltum 2¼ lbs.; put them into an iron kettle which will fit upon a stove, and dissolve the gum by heat. When dissolved and a little cool, add copal varnish 1 pt., and boiled linseed-oil ¼ pt.; when cold it is ready for use. Perhaps a little lamp-black would make it a more perfect black.

If done over a common fire, the turpentine will be very likely to take fire and be lost ; and, perhaps, fire the house or your clothes.

This is valuable for wood, iron, or leather ; but for cloth, first make a sizing by boiling flax-seed one quart, in water one gallon ; applying of this for the first coat ; the second coat of common thick black paint ; and lastly a coat of the varnish. Some think that sperm oil, the same quantity, makes a little better gloss.

3. VARNISH, TRANSPARENT, FOR WOOD.—Best alcohol 1 gal.; nice gum shellac 2¼ lbs. Place the jug or bottle in a situation to keep it just a little warm, and it will dissolve quicker than if hot, or left cold.

This varnish is valuable for plows, or any other article where you wish to show the grain of the wood, and for pine, when you wish to finish up rooms with white, as the " Porcelain Finish ;" a coat or two of it effectually prevents the pitch from oozing out, which would stain the finish.

If this stands in an open dish, it will become thick by evaporation ; in such cases add a little more alcohol, and it is as good as before. Some do use as much as three and a half pounds of shellac, but it is too thick to spread well, better apply two or more coats, if necessary. When a black varnish is wanted, you can rub lamp-black with this, for that purpose, if preferred before the asphaltum, last given.

BARBERS' AND TOILET DEPARTMENT.

HAIR DYE—IN TWO NUMBERS.—No. 1. Take gallic acid ¼ oz.; alcohol 8 ozs.; soft water 16 ozs.; put the acid in the alcohol, then add the water.

No. 2. Take for No. 2, crystalized nitrate of silver 1 oz.: ammonia, strongest kind, 3 ozs.; gum arabic ½ oz.; soft water 6 ozs. Observe, in making it, that the silver is to be put into the ammonia, and not corked until it is dissolved; the gum is to be dissolved in the water, then all mixed, and it is ready for use.

Barbers will probably make this amount at a time, as it comes much cheaper than in small quantities; but if families or others, for individual use, only wish a little, take drachms, instead of ounces, which you see will make only one-eighth of the amount.

DIRECTIONS FOR APPLYING.—First, wash the whiskers or hair with the "shampoo," and rinse out well, rubbing with a towel until nearly dry; then with a brush apply No. 1, wetting completely, and use the dry towel again to remove all superfluous water; then with another brush, (tooth-brushes are best,) wet every part with No. 2, and it becomes instantaneously black; as soon as it becomes dry, wash off with hard water, then with soap and water; apply a little oil, and all is complete.

The advantages of this dye are, that if you get any stain upon the skin, wipe it off with a cloth at the time, and the washing removes all appearances of stain; and the whiskers or hair never turn red, do not crock, and are a beautiful black.

However, cyanuret of potassium 1 dr., to 1 oz. of water, will take off any stain upon the skin, arising from nitrate of silver; but it is poison, and should not touch sore places nor be left where children may get at it.

Persons whose hair is prematurely gray, will find dye less trouble in using, than the restoratives; for when once applied, nothing more needs being done for several weeks; whilst the restoratives are only slow dyes, and yet need several applications. But that all may have the chance of choosing for themselves, I give you some of the best restoratives in use.

HAIR RESTORATIVES AND INVIGORATORS.—EQUAL TO WOOD'S, FOR A TRIFLNIG COST.—Sugar of lead, borax, and lac-sulphur, of each 1 oz.; aqua ammonia ½ oz.; alcohol 1 gill. These articles to stand mixed for 14 hours; then add bay rum 1 gill; fine table salt 1 table-spoon; soft water 3 pts.; essence of bergamot 1 oz.

This preparation not only gives a beautiful gloss, but will cause hair to grow upon bald heads arising from all common causes; and turn gray hair to a dark color.

MANNER OF APPLICATION.—When the hair is thin or bald, make two applications daily, until this amount is used up, unless the hair has come out sufficiently to satisfy you before that time; work it to the roots of the hair with a soft brush or the ends of the fingers, rubbing well each time. For gray hair one application daily is sufficient. It is harmless and will do all that is claimed for it, does not cost only a trifle in comparison to the advertised restoratives of the day; and will be found as good or better than most of them.

2 INVIGORATOR.—Vinegar of cantharides 1 oz.; cologne-water 1 oz.; and rose-water 1 oz.; mixed and rubbed to the roots of the hair, until the scalp smarts, twice daily, has been very highly recommended for bald heads, or where the hair is falling out.

If there is no fine hair on the scalp, no restorative, nor invigorator on earth can give a head of hair. See remarks after No. 5.

3. ANOTHER.—Lac-sulphur and sugar of lead, of each 1 dr.; tannin and pulverized copperas, each 32 grs.; rose-water 4 ozs.; wetting the hair once a day for 10 or 12 days, then once or twice a week will keep up the color.

If it is only desired to change gray hair to a dark color the last will do it; but where the hair is falling out or has already fallen, the first is required to stimulate the scalp to healthy action.

4. ANOTHER.—Lac-sulphur and sugar of lead, of each 1 oz.;

pulverized litharge, (called lithrage) 1¼ ozs.; rain water 1 qt ; applying 3 mornings and skipping 3, until 9 applications—gives a nice dark color.

I obtained this of one of the Friends, at Richmond, Ind., and for turning white or gray hair, it is a good one. The litharge sets the color, as the sulphate of iron does in the next. There is but little choice between them.

5. ANOTHER.—Rain water 6 ozs.; lac-sulphur ½ oz.; sugar of lead ¼ oz.; sulphate of iron (copperas,) ¼ oz; flavor with berga-mot essence, if desired; and apply to the hair daily until suffi-ciently dark to please.

All the foregoing restoratives will change, or color the gray or white hair black, or nearly so; but let who will tell you that his restorative will give your hair its original color, just let that man go for all he is worth at the time; for as time advances his worth will be beautifully less.

6. HAIR INVIGORATOR.—A Wheeling barber makes use of the following invigorator to stop hair from falling out, or to cause it to grow in; it is a good one, so is the one follow-ing it :

Take bay rum 1 pt.; alcohol ½ pt.; castor oil ½ oz.; carbonate of ammonia ¼ oz.; tincture of cantharides ½ oz. Mix, and shake when used. Use it daily, until the end is attained.

7. ANOTHER.—Carbonate of ammonia 1 oz.; rubbed up in 1 pt. of sweet oil. Apply daily until the hair stops falling out, or is sufficiently grown out.

This last is spoken of very highly in England, as a pro-ducer of hair, "Where the hair ought to grow," and does not.

8. STRONG sage tea, as a daily wash is represented to stop hair from falling out; and what will stop it from falling, is an invigorator and consequently good.

There is not a liniment mentioned in this book, but which, if well rubbed upon the scalp daily for two or three months, will bring out a good head of hair; when the scalp has be-come glossy and shining, however, and no fine hair growing, you may know that the hair follicle or root, is dead; and nothing can give a head of hair in such cases, any more than grain can grow from ground which has had none scat-tered upon it. This condition may be known by the shin-ing or glistening appearance of the scalp

All heads as well as bodies should be often washed with soap and clean water; but if that is neglected too long, it becomes necessary to use something stronger to remove the grease and dandruff—then the following will be found just the thing to be desired.

SHAMPOOING MIXTURES—FOR FIVE CENTS PER QUART. —Purified carbonate of potash, commonly called, salts of tartar 1 oz.; rain water 1 qt.; mix, and it is ready for use.

Apply a few spoons of it to the head, rubbing and working it thoroughly; then rinse out with clean soft water, and dry the hair well with a coarse, dry towel, applying a little oil or pomatum to supply the natural oil which has been saponified and washed out by the operation of the mixture. A barber will make at least five dollars out of this five cents worth of material.

2. ANOTHER excellent shampoo is made by using aqua ammonia 3 ozs.; salts of tartar ¼ oz.; alcohol ½ oz.; and soft water 2½ pts. and flavoring with bergamot. In applying, rub the head until the lather goes down; then wash out.

The next recipe also, makes as good a shampoo mixture as I wish; for it kills so many birds at one throw that I do not wish to throw any other.

RENOVATING MIXTURES—FOR GREASE SPOTS, SHAMPOOING, AND KILLING BED-BUGS.—Aqua ammonia 2 ozs.; soft water 1 qt.; saltpetre 1 tea-spoon; variegated shaving soap 1 oz., or one 3 cent cake, finely shaved or scraped; mix all, shake well, and it will be a little better to stand a few hours or days before using, which gives the soap a chance to dissolve.

DIRECTIONS.—Pour upon the place a sufficient amount to well cover any grease or oil which may get spilled or daubed upon coats, pants, carpets, &c., sponging and rubbing well and applying again if necessary to saponify the grease in the garment; then wash off with clear cold water.

Don't squirm now, for these are not half it will do—some people fly entirely off the handle when a preparation is said to do many things—for my part, however, I always admire an article in proportion to the labor which can be performed by it or with it. This preparation will shampoo like a charm; raising the lather in proportion to the amount of grease and dandruff in the hair. It will remove paint, even from a board, I care not how long it has been applied, if oil was used in the paint—and yet it does not injure the finest textures, for the simple reason that its affinity is for grease or oil, changing them to soap, and thus loosening any substance with which they may be combined.

If it is put upon a bed-bug he will never step afterwards· and if put into their crevices, it destroys their eggs and thus drives them from the premises.

A cloth wet with it will soon remove all the grease and dirt from doors which are much opened by kitchen-hands.

2. RENOVATING CLOTHES—GENTLEMEN'S WEAR.—To warm soft water 4 gals., put in 1 beef's gall; saleratus ¼ lb. Dissolve.

Lay the garment on a bench and scour every part thoroughly by dipping a stiff brush into the mixture; spots of grease and the collar must be done more thorough, and longer continued than other parts, and rinse the garment in the mixture by raising up and down a few times, then the same way in a tub of soft cold water; press out the water and hang up to dry; after which it needs brushing the way of the nap and pressing well under a damp cloth.

Beef's gall will set the color on silks, woolen, or cotton— one spoon to a gallon of water is sufficient for this purpose. Spotted bombazine or bombazette washed in this will also look nearly equal to new.

3. FADED AND WORN GARMENTS—TO RENEW THE COLOR.— To alcohol 1 qt., add extract of logwood ¼ lb.; loaf sugar 2 oz.; blue vitriol ¼ oz.; heat gently until all are dissolved; bottle for use.

DIRECTIONS.—To one pint of boiling water put three or four tea-spoons of the mixture, and apply it to the garment with a clean brush; wetting the fabric thoroughly; let dry: then suds out well and dry again to prevent crocking; brush with the nap to give the polish. This may be applied to silks and woolen goods having colors; but is most applicable to gentlemen's apparel.

COLOGNES—IMPERIAL.—Take oils of bergamot 1 oz.; neroli 1 dr.; jessamine ¼ oz.; garden lavender 1 dr.; cinnamon 5 drops; tincture of benzoin 1½ ozs.; tincture of musk ¼ oz.; deodorized or cologne alcohol 2 qts.; rose water 1 pt. Mix.

Allow the preparation to stand several days, shaking occasionally, before filtering for use or bottling. This is rather expensive, yet a very nice article. See "Rose-Water."

2. COLOGNE FOR FAMILY USE—CHEAPER.—Oils of rosemary

and lemon, each ¼ oz.; bergamot and lavender, each 1 dr.; cinnamon 8 drops; clove and rose, each 15 drops; common alcohol 2 qts. Mix, and shake 2 or 3 times daily for a week.

Colognes need only be used in very small quantities; the same is true of highly flavored oils or pomades; as too much, even of a good thing, soon disgusts those whom they were intended to please.

HAIR OILS—NEW YORK BARBERS', STAR.—Castor oil 6½ pts.; alcohol 1½ pts.; oil of citronella ¼ oz.; lavender ¼ oz.; mixed and shaken when used, makes one of the finest oils for the hair in use.

I have been told that this amount of alcohol does not cut the oil. Of course, we know that; that is, it does not become clear, neither do we want it to do so; it combines with the oil, and destroys all the gumminess and flavor peculiar to castor oil, by which it becomes one of the best oils for the hair which can be applied. Gills, spoons, or any other measure will do as well, keeping the proportion of flavoring oils; and if the citronella cannot be got, use some other oil in its place; none are equal to it, however.

2. MACASSAR, OR ROSE.—Olive oil 1 qt.; alcohol 2½ ozs.; rose oil ½ dr.; tie chipped-alkanet root 1 oz., into 2 or 3 little muslin bags; let them lie in the oil until a beautiful red is manifested; then hang them up to drain, for if you press them you get out a sediment you do not wish in the oil.

3. FRAGRANT, HOME-MADE.—Collect a quantity of the leaves of any of the flowers that have an agreeable fragrance; or fragrant leaves, as the rose-géranium, &c.; card thin layers of cotton, and dip into the finest sweet oil; sprinkle a small quantity of salt on the flowers; a layer of cotton and then a layer of flowers, until an earthen-ware vessel, or a wide-mouthed glass bottle is full.

Tie, over it, a piece of a bladder; then place the vessel in the heat of the sun; and in fifteen days a fragrant oil may be squeezed out, resembling the leaf used. Or, an extract is made by putting alcohol upon the flowers or leaves, in about the same length of time. These are very suitable for the hair, but the oil is undoubtedly the best.

4. POMADE—OX MARROW.—One of the most beautiful pomades, both in color and action, is made as follows:

Take beef's marrow 1 lb.; alkanet root, not chipped, 1 oz.; put them into a suitable vessel and stew them as you would render tallow; strain through two or three thicknesses of muslin, and

then add, of castor oil ⅜ lb.; bay rum 1 gill; which takes away
the peculiar freshness of the marrow; then use the extract of
the common rose-geranium to give it the flavor desired.

Half as much suet as marrow, also makes a very nice
article; and can be used where the marrow is not easily ob
tained.

BALM OF A THOUSAND FLOWERS.

—As strange
as it may seem, some of the most astonishingly named articles, are the most simple in their composition. Although
thousands of dollars have been made out of the above
named article, it is both cheap and simple :

Deodorized alcohol 1 pt.; nice white-bar soap 4 ozs.; shave the
soap when put in; stand in a warm place until dissolved; then
add oil of citronella 1 dr.; and oils of neroli and rosemary, of
each ½ dr.

It is recommended as a general perfume; but it is more
particularly valuable to put a little of it into warm water,
with which to cleanse the teeth.

RAZOR STROP-PASTE.

—Take the very finest superfine
flour of emery and moisten it with sweet oil; or you may moist-
en the surface of the strop with the oil, then dust the flour of
emery upon it, which is perhaps the best way.

Nothing else is needed. You must not take any of the
coarse flours, nothing but the finest will do. It is often
mixed with a little oil and much other stuff which is of no
use, and put up in little boxes and sold at two shillings, not
having more than three cent's worth of emery.

BAKERS' AND COOKING DEPARTMENT

REMARKS.—It may not be considered out of place to
make a few remarks here, on the art, as also on the principles, of cookery. For nearly all will acknowledge cooking
not only to be an art, but a science, as well. To know how
to cook economically is an art. Making money is an art.
Now is there not more money made and lost in the kitchen
than almost any where else ? Does not many a hard-work-
ing man have his substance wasted in the kitchen ? Does

not many a shiftless man have his substance saved in the kitchen? A careless cook can waste as much as a man can earn, which might as well be saved. It is not what we earn, as much as what we save, that makes us well-off. A long and happy life is the reward of obedience to nature's laws; and to be independent of want, is not to want what we do not need. Prodigality and idleness constitute a crime against humanity. But frugality and industry, combined with moral virtue and intelligence, will insure individual happiness and national prosperity. Economy is an institute of nature and enforced by Bible precept: "Gather up the fragments, that nothing be lost." Saving is a more difficult art than earning. some people put dimes into pies and puddings, where others only put in cents; the cent dishes are the most healthy.

Almost any woman can cook well, if she have *plenty* with which to do it; but the real *science* of cooking is to be able to cook a good meal, or dish, with but *little* out of which to make it. This is what our few recipes shall assist you in doing.

As to the principles of cooking, remember that water can. not be made more than boiling hot—no matter how much you hasten the fire, you cannot hasten the cooking, of meat potatoes, &c., one moment : a brisk boil is sufficient. When meat is to be boiled for eating, put it into boiling water at the beginning, by which its juices are preserved But if you wish to extract these juices for soup or broth, put the meat. in small pieces, into cold water, and let it simmer slowly.

The same principle holds good in baking, also. Make the oven the right heat, and give it *time* to bake through, is the, true plan; if you attempt to hurry it, you only *burn*, instead of cooking it *done*.

If you attempt the boiling to hurry, the wood only is wasted ·
But, in attempting the baking to hurry, the food, as well, isn t fit to be tasted.

CAKES—FEDERAL CAKE.—Flour 2½ lbs.; pulverized white sugar 1¼ lbs.; fresh butter 10 ozs ; 5 eggs well beaten ; carbonate of ammonia ⅛ oz.; water ½ pt., or milk is best, if you have it.

Grind down the ammonia, and rub it with the sugar. Rub the butter into the flour; now make a bowl of the flour, (unless you choose to work it up in a dish,) and put in the eggs, milk, sugar, &c., and mix well, and roll out to about a quarter of an inch in thickness ; then cut out with a round cutter, and place on tins so they touch each other and instead of rising up thicker, in baking, they fill up the space between, and make a square-looking cake, all attached together.   While they are yet warm, drench over with white coarsely-pulverized sugar.   If they are to be kept in a show-case, by bakers, you can have a board as large as the tin on which you bake them, and lay a dozen or more tins-ful on top of each other, as you sprinkle on the sugar.   I cannot see why they are called "Federal," for really, they are good enough for any "Whig."

Ammonia should be kept in a wide-mouthed bottle, tight-ly corked, as it is a very volatile salt.   It is known by various names, as "volatile salts," "sal volatile," "hartshorn," "hartshorn-shavings," &c., &c.   It is used for smelling-bot-tles, fainting, as also in baking.

2. ROUGH-AND-READY CAKE.—Butter or lard 1 lb.; molasses 1 qt.; soda 1 oz.; milk or water ½ pt.; ground ginger 1 table-spoon; and a little oil of lemon; flour sufficient.

Mix up the ginger in flour, and rub the butter or lard in also ; dissolve the soda in the milk or water; put in the molasses, and use the flour in which the ginger and butter is rubbed up, and sufficient more to make the dough of a proper consistence to roll out ; cut the cakes out with a long and narrow cutter, and wet the top with a little mo-lasses and water, to remove the flour from the cake ; turn the top down, into pulverized white sugar, and place in an oven sufficiently hot for bread, but keep them in only to bake, not to dry up.   This, and the "Federal," are great favorites in Pennsylvania, where they know what is good, and have the means to make it ; yet they are not expen-sive.

3. SPONGE CAKE, WITH SOUR MILK.—Flour 3 cups; fine white sugar 2 cups; 6 eggs; sour milk ½ cup, with saleratus 1 tea-spoon.

Dissolve the saleratus in the milk ; beat the eggs sepa-rately ; sift the flour and sugar ; first put the sugar into the milk and eggs, then the flour, and stir all well together, using any flavoring extract which you prefer, 1 tea-spoon— lemon, however, is the most common   As soon as the flour

It stirred in, put it immediately into a quick oven; and if it is all put into a common square bread-pan, for which it makes the right amount, it will require about twenty to thirty minutes to bake; if baked in small cakes, proportion ately less.

4. SPONGE CAKE WITH SWEET MILK.—As sour milk cannot always be had, I give you a sponge cake with sweet milk

Nice brown sugar 1½ cups; 3 eggs; sweet milk 1 cup; flour 3½ cups; cream of tartar and soda, of each 1 tea-spoon; lemon essence 1 tea-spoon.

Thoroughly beat the sugar and eggs together; mix the cream of tartar and soda in the milk, stirring in the flavor also; then mix in the flour, remembering that all cakes ought to be baked soon after making. This is a very nice cake, notwithstanding what is said of " Berwick," below.

5. BERWICK SPONGE CAKE WITHOUT MILK.—Six eggs, powdered white sugar 3 cups; sifted flour 4 even cups; cream of tartar 2 tea-spoons; cold water 1 cup; soda 1 tea spoon; one lemon.

First, beat the eggs two minutes, and put in the sugar and beat five minutes more; then stir in the cream of tartar and two cups of the flour, and beat one minute; now dissolve the soda in the water and stir in, having grated the rind of the lemon, squeeze in half of the juice only; and finally add the other two cups of flour and beat all one minute, and put into deep pans in a moderate oven. There is considerable beating about this cake, but if *itself* does not beat all the sponge cakes you ever beat, we will acknowl edge it to be the *beating* cake, all around.

6. SURPRISE CAKE.—One egg; sugar 1 cup; butter ½ cup; sweet milk 1 cup; soda 1 tea-spoon; cream of tartar 2 teaspoons.

Flavor with lemon, and use sufficient sifted flour to mak the proper consistence, and you will really be surprised t see its bulk and beauty.

7. SUGAR CAKE.—Take 7 eggs and beat the whites and yolks separately; then beat well together; now put into them sifted white sugar 1 lb.; with melted butter ½ lb., and a small teaspoon of pulverized carbonate of ammonia.

Stir in just sufficient sifted flour to allow of its being rolled out and cut into cakes.

8. GINGER CAKE.—Molasses 2 cups; butter, or one-half lard if you choose, 1½ cups; sour milk 2 cups; ground ginger 1 tea-spoon, saleratus 1 heaping tea-spoon.

Mash the saleratus, then mix all these ingredients together in a suitable pan, and stir in flour as long as you can with a spoon; then take the hand and work in more, just so you can roll them by using flour dusting pretty freely; roll out thin, cut and lay upon your buttered or floured tins; then mix one spoon of molasses and two of water, and with a small brush or bit of cloth wet over the top of the cakes; this removes the dry flour, causes the cakes to take a nice brown and keep them moist; put into a quick oven, and ten minutes will bake them if the oven is sufficiently hot. Do not dry them all up, but take out as soon as nicely browned.

We have sold cakes out of the grocery for years, but never ound any to give as good satisfaction as these, either at table for counter. They keep moist, and are sufficiently rich and ight for all cake eaters.

9 TEA OR CUP CAKE.—Four eggs; nice brown sugar 2 cups; saleratus 1 tea-spoon; sour milk 3 cups; melted butter or half lard 1 cup; half a grated nutmeg; flour.

Put the eggs and sugar into a suitable pan and beat together· dissolve the saleratus in the milk and add to the eggs and sugar· put in the butter and nutmeg also stir all well: then sift in flour sufficient to make the mass to such a consistence that it will not run from a spoon when ifted upon it. Any one preferring lemon can use that in place of nutmeg. Bake rather slowly.

10 CAKE, NICE, WITHOUT EGGS OR MILK.—A very nice cake is made as follows, and it will keep well also:

Flour 3½ lbs.; sugar 1¼ lb; butter 1 lb; water ½ pt: having 1 tea-spoon of saleratus dissolved in it.
Roll thin and bake on tin sheets.

11. PORK CAKE, WITHOUT BUTTER, MILK, OR EGGS.—Al most delightful cake is made by the use of pork, which saves the expense of butter, eggs, and milk. It must be tasted to appreciated; and another advantage of it is that you cabe make enough, some leisure day, to last the season through for I have eaten it two months after it was baked, still nice, and moist.

Fat, salt pork, entirely free of lean or rind, chopped so fine as to be almost like lard 1 lb.; pour boiling water upon it $\frac{1}{2}$ pt.; raisins seeded and chopped 1 lb.; citron shaved into shreds $\frac{1}{4}$ lb.; sugar 2 cups; molasses 1 cup; saleratus 1 tea-spoon, rubbed fine and put into the molasses. Mix these all together, and stir in sifted flour to make the consistence of common cake mixtures; then stir in nutmeg and cloves finely ground 1 oz. each; cinnamon, also fine, 2 ozs.; be governed about the time of baking it by putting a sliver into it—when nothing adheres it is done. It should be baked slowly.

You can substitute other fruit in place of the raisins, if desired, using as much or as little as you please, or none at all, and still have a nice cake. In this respect you may call it the accommodation cake, as it accommodates itself to the wishes or circumstances of its lovers.

When *pork* will do all we here claim for it, who will longer contend that it is not fit to eat? Who!

12. CIDER CAKE.—Flour 6 cups; sugar 3 cups; butter 1 cup; 4 eggs; cider 1 cup; saleratus 1 tea-spoon; 1 grated nutmeg.

Beat the eggs, sugar, and butter together, and stir in the flour and nutmeg; dissolve the saleratus in the cider and stir into the mass and bake immediately, in a quick oven.

13. GINGER SNAPS.—Butter, lard, and brown sugar, of each $\frac{1}{4}$ lb.; molasses 1 pt.; ginger 2 table-spoon; flour 1 qt.; saleratus 2 tea-spoons; sour milk 1 cup.

Melt the butter and lard, and whip in the sugar, molasses, and ginger; dissolve the saleratus in the milk and put in; then the flour, and if needed, a little more flour, to enable you to roll out very thin; cut into small cakes and bake in a slow oven until *snappish*.

14. JELLY CAKE.—Five eggs; sugar 1 cup; a little nutmeg; saleratus 1 tea-spoon; sour milk 2 cups; flour.

Beat the eggs, sugar, and nutmeg together; dissolve the saleratus in the milk, and mix; then stir in flour to make only a thin batter, like pan-cakes; three or four spoons of the batter to a common round tin; bake in a quick oven Three or four of these thin cakes, with jelly between, form one cake, the jelly being spread on while the cake is warm

15. ROLL, JELLY CAKE.—Nice brown sugar 1$\frac{1}{2}$ cups; 3 eggs; sweet skim milk 1 cup; flour 2 cups, or a *little* more only; cream of tartar and soda, of each 1 tea-spoon; lemon essence 1 tea-spoon.

Thoroughly beat the eggs and sugar together; mix the

cream of tartar and soda with the milk, stirring in the flavor also ; now mix in the flour, remembering to bake soon, spreading thin upon a long pan ; and as soon as done spread jelly upon the top and roll up ; slicing off only as used ; tho jelly does not come in contact with the fingers, as in the last, or flat cakes.

CAKE TABLE, FIFTEEN KINDS.

	Flour.	Butter.	Sugar.	Milk.	Eggs.	
16. Pound,	1 lb.	1 lb.	1 lb.	—	8	rose-water three spoons, mace, &c.
17. Genuine Whig,	2 "	8 ozs.	8 ozs.	1 pt.	—	raise with yeast.
18. Shrewsbury,	1 "	1 lb.	¾ lb.	—	—	rose-water, &c.
19. Training,	3 "	¾ "	¾ "	—	—	cin'n, nutmeg.
20. Nut-Cake,	7 "	¾ "	2 "	—	7	cin'n, wet with milk, raise with yeast, or wet and raise with sour milk & saleratus.
21. Short-Cake,	5 "	8 ozs.	¾ "	—	8	rose-water and nutmeg.
22. Cymbals,	2 "	8 "	½ "	—	6	rose-water and a little spice.
23. Burk Cake,	5 "	8 "	¾ "	1 pt.	9	rose-water, raise with yeast.
24. Jumbles,	5 "	1 lb.	2 "	—	6	roll out in loaf sugar.
25. Ginger-Bread,	1 "	½ "	½ "	—	3	yolks only—ginger to suit.
26. Wonders,	2 "	¼ "	½ "	—	10	cinnamon.
27. Cookies,	3 "	¾ "	¾ "	—	3	or without eggs —wet up, raise with saleratus and sour milk.
28. York Biscuit,	3 "	½ "	¾ "	—	—	wet up, and raise with sour milk and saleratus.
29. Common,	12 "	3 "	3 "	2 qts.	—	yeast, spice to taste.
30. Loaf,	9 qts.	3 "	4 "	1 gal.	—	wine 1 pt. yeast 1 pint.

31. MOLASSES CAKE.—Molasses 1½ cups ; saleratus 1 tea spoon ; sour milk 2 cups ; 2 eggs ; butter, lard, or pork gravy, what you would take up on a spoon ; if you use lard add, a little salt.

Mix all by beating a minute or two with a spoon, dissolving the saleratus in the milk; then stir in flour to give the consistence of soft-cake, and put directly into a hot oven, being careful not to dry them up by over-baking, as it is a soft, moist cake, that we are after.

32. MARBLED CAKE.—Those having any curiosity to gratify upon their own part, or on the part of friends. will be highly pleased with the contrast seen when they take a piece of a cake made in two parts, dark and light, as follows:

LIGHT PART.—White sugar 1½ cups; butter ¼ cup; sweet milk ¼ cup; soda ½ tea-spoon; cream of tartar 1 tea-spoon. whites of 4 eggs; flour 2¼ cups; beat and mixed as "Gold Cake."

DARK PART.—Brown sugar 1 cup; molasses ½ cup; butter ½ cup, sour milk ¼ cup; soda ½ tea-spoon; cream of tartar 1 tea-spoon; flour 2¼ cups; yolks of 4 eggs; cloves, allspice, cinnamon, and nutmeg, ground, of each ½ table-spoon; beat and mixed as "Gold Cake."

DIRECTIONS.—When each part is ready, drop a spoon of dark, then a spoon of light, over the bottom of the dish, in which it is to be baked, and so proceed to fill up the pan dropping the light upon the dark as you continue with the different layers.

33. SILVER CAKE.—Whites of 1 doz. eggs; flour 5 cups; white sugar and butter, of each 1 cup; cream or sweet milk 1 cup; cream of tartar 1 tea-spoon; soda ½ tea-spoon; beat and mix as the "Gold Cake." Bake in a deep pan

34. GOLD CAKE.—Yolks of 1 doz. eggs; flour 5 cups; white sugar 3 cups; butter 1 cup; cream or sweet milk 1½ cups; soda ½ tea-spoon · cream of tartar 1 tea-spoon. Bake in a deep loaf pan.

Beat the eggs with the sugar, having the butter softened by the fire; then stir it in; put the soda and cream of tartar into the cream or milk, stirring up and mixing all together; then sift and stir in the flour.

The gold and silver cakes dropped as directed in the "Marbled Cake," gives you still another variety.

35. BRIDE CAKE.—Presuming that this work may fall into the hands of some persons who may occasionally have a wedding amongst them, it would be imperfect without a "wedding cake," and as I have lately had an opportunity to test this one, upon "such an occasion," in my own family, I can bear testimony, so can the "printer," to its adaptation for all similar displays.

Take butter 1½ lbs.; sugar 1½ lbs., half of which is to be Orleans sugar; eggs well beaten, 2 lbs.; raisins 4 lbs.; having the seeds taken out, and chopped; English currants having the grit picked out and nicely washed 5 lbs.; citron, cut fine, 2 lbs. sifted flour 2 lbs.; nutmegs 2 in number, and mace as much in bulk; alcohol 1 gill to ½ pt., in which a dozen or fifteen drops of oil of lemon have been put.

When ready to make your cake, weigh your butter and cut it in pieces, and put it where it will soften, but not melt Next, stir the butter to a cream, and then add the sugar, and work till white. Next beat the yolks of the eggs, and put them to the sugar and butter. Meanwhile another person should beat the whites to a stiff froth and put them in. Then add the spices and flour, and, last of all, the fruit, except the citron, which is to be put in about three layers, the bottom layer about one inch from the bottom, and the top one, an inch from the top, and the other in the middle, smoothing the top of the cake by dipping a spoon or two of water upon it for that purpose.

The pan in which it is baked should be about thirteen inches across the top, and five and a half or six inches deep, without scollops, and two three-quart pans also, which it will fill; and they will require to be slowly baked about three to four hours. But it is impossible to give definite rules as to the time required in baking cake. Try whether the cake is done, by piercing it with a broom splinter, and if nothing adheres, it is done.

Butter the cake pans well; or if the pans are lined with buttered white paper, the cake will be less liable to burn. Moving cakes while baking tends to make them heavy.

The price of a large "Bride Cake," like this, would be about twelve dollars, and the cost of making it would be about three dollars only, with your two small ones, which would cost as much to buy them as it does to make the whole three.

The foregoing was written and printed over a year ago. The daughter came home, and took dinner with us, one year from the marriage; and her mother set on some of the cake as nice and moist as when baked.

36. FRUIT CAKE.—As side accompaniments to the "Bride Cake," you will require several "Fruit Cakes," which are to be made as follows:

Butter, sugar, English currants, eggs, and flour, of each 5 lbs Mix as ir the "Bride Cake."

Bake in about six cakes, which would cost from one dol lar and fifty cents to two dollars a-piece, if bought for the occasion.

37. FROSTING, OR ICING, FOR CAKES.—The whites of 8 eggs beat to a perfect froth and stiff; pulverized white sugar 2 lbs.; starch 1 table-spoon; pulverized gum arabic ¼ oz.; the juice of 1 lemon.

Sift the sugar, starch, and gum arabic into the beaten egg, and stir well and long. When the cake is cold lay on a coat of the frosting; it is best not to take much pains in putting on the first coat, as little bits of the cake will mix up with it, and give the frosting a yellow appearance; but on the next day, make more frosting the same as the first, and apply a second coat, and it will be white, clear, and beautiful. And by dipping the knife into cold water as applying, you can smooth the frosting very nicely.

38. EXCELLENT CRACKERS.—Butter 1 cup; salt 1 tea-spoon; flour 2 qts.

Rub thoroughly together with the hand, and wet up with cold water; beat well, and beat in flour to make quite brittle and hard; then pinch off pieces and roll out each cracker by itself, if you wish them to resemble bakers' crackers.

39. SUGAR CRACKERS.—Flour 4 lbs.; loaf sugar and butter, of each ¼ lb.; water 1¼ pts. Make as above.

40. NAPLES BISCUIT.—White sugar, eggs, and flour, of eacn 1 lb.

If properly pulverized, sifted, beat, mixed, and baked the size of Boston crackers, you will say it is nice indeed.

41. BUCKWHEAT SHORT-CAKE.—Take 3 or 4 tea-cups of nice sour milk, 1 tea-spoon of soda-saleratus dissolved in the milk; if the milk is very sour, you must use saleratus in proportion, with a little salt; mix up a dough with buckwheat flour, *thicker* than you would mix the same for griddle-cakes, say quite stiff; put into a buttered tin, and put directly into the stove oven and bake about 30 minutes; or as you would a short-cake from common flour.

It takes the place of the griddle-cake, also of the short-cake, in every sense of the word—nice with meat, butter, honey, molasses, &c No shortening is used, and no need of setting your dish of batter over night, for a drunken

10

husband to set his foot in. Wet the top a little, and warm it up at next meal, if any is left—it is just as good as when first made, while griddle-cakes have to be thrown away. It is also very good, cold.

Was the beauty of this cake known to the majority of persons, throughout the country generally, buckwheat would become as staple an article of commerce as the common wheat. Do not fail to give it a trial. Some persons, in trying it, have not had good luck the first time; they have failed from the milk's being too sour for the amount of saleratus used, or from making the dough too thin. I think I can say we have made it *hundreds* of times with success, as I could eat it while dyspeptic, when I could eat no other warm bread.

42. YEAST CAKE.—Good lively yeast 1 pt.; rye or wheat flour to form a thick batter; salt 1 tea-spoon; stir in and set to rise when risen, stir in Indian meal, until it will roll out good.

When again risen, roll out very thin; cut them into cakes and dry in the shade; if the weather is the least damp, by the fire or stove. If dried in the sun, they will ferment.

To use: Dissolve one in a little warm water, and stir in a couple of table-spoons of flour; set near the fire, and when light, mix into the bread. If made perfectly dry, they will keep for six months.

BREADS—YANKEE BROWN BREAD.—For each good sized loaf being made, take 1½ pts. corn meal, and pour boiling water upon it, to scald it properly; let stand until only blood warm, then put about 1 qt. of rye flour upon the meal, and pour in a good bowl of emptyings, with a little saleratus dissolved in a gill of water, kneading in more flour, to make of the consistence of common bread. If you raise it with yeast, put a little salt in the meal, but if you raise it with salt-risings, or emptyings which I prefer, no more salt is needed.

Form into loaves, and let them set an hour and a half, or until light; in a cool place, in summer, and on the hearth, or under the stove, in winter; then bake about two hours. Make the dough fully as stiff as for wheat bread, or a little harder; for if made too soft it does not rise good. The old style was to use only one-third rye flour, but it does not wear if made that way; or, in other words, most persons get tired of it when mostly corn meal, but I never do when mostly rye flour.

Let all persons bear in mind that bread should never be eaten the day on which it is baked, and *positively* must this be observed by *dyspeptics*. Hotels never ought to be without this bread, nor families who care for health.

2 GRAHAM BREAD.—I find in Zion's Herald, of Boston, edited by Rev. E O. Haven, formerly a Professor in the University at this city, a few remarks upon the " Different Kinds of Bread," including Graham, which so full explain the *philosophy*, and true principles of bread-making, that I give them an insertion, for the benefit of bread-makers. It says:

" Rice flour added to wheat flour, enables it to take up an increased quantity of water." [See the "New French Method of Making Bread."] "Boiled and mashed potatoes mixed with the dough, cause the bread to retain moisture, and prevent it from drying and crumbling. Rye makes a dark-colored bread; but it is capable of being fermented and raised in the same manner as wheat. It retains its freshness and moisture longer than wheat. An admixture of rye flour with that of wheat, decidedly improves the latter in this respect. Indian corn bread is much used in thi. country. Mixed with wheat and rye, a dough is produced capable of fermentation, but pure maize meal cannot be fermented so as to form a light bread. Its gluten lacks the tenacious quality necessary to produce the regular cell-structure. It is most commonly used in the form of cakes, made to a certain degree light by eggs or sour milk, and saleratus, and is generally eaten warm. Indian corn is ground into meal of various degrees of coarseness, but is never made so fine as wheaten flour. Bread or cakes from maize require a considerably longer time to be acted upon by heat in the baking process, than wheat or rye. If ground wheat be unbolted, that is, if its bran be not separated, wheat meal or Graham flour results, from which Graham or dyspepsia bread is produced. It is made in the same general way as other wheaten bread, but requires a little peculiar management. Upon this point, Mr. Graham remarks:

The wheat meal, and especially if it is ground coarsely, swells consiuerably in the dough, and therefore the dough should not at first be made quite so stiff as that made of superfine flour; and when it is raised, if it is found too soft to mould well, a little more meal may be added It should be remarked that dough made of wheat meal will take on the acetous fermentation, or become sour sooner than that made of fine flour. It requires a hotter oven, and to be baked longer, but must not stand so long after being mixed before baking, as that made from flour.

3. BROWN BREAD BISCUIT.—Take corn meal 2 qts.; rye flour 8 pts.; wheat flour 1 pt.; molasses 1 table-spoon ; yeast 3 table spoons, having soda 1 tea-spoon mixed with it.

Knead over night for breakfast. If persons will eat warm bread, this, or buckwheat short-cake, should be the only kinds eaten.

4. DYSPEPTICS' BISCUIT AND COFFEE.—Take Graham-flour (wheat coarsely ground, without bolting,) 2 qts.; corn meal sifted, 1 qt.; butter ½ cup ; molasses 1 cup; sour milk to wet it up with saleratus' as for biscuit.

Roll out and cut with a tea-cup and bake as other biscuit , and when cold they are just the thing for dyspeptics. And if the flour was sifted, none would refuse to eat them :

FOR THE COFFEE.—Continue the baking of the above biscuit in a slow oven for six or seven hours, or until they are browned through like coffee.

DIRECTIONS.—One biscuit boiled ¾ of an hour will be plenty for 2 or 3 cups of coffee, and 2, for 6 persons ; serve with cream and sugar as other coffee.

Dyspeptics should chew very fine, and slowly, not drinking until the meal is over ; then sip the coffee at their leisure, not more than one cup, however. This will be found very nice for common use, say with one-eighth coffee added ; hardly any would distinguish the difference between it and that made from coffee alone. The plan of buying ground coffee is bad ; much of it is undoubtedly mixed with peas, which you can raise for less than fifteen or twenty cents a pound, and mix for yourself.

5. LONDON BAKER'S SUPERIOR LOAF BREAD. -The *Michigan Farmer* gives us the following ; any one can see that it contains sound sense :

"To make a half-peck loaf, take ¼ lb. of well boiled mealy potatoes, mash them through a fine cullender or coarse sieve, add ½ pt. of yeast, or ¼ oz. of German dried-yeast, and 1½ pts. of luke-warm water, (88 deg. Fahr.) together with ¼ lb. of flour, to render the mixture the consistence of thin batter; this mixture is to be set aside to ferment : if set in a warm place it will rise in less than 2 hours, when it resembles yeast, except in color.

The sponge so made is then to be mixed with 1 pt. of water, nearly blood warm—viz. 92 deg. Fahr., and poured into a half, peck of flour, which has previously had 1¼ ozs. of salt mixed into it; the whole should then be kneaded into dough, and allowed to rise in a warm place for 2 hours, when it should be kneaded into loaves and baked."

The object of adding the mashed potatoes is to increase the amount of fermentation in the sponge, which it does to a very remarkable degree, and consequently, renders the bread lighter and better. The potatoes will also keep the bread moist.

6. OLD BACHELOR'S BREAD, BISCUIT, OR PIE-CRUST.—Flour 1 qt.; cream of tartar 2 tea-spoons; soda ¼ tea-spoon; sweet milk to wet up the flour to the consistence of biscuit dough.

Rub the flour and cream of tartar well together; dissolve the soda in the milk, wetting up the flour with it and bake *immediately*. If you have no milk, use water in its place, adding a spoon of lard to obtain the same richness. It does well for pie-crust where you cannot keep up sour milk.

7. NEW FRENCH METHOD OF MAKING BREAD.—Take rice ¾ lb.; tie it up in a thick linen bag, giving ample room for it to swell; boil it from 3 to 4 hours, or until it becomes a perfect paste; mix this while warm with 7 lbs. of flour adding the usual quantities of yeast and salt; allow the dough to work a proper time near the fire, then divide into loaves. Dust them in, and knead vigorously.

This quantity of flour and rice makes about thirteen and one-half lbs. of bread, which will keep moist much longer than without the rice. It was tested at the London Polytechnic Institute, after having been made public in France, with the above results.

8. BAKING POWDERS, FOR BISCUIT WITHOUT SHORTENING. —Bi-carbonate of soda 4 ozs.; cream of tartar 8 ozs.; and properly dry them, and thoroughly mix. It should be kept in well corked bottles to prevent dampness which neutralizes the acid.

Use about three tea-spoons to each quart of flour being baked; mix with milk, if you have it, if not, wet up with cold water and put *directly* into the oven to bake.

PIES.—LEMON PIE, EXTRA NICE.—One lemon; water 1 cup; brown sugar 1 cup; flour 2 table-spoons; 5 eggs; white sugar 2 table-spoons.

Grate the rind from the lemon, squeeze out the juice, and chop up the balance very fine; put all together and add the water, brown sugar, and flour, working the mass into a smooth paste; beat the eggs and mix with the paste, saving the whites of two of them; make two pies, baking with no top crust; while these are baking, beat the whites of the two eggs, saved for that purpose, to a stiff froth and stir in the white sugar; when the pies are done, spread this frosting evenly over them, and set again in the oven and brown slightly.

2. Pie-Crust Glaze.—In making any pie which has a juicy mixture, the juice soaks into the crust, making it soggy and unfit to eat; to prevent this:

Beat an egg well; and with a brush or bit cf cloth, wet the crust of the pie with the beaten egg, just before you put in the pie mixture.

For pies which have a top crust also, wet the top with the same before baking, which gives it a beautiful yellow brown. It gives beauty also to biscuit, ginger cakes, and is just the thing for rusk, by putting in a little sugar.

3. Apple Pie which is Digestible.—Instead of mixing up your crust with water and lard, or butter, making it very rich, with shortening, as customary for apple pies:

Mix it up every way just as you would for biscuit, using sour milk and saleratus, with a *little* lard or butter only; mix the dough quite stiff, roll out rather thin, lay it upon your tin, or plate; and having ripe apples sliced or chopped nicely and laid on, rather thick, and sugar according to the acidity of the apples, then a top crust, and bake well, putting the egg upon the crusts, as mentioned in the " Pie Crust Glaze," and you have got a pie that is fit to eat.

But when you make the rich crust, and cook the apples and put them on, it soaks the crust, which does not bake, and no stomach can digest it, whilst our way gives you a nice light crust, and does not take half the shortening of the other plan; yet perhaps nothing is saved pecuniarily, as butter goes as finely with the biscuit-crust-pies, when hot, as it does with biscuit; but the pie is digestible, and wher it is cold, does not taste bad to cut it up on your plate, with plenty of sweetened cream.

4. Apple Custard Pie—The Nicest Pie ever Eaten.— Peel sour apples and stew until soft and not much water left in them; then rub them through a cullender—beat 3 eggs for each pie to be baked; and put in at the rate of 1 cup of butter and 1 of sugar for 3 pies; season with nutmeg

My wife has more recently made them with only 1 egg to each pie, with only half of a cup of butter and sugar each, to 4 or 5 pies; but the amount of sugar must be governed somewhat by the acidity of the apples.

Bake as pumpkin pies, which they resemble in appearance; and between them and apple pies in taste; very nice indeed. We find them equally nice with dried apples by making them a little more juicy.

If a frosting was put upon them, as in the "Lemon Pie," then returned, for a few moments, to the oven, the appearance, at least, would be improved.

5. APPLE CUSTARD, VERY NICE.—Take tart apples, that are quite juicy, and stew and rub them, as in the recipe above, and to 1 pt. of the apple, beat 4 eggs and put in, with 1 table-spoon of sugar, 1 of butter, and ½ of a grated nutmeg.

Bake as other custards. It is excellent; and makes a good substitute for butter, apple butter, &c.

6. PASTE FOR TARTS.—Loaf sugar, flour, and butter, equal weights of each; mix thoroughly by beating with a rolling-pin, for half an hour; folding up and beating again and again.

When properly mixed, pinch off small pieces and roll out each crust by itself, which causes them to dish so as to hold the tart-mixture. And if you will have a short pie-crust, this is the plan to make it.

PUDDINGS—BISCUIT PUDDING, WITHOUT RE-BAKING.— Take water 1 qt.; sugar ¼ lb.; butter the size of a hen's egg; flour 4 table-spoons; nutmeg, grated ½ of one.

Mix the flour with just sufficient cold water to rub up all the lumps while the balance of the water is heating, mix all, and split the biscuit once or twice, and put into this gravy while it is hot, and keep hot until used at table. It uses up cold biscuit, and I prefer it to richer puddings. It is indeed worth a trial. This makes a nice dip gravy also for other puddings.

2. OLD ENGLISH CHRISTMAS PLUM PUDDING.—The Harrisburg *Telegraph* furnishes its readers with a recipe for the real "Old English Christmas Plum Pudding." After having given this pudding a fair test, I am willing to endorse every word of it; and wish for the holiday to come oftener than once a year:

"To make what is called a pound pudding; take of raisins

well stoned but not chopped, currants thorough.~ washed, 1 lb.
each; chop suet 1 lb. very finely, and mix with tnem; add ¼ lb.
of flour or bread very finely crumbled; 3 ozs. of sugar; 1½ ozs
of grated lemon peel, a blade of mace, ½ of a small nutmeg, 1
tea-spoon of ginger, ½ doz. of eggs, well beaten; work it well together, put it in a cloth, tie it firmly, allowing room to swell; put
it into boiling water, and boil not less than two hours. It should
not be suffered to stop boiling.

The cloth, when about to be used, should be dipped into
oiling water, squeezed dry, and floured; and when the
pudding is done, have a pan of cold water ready, and dip
it in for a moment, as soon as it comes out of the pot, which
prevents the pudding from sticking to the cloth. For a dip-
gravy for this or other puddings, see the "Biscuit Pudding,
without Re-Baking," or "Spreading Sauce for Puddings."

3. INDIAN PUDDING, To BAKE.—Nice sweet milk 1 qt.; butter 1 oz.; 4 eggs, well beaten; Indian meal 1 tea-cup; raisins ½
lb.; sugar ¼ lb.

Scald the milk, and stir in the meal whilst boiling; then
let it stand until only blood-warm, and stir all well together, and bake about one and a half hours. Eaten with sweetened cream, or either of the pudding sauces mentioned in
the "Christmas Pudding."

4. INDIAN PUDDING, To BOIL.—Indian meal 1 qt., with a
little salt; 6 eggs; sour milk 1 cup; saleratus 1 tea-spoon; rai
sins 1 lb.

Scald the meal, having the salt in it; when cool stir in
the beaten eggs; dissolve the saleratus in the milk and stir
in also, then the raisins; English currants, dried. currants,
or dried berries, of any kind, answer every purpose, and are,
in fact, very nice in place of the raisins. Boil about one
and a half hours. Eaten with sweetened cream or any of
the pudding sauces. Any pudding to be boiled must not
be put into the water until it boils, and taken out as soon as
'one, or they become soggy and unfit to eat.

5. QUICK INDIAN PUDDING.—Take 1½ cups of sour milk; 3
eggs well beaten; 1 small tea-spoon of saleratus; dissolved in
the milk; then sift in dry corn meal, and stir to the consistence
of corn bread; then stir in ½ lb. of any of the fruits mentioned
above; or, if you have no fruit, it is quite nice without;

Tie up and boil one hour; sweetened cream with a little
nutmeg makes a nice sauce. As I have just eaten of this
for my dinner, I throw it in extra, for it is worthy.

6. FLOUR PUDDING, To BOIL.—When persons have plenty of dried apples or peaches, and not much of the smaller fruits; or desire to change from them in puddings:

Take wheat flour sufficient to make a good pan of biscuit, and mix it up as for biscuit, with sour milk, saleratus, and a little butter or lard, roll out rather thicker than for pie-crust; now having your apples or peaches nicely stewed wet the crust over with the "Pie Crust Glaze," then spread a layer of the fruit upon it, adding a little sugar, as it lies upon the table; and if you choose, scatter over them a handful of raisins, or any other of the dried fruits mentioned; roll up the whole together, and boil 1 hour.

Eaten with any sauce which you may prefer, but the corn meal puddings are much the most healthy, and I prefer their taste to those made from flour.

7. POTATO PUDDING.—Rub through a cullender 6 large or 12 middle sized potatoes; beat 4 eggs, mix with 1 pt. of good milk; stir in the potatoes, sugar and seasoning to taste; butter the dish; bake ¼ an hour.

This recipe is simple and economical, as it is made of what is wasted in many families, namely, cold potatoes; which may be kept two or three days, until a sufficient quantity is collected. To be eaten with butter.

8. GREEN CORN PUDDING.—Green corn, raw, 2 doz. ears; sweet milk 3 to 4 qts.; 6 eggs; sugar 1 to 2 cups. Salt to suit the taste.

Split the kernels lengthwise of the ear with a sharp knife; then with a case knife scrape the corn from the cob, which leaves the hulls on the cob; mix it with the milk and other articles, and bake from two to three hours. To be eaten with butter and sugar.

9. STEAMED PUDDING.—Two eggs; sugar 1 cup; sour milk 1 cup; saleratus ½ tea-spoon; a little salt; dried whortleberries, currants, raisins, or other fruit 1 cup; flour.

Beat the eggs and stir in the sugar; dissolve the saleratus in the milk, and mix in also the fruit and salt; then thicken with flour, rather thicker than for cake; put into a two-quart pan and set in the steamer, and steam an hour and a half; and I think it will crack open on the back—if not, try again. It is worth the trouble, especially if you have plenty of sweetened cream.

10. SPREADING SAUCE FOR PUDDINGS.—Butter 4 ozs.; sugar 6 ozs.; 1 nutmeg.

Grate the nutmeg, and rub all together; these are about the proper proportions, but more or less can be made, as desired, and more or less nutmeg can also be used; or any other flavoring in their place. This sauce is nice on baked puddings, hot or cold; and to tell it all, it is not bad or bread. See the "Biscuit Pudding," for dip-sauces.

DOMESTIC DISHES—GREEN CORN OMELET.—Green corn boiled 1 doz. ears; 5 eggs; salt and pepper to suit the taste.

Remove the corn from the cob, as mentioned in the "Green Corn Pudding." The splitting allows the escape of the pulp, whilst the hull is held by the cob; season, form into small cakes, and fry to a nice brown, and you have a very nice omelet.

2. APPLES—TO BAKE—STEAMBOAT STYLE—BETTER THAN PRESERVES.—Take moderately sour apples, when ripe; and with a pocket-knife cut out the stem, and flower-end also, so as to remove the skin from these cup-shaped cavities; wash them, and place them in a dripping-pan; now fill these cavities with brown sugar, and pretty freely between them also, with sugar; then lay on a few lumps of butter over the sugar; place them, thus arranged, into the oven when you begin to heat up the stove for breakfast or dinner, and keep them in until perfectly baked through and soft.

Take them up on plates, while hot, by means of a spoon. and dip the gravy, arising from the apple-juice, sugar and butter, over them. Should any of them be left, after the meal is over, set them by until the next meal, when they may be placed in the stove oven until hot, and they will have all the beauty of the first baking. Or perhaps some persons may prefer them fried, as follows:

3. FRIED APPLES—EXTRA NICE.—Take any nice sour cooking apples, and, after wiping them, cut into slices about one-fourth of an inch thick; have a frying-pan ready, in which there is a small amount of lard, say ¼ or ½ of an inch in depth. The lard must be hot before the slices of apples are put in. Let one side of them fry until brown; then turn, and put a small quantity of sugar on the browned side of each slice. By the time the other side is browned, the sugar will be melted and spread over the whole surface.

Serve them up hot, and you will have a dish good enough for kings and queens, or any poor man's breakfast; and I think that even the President would not refuse a few slices, if properly cooked. There is but little choice between frying and baking by these plans; either one is very nice.

4. APPLE FRITTERS.—Sour milk 1 pt.; saleratus 1 tea-spoon; flour to make a batter not very stiff; 6 apples, pared and cored, 3 eggs.

Dissolve the saleratus in the milk; beat the eggs, and put in; then the flour to make a soft batter; chop the apples to about the size of small peas, and mix them well in the batter. Fry them in lard, as you would dough-nuts Eaten with butter and sugar.

5. APPLE MERANGE.—AN EXCELLENT SUBSTITUTE FOR PIE OR PUDDING.—First, take a deep dish and put a bottom crust into it, as for a pie; have nice sour apples, pared, sliced, and stewed, sweetening slightly; place a layer of the stewed apple upon the crust, say about half an inch in thickness, then put on a layer of nice bread, spread with butter, as for eating, then another layer of the apple; now place in the oven and bake as a pudding, or pie; when done, have the whites of eggs beaten and mixed with a little loaf or other white sugar, say 2 eggs for a 2-quart dish; place this upon the merange and return it to the oven for a few minutes, to brown the egg mixture, or frosting. Serve with sugar dissolved in a little water, adding a little butter, with nutmeg, or lemon, as desired or preferred.

6 BREAD, TO FRY—BETTER THAN TOAST.—Take bread that is dry; the dryer the better, so it is not mouldy; first dip it rather quickly into cold water, then into eggs which are well beat, having a little salt in them; then immediately fry for a short time in hot lard until the surface is a pretty yellow or light brown, according to the heat of the lard.

I have never eaten bread cooked in any form which suits me as well as this. But the following is very nice.

7. TOAST—GERMAN STYLE.—Bakers' bread 1 loaf, cut into slices of half an inch in thickness; milk 1 qt.; 3 eggs, and a little salt; beat the eggs and mix them with the milk, and flavor as for custard, not cooking it however. Dip the sliced bread into the mixture occasionally until it is all absorbed; then fry the pieces upon a buttered griddle. Serve, for dinner, with sugar syrup, flavored with lemon.

This is the German style of making toast; but is quite good enough for an American. And I have no doubt that home-made bread will answer all purposes; ours does, certainly.

8. BACK-WOODS PRESERVES.—Moderately boil a pint of molasses, from 5 to 20 minutes, according to its consistency; then

add 3 eggs, thoroughly beaten, hastily stirring them in, and continue boil a few minutes longer; then season with a nutmeg or lemon.

Do not fail to give it a trial.

9. FRENCH HONEY.—White sugar 1 lb.; 6 eggs, leaving out the whites of 2; the juice of 3 or 4 lemons, and the grated rind of 2; and ¼ lb. of butter. Stir over a slow fire until it is about the consistency of honey.

This and the last, will be found to come much nearer what they represent, than the Yankee's "Wooden nutmegs" did, upon trial.

10. MUFFINS.—To each qt. of sweet milk add 2 eggs well beaten; a lump of butter half the size of an egg, and flour enough to make a stiff batter. Stir in ¼ pt. of yeast; let them stand until perfectly light, and then bake on a griddle, in tin rings, made for that purpose.

These are merely strips of tin, three-quarters of an inch wide, made into rings from two and a half to three inches in diameter, without bottom—the ring being simply placed on a griddle, and the batter poured in to fill it.

11. MOCK OYSTERS.—Six, nice, plump, ears of sweet corn, uncooked; grate from the cob; beat 1 egg, stirring into it flour and milk, of each 1 table-spoon; season with a little salt and pepper. Put about a tea-spoon of butter into a suitable pan for frying, having mixed in the corn also, drop the mixture into the hot butter, one spoon of it in a place, turning them so as to fry brown. Serve hot, for breakfast.

Whether they imitate oysters or not, no one need regret giving them a trial.

12. FRUIT JAMS, JELLIES, AND PRESERVES —The difference between common preserves, jellies, and jams, is this : Preserves are made by taking fruit and sugar, pound for pound, and simply cooking them together until the fruit is done.

13. JELLIES are made by squeezing and straining out the juice only, of the fruit; then taking a pound of sugar for a pound of juice, and cooking until it jells, which is told by taking out a little upon a cold plate.

14. JAMS are made by weighing the whole fruit, washing, slicing, and putting in sufficient water to cook it well, then when cool, rubbing it through a fine sieve, and with this pulp, putting in as much sugar as there was of the

fruit only, and cooking it very carefully, until the weight
of the jam is the same as the fruit and added sugar; the
water, you see, is all gone; and this is easily told by having
previously weighed the kettle in which you are cooking it.
The jam, if nicely done, contains more of the fruit flavor
than the jell, and is as valuable as the jell to put into water as
a drink for invalids; and better for flavoring syrups for
soda-fountains, &c.   Strawberries, raspberries, blackberries
peaches, and pine-apples, make very nice jams for flavoring
syrups.   Much of the flavor of the fruit resides in the
skin, pits, &c.   And jams made in this way, from the blackberry, are good for sore mouth, diarrhea, dysentery, &c.

15. FRUIT EXTRACTS.—Best alcohol 1 pt.; oil of lemon 1 oz.;
peel of 2 lemons.

Break the peels, and put in with the others for a few
days: then remove them, and you will have just what you
desire, for a trifling cost, compared with the twenty-five
cent bottles, which are so prominently set out as the nicest
thing in the world.

This rule holds good for all fruit oils; but for fruits,
such as peaches, pine-apples, strawberries, raspberries,
blackberries, &c., you will take alcohol and water equal
parts, and put upon them sufficient to handsomely cover;
and in a few days you have the flavor and juices of the
fruit, upon the principle of making " Bounce," which most
men know more or less about.   If persons will act for
themselves, using common sense, working from known facts
like these, they will not need to run after every new-fangled
thing which is seen blazing forth in almost every advertisement of the day.

Vanilla, nutmeg, mace, cinnamon, &c., are made by cutting up the vanilla bean, or bruising the nutmegs, cinnamon,
&c., and putting about two ounces to each pint of pure
spirit, or reduced alcohol, frequently shaking for about two
weeks, and filtering or pouring off very carefully; if for
sale, however, they must be filtered; for coloring any of
the extracts see the "Essences," and "Syrups."   For cakes
and pies, however, it is just as well to pulverize nutmegs,
mace, cinnamon, &c., and use the powder, for the quantity
required is so small that it will never be seen in the cake or
pie.

MEDICATED WATERS—Rose Water —Take carbonate of magnesia ⅛ oz.; oil of rose 30 drops; drop the oil upon the magnesia, and rub it together; then add, rubbing all the time, of distilled water, if you can get it, 1 qt., if not, take the purest rain or snow water,—a porcelain mortar is best, but a bowl does very well,—then filter through filtering paper.

The magnesia breaks up the oil globules and enables the water to take it up; and the filtering removes the magnesia.

2. Cinnamon Water.—Use the same amount of o_ magnesia, and water, and treat the same as the "Rose Water."

3. Peppermint, Spearmint and Pennyroyal Waters are made the same as above.

4. Camphor Water.—To make camphor water, you must first put on a few drops of alcohol; say 40 or 50 drops, to camphor gum ¼ oz.; and rub the camphor fine, which enables you to work it up with magnesia ⅛ oz.; then gradually add water 1 qt., as mentioned in the waters above, and filtered.

The rose and cinnamon waters are used for cooking but the others for medical purposes.

MISCELLANEOUS DEPARTMENT.

WASHING FLUID—Saving Half the Wash-Board La bor.—Sal-soda 1 lb.; stone lime ½ lb.; water 5 qts.; boil a short time, stirring occasionally; then let it settle and pour off the clear fluid into a stone jug and cork for use; soak your white clothes over night, in simple water; wring out, and soap wrist-bands, collars, and dirty or stained places; have your boiler half filled with water, and when at scalding heat, put in one common tea-cup of the fluid, stir and put in your clothes, and boil for half an hour; then rub lightly through one suds only, rinsing well in the bluing water, as usual, and all is complete.

If you wish to wash on Monday, put warm suds to the clothes whilst breakfast is being got ready; then wring out and soap as above, will do just as well as soaking them over night, and my wife thinks better.

For each additional boiler of clothes add half a cup of the fluid only; of course boiling in the same water through the whole washing. If more water is needed in the boiler for the last clothes, dip it from the sudsing tub. Soak your woolen and calico in the suds from which you have washed the white clothes, whilst hanging them out, dipping in some of the boiling water from the boiler, if necessary; then wash out the woolen and calico as usual—of course, washing out woolen goods before you do the calico. The fluid brightens instead of fading the colors in calico.

This plan not only saves the two rubbings which women give their clothes before boiling, and more than half of the soap—does not injure the clothes, but saves their wear in two rubbings before boiling; and is a good article for removing grease from floors, doors, and windows, and to remove tar or grease from the hands, &c.

I hope every lady into whose hands this recipe may fall, will give it a trial, as my family have now used it over seven years, not missing only two washings. It does not rot clothes, but makes them wash full or more than one-half easier than the old way. Seven years ought to be considered a sufficient test.

The honor of this recipe is accredited to Prof. Liebig, of Germany.

I have found many women using turpentine, alcohol, ammonia, camphor gum, &c., in their washing fluids; but none of them ought ever to be used for such purposes (one woman lost the use of her arm, for six months, by using a fluid containing turpentine); the turpentine and alcohol especially, tend to open the pores of the skin, and thus make the person more liable to take cold in hanging out the clothes, as also to weaken the arm.

And here let me say, if it is possible to avoid it, never allow the woman who washes the clothes, and thus becomes warm and sweaty, to hang them out; and especially ought this to be regarded in the winter or windy weather. Many consumptions are undoubtedly brought on by these frequently repeated colds, in this way. It works upon the principle that two thin shoes make one cold, two colds an attack of bronchitis, two attacks of bronchitis one consumption—the end, a coffin.

LIQUID BLUING—For Clothes.—Most of the bluing sold is poor stuff, leaving specks in the clothes. To avoid this:

Take best Prussian-blue, pulverized, 1 oz.; oxalic acid, also pulverized, ¼ oz.; soft water 1 qt. Mix. The acid dissolves the blue and holds it evenly in the water, so that specking will never take place. One or two table-spoons of it is sufficient for a tub of water, according to the size of the tub.

Chinese-blue, when it can be got, is the best, and only costs one shilling an ounce, with three cents for the acid, will give better satisfaction than fifty cents worth of the common bluing. This amount has now lasted my family over a year

SOAPS—Soft Soap—For Half the Expense and One Fourth the Trouble of the Old Way —Take white-bar soap 4 lbs., cut it fine and dissolve, by heating in soft water 4 gal.; adding sal-soda 1 lb. When all is dissolved and well mixed it is done.

Yellow soap does very well, but Colgate's white, is said to be the best. But our " White Hard Soap" is the same kind.

This soap can be made thicker.or more thin, by using more or less water, as you may think best after once making it. Even in common soft soap, if this amount of sal-soda is put into that number of gallons, washing will be done much easier, and the soap will more than compensate for the ex pense and trouble of the addition.

2. German Erasive, or Yellow Soap.—Tallow and sal-soda, of each 112 lbs.; rosin 56 lbs.; stone lime 28 lbs.; palm-oil 8 lbs.; soft water 28 gals.; *or for small quantities*, tallow and sal-soda, of each 1 lb.; rosin 7 ozs.; stone lime 4 ozs.; palm-oil 1 oz.; soft water 1 qt.

Put soda, lime, and water into a kettle and boil, stirring well; then let it settle and pour off the lye. In another kettle, melt the tallow, rosin and palm-oil; having it hot, the lye being also boiling hot; mix all together stirring well, and the work is done.

3. Hard Soap, with Lard.—Sal-soda and lard, of each 6 lbs. stone lime 3 lbs.; soft water 4 gals.; dissolve the lime and soda in the water, by boiling, stirring, settling and pouring off; then return to the kettle (brass or copper) and add the lard and boil until it becomes soap; then pour into a dish or moulds, and when cold, cut it into bars and let it dry.

This recipe was obtained by finding an over-coat with it in the pocket, and also a piece of the soap; the man kept it with him, as it irritated his salt-rheum so much less than other soaps. It has proved valuable for washing generally;

and also for shaving purposes. It would be better than half the toilet soaps sold, if an ounce or two of sassafras oil was stirred into this amount; or a little of the soap might be put in a separate dish, putting in a little of the oil, to correspond with the quantity of soap.

4. WHITE HARD SOAP, WITH TALLOW.—Fresh slacked lime, sal-soda, and tallow, of each 2 lbs.; dissolve the soda in 1 gal. boiling soft water; now mix in the lime, stirring occasionally or a few hours; after which let it settle, pouring off the clear liquor and boiling the tallow therein until it is all dissolved; cool it in a flat box or pan, and cut into bars, or cakes, as preferred.

It can be flavored with sassafras oil, as the last, by stirring it in when cool; it can be colored also if desired as mentioned in the "Variegated Toilet Soap."

. When any form of soda is used in making soap, it is necessary to use lime to give it causticity; or, in other words, to make it caustic; which gives it much greater power upon the grease, by removing the carbonic acid; hence the benefit of putting lime in the bottom of a leach when making soap from common ashes.

5. TRANSPARENT SOAP.—Take nice yellow bar soap 6 lbs.; cut it thin and put into a brass, tin, or copper kettle, with alcohol ¼ gal.; heating gradually over a slow fire, stirring until all is dissolved; then add an ounce of sassafras essence, and stir until well mixed; now pour into pans about 1½ inches deep and when cold, cut into square bars, the length or width of the pan, as desired.

This gives you a nice toilet soap for a trifling expense, and when fully dry it is very transparent.

6. ONE HUNDRED POUNDS OF GOOD SOAP FOR $1.30.—Take potash 6 lbs., 75 cts.; lard 4 lbs., 50 cts.; rosin ¼ lb., 5 cts.

Beat up the rosin, mix all together, and set aside for five days; then put the whole into a ten gallon cask of warm water, and stir twice a day for ten days; at the expiration of which time you will have one hundred pounds of excellent soap.

7. CHEMICAL SOFT SOAP.—J. Hamilton, an English gentleman, and proprietor of the Eagle Hotel, Aurora, Indiana, makes his soap for house use, as follows:

Take grease 8 lbs.; caustic soda 8 lbs.; sal-soda 1 lb.; melt the grease in a kettle, melt the sodas in soft water 4 gals., and pour all into a barrel holding 40 gals. and fill up with soft water, and the labor is done.

When the caustic soda cannot be obtained of soap-makers, you will make it by taking soda-ash and fresh slacked lime, of each eight pounds; dissolving them in the water with the sal-soda, and when settled, pouring off the clear liquid as in the "White Hard Soap with Tallow."

8. SOAP WITHOUT HEAT.—Mr. Tomilson, writing to Judge Buel, says :

"My wife has no trouble about soap. The grease is put into a cask, and strong lye added. During the year, as the fat increases, more lye is stirred in; and occasionally stirred with a stick that is kept in it. By the time the cask is full, the soap is made for use."

There is no mistake about this manner of making soap. The only object of boiling is to increase the strength of *weak* lye and hasten the process.

9. WINDSOR, OR TOILET SOAP.—Cut some new, white bar soap into thin slices, melt it over a slow fire, and scent it with oil of caraway; when perfectly dissolved, pour it into a mould and et it remain a week, then cut it into such sized squares as you may require.

10. VARIEGATED TOILET SOAP.—Soft water 3 qts.; nice white bar soap 3 lbs.; sal-soda 2 ozs.; Chinese vermilion, and Chinese blue, of each, as much as will lie on a 5-cent piece; oil of sassafras ¼ oz.

Shave the soap fine, and put it into the water as it begins to boil; when dissolved, set it from the fire; take out a cup of the soap and stir in the vermilion; take out another cup of the soap and stir in the blue; then pour in one of the cups and give two or three turns only with the stirring stick; then put in the other in the same way; and finally pour into a suitable box; and when cold it can be cut into bars; or it can be run in moulds, if desired; it will become hard in a short time; giving most excellent satisfaction. If stirred thoroughly, after putting in the colors, it would be all of a mixed color; but giving it only two or three turns, leaves it in streaks, most beautiful.

Soap manufacturers generally use soda, in preference to wood-ashes, because less troublesome; and to make it more caustic, or, in other words, to absorb the carbonic-acid-gas, they must put about pound for pound of recently slacked lime with soda-ash, or sal-soda; dissolving by heat or stirring; or by both; using sufficient water to make the lye support a fresh lain egg, and drawing it off clear of the lime sediment.   Thirteen hundred pounds of the tallow, or thereabouts, with the lye, makes one ton of white soap; and yellow soap, by using ten hundred of tallow and three hundred and fifty of yellow rosin, for each ton, boiling with the lye until they unite; then pouring into frames, made to fit one upon another, to cool and harden; finally taking off one frame at a time, and with a wire, having a handle at each end to draw it with, cut into slices, then bars, and cording up, as wood, to dry.   If wood-ashes are used, plenty of lime must be put into the bottom of the leach.

TALLOW   CANDLES—For   Summer   Use.—Most tallow, in summer, is more or less soft and often quite yellow, to avoid both:

Take your tallow and put a little bees-wax with it, especially it your bees-wax is dark and not fit to sell; put into a suitable kettle, adding *weak* lye and gently boil, an hour or two each day for 2 days, stirring and skimming well; each morning cutting it out and scraping off the bottom which is soft, adding fresh lye (be sure it is not too strong) 1 or 2, or 3. gals., according to the amount of tallow.   The third morning use water in which alum and saltpetre is dissolved, at the rate of 1 lb. each, for 30 lbs. of tallow; then simmer, stir, and skim again; let cool, and you can take it off the water for use.

They may be dipped or run in moulds; for dipping, allow two pounds for each dozen candles.

Saltpetre and alum are said to harden *lard* for candles; but it can be placed amongst the humbugs of the day But I will give you a plan which is a little shorter for hardening tallow; either will work well, take your choice:

2 Tatlow—To Cleanse and Bleach.—Dissolve alum 5 lbs., in water 10 gals., by boiling; and when it is all dissolved, add tallow 20 lbs.; continue the boiling for an hour, constantly stirring and skimming; when sufficiently cool to allow it, strain through thick muslin; then set aside to harden; when taken from the water, lay it by for a short time to drip.

Dip or mould, as you please, not expecting them to "run" in summer nor "crack" in winter.   They will also burn very brilliantly, at which, however, you will not be surprised when you consider the amount of filth thrown off in cleansing.

FENCE POSTS—To Prevent Rotting.—A correspondent of the *American Agriculturalist* says :

"I think it would be well to call the attention of farmers to the use of coal-tar as a paint. The tar produced in coal gas-works is extensively used in England for painting fences, out buildings, &c.; and is being introduced in this country, also. It *never* alters by exposure to the weather; and one or two good coats will last for many years. It is the cheapest and best black paint that can be used. Our buildings are painted with it; all our apparatus also; and even the wrought-iron pipe we place in the ground is coated with it. I think if its advantages were fully known, it would be generally used throughout the United States. The Government soak the brick used in building the fort at Throg's Neck in this tar, which renders them impervious to water; and posts painted with it are protected from rot, when in the ground, as effectually as if they had been charred."

I know this tar is much more effectual than charring, and is not one-tenth the trouble. There are posts near this city, which have now been set over ten years, and yet no appearance of decay. The coating is still perfect also.

The only objection to it as a paint above ground, is its offensive smell, from the heat of the sun.

No persons should allow themselves to set a single post without its application, and farmers who are putting out much fence, cannot possibly be so short-sighted as to neglect it after it once comes to their notice.

It is doubly important to Railroad-Companies from the fact that these roads run through the most level portions of country, and consequently the most swampy and wet, therefore fence posts are the more liable to rot. The mode of application is as follows :

Have a large iron kettle so arranged that you can make and keep the tar hot, then, after having removed the bark, if any, set the end of the post into the tar; and if the tar is not sufficiently deep to take the post into it as far as you wish to tar it have a swab of cloth tied upon a broom-handle or other stick, and swab it up at least 6 to 10 inches above the ground-line when the post is set; then lift up the post, letting it drip a mo ment, and lay it away upon rails or poles placed for that pur pose, not allowing them to touch each other until dry.

Two men will tar about five hundred posts in one day ; and one barrel of tar will be sufficient for that number Who then will hesitate to adopt its use ? especially when the tar can be purchased at the gas-works for about two dollars per barrel

MEATS—TO PRESERVE—BEEF—TO PICKLE FOR LONG KEEPING.—FIRST, thoroughly rub salt into it and let it remain in bulk for 24 hours to draw off the blood. SECOND, take it up leaving it drain, and pack as desired. THIRD, have ready a pickle prepared as follows:—For every 100 lbs. of beef, use 7 lbs. of salt; saltpetre and cayenne pepper, of each 1 oz.; molasses 1 qt., and soft water 8 gals.; boil and skim well; and when cold pour it over the beef.

This amount will cover one hundred pounds, if it ha been properly packed. I have found persons who use noth ing but salt with the water, and putting on hot, scalding again at the end of three weeks and putting on hot again. The only object claimed for putting the brine on the meat while hot, is, that it hardens the surface, which retains the juices, instead of drawing them off.

2. THE MICHIGAN FARMER'S METHOD.—Is, " for each 100 lbs. of beef, use salt 5 lbs.; saltpetre ¼ oz.; brown sugar 1 lb.; dissolve in sufficient water to cover the meat—two weeks after take up, drain—throw away the brine—make more the same as first, it will keep the season through—when to be boiled for eating, put into boiling water—for soups into cold water."

I claim a preference for the first plan, of drawing off the blood before pickling, as saving labor; and that the cayenne and saltpetre improves the flavor and helps preserve; and that boiling and skimming cleanse the brine very much. Of late years I pursue the following :

3. BEEF—TO PICKLE FOR WINTER OR PRESENT USE, AND FOR DRYING.—Cut your beef into sizable pieces, sprinkle a little salt upon the bottom of the barrel only, then pack your beef without salt amongst it, and when packed pour over it a brine made by dissolving 6 lbs. of salt for each 100 lbs. of beef in just sufficient cold water to handsomely cover it.

You will find that you can cut and fry as nice as fresh, for a long time ; just right for boiling, also ; and when it gets a little too salt for frying, you can freshen it nearly as nicely as pork, for frying purposes, or you can boil of it, then make a stew for breakfast, very nice indeed. By the other plan it soon becomes too salt for eating, and the juices are drawn off by the salt. In three weeks, perhaps a little less, such pieces as are designed for drying will be ready to hang up, by soaking over night to remove the salt from the outside. Do not be afraid of this way; for it is very nice for winter and drying purposes; but if any is left until warm weather, throw away this brine, put salt amongst what is left and cover with the first brine, and all is right for long keeping.

4. MUTTON HAMS—TO PICKLE FOR DRYING.—First take weak brine and put the hams into it for 2 days, then pour off and apply the following, and let it remain on from 2 to 3 weeks. according to size: For each 100 lbs.; take salt 6 lbs.; saltpetre 1 oz.; saleratus 2 ozs.; molasses 1 pt.; water 6 gals., will cover these if closely packed.

The saleratus keeps the mutton from becoming too hard.

5. CURING, SMOKING, AND KEEPING HAMS.—ROSE COTTAGE, MUNCIE, Ind., Nov. 26th, 1859: I noticed an article in the *Gazette* of yesterday, headed as above, from the pen of Mr. Alexander Brooks, taken from the *Rural New Yorker*, and as I have some useful experience in that line, I desire to suggest my plan for curing and keeping:

To a cask of hams, say from 25 to 30, after having packed them closely and sprinkled them slightly with salt, I let them lie thus for 3 days; then make a brine sufficient to cover them, by putting salt into clear water, making it strong enough to bear up a sound egg or potatoe. I then add ¼ lb. of saltpetre, and a gallon of molasses; let them lie in the brine for 6 weeks—they are then exactly right. I then take them up and let them drain; then while damp, rub the flesh side and the end of the leg with finely pulverized black, red, or cayenne pepper; let it be as fine as dust, and dust every part of the flesh side, then hang them up and smoke. You may leave them hanging in the smoke-house or other cool place where the rats cannot reach them, as they are perfectly safe from all insects; and will be a dish fit for a Prince, or an American citizen, which is better.

Respectfully yours,

TIIO'S. J. SAMPLE.

I find that Mr. Sample uses twice as much saltpetre and double the time, for my eating, but perhaps not for general market.

If Grocers will take this plan for preparing their hams and shoulders, there will be no need of sacking; and such as they buy in during the summer should recieve a coat of pepper immediately, to prevent annoyance from flies.

6. T. E. HAMILTON'S MARYLAND METHOD.—The hams of Maryland and Virginia have long enjoyed a wide celebrity. At one of the exhibitions of the Maryland State Agricultural Society, four premiums were awarded for

hams. The one which took the first premium, was cured by Mr. T. E. Hamilton, from the following recipe :

"To every 100 lbs. take best coarse salt 8 lbs.; saltpetre 2 ozs; brown sugar 2 lbs.; potash 1¼ ozs.; and water 4 gals. Mix the above, and pour the brine over the meat, after it has lain in the tub for some 2 days. Let the hams remain 6 weeks in the brine, and then dry several days before smoking. I have generally had the meat rubbed with fine salt, when it is packed down."

The meat should be perfectly cool before packing. The potash keeps it from drying up and becoming hard.

7. PORK—TO HAVE FRESH FROM WINTER KILLING, FOR SUMMER FRYING.—Take pork when killed in the early part of the winter, and let it lay in pickle about a week or 10 days; or until just sufficiently salted to be palatable; then slice it up and fry it about half or two-thirds as much as you would for present eating; now lay it away in its own grease, in jars properly covered, in a cool place, as you would lard.

When desired, in spring or summer, to have fresh pork, take out what you wish and re-fry suitable for eating, and you have it as nice as can be imagined. Try a jar of it, and know that some things can be done as well as others. It is equally applicable to hams and shoulders, and I have no doubt it will work as well upon beef, using lard sufficient to cover it. So well satisfied am I of it that I have put in beef-steak, this spring, with my fresh ham, in frying for summer use. It works upon the principle of canning fruits to exclude the air. I put in no bone.

8. SALT PORK FOR FRYING—NEARLY EQUAL TO FRESH.—For the benefit of those who are obliged to use considerable salt pork, the following method much improves it for frying :

Cut as many slices as may be needed; if for breakfast, the night previous, and soak till morning in a quart or two of milk and water, about one-half milk, skimmed-milk, sour milk, or buttermilk;—rinse till the water is clear and then fry. It is nearly or quite as nice as fresh pork,—both the fat and lean parts.

Occasionally I like to have this rolled in corn meal before frying, as it makes such a nice imitation of fresh fish.

9. FRESH MEAT—TO KEEP A WEEK OR TWO, IN SUMMER.— Farmers or others, living at a distance from butchers, can keep fresh meat very nicely, for a week or two, by putting it into sour milk, or butter-milk, placing it in a cool cellar. The bone or fat need not be removed.

Rinse well when used.

10. SMOKED MEAT—TO PRESERVE FOR YEARS, OR FOR SEA VOYAGES.—How often are we disappointed in our hopes of having sweet hams during the summer? After carefully curing and smoking, and sewing them up in bags, and white-washing them; we often find that either the fly has commenced a family in our hams, or that the choice parts around the bone are tainted, and the whole spoiled.

Now this can be easily avoided, by packing them in pulver ized charcoal. No matter how hot the weather, nor how thick the flies; hams will keep, as sweet as when packed, for years. The preservative quality of charcoal will keep them till charcoal decays; or sufficiently long to have accompanied Cook three times around the world.

11. THE RURAL NEW YORKER'S METHOD.—It says: "In the Spring, cut the smoked ham in slices, fry till partly done, pack in a stone jar alternate layers of ham and gravy. If the ham should be very lean, use lard for gravy. Be sure and fry the ham in the lard, so that it will be well seasoned. When wanted for use, take up, finish frying, and it is ready for the table."

The only trouble is, that we can't keep it half long enough, it is so good and handy.

12. THE NEW ENGLAND FARMER'S "SAVING HIS BACON."—About a couple of years ago, we were entertained, at the house of a friend, with a dinner of eggs and bacon. We complimented our host on the superior quality of his bacon; and were curious to inquire the way to like success in the preparation of a dainty article of diet, though one that is better fitted for the palate of an epicure than for the stomach of a dyspeptic. To our surprise we were informed that that portion of our meal was cooked eight months before.

Upon asking for an explanation, he stated that it was his practice to slice and fry his bacon immediately on its being cured, and then pack it in its own fat. When occasion came for using it, the slices, slightly re-fried, have all the freshness and flavor of new bacon just prepared. By this precaution, our friend always succeeded in " Saving *his* bacon," fresh and sweet, through the hottest of weather.—*New England Farmer*.

I have no doubt but what it will do as well to pack meats fried in this way, in tubs or barrels as in jars; but I rather prefer covered jars, putting a couple of thicknesses of cloth over the jar before putting on the cover; placed in a cool cellar.

I also find it necessary to put in lard occasionally as you are frying, as there is not generally enough brought out by the frying to fill the crevices between the slices, which mus' be filled.

CANNING FRUITS—PEACHES AND PEARS.—After paring and coring, put amongst them sufficient sugar to make them palatable for present eating,—about 3 to 4 lbs. only for each bushel; let them stand a while to dissolve the sugar, not using any water; then heat to a boil, and continue the boiling, with care, from 20 to 30 minutes; or sufficiently long to heat through which expels the air.

Have ready a kettle of hot water, into which dip the can long enough to heat it; then fill in the fruit while hot, corking it immediately, and dip the end of the cork into the "Cement for Canning Fruits." When cold it is bes to dip the second time to make sure that no air holes are left which would spoil the fruit. All canned fruits are to be kept in a very cool cellar.

We have, yesterday and to-day, been eating peaches put up in this way, two years ago, which were very nice indeed. See "Peaches, To Peel."

2. BERRIES, PLUMS, CHERRIES, &c.—Raspberries, blackberries, whortleberries, currants, cherries, and plums, need not be boiled over 10 to 15 minutes; using sugar to make palatable, in all cases; as it must be put in some time, and it helps to preserve the fruit.

They require the same care in heating cans, &c., as above, for peaches.

3. STRAWBERRIES.—For strawberries, put sugar ¼ lb. for each lb. of berries; and proceed as for berries above.

Strawberries are so juicy, and have such a tendency to fermentation, that it is almost impossible to keep them   I have found it absolutely so, until I adopted the plan of using the amount of sugar above named; if others can do with less, they can benefit the public by telling me how they do it.

5. TOMATOES.—For tomatoes, scald and peel them as for other cooking; then scald, or rather boil for about 15 minutes only, and can as above.

Or what I think best, is to use a little salt, and put them into half-gallon jugs; for we want them in too great quantities to stop on a few glass jars, such as we use for other fruits; as for tin cans, I never use them; if you do use tin cans for tomatoes it will not do to use salt with them, as it has a tendency to cause rust.

6. CEMENT FOR CANNING FRUITS.—Rosin 1 lb.; lard, tallow and bees-wax, of each 1 oz.

Melt and stir together; and have it hot, ready to dip into when canning.

7. RURAL NEW YORKER'S METHOD.—The editor says :

From four years experience with, not only strawberries, but peaches, cherries, raspberries, pine-apples, &c., without losing a single jar, the flavor being also perfect: Use only self-sealing *glass jars.* Put into a porcelain preserving kettle, enough to fill two, quart jars; sprinkle on sugar ¼ lb.; place over a slow fire and heat through, *not cooked.* While the fruit is heating, keep the jars filled with hot water. Fill up to the brim, and seal immediately.

As it cools a vacuum is formed which prevents bursting. In this way every kind of fruit will retain its flavor. Sometimes a thick leathery mould form, on the top—if so, all the better.

CATCHUP—TOMATO CATCHUP.—Take perfectly ripe tomatoes ¼ bushel; wash them clean and break to pieces; then put over the fire and let them come to a boil, and remove from the fire; when they are sufficiently cool to allow your hands in them, rub through a wire sieve; and to what goes through, add salt 2 tea-cups; allspice and cloves, of each, ground, 1 tea-cup; best vinegar 1 qt. Put onto the fire again and cook 1 hour, stirring with great care to avoid burning. Bottle and seal for use. If too thick when used, put in a little vinegar. If they were very juicy they may need boiling over an hour.

This recipe is from Mrs. Hardy, of the American Hotel, Dresden, O., and is decidedly the best catchup which I have ever tasted; the only fault I have ever heard attributed to it was, "I wish we had made more of it." "We have not got half enough of it," &c. But there are those who cannot use tomatoes in any shape; such persons will, undoubtedly like the following :

2. CURRANT CATCHUP.—Nice fully ripe currants 4 lbs.; sugar 1½ lbs.; cinnamon, ground 1 table-spoon; salt, with ground cloves and pepper, of each 1 tea-spoon; vinegar 1 pt.

Stew the currants and sugar until quite thick; then add the other ingredients, and bottle for use.

PRESERVES—TOMATO PRESERVES.—As some persons will have preserves, I give them the plan of making the most healthy of any in use :

Take ripe, scalded and peeled tomatoes 13 lbs. ; nice, scalding hot molasses 1 gal. ; pour the molasses upon them and let stand 12 hours ; then boil until they are properly cooked ; now skim out the tomatoes, but continue boiling the syrup until quite thick ; then pour again upon the tomatoes and put away as other preserves. A table-spoon of ginger tied up in a bit of cloth and boiled in them, gives a nice flavor ; or the extracts can be used ; or lemon peel, as preferred—if sugar is used, pound for pound is the amount.

But I prefer to put them, or any other fruit, into jugs, cans, or bottles, which retains the natural flavor and does not injure the stomach, which all preserves do, to a greater or less extent. Yet I give you another, because it does so nicely in place of citron, in cakes.

2. PRESERVED WATER-MELON IN PLACE OF CITRON, FOR CAKES.—The harder part of water-melon, next the skin, made into preserves with sugar, equal weights ; cooking down the syrup rather more than for common use, causes it to granulate, like citron, which is kept for sale.

This chopped fine, as citron, makes an excellent substitute for that article ; and for very much less cost. Call in the neighbors, to help eat about a dozen good sized melons, and you have outside enough for the experiment ; and if the Doctor is near he will help without a fee. They are nice, also, in mince-pies in place of raisins.

CURRANTS—TO DRY WITH SUGAR.—Take fully ripe currants, stemmed, 5 lbs.; sugar 1 lb.; put into a brass kettle, stirring at first, then as the currants boil up to the top, skim them off ; boil down the juicy syrup until quite thick and pour it over the currants, mixing well ; then place on suitable dishes, and dry them by placing in a low box over which you can place musketo-bar, to keep away flies.

When properly dried, put in jars and tie paper over them. Put cold water upon them and stew as other fruit for eating or pie-making, adding more sugar if desired.

TIN-WARE—TO MEND BY THE HEAT OF A CANDLE.—Take a vial about two-thirds full of muriatic acid, and put into it, little bits of sheet zinc, as long as it dissolves them ; then put in a crumb of sal-ammoniac and fill up with water, and it is ready to use.

With the cork of the vial wet the place to be mended,

with the preparation; then put a piece of sheet zinc over the hole and hold a lighted candle or spirit lamp under the place, which melts the solder on the tin and causes the zinc to adhere without further trouble. Wet the zinc also with the solution. Or a little solder may be put on in place of the zinc, or with the zinc.

WATER FILTER—HOME-MADE.—Rain water is much healthier than hard water as a beverage; and the following will be found an easy and cheap way to fit it for drinking purposes:

Have an oak tub made, holding from half, to a barrel, according to the amount of water needed in the family; let it stand on end, with a faucet near the bottom; or, I prefer a hole through the bottom, near the front side, with a tube in it which prevents the water from rotting the outside of the tub; then put clean pebbles 3 or 4 inches in thickness over the bottom of the tub; now have charcoal pulverized to the size of small peas (that made from hard maple is best) and put in half a bushel or so at a time; pound it down quite firmly, then put in more and pound again until the tub is filled to within 8 inches of the top; and again put on 2 inches more of pebbles; then put a piece of clean white flannel over the whole top as a strainer.

The flannel can be washed occasionally, to remove the impurities collected from the water, and it might be well to put a flannel between the pebbles and flannel at the bottom also. When the charcoal becomes foul, it can be renewed as before, but will work a whole season without renewing. Put on your water freely until it becomes clear; when you will be as well satisfied as you would be if it run through a *patent* filter, costing six times as much as this.

A large jar to hold the filtered water can be set in an ice-box if preferred; or an occasional piece of ice can be put in the water; but if the filter is set in the cellar, as it should be, the water will be sufficiently cool for health. This makes a good cider filter, also, first straining the cider through cotton to free it from the coarsest pomace.

TIRE—TO KEEP ON THE WHEEL.—A correspondent of the *Southern Planter* says: "I ironed a wagon some years ago for my own use, and before putting on the tires I filled the fellies with linseed-oil; and the tires have worn out, and were never loose. I ironed a buggy for my own use seven years ago, and the tires are now as tight as when put on

My method of filling the fellies with the oil is as follows.

I use a long, cast iron oil-heater, made for the purpose; the oil is brought to a boiling heat, the wheel is placed on a stick, so as to hang in the oil, each felly an hour, for a common sized felly. The timber should be dry, as green timber will not take oil. Care should be taken that the oil be not made hotter than a boiling heat, in order that the timber be not burnt. Timber filled with oil is not susceptible to water, and is much more durable."

I was amused some time ago when I told a blacksmith how to keep tires tight on wheels, by his telling me it was a profitable business to tighten tires; and the wagon maker will say it is profitable to him to make and repair wheels— but what will the farmer, who supports the wheel-wright and the blacksmith say? The greatest good to the greatest number, is my motto.

WEEDS—To Destroy in Walks.—The following method to destroy weeds is pursued at the mint in Paris, with good effect:

Water 10 gals.; stone lime 20 lbs.; flour of sulphur 2 lbs Boil in an iron kettle; after settling, the clear part is to be poured off and sprinkled, freely, upon the weedy walks.

Care must be taken, for it will destroy weeds; and as certainly destroy edging and border flowers, if sprinkled on them.

CEMENTS—Cement for China, &c., which Stands Fire and Water.—With a small camel's-hair brush, rub the broken edges with a little carriage oil-varnish.

If neatly put together, the fracture will hardly be perceptible, and when thoroughly dry, will stand both fire and water.

2. Russian Cement.—Much is said about cements; but there is probably nothing so white and clear, and certainly nothing better than he following:

Russian isinglass dissolved in pure soft water, snow water is best; for it takes 12 hours to soften it by soaking in pure soft water, then considerable heat to dissolve it; after which it is applicable to statuary, china, glass, alabaster, &c., &c.

In all cements the pieces must be secured until dry. It is easy to reason that if twelve to fifteen hours are required to soften this isinglass that no dish-washing will ever effect it. You may judge from the price whether you get the Russian, for thirty-seven cents per ounce, is as low as the genuine article can be purchased in small quantities, whilst the common, bear a price of only from ten to twelve cents and even less.

3. CEMENT, CHEAP AND VALUABLE.—A durable cement is made by burning oyster-shells and pulverizing the lime from them very fine; then mixing it with white of egg to a thick paste and applying it to the china or glass, and securing the pieces together until dry.

When it is dry, it takes a very long soaking for it to become soft again. I have lifted thirty pounds by the stem of a wine-glass which had been broken, and mended with this cement. Common lime will do, but it is not so good; either should be fresh burned, and only mix what is needed, for when once dry you cannot soften it.

4. CEMENT—WATER-PROOF, FOR CLOTH OR BELTING.— Take ale 1 pt.; best Russia isinglass 2 ozs.; put them into a common glue kettle and boil until the isinglass is dissolved; then add 4 ozs. of the best common glue, and dissolve it with the other; then slowly add 1½ ozs. of boiled linseed-oil, stirring all the time while adding, and until well mixed. When cold it will resemble India-rubber. When you wish to use this, dissolve what you need in a suitable quantity of ale to have the consistence of thick glue. It is applicable for earthenware, china, glass, or leather; for harness; bands for machinery; cloth belts for cracker machines for bakers, &c., &c. If for leather, shave off as it for sewing, apply the cement with a brush while *hot*, laying a weight to keep each joint firmly for 6 to 10 hours, or over night.

This cement will supersede "Spaulding's Prepared Glue," and all the white cements you can scare up, if you use good articles to make it of,—not less than thirty or forty cents a pound for common glue, and three shillings per ounce for the Russian isinglass; but the expense of this will cause it only to be used when dampness is to be contended with.

If you have not a glue kettle, take an oyster can and punch some holes through the top of it, putting in a string to suspend it on a stick in a common kettle of boiling water, and keep it boiling in that way.

5. CEMENT, OR FURNITURE GLUE, FOR HOUSE USE.—To mend marble, wood, glass, china and ornamental ware—take water 1 gal.; nice glue 3 lbs; white lead 4 ozs.; whisky 3 qts.

Mix by dissolving the glue in the water; remove from the fire and stir in the white lead, then add the whisky, which keeps it fluid, except in the coldest weather. Warm and stir it up when applied.

6. WHITE CEMENT.—Take white (fish) glue, 1 lb. 10 ozs.; dry white lead 6 ozs.; soft water 3 pts.; alcohol 1 pt.

Dissolve the glue by putting it into a tin kettle, or dish, containing the water, and set this dish into a kettle of water, to prevent the glue from being burned; when the glue is all dissolved, put in the lead and stir and boil until all is thoroughly mixed; remove from the fire, and, when cool enough to bottle, add the alcohol, and bottle while it is yet warm, keeping it corked. This last recipe has been sold about the country for from twenty-five cents to five dollars, and one man gave a horse for it.

7. GERMAN CEMENT.—Two measures of litharge, and 1 each of unslacked lime and flint glass; each to be pulverized separately before mixing; then to use it, wet it up with old drying-oil.

The Germans use it for glass and china ware only. Water hardens it instead of softening.

8. SCRAP-BOOK PASTE, OR CEMENT.—A piece of common glue, 2 square inches; dissolve it in water, adding as much pulverized alum, in weight, as of the glue; now mix flour ¼ teaspoon in a little water; stir it in and boil. When nearly cool stir in oil of lavender 2 tea-spoons.

This should make a pint of paste, which will keep a long time if tightly covered when not in use.

CEMENT— PREVENTING LEAKS ABOUT CHIMNEYS, &c.—Dry sand 1 pt.; ashes 2 pts.; clay dried and pulverized 3 pts.; all to be pulverized and mixed into a paste with linseed-oil.

Apply it while soft, as desired, and when it becomes hard, water will have no effect upon it. It may be used for walks, and I think it would do well in cisterns, and on roofs, &c.

MAGIC PAPER.—USED TO TRANSFER FIGURES IN EMBROIDERY, OR IMPRESSIONS OF LEAVES FOR HERBARIUMS.—Take lard-oil, or sweet-oil, mixed to the consistence of cream, with either of the following paints, the color of which is desired: Prussian blue, lamp-black, Venitian red or chrome green, either of which should be rubbed, with a knife on a plate or stone until smooth. Use rather thin, but firm paper; put on with a sponge and wipe off as dry as convenient; then lay them between uncolored paper, or between newspapers, and press by laying books or some other flat substance upon them, until the surplus oil is absorbed, when it is ready for use.

DIRECTIONS.—For taking off patterns of embroidery place a piece of thin paper over the embroidery to prevent soiling; then lay on the magic paper, and put on the cloth you wish to take the copy on, to embroider; pin fast, and rub over with a spoon handle; and every part of the raised figure will show upon the plain cloth. To take impressions of leaves on paper, place the leaf between two sheets of this paper, and rub over it hard, then take the leaf out and place it between two sheets of white paper; rub again, and you will have a beautiful impression of both sides of the leaf or flower. Persons traveling without pen or ink, can write with a sharp stick, placing a sheet of this paper over a sheet of white paper.

RAT DESTROYERS—RAT EXTERMINATOR.—Flour 3 lbs; water only sufficient to make it into a thick paste; then dissolve, phosphorus 1 oz., in butter 1½ oz., by heat. Mix.

This you will leave, thickly spread on bread, where rats can get at it; or make into balls, which is preferable, covered or rolled with sugar. If it is desired to sell this article and you wish to color to hide its composition, work into it pulverized turmeric 2 oz. Or:

2. Take warm water 1 qt.; lard 2 lbs.; phosphorus 1 oz. Mix, and thicken with flour.

It is found best to make only in small quantities, as the phosphorus loses its power by exposure. Some will object to killing rats about the house; but I had rather *smell* their dead carcasses than *taste* their tail-prints, left on every thing possible for them to get at, or suffer loss from their *tooth*-prints on *all* things possible for them to devour, or destroy.

3. DEATH FOR THE OLD SLY RAT.—Some rats get so cunning that it is almost impossible to overcome their shrewdness.

Then get a few grains of strychnine, having a little fresh lean meat broiled; cut it into small bits, by using a fork to hold it, for if held by the fingers, they will smell them and not eat it; cutting with a sharp penknife; then cut a little hole into the bits, and put in a little of the strychnine, and close up the meat together again.

Put these on a plate where they frequent, but not near their holes, laying a piece of paper over the meat; when those are eaten put more, for three or four days, and you are soon done with the wisest of them.

4 RATS—TO DRIVE AWAY ALIVE.—If you choose to drive them away alive, take potash pulverized, and put quite plenty of it into all their holes about the house. If the potash is pulverized and left in the air, it becomes pasty; then it can be daubed on the boards or planks, where they come through into rooms.

They will sooner leave, than be obliged to have a continual re-application of this " Doctor Stuff," every time they go through their holes.   See " Potash to Make."

5. Scotch snuff, or pulverized cayenne pepper, mixed together, or separate; if freely put into their burrowing-holes, will certainly send them off, at a sneezing pace.

6. RAT POISON—FROM SIR HUMPHREY DAVY.—A tasteless, odorless and infallible rat poison, he says, is made as follows :

" Mix carbonate of barytes 2 ozs., with grease 1 lb."

It produces great thirst, consequently water must be set by it, for death takes place immediately after drinking, not giving them time to go back to their holes.   I obtained this at such a late day, that I have not had opportunity of testing it   Be sure that no other animal can get at it, except rats and mice; for it is a most deadly poison. Should this be found as effectual as recommended, it will prove just the thing for rat-killing, as they can be gathered up and carried away, thus avoiding the stench arising from their dead carcasses.

FISH—ART OF CATCHING.—Mix the juice of lovage or smellage, with any kind of bait, or a few drops of the oil of rhodium. India cockle also, (Coculus Indicus,) is sometimes mixed with flour dough and sprinkled on the surface of still water.   This intoxicates the fish and makes them turn up, on top of the water.   Mullein seed, pulverized, and used in place of the India seckle is about equal to that article.

They may be eaten without fear, but this will destroy many fish.   Oil of rhodium is the best plan.

" It is generally supposed," says Mr. R. I. Pell, " that fish are not possessed of the sense of smell.   From the following experiments I am convinced they are: I placed a hook, well baited with an angle-worm, enticingly before a perch weighing one and a half pounds; he did not take the

least notice of it. It was withdrawn, and a drop of rhodium
brought in contact with it, when it was dropped very carefully several feet behind him; he immediately turned and
seized the bait. This experiment was several times repeated, with like success. It has been denied that fish have
the sense of hearing. I find many varieties very sensitive
to noise, and by numerous experiments am convinced that
their sense of hearing is acute."

STRAW AND CHIP HATS—To VARNISH BLACK.—Best
alcohol 4 ozs.; pulverized, black sealing-wax 1 oz.; put them into
a vial, and put the vial into a warm place, stirring or shaking
occasionally, until the wax is dissolved; apply it when warm
by means of a soft brush, before the fire or in the sun.

It gives stiffness to old straw hats or bonnets, makes a
beautiful gloss, and resists wet; if anything else is required,
just apply it to small baskets also, and see how nicely they
will look.

2. STRAW BONNETS—TO COLOR A BEAUTIFUL SLATE.—First
soak the bonnet in rather strong warm suds for fifteen minutes,
this is to remove sizing or stiffening; then rinse in warm water
o get out the soap; now scald cudbear 1 oz., in sufficient water
o cover the hat or bonnet—work the bonnet in this dye at 180
.egrees of heat, until you get a light purple; now have a bucket
of cold water blued with the extract of indigo, about ¼ oz., and
work or stir the bonnet in this, until the tint pleases.

Dry, then rinse out with cold water and dry again, in
the shade. If you get the purple too deep in shade, the
final slate will be too dark. See "Extract of Indigo, or
Chemic."

STUCCO PLASTERING—FOR BRICK AND GRAVEL HOUSES.
—First make up as much mortar as you need for the job, with
good common lime; using only ¾ or four-fifths, at most, as much
lime as needed for common work—the other fourth or fifth is to
be water-lime; and not to be put in only as used. The sand
must be coarse, and free from loam or dirt.

To prepare the white and colored washes, run off common
lime enough with hot water, to make a white-wash to go over
the whole job. This white-wash is to be colored the tint desired for the work. Be sure to make color-wash enough at one
time, or you will find it hard to get the shades alike; saving a
little of the white-wash without color, to pencil the seams, and
also for specking, as mentioned below. The colors used are
lamp-black, Spanish-brown, or Venetian-red, as preferred, and
these are cut or dissolved in whisky; then putting into the
white-wash to suit

When these washes are all prepared, wet up as much of the mortar as can be put on in 20 to 40 minutes, and mix in the fourth or fifth of the cement, and put on as fast as possible; first wetting the wall very wet with water. Some cement will set in 20 and some in 40 to 50 minutes. When you see the time necessary for the kind you are using, act accordingly, and only mix the cement into as much mortar as your help will put on before it sets; beginning at the top of the wall with your scaffolding and working down, which prevents too much specking from the colors. Have a man to follow right after with a float, keeping the stucco very wet while floating down level and smooth; and the longer it is floated and wet, the better will be the job. Even after it is floated down well, keep a man wetting it with a brush until you get the whole line on, around the house, as the water-ime must be kept quite wet for some considerable time, to set properly. Heed this caution, and if water never gets in be .ind the plastering from bad cornice or leaky roofs, it will neve peel off. When this line of scaffolding is plastered, take cut e .ough of the color-wash, running it through a sieve, and go over the plastering; lamp-black alone gives it a bluish slate color; if a little of the brown is added with the black, it will be a little reddish, and if the red is used without the brown, it will be quite red. I prefer sufficient of the black only to make a gray stone color. A brown, however, looks exceedingly well. If you choose, you can make one-half of the color-wash darker than the other—having laid it off into blocks resembling stone, by means of a straight-edge, and piece of board about half an inch thick, paint every other block with the darker wash to represent different shades of stone. Some of our best buildings are done in this way, and look well.

Then to give it a granite appearance, take a small paint-brush and dip it into the white-wash, saved for this purpose; strike it across a hammer-handle so as to throw the specks from the brush upon the wall, then the same with black and red. Pencil the seams with the white-wash, which gives it the appearance of mortar, as in real stone-work.

Now you are ready to move down the scaffold, and go over the same thing as before. After the colors have been dissolved with spirits. they can be reduced with water, or what is better for them and the color-wash also, is skimmed-milk; and where milk is plenty, it ought to be used in place of water, for white-wash or color-washes, as it helps to resist the weather, and prevents the colors from fading—see "Paint, to Make without Lead or Oil," which gives you the philosophy of using milk. Speck quite freely with the white, then about half as much with the black, and then rather free again with the red. The proportion of lime,

probably, should not exceed one, to six or seven of sand
Our University buildings, represented in the frontispiece,
except the Laboratory, and Law-building, which have been
more recently put up, are finished with it, and also whole
blocks in the business part of our city

Prof. Douglass' house is probably the prettiest color of
ny in the city—an imitation of "Free-stone," made with
amp-black, yellow ochre, and a larger proportion of Spanish
grown, But all will have a preference for some special color ;
then, with a little ingenuity and patience, nearly any colored
stone can be imitated.

GRAVEL HOUSES—To Make—Proportions of
Lime, Sand, and Gravel.—It has become quite common
to put up gravel houses; and many persons are at a great
loss to know what proportion of materials to use. Various
proportions have been proposed ; but from the fact that the
philosophy was not explained, no real light was given upon
the subject.

All that is required to know, is, that sand and lime are to be
used in proportion to the size of the gravel,—say for 15 bushels
of clean gravel, from the size of peas up to that of hen's eggs,
it will take about 3 bushels of clean sharp sand and 1 of lime to
fill the crevices without swelling the bulk of the gravel. If the
gravel is coarse, up to 5 bushels of sand may be required, but
the lime will not need to be increased but very little, if any.
Then the philosophy of the thing is this--about 1 to 1¼ bushels
of lime to 15 bushels of gravel, and just send enough to fill the
crevices without increasing the bulk as above mentioned.

If the gravel is free of dirt, the sand also clean, and the
weather dry, the walls can be raised one foot each day, if
you have help to do that amount of labor.

Some prefer to make the gravel and sand into mortar and
press it into bricks ; then lay into walls, but the wall must
be stronger if laid up solid, in board frames, made to raise
up as required.

Many persons argue for the eight-square or octagon house ;
but I like the square form much the best, carrying up the
hall and main partiton walls of the same material. The
eight square house looks like an old fort, or water tank, and
is very expensive to finish ; costing much more than the
same room with square an, es; for mechanics cannot put
up cornice outside, or in, in ass than double the time required for making the common square mitre.

Prof. Winchell, of the University, and State Geologist, in this city, has put up one of the octagons which looks well, however, for the style of *finish* is what attracts attention, instead of the style of form.

WHITEWASHES AND CHEAP PAINTS.—Brilliant Stucco Whitewash—Will Last on Brick or Stone, Twenty to Thirty Years.

—Many have heard of the brilliant stucco whitewash on the east end of the President's house at Washington. The following is a recipe for it, as gleaned from the *National Intelligencer*, with some additional improvements learned by experiments:

Nice unslaked lime ½ bushel; slake it with boiling water; cover it during the process, to keep in the steam. Strain the liquid through a fine sieve or strainer, and add to it, salt 1 peck; previously well dissolved in water; rice 3 lbs.—boiled to a thin paste, and stirred in boiling hot; Spanish whiting ½ lb.; clean nice glue 1 lb., which has been previously dissolved by soaking it well, and then hanging it over a slow fire, in a small kettle, immersed in a larger one filled with water. Now add hot water 5 gals., to the mixture, stir it well, and let it stand a few days covered from the dirt.

It should be put on not. For this purpose it can be kept in a kettle on a portable furnace. Brushes more or less small may be used, according to the neatness of job required. It answers as well as oil paint for brick or stone, and is much cheaper.

There is one house in our city which had this applied twelve years ago, and is yet nice and bright. It has retained its brilliancy over thirty years.

Coloring matter, dissolved in whisky, may be put in and made of any shade you like; Spanish brown stirred in will make red-pink, more or less deep, according to quantity. A delicate tinge of this is very pretty for inside walls. Finely pulverized common clay, well mixed with Spanish brown, makes reddish stone color. Yellow-ochre stirred in makes yellow wash, but chrome goes further, and makes a color generally esteemed prettier. In all these cases the darkness of the shade, of course, is determined by the quantity of the coloring used. It is difficult to make rules, because tastes are different—it would be best to try experiments on a shingle and let it dry. Green must not be mixed with lime. The lime destroys the color, and the color has an effect on the whitewash, which makes it crack and peel. When inside walls have been badly smoked, and you wish to make them a clean, clear white, it is well to squeeze indigo plentifully through a bag into the water you use, be fore it is stirred into the whole mixture, or blue vitriol pulverized and dissolved in boiling water and put into whitewash, gives a beautiful blue tint. If a larger quantity than five gallons be wanted, the same proportions should be observed.

2. WHITEWASH—VERY NICE FOR ROOMS.—Take whiting 4 lbs.; white or common glue 2 ozs.; stand the glue in cold water over night; mix the whiting with cold water, and heat the glue until dissolved; and pour it into the other, hot. Make of a proper consistence to apply with a common whitewash brush.

Use these proportions for a greater or less amount. In England scarcely any other kind of whitewash is used

A lady, of Black River Falls, Wis., who had one of my books, wrote to me, expressing her thankfulness for the beauty of this whitewash.

3. PAINT—TO MAKE WITHOUT LEAD OR OIL.—Whiting 5 lbs; skimmed milk 2 qts.; fresh slaked lime 2 ozs. Put the lime into a stone-ware vessel, pour upon it a sufficient quantity of the milk to make a mixture resembling cream; the balance of the milk is then to be added; and lastly the whiting is to be crumbled upon the surface of the fluid, in which it gradually sinks. At this period it must be well stirred in, or ground as you would other paint, and it is fit for use.

There may be added any coloring matter that suits the fancy, (see the first whitewash for mixing colors,) to be applied in the same manner as other paints, and in a few hours it will become perfectly dry. Another coat may then be added and so on until the work is done. This paint is of great tenacity, bears rubbing with a coarse cloth, has little smell, even when wet, and when dry is inodorous. The above quantity is sufficient for fifty-seven yards.—*Annapolis Republican.*

"We endorse the recipe. The casein or curd of the milk, by the action of the caustic-lime, becomes insoluble, and has been used, for time immemorial, as a lute for chemical experiments. It is a good, and, in comparison with white lead, a durable paint."—*Moore's Rural New Yorker*

Most of the cheap paints will require about three coats.

White lead always requires two, but some people think because they get a cheap paint that one coat ought to make a good job. Two will generally do with any except white.

4. White Paint—A New Way of Mafnuacturing.—The following was communicated by a man who was formerly a carpenter in the U. S. Navy.

" During a cruise in the South Pacific, we went into the harbor of Coquimbo ; and as the ship had been out a long time, she was covered with rust from stem to stern. It was the anxious wish of the commander that she should be restored to her original colors; but on examining the storeroom, it was ascertained that there was not a pound of white lead in the ship. In this emergency I bethought me of an expedient which concocted an admirable substitute, composed of the following ingredients :

" Air-slaked lime, pulverized until it was of the fineness of flour, which was then passed through a seive. Rice boiled in a large kettle until the substance was drawn entirely out of the grain ; the water, then of a plastic nature, was strained to separate the grain, &c., from the clear liquid. A tub, about the size of a half barrel, of the prepared lime and rice-water, was mixed with 1 gallon of linseed-oil ; and the material had so much the appearance of paint that a novice could not have told the difference.

" The ship was painted outside and inboard with the above mixture (which cost next to nothing,) and never presented a finer white streak on her bends, or cleaner bulwarks and berth-deck than on that occasion, and no other kind of white paint was used during the remainder of the cruise."

If this is good for ships out and inboard, it is worth trying for fences and out-work requiring a cheap white paint.

5. Black and Green Paint—Durable and Cheap, for Out-Door Work.—Any quantity of charcoal, powdered ; a sufficient quantity of litharage as a dryer, to be well levigated (rubbed smooth) with linseed-oil ; and when used, to be thinned with well boiled linseed-oil. The above forms a good black paint.

By adding yellow ochre, an excellent green is produced, which is preferable to the bright green, used by painters, for all garden work, as it does not fade with the sun.

This composition was first used by Dr. Parry, of Bath, on some spouts ; which, on being examined, fourteen years afterwards, were found to be as perfect as when first put

6. MILK PAINT, FOR BARNS—ANY COLOR.— 'Mix water lime with skim-milk, to a proper consistence to apply with a brush, and it is ready to use. It will adhere well to wood, whether smooth or rough, to brick, mortar or stone, where oil has not been used, (in which case it cleaves to some extent,) and forms a very hard substance, as durable as the best oil paint. It is too cheap to estimate, and any one can put it on who can use a brush."—*Country Gentleman.*

Any color may be given to it, by using colors of the tinge desired, dissolving in whisky first, then adding in to suit the fancy, as in the first recipe.

If a red is preferred, mix Venetian-red with milk, not using any lime. It looks well for fifteen years.

LIQUID, AND WATER-PROOF GLUES.—LIQUID GLUE. —To have a good glue always ready for use, just put a bottle two-thirds full of best common glue, and fill up the bottle with common whisky; cork it up, and set by for 3 or 4 days, and it will dissolve without the application of heat.

It will keep for years, and is always ready to use without heat, except in very cold weather, when it may need to be set a little while in a warm place, before using.

2. IMITATION OF SPALDING'S GLUE.—First, soak in cold water all the glue you wish to make at one time, using only glass, earthen, or porcelain dishes; then by gentle heat dissolve the glue in the same water, and pour in a little nitric acid, sufficient to give the glue a sour taste, like vinegar, or from $\frac{1}{4}$ oz. to 1 oz. to each pound of glue.

The acid keeps it in a liquid state, and prevents it from spoiling; as nice as Spalding's or any other, for a very trifling expense. If iron dishes are used, the acid corrodes them and turns the glue black. Or :

3. Acetic acid 1 oz.; pure soft water 6 oz.; glue 3 oz.; gum tragacanth 1 oz. Mix, and if not as thick as desired, add a little more glue.

This keeps in a liquid state, does not decompose ; and is valuable for Druggists in labeling ; also for house use ; and if furniture men were not prejudiced, they would find it valuable in the shop.

4. WATER-PROOF GLUE—Is made by first soaking the glue in cold water, for an hour or two, or until it becomes a little soft, yet retaining its original form; then taking it from the water and dissolving it by gentle heat, stirring in a little boiled lin-seed-oil.

If mahogany veneers were put on with this glue, they would not fall off, as they now do, by the action of the atmosphere.

FIRE KINDLERS.—To make very nice fire kindlers, take rosin, any quantity, and melt it, putting in for each pound being used, from 2 to 3 ozs. of tallow, and when all is hot, stir in pine saw-dust to make very thick ; and, while yet hot, spread it out about 1 inch thick, upon boards which have fine saw-dust sprinkled upon them, to prevent it from sticking. When cold, break up into lumps about 1 inch square. But if for sale, take a thin board and press upon it, while yet warm, to lay it off into 1 inch squares ; this makes it break regularly, if you press the crease sufficiently deep, greasing the marking-board to prevent it from sticking.

One of these blocks will easily ignite with a match, and burn with a strong blaze long enough to kindle any wood fit to burn. The above sells readily in all our large towns and cities, at a great profit.

2. Most of the published recipes call for rosin 3 lbs.; tar 1 qt.; and 1 gill of turpentine ; but they make a black, sticky mess of stuff, which always keep the hands daubed. On the other hand, this makes a rosin-colored kindler, which breaks nicely also when cold ; and they are decidedly a nice thing; and much more certain to start a fire than shavings. If the tar plan is used, 1 pt. is enough for 5 lbs of rosin.

STARCH POLISH.—White-wax 1 oz.; spermaceti 2 ozs.; melt them together with a gentle heat.

When you have prepared a sufficient amout of starch, in the usual way, for a dozen pieces—put into it a piece of the polish the size of a large pea ; more or less, according to large or small washings. Or, thick gum solution (made by pouring boiling water upon gum arabic,) one table-spoon to a pint of starch, gives clothes a beautiful gloss.

PERCUSSION MATCHES—OF THE BEST QUALITY.—Chlorate of potash ¼ lb.; glue 3 lbs.; white lead, dry, 5 lbs.; red lead ½ lb ; phosphorus 2¼ lbs. DIRECTIONS.—First put the chlorate into a dish made for the purpose, deep, and of a suitable size to set into a kettle of water, which can be kept on the fire for 2 or 3 days, having 2 qts. of water on the chlorate; then put the glue on top of the chlorate water, and let soak until all is perfectly dissolved ; then add the leads and heat up quite hot, and thoroughly mix; let cool and add the phosphorus, let it dissolve and be careful never to heat hot after the phosphorus is added; stir occasionally while dipping, and if little particles of phosphorus fires, push it down into the mixture, or put on warm water; if you put on cold water, it will fly all over you. Keep it rather thin after the phosphorus is put in, and there will be no danger; although the chlorate of potash is considered a dangerous article to work with; so is powder, yet when you know how to work with them, you can do as safely with one as the other. When dry give them a coat of varnish.

I have been acquainted with a man for about fourteen years who makes them, and several others for a less time, without trouble or accident. A better match was never made to stand dampness, or bear transportation without setting on fire. I have used and sold them much of the time, and speak from knowledge. One explosion has since taken place.

The plan pursued here in preparing the splints is as follows: Sawed pine timber from four to eight inches each way, is cut off the right length for the match, then one end of it is shaved smooth, with a drawing-knife; the block is held upon the horse by a brace from the top of the horse head against the back side of the block, so as to be out of the way of the knife instead of putting the block under the jaws of the horse head, as the dents made in the end of match timber would not answer; the front edge comes against a strip put on for that purpose; then glue the other end and put on brown paper, which holds them together when split; machines are used to split with which feeds up the block enough each time the knife is raised, to make the size of the match when split the other way, or about ten to the inch. These machines cost about fifty dollars, and the work goes ahead like a young saw-mill, by simply turning a crank as shown in the figure.

A A, shows two standards bolted upon a base plank, four feet in length; these standards support a shaft, with crank and balance wheel D, which is two feet in diameter, the shaft has upon it an oval wheel, G, which sinks the knife, F, twice in each revolution, the knife passing down through a space in a thin iron strip, H, standing out from the two blocks, C C, under which the match block passes by the drawing of the chain seen to pass over a small drum, P, upon the shaft of the rag wheel, B, the notches being only one-fourth inch apart, and fed up by the hand, M, attached to

the iron frame, L, being kept back to the cam wheel, E, which
has two swells upon it, by a light spring which is not shown

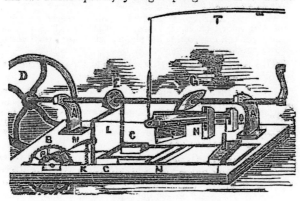

MATCH SPLITTING MACHINE.

The hand, M, is kept down into the cogs or notches by the
little spiral wire spring, K ; the match block, to be split, sets
in the frame forward of the block, I, which has a pin in it
to draw back the frame. When the block of matches is
split, this frame goes forward to touch a catch, the same as
a saw-mill, which lets another spring not seen, raise the
hand, M, when the feeding operation ceases. The frame is
then drawn back and the same repeated. As the match is
split they open and require a rounding mortise made through
the base plank between the blocks, C C, which allows them
to remain in a half circular form—the knife is raised by a
line attached to a spring pole, T, the knife is screwed upon
a piece of cast iron which works in the guide, N, having the
back end firmly fastened by a bolt through the standard, O
This knife stands at right angles with the shaft.   When the
matches are split and sufficiently dry to work upon, they are
dipped in melted brimstone, kept hot, and the match also
kept hot on a sheet iron stove, and all the brimstone is thrown
off which can possibly be by jerking the block with the
hand.   If any brimstone remains upon the end it must be
scraped off before dipping into the match composition.
Without the chlora‘e, the composition makes a first class

'Friction Match." It ought to be known, however, that the match business is an unhealthy occupation, from the poisonous effects of the phosphorus.

STEAM BOILERS—To Prevent Lime Deposits.—Put into your cistern or tank, from which the boiler is fed, a sufficient amount of oak tan-bark, in the piece, to color the water rather dark ; run 4 weeks and renew.

This plan has been much used, in the lime-stone sections of Washington, O., giving general satisfaction.

2. Ohio River Plan.—Sprouts from barley, in malting, are recommended by Capt. Lumm, part owner of a steamboat, and engineer on the Ohio and Mississippi rivers, to prevent the deposit of lime upon boilers, and he says tightens up old leaky boilers, also. It may be used in quantities of from 3 pts. to 2 or 3 qts., according to the size of boilers.

When it is put in you must know the quantity of water in the boiler, for unless you heat up quite slow it causes a foaming of the water, and might deceive the engineer about the amount of water in the boiler, but if heat up slow there is no danger of this deception.

3. To Prevent Explosion, with the Reason why they Explode.—At a recent meeting of the Association for the Advancement of Science, Mr. Hyatt, of New York, presented what we believe to be the true cause. He presented the following table, showing the rapidity with which pressure is *doubled* by only a slight increase of heat.

At 212 degrees of heat water begins to boil; at 868 degrees iron becomes of a red heat :

212 degrees of heat,	15 pounds to square inch.		
251   "   "   30   "   "   "
294   "   "   60   "   "   "
342   "   "   120   "   "   "
398   "   "   240   "   "   "
464   "   "   480   "   "   "
868   "   "   7680 "   "   "

It was stated by Mr. Hyatt, that, from experiments he had made, this great increase of pressure could be obtained in *six to seven minutes*, with an engine at rest. This rapid doubling of pressure, with but a small increase of heat, is due to the conversion of what is termed latent heat, in steam, into sensible heat. If we immerse a thermometer into boiling water, it stands at 212; if we place it in steam immediately above the water, it indicates the same temperature. The question then arises, what becomes of all the heat which is communicated to the water, since it is neither indicated by the water nor by the steam formed from it? The answer is, it enters the water and converts it into steam without raising its temperature. One *thousand* degrees of heat are absorbed in the conversion of water into steam, and this is called its *latent* heat. And it is the *sudden* conversion of *latent* heat into *sensible* heat that produces the explosion. If an engine is stopped, even if there is but a moderate fire, if the escape valve is closed, there is a rapid absorption or accumulation of latent heat. The pressure rises with great rapidity, and when the engineer thinks everything is safe, the explosion comes.

That this is the true cause of nearly all the explosions that occur, will be plain to every one who will look at the relations between latent and sensible heat. Prof. Henry and Prof. Silliman, Jr., endorse the view. What, then, is the security against explosions? We know of no securities but these—a sufficiency of water in the boilers, and the *escape valves open* at light pressure, when the engine is at rest.—*Springfield Republican.*

There is no question about the foregoing explanations being founded in *true* philosophy; and if engineers will be *governed* by them, instead of by a desire to hold on to steam for the purpose of getting *ahead* or of *keeping* ahead, as the case may be, of some other boat; or on land, to save the expense of fuel, not *one* explosion would take place where now there is, at least, a *hundred.*

Awful will be the reckoning with these *murderers;* for in Heaven's sight they are one and the same.

A series of experiments have recently been concluded on the U. S. Steamer Michigan, and a full but voluminous report laid before the Navy Department, upon the subject of steam expansion. It would pay all interested in steam works to obtain and read it.

PLUMS AND OTHER FRUIT—To Prevent Insects from Stinging.—Take new, dry lime, sulphur, and gunpowder, equal parts, pulverized very fine, and throw it amongst the flowers when in full bloom; use it freely so that all may catch a little.

This has been tried with success. Working upon the principle of pepper, to keep flies from meat. The injury to fruit being done while in blossom.

BED-ROOM CARPETS—For Twelve and a half Cents per Yard.—Sew together the cheapest cotton cloth, the size of the room, and tack the edges to the floor. Now paper the cloth as you would the sides of a room, with cheap room paper; put

ting a border around the edge if desired. The paste will be t *s*
better if a little gum arabic is m. xed with it. When thoroughly
dry, give it two coats of furniture or carriage varnish, and when
dry it is done.

It can be washed; and looks well in proportion to the
quality and figure of the paper used. It could not be expected to stand the wear of a kitchen, for any length of
time, but for bed-rooms it is well adapted.

COFFEE—More Healthy and Better Flavored, for
One-Fourth the Expense of Common.—Coffee, by weight or
measure, one-fourth, rye three-fourths.

Look them over separately, to remove bad grains; then
wash to remove dust, draining off the water for a moment
as you take it with the hands, from the washing water,
putting directly into the browning skillet, carefully stirring,
all the time, to brown it evenly. Brown each one separately; then mix evenly, and grind only as used; settling
with a beaten egg, seasoning with a little cream and sugar
as usual.

And I do sincerely say the flavor is better, and it is one
hundred per cent. more healthy than all coffee.

You may try barley, peas, parsnips, dandelion roots, &c.,
but none of their flavors are equal to rye. Yet all of them
are more or less used for coffee.

PICKLING FRUITS, AND CUCUMBERS—Pickling Ap
ples.—Best vinegar 1 gal.; sugar 4 lbs.; apples all it will cover
handsomely; cinnamon and cloves, ground, of each 1 table-
spoon.

Pare and core the apples, tying up the cinnamon and
cloves in a cloth and putting with the apples, into the vinegar and sugar and cooking until done, only. Keep in jars.
They are nicer than preserves, and more healthy, and keep
a long time; not being too sour, nor too sweet, but an agreeable mixture of the two. It will be seen below that the
different fruits require different quantities of sugar and
vinegar, the reason for it, is, the difference in the fruit.

2. Pickling Peaches.—Best vinegar 1 qt.; sugar 4 lbs.;
peaches, peeled and stoned 8 lbs.; spices as desired, or as for
apples.

Treated every other way as apples. If they should begin
to ferment, at any time, simply boil down the juice; then
boil the peaches in it for a few minutes only.

3. PEACHES—TO PEEL.—In peeling small peaches with a knife, too much of the peach is wasted; but by having a wire-cage, similar to those made for popping corn; fill the cage with peaches and dip it into boiling water, for a moment, then into cold water for a moment and empty out · going on in the same way for all you wish to peel. This toughens the skin and enables you to strip it off, saving much in labor, as also the waste of peach. Why not, as well as tomatoes?

4. PICKLING PLUMS.—Best vinegar 1 pt.; sugar 4 lbs.; plums 8 lbs.; spices to taste.

Boil them in the mixture until soft; then take out the plums, and boil the syrup until quite thick and pour it over them again.

5. PICKLING CUCUMBERS.—Pick each morning; stand in weak brine 3 or 4 days, putting in mustard pods and horseradish leaves to keep them green. Then take out and drain, covering with vinegar for a week; at which time take out and drain again, putting into new vinegar, adding mustard seed, ginger root, cloves, pepper and red pepper pods, of each about 1 or 3 oz.; or to suit different tastes, for each barrel.

The pickles will be nice and brittle, and pass muster a any man's table, or market. And if it was generally known that the greenness of pickles was caused by the action of the vinegar on the copper kettle, producing a *poison*, (verdigris,) in which they are directed to be scalded, I think no one would wish to have a nice *looking* pickle at the expense of HEALTH; if they do, they can continue the bad practice of thus scalding; if not, just put your vinegar on cold, and add your red peppers, or cayennes, cloves, and other spices, as desired; but the vinegar must be changed once, as the large amount of water in the cucumber reduces the vinegar so much that this change is absolutely necessary; and if they should seem to lose their sharp taste again, just add a little molasses, or spirit, and all will be right.

SANDSTONE—TO PREVENT SCALING BY FROST.—Raw linseed-oil, 2 or 3 coats.

Apply in place of paint, not allowing the first coat to get entirely dry until the next is applied; if it does, a skin is formed which prevents the next from penetrating the stone. Poorly burned brick will be equally well preserved by the same process.

SEALING WAX—RED, BLACK, AND BLUE.—Gum Shellac 3 oz.; Venice turpentine 4 ozs.; vermillion 2½ ozs.; alcohol 2 ozs.; camphor gum ¼ oz.   Dissolve the camphor in the alcohol, then the shellac, adding the turpentine, and finally the vermillion, be-ing very careful that no blaze shall come in contact with its fumes; for if it does, it will fire very quickly.

BLUE.—Substitute fine Prussian-blue for the vermillion, same quantity.

BLACK.—Lamp-black only sufficient to color.   Either color must be well rubbed into the mixture.

ADVICE—TO YOUNG MEN AND OTHERS, OUT OF EM-PLOYMENT.—ADVICE—How few there are that will hear advice at all; not because it is advice, but from the fact that those who attempt to give it are not qualified for the work they assume; or that they endeavor to thrust it upon their notice at an inappropriate time; or upon persons over whom no control is acceded, if claimed.   But a book or paper never give offense from any of these causes; there-fore, they are always welcomed with a hope that real benefit may be derived from their suggestions.   Whether that end will be attained in this case, I leave to the judgment of those for whom it is intended; hoping they may find them-selves sufficiently interested to give it a careful perusal, and candid consideration.   And although my remarks must, in this work, be necessarily short, yet every sentence shall be a text for your own thoughts to contemplate and enlarge upon; and perhaps, in some future edition of the work, I may take room and time to give the subject that attention which is really its due; and which would be a pleasure to devote to its consideration.

First, then, let me ask why are so many young men and other persons out of employment?   The answer is very positive as well as very plain.   It is this—indolence, coupled with a determination that they will do some *great* thing, only And because that great thing does not turn up without effort, they are doing nothing.   The point of difficulty is simply this; they look for the end, before the beginning.   But just consider how few there are that really accomplish any great thing, even with a whole life of industry and economi-cal perseverance.   And yet most of our *youth* calculate that their *beginning* shall be amongst the *greats*.   But as no one comes to offer them their expectations, indolence says wait;

and so they are still waiting. Now mind you, as long as your expectations are placed upon a chance offer of something very remunerative, or upon the assistance of others; even in a small way, so long will you continue to wait in vain. At this point, then, the question would arise, what can be done? and the answer is equally plain with the other. Take hold of the first job you can find, for it will not find you. No matter how insignificant it may be, it will be better than longer idleness; and when you are seen doing something for yourselves, by those whose opinions are worth any consideration, they will soon offer you more and better jobs; until, finally, you will find something which agrees with your taste or inclination, for a life business. But remember that the *idle* never have good situations offered them. It is the industrious and persevering or·ly, who are needed to assist in life's great struggle.

There are a few lines of poetry called "The Excellent Man," which advocates the principles I am endeavoring to advance, so admirably that I cannot deny myself the pleasure of quoting them. The old proverb, "God helps those who help themselves," is as true as it is old, and after all that is said and done, in this country, if in no other, a man must depend on his own exertions, not on patronage, if he would have or deserve success:

> "They gave me advice and counsel in store,
> Praised me and honored me more and more
> Said that I only should 'wait awhile,'
> Offered their patronage, too, with a smile
>
> But with all their honor and approbation,
> I should long ago have died of starvation,
> Had there not come an *excellent* man,
> Who, bravely to help me along began
>
> Good-fellow! he got me the food I ate,
> His kindness and care I shall never forget;
> Yet I cannot embrace him—though other folks can,
> For I, *myself*, am this excellent man!".

Up, then, and at it, for there is

> Knitting and sewing, and reaping and mowing,
> And all kinds of work for the people to do,
> To keep themselves busy, both Abram and Lizzie;
> Begin, then, ye idle, there is plenty for you.

When you have found a situation or a job of work, prove

yourself honest, industrious, persevering, and faithful in every trust, and no fears need be apprehended of your final success. Save a part of your wages as a sinking fund, or rather as a floating fund, which shall keep your head above water in a storm; or to enable you, at no distant day, to commence a business of your own.

A poor orphan boy, of fourteen, once resolved to save half of his wages, which were only four dollars per month, for this purpose; and actually refused, even in sickness, although really suffering for comforts, to touch this business fund. He was afterwards the richest man in St. Louis.

His advice to young men was always this: "Go to work; save half your wages; no matter how small they may be, until you have what will enable you to begin what you wish to follow; then begin it, stick to it; be economical, prudent, and careful, and you cannot fail to prosper."

My advice is the same, with this qualification, however; that in choosing your occupation, you should be governed by the eternal principles of right! never choosing that which, when done, injures a fellow creature more than it can possibly benefit yourself—I mean the liquor traffic. But with the feeling of St. Paul, when he saw the necessity of doing something different from what he had been doing, he cried out, "Lord, what wilt thou have me to do?" Ask your own tastes, being governed by conscience, under the foregoing principles; knowing that if a person has to learn a trade or business *against* his own inclination, it requires double dilligence to make only half speed, and hardly ever meeting with success.

The question to be settled, then, is this: Shall I work the soil: Shall I be a mechanic, teacher, divine, physician, lawyer, merchant, druggist, or grocer, or shall it be something else? Whenever you make up your mind what it shall be, make it up, also, to be the best one in that line of business. Set your mark high, both in point of moral purity and literary qualifications.

If you choose any of the occupations of trade, you must save all that it is possible for economy and prudence to do, for your beginning.

But if you choose one of the learned professions, you must work with the same care and prudence until you have accumulated sufficient to make a fair commencement in your studies ; then prosecute them . in all faithfulness as far as the accumulated means will advance you ; realizing that this increase of knowledge will give you increased power in obtaining the further means of prosecuting your studies, necessary to qualify you to do one thing only in life.

Nearly all of our best men are self-made, and men of one idea, *i, e.*, they have set themselves to be mechanics, physicians, lawyers, sculptors, &c., and have bent their whole energies and lives to fit themselves for the great work before them. Begin, then ; offer no excuse. Be sure you are on the right track, then go ahead :

"Live for something ;" slothful be no longer, look around for some employ ;
Labor always makes you stronger, and also gives you sweetest joy.
Idle hands are always weary ; faithful hearts are always gay ;
Life for us, should not be dreary ; nor can it, to the active, every day.

Always remembering that industry, in study or labor, will keep ahead of his work, giving time for pleasure and enjoyment ; but indolence is ever behind ; being driven with her work, and no prospect of its ever being accomplished.

When you have made your decision, aside from what time you must necessarily devote to labor, let all possible time be given to the study of the best works upon the subject of your occupation or profession, knowing that one hour's reading in the morning, when the mind is calm and free from fatigue, thinking and talking with your companions through the day upon the subjects of which you have been reading, will be better than twice that time in evening reading, yet if both can be enjoyed, so much the better ; but one of them must certainly be occupied in this way.

If you choose something in the line of mercantile or trade life, do not put off, too long, commencing for yourself. Better begin in a small way and learn, as your capital increases, how to manage a larger business.

I knew a gentleman to commence a business with five dollars, and in two weeks his capital was seventeen dollars, besides feeding his family.

I knew one also to begin with sixty dollars, and in fifteen months he cleared over four hundred and fifty dollars, besides supporting his family ; then he sold out and lost all, before he again got into successful business.

No person should ever sell out, or quit an honorable paying business.

Those who choose a professional life, will hardly find a place in the West, equal to the University of Michigan, Ann Arbor, to obtain their literary qualifications. An entrance fee of Ten Dollars, with Five Dollars yearly, pays for a full Literary, Law, Medical, or Civil Engineering course; the first requiring four, the two next, two, and the last, three years. [See Frontispiece.]

Or, in the words of the Catalogue: "The University, having been endowed by the General Government, affords education, without money and without price. There is no young man, so poor, that industry, diligence, and perseverance, will not enable him to get an education here.

"The present condition of the University confirms this view of its character. While the sons of the rich, and of men of more or less property, and, in large proportion, the sons of substantial farmers, mechanics, and merchants, are educated here, there is also a very considerable number of young men dependent *entirely* upon their own exertions—young men who, accustomed to work on the farm, or in the mechanic's shop, have become smitten with the love of knowledge, and are manfully working their way through, to a liberal education, by appropriating a portion of their time to the field or the workshop."

Persons wishing to qualify themselves for teaching in this State, will find the Normal School, Ypsilanti, undoubtedly preferable.

And that none may excuse themselves from an effort because somewhat advanced in life, let me say that Doctor Eberle, who wrote several valuable medical works, did not begin his medical studies until forty-five years of age; and, although I could mention many more, I will only add that I, myself, always desired to become a physician, yet circumstances did not favor nor justify my commencement until I was thirty-eight. See the remarks following " Eye Water."

There is no occupation, however, so free and independent as that of the farmer; and there is none, except parents, capable of using so great an influence, for good or for evil, as that of teacher.

All might and ought, to a greater or less extent, be farmers; but all cannot be teachers. Then let those whose taste inclines them to teach, not shrink the responsibility, but fully qualify for the work; learning also the ways of Truth and Righteousness for themselves; teaching it through the week-school, by action as well as by word, and in the Sabbath-school, fail not to take their stand for the right, like our President *elect;* then when it comes your turn to assist in the government of the State, or Nation, the people will come to your support, as you do to your work— as they have just done to his, (1860); feeling, as now, that the government must be safe in the hands of those who love God—deal honestly with their fellows; and who, in remembering the Sabbath to keep it holy themselves, are not ashamed—nor forget, to teach the children to love the same God, and reverence His Word. Only think—a Sabbath-School Teacher—*a Rail-Splitter*—*a Boat-man*, President of the United States !

Who will hereafter be afraid of common labor; or, let indolence longer prevent their activity? when it is only those who begin with *small* things, and persevere *through* life, that reach the final goal of greatness; and, as in this case, are crowned with the greatest honor which man can receive—the *confidence* of his Nation.

Then let *Industry* take the place of *Indolence*, beginning to be great, by grappling with the small things of life—be faithful to yourself, and, you may reasonably expect, the end shall, indeed, be great.

And although it could not be expected, in a work of this kind, that much could, or would be said, directly, regarding a future life, yet I should be recreant to duty if I did not say a word more upon that subject. It shall be only a word . Be as faithful to GOD, as I have recommended you to be to yourselves, and all things pertaining to a future, will be equally prosperous, and glorious in its results.

GRAMMAR IN RHYME—FOR THE LITTLE FOLKS.
—It is seldom that one sees so much valuable matter as the following lines contain, comprised in so brief a space Every young grammarian, and many older heads, will find it highly advantageous to commit the " poem " to memory;

for with these lines at the tongue's end, none need ever mistake a part of speech :

1. "Three little words you often see,
   Are articles—*a, an,* and *the.*
2. A Noun's the name of any thing,
   As *school,* or *garden, hoop,* or *swing.*
3. Adjectives tell the kind of Noun,
   As *great, small, pretty, white,* or *brown.*
4. Instead of Nouns the Pronouns stand—
   Her head, *his* face, *your* arm, *my* hand.
5. Verbs tell of something to be done—
   To *read, count, sing, laugh, jump,* or *run.*
6. How things are done, the adverbs tell,
   As *slowly, quickly, ill,* or *well.*
7. Conjunctions join the words together—
   As men *and* women, wind *or* weather.
8. The Preposition stands before
   A Noun, as *in,* or *through* a door.
9. The Interjection shows surprise,
   As *oh!* how pretty—*ah!* how wise.

The whole are called Nine Parts of Speech,
Which reading, writing, speaking, teach.

MUSICAL CURIOSITY—Scotch Genius in Teaching.—A Highland piper, having a scholar to teach, disdained to crack his brains with the names of semibreves, minims, crotchets and quavers. "Here, Donald," said he, "tak yer pipes, lad, and gie us a blast. So—verra weel blawn, indeed; but what's a sound, Donald, without sense? Ye maun blaw forever without making a tune o't, if I dinna tell you how the queer things on the paper maun help you. You see that big fellow wi' a round, open face? (pointing to a semibreve between two lines of a bar). He moves slowly from that line to this, while ye beat ane wi' yer fist, and gie us a long blast. If, now, ye put a leg to him, ye mak' twa o' him, and he'll move twice as fast; and if ye black his face, he'll run four times faster than the fellow wi' the white face; but if, after blacking his face, ye'll bend his knee or tie his leg, he'll hop eight times faster than the white-faced chap I showed you first. Now, whene'er ye blaw yer pipes, Donald, remember this—that the tighter those fellows' legs are tied, the faster they'll run, and the quicker they're sure to dance."

That is, the more legs they have bent up, contrary to nature, the faster goes the music.

COLORING DEPARTMENT.

REMARKS.—It may be necessary to remark, and I do ¿ here, once for all, that every article to be dyed, as well as everything used about dyeing, should be perfectly clean.

In the next place, the article to be dyed should be well scoured in soap, and then the soap rinsed out. It is also an advantage to dip the article you wish to dye into warm water, just before putting it into the alum or other preparation; for the neglect of this precaution it is nothing uncommon to have the goods or yarn spotted. *Soft* water should always be used, if possible, and sufficient to cover the goods handsomely.

As soon as an article is dyed it should be aired a little, then well rinsed, and afterwards hung up to dry.

When dyeing or scouring silk or merino dresses, care should be taken not to wring them, for this has a tendency to wrinkle and break the silk.

In putting dresses and shawls out to dry, that have been dyed, they should be hung up by the edge so as to dry evenly.

Great confidence may be placed in these coloring recipes, as the author has had them revised by Mr. Storms, of this city, who has been in the business over thirty years.

COLORS ON WOOLEN GOODS.

1. CHROME BLACK—Superior to Any in Use.—For 5 lbs. of goods—blue vitriol 6 ozs.; boil it a few minutes, then dip the goods ¾ of an hour, airing often; take out the goods, and make a dye with logwood 3 lbs.; boil ½ hour; dip ¾ of an hour and air the goods, and dip ¾ of an hour more. Wash in strong suds.

N. B.—This will not impart any of its color in fulling, nor fade by exposure to the sun.

2. BLACK ON WOOL—Fo Mixtures.—For 10 lbs. of wool –bi-chromate of potash 4 ozs.; ground argal 3 ozs.; boil together and put in the wool; stir well and let it remain in the dye 4 hours. Then take out the wool, rinse it slightly in clear water; then make a new dye, into which

put logwood 3½ lbs. Boil 1 hour and add chamber-lye 1 pt., and let the wool lie in all night. Wash in clear water

3. STEEL MIX—Dark.—Black wool—it may be natural or colored, 10 lbs.—white wool 1¼ lbs. Mix evenly together and it will be beautiful.

4. SNUFF BROWN—Dark, for Cloth or Wool.— For 5 lbs. goods—camwood 1 lb.; boil it 15 minutes, then dip the goods for ¾ hour; take out the goods, and add to the dye, fustic 2½ lbs.; boil 10 minutes, and dip the goods ¾ hour; then add blue vitriol 1 oz.; copperas 4 ozs.; dip again ½ hour; if not dark enough, add more copperas. It is dark and permanent.

5. WINE COLOR.—For 5 lbs. goods—camwood 2 lbs.; boil 15 minutes and dip the goods ½ hour; boil again and dip ½ hour; then darken with blue vitriol 1½ ozs.; if not dark enough, add copperas ½ oz.

6. MADDER RED.—To each lb. of goods—alum 5 ozs.; red, or cream of tartar 1 oz.; put in the goods and bring your kettle to a boil for ½ hour; then air them and boil ½ hour longer; then empty your kettle and fill with clean water, put in bran 1 peck; make it milk warm and let it stand until the bran rises, then skim off the bran and put in madder ½ lb.; put in your goods and heat slowly until it boils and is done. Wash in strong suds.

7. GREEN—On Wool or Silk, with Oak Bark.— Make a strong yellow dye of yellow oak and hickory bark, in equal quantities. Add the extract of indigo, or chemic, (which see,) 1 table-spoon at a time, until you get the shade of color desired. Or:

8. GREEN—With Fustic.—For each lb. of goods— fustic 1 lb.; with alum 3½ ozs. Steep until the strength is out, and soak the goods therein until a good yellow is obtained; then remove the chips, and add extract of indigo or chemic, 1 table-spoon at a time, until the color suits.

9. BLUE—Quick Process.—For 2 lbs. of goods,—alum 5 ozs.; cream of tartar 3 ozs.; boil the goods in this for 1 hour; then throw the goods into warm water, which has more or less of the extract of indigo in it, according to the depth of color desired, and boil again until it suits, adding more of the blue if needed. It is quick and permanent.

10. STOCKING YARN, OR WOOL TO COLOR—
BETWEEN A BLUE AND PURPLE.—For 5 lbs. of wool bichromate of potash 1 oz.; alum 2 ozs.; dissolve them and bring the water to a boil, putting in the wool and boiling 1 hour; then throw away the dye and make another dye with logwood chips 1 lb., or extract of logwood 2½ ozs., and boil 1 hour. This also works very prettily on silk.

N B.—Whenever you make a dye with logwood chips either boil the chips ½ hour and pour off the dye, or tie up the chips in a bag and boil with the wool or other goods or take 2½ ozs. of the extract in place of 1 lb. of the chips is less trouble and generally the better plan. In the above recipe the more logwood that is used the darker will be the shade

11. SCARLET, WITH COCHINEAL—For YARN OR CLOTH.—For 1 lb. of goods—cream of tartar ½ oz.; cochineal, well pulverized, ¼ oz.; muriate of tin 2½ ozs.; then boil up the dye and enter the goods; work them briskly for 10 or 15 minutes, after which boil 1½ hours, stirring the goods slowly while boiling, wash in clear water and dry in the shade.

12. PINK.—For 3 lbs. of goods—alum 3 ozs., boil and dip the goods 1 hour; then add, to the dye, cream of tartar 4 ozs., cochineal, well pulverized, 1 oz.; boil well and dip the goods while boiling, until the color suits.

13. ORANGE.—For 5 lbs. goods—muriate of tin 6 table-spoons; argal 4 ozs.; boil and dip 1 hour; then add, to the dye, fustic 2½ lbs.; boil 10 minutes, and dip ½ hour, and add, again, to the dye, madder 1 tea-cup; dip again ½ hour.

N. B.—Cochineal in place of madder makes a much brighter color, which should be added in small quantities until pleased. About 2 ozs.

14. LAC RED.—For 5 lbs. goods—argal 10 ozs.; boil a few minutes; then mix fine ground lac 1 lb. with muriate of tin 1¼ lbs., and let them stand 2 or 3 hours; then add half of the lac to the argal dye, and dip ½ hour; then add the balance of the lac and dip again 1 hour; keep the dye at a boiling heat, until the last half hour, when the dye may be cooled off.

15. PURPLE.—For 5 lbs. goods—cream of tartar 4 ozs.; alum 6 ozs.; cochineal, well pulverized, 2 ozs.; muriate of tin ¼ tea-cup. Boil the cream of tartar, alum and tin, 15 minutes; then put in the cochineal and boil 5 minutes; dip the goods 2 hours; then make a new dye with alum 4 ozs.; Brazil wood 6 ozs.; logwood 14 ozs.; muriate of tin 1 tea-cup, with a little chemic; work again until pleased.

16. SILVER DRAB—Light.—For 5 lbs. goods—alum 1 small tea-spoon, and logwood about the same amount; boil well together, then dip the goods 1 hour; if not dark enough, add in equal quantities alum and logwood, until suited.

17. SLATE, ON WOOLEN OR COTTON—With Beach Bark.—Boil the bark in an iron kettle, skim out the chips after it has boiled sufficiently, and then add copperas to set the dye. If you wish it very dark add more copperas. This is excellent for stockings.

18. EXTRACT OF INDIGO OR CHEMIC—To Make.—For good chemic or extract of indigo, take oil of vitriol ½ lb., and stir into it indigo, finely ground, 2 ozs., continuing the stirring at first for ½ hour; now cover over, and stir 3 or 4 times daily for 2 or 3 days; then put in a crumb of saleratus and stir it up, and if it foams, put in more and stir, and add as long as it foams; the saleratus neutralizes any excess of acid; then put into a glass vessel and cork up tight. It improves by standing. Druggists keep this prepared.

19. WOOL—To Cleanse.—Make a liquid of water 3 parts and urine 1 part; heat it as hot as you can bear the hand in it; then put in the wool, a little at a time, so as not to have it crowd; let it remain in for 15 minutes; take it out over a basket to drain; then rinse in running water, and spread it out to dry; thus proceed in the same liquor; when it gets reduced fill it up, in the same proportions, keeping it at hand heat, all the time not using any soap.

20. DARK COLORS—To Extract and Insert Light. —This recipe is calculated for carpet rags. In the first place let the rags be washed clean—the black or brown rags can be colored red, or purple, at the option of the dyer; to do

this, take, for every 5 lbs black or brown rags muriate of tin ¾ lb.; and the lac ½ lb.; mixed with the same, as for the lac red; dip the goods in this dye 2 hours, boiling ½ of the time, if not red enough add more tin and lac. The goods can then be made a purple, by adding a little logwood; be careful, and not get in but a very small handful, as more can be added if not enough. White rags make a beautiful appearance in a carpet, by tying them in the skein and coloring them red, green or purple; gray rags will take a very good green,—the coloring will be in proportion to the darkness of mix.

DURABLE COLORS ON COTTON.

1. BLACK.—For 5 lbs. goods—sumac, wood and bark together, 3 lbs.; boil ½ hour, and let the goods steep 12 hours; then dip in lime water ½ hour; then take out the goods and let them drip an hour; now add to the sumac liquor, copperas 8 ozs., and dip another hour; then run them through the tub of lime water again for 15 minutes · now make a new dye with logwood 2½ lbs., by boiling 1½ hour, and dip again 3 hours; now add bi-chromate of potash 2 ozs., to the logwood dye, and dip 1 hour. Wash in clear cold water and dry in the shade. You may say this is doing too much. You cannot get a permanent black on cotton with less labor.

2. SKY BLUE.—For 3 lbs. goods—blue vitriol 4 ozs.; boil a few minutes; then dip the goods 3 hours, after which pass them through strong lime water. You can make this color a beautiful brown by putting the goods through a solution of Prussiate of potash.

3. LIME WATER, AND STRONG LIME WATER.— For Coloring.—Lime water is made by putting stone lime 1 lb., and strong lime water, 1½ lbs. into a pail of water, slacking, stirring, and letting it stand until it becomes clear, then turn into a tub of water, in which dip the goods.

4. BLUE, ON COTTON OR LINEN—With Logwood In all cases, if new, they should be boiled in a strong soap suds or weak-lye and rinsed clean; then for cotton 5 lbs. or linen 3 lbs., take bi-chromate of potash ¾ lb.; put in the goods and dip 2 hours, then take out, rinse; make a

dye with logwood 4 lbs. ; dip in this 1 hour, air, au l let stand in the dye 3 or 4 hours, or till the dye is almost cold, wash out and dry.

5. BLUE ON COTTON—WITHOUT LOGWOOD.—For 5 lbs. of rags—copperas 4 ozs.; boil and dip 15 minutes; then dip in strong suds, and back to the dye 2 or 3 times; then make a dye with prussiate of potash 1 oz.; oil of vitriol 3 table-spoons ; boil 30 minutes and rinse ; then dry.

6. GREEN.—If the cotton is new, boil in weak-lye or strong suds; then wash and dry; give the cotton a dip in the home-made blue dye-tub until blue enough is obtained to make the green as dark as required, take out, dry, and rinse the goods a little ; then make a dye with fustic ¾ lb.; logwood 3 ozs. to each lb. of goods, by boiling the dye 1 hour; when cooled so as to bear the hand, put in the cotton, move briskly a few minutes, and let lay in 1 hour; take out and let it thoroughly drain; dissolve and add to the dye, for each lb. of cotton, blue-vitriol ½ oz., and dip another hour; wring out and let dry in the shade. By adding or diminishing the logwood and fustic, any shade of green may be obtained.

7. YELLOW.—For 5 lbs. of goods—sugar of lead 7 ozs.; dip the goods 2 hours; make a new dye with bi-chromate of potash 4 ozs.; dip until the color suits, wring out and dry, if not yellow enough repeat, the operation.

8. ORANGE.—For 5 lbs. goods—sugar of lead 4 ozs.; boil a few minutes, and when a little cool put in the goods, dip 2 hours, wring out; make a new dye with bi-chromate of potash 8 ozs.; madder 2 ozs.; dip until it suits; if the color should be too red, take off a small sample and dip it into lime water, when the choice can be taken of the sam ple dipped in the lime or the original color.

8. RED.—Take muriate of tin ¾ of a tea-cup; add suffi- ient water to cover the goods well, bring it to a boiling heat, putting in the goods 1 hour, stirring often; take out the goods and empty the kettle and put in clean water, witn nic-wood 1 lb., steeping it for ½ hour, at hand heat; then put in the goods and increase the heat for 1 hour, not bring- ing to a boil at all; air the goods and dip an hour as be fore ; wash without soap.

9. MURIATE OF TIN—TIN LIQUOR.—If druggists keep it, it is best to purchase of them already made; but if you prefer, proceed as follows:

Get at a tinner's shop, block tin; put it in a shovel and melt it. After it is melted, pour it from the hight of 4 or 5 feet into a pail of clear water. The object of this is to have the tin in small particles, so that the acid can dissolve it. Take it out of the water and dry it; then put it into a strong glass bottle; pour over it muriatic acid 12 ozs.; then slowly, add sulphuric acid 8 ozs. The acid should be added about a table-spoon at a time, at intervals of 5 or 8 minutes, for if you add it too rapidly you run the risk of breaking the bottle by heat. After you have all the acid in, let the bottle stand until the ebullition subsides; then stop it up with a bees-wax or glass stopper, and set it away, and it will keep good for a year or more, or will be fit for use in 24 hours.

COLORS ON SILK GOODS.

GREEN—VERY HANDSOME WITH OAK BARK.—For 1 lb. of silk—yellow oak bark 8 ozs.; boil it ½ hour; turn off the liquor from the bark and add alum 6 ozs.; let stand until cold; while this dye is being made, color the goods in the blue dye-tub, a light blue; dry and wash; then dip in the alum and bark dye; if it does not take well, warm the dye a little.

2. GREEN OR YELLOW—ON SILK OR WOOL, IN FIVE TO FIFTEEN MINUTES.—For 5 lbs. of goods—black oak bark or peach leaves ½ peck; boil well; then take out the bark or leaves, and add muriate of tin ½ tea-cup, stirring well; then put in the goods and stir them round, and it will dye a deep yellow in from 5 to 15 minutes, according to the strength of the bark; take out the goods, rinse and dry immediately

N B.—For a green, add, to the above dye, extract of indigo, or chemic 1 table-spoon only, at a time, and work the goods 5 minutes, and air; if not sufficiently dark use the same amount of chemic as before, and work again until it suits.

3. MULBERRY—For 1 lb. of silk—alum 4 ozs.; dip 1

hour; wash out, and make a dye with Brazil wood 1 oz., and logwood ¼ oz. by boiling together; dip in this ½ hour, then add more Brazil wood and logwood, in equal proportions, until the color is dark enough.

4. BLACK.—Make a weak dye as you would for black on woolens, work the goods in bi-chromate of potash, at a little below boiling heat, then dip in the logwood in the same way; if colored in the blue vitriol dye, use about the same heat.

5. SPOTS—To Remove and Prevent when Coloring Black on Silk or Woolen.—N. B. In dyeing silk or woolen goods, if they should become rusty or spotted, all that is necessary is to make a weak-lye, and have it scalding hot, and put your goods in for 15 minutes; or throw some ashes into your dye, and run your goods in it 5 minutes, and they will come out a jet black, and an even color. I will warrant it.—*Storms.*

The reason that spots of brown, or rust, as it is generally called, appear on black cloths, is that these parts take the color faster than the other parts; but I have no doubt Mr. Storms' plan will remove them, for he regretted much to make public the information, which he says is not generally known. And if the precaution, given in our leading remarks on coloring, are heeded, there will be but very little danger of spotting at all.

6. LIGHT CHEMIC BLUE.—For cold water 1 gal., dissolve alum ½ table-spoon, in hot water 1 tea-cup, and add to it; then add chemic 1 tea-spoon at a time, to obtain the desired color,—the more chemic that is used, the darker will be the color.

7 PURPLE.—For 1 lb. of silk—having first obtained a light blue by dipping in the home-made blue dye-tub. and dried, dip in alum 4 ozs., to sufficient water to cover, when a little warm; if the color is not full enough add a little chemic.

6. YELLOW.—For 1 lb. of silk—alum 3 ozs.; sugar of lead ¾ ozs; immerse the goods in the solution over night; take out, drain, and make a new dye with fustic 1 lb.; dip until the required color is obtained.

N. B. The yellow or green, for wool, works equally well on silk.

9. ORANGE.—Take anotta and soda, and add in equal quantities, according to the amount of goods and darkness of the color wanted : Say 1 oz. of each, to each pound of silk, and repeat as desired.

10. CRIMSON.—For 1 lb. of silk—alum 3 ozs.; dip at hand-heat 1 hour ; take out and drain, while making a new dye, by boiling 10 minutes, cochineal- 3 ozs. ; bruised nut-galls 2 ozs. ; and cream- of tartar ¼ oz., in one pail of water; when a little cool, begin to dip, raising the heat to a boil, continuing to dip 1 hour; wash and dry.

11. CINNAMON OR BROWN ON COTTON AND SILK.—By a New Process—Very Beautiful.—Give the goods as much color, from a solution of blue vitriol 2 ozs., to water 1 gallon, as it will take up in dipping 15 minutes ; then run it through lime-water ; this will make a beautiful sky-blue, of much durability ; it has now to be run through a solution of Prussiate of potash 1 oz., to water 1 gal.

TABLES AND EXPLANATIONS OF INTEREST.

INTEREST—LEGAL RATES ALLOWED IN EACH OF THE DIFFERENT STATES; ALSO, SHOWING WHAT RATES MAY BE CONTRACTED FOR, AND COLLECTED; AND GIVING THE FORFEITURES WHEN ILLEGAL RATES ARE ATTEMPTED TO BE COLLECTED.—FIRST, then *Six* per cent is the *Legal* rate in the States of Maine, New Hampshire, Rhode Island, Connecticut, Vermont, Delaware, Maryland, Pennsylvania, Virginia, North Carolina, Florida, (*Eight* per cent. is allowed in this State if agreed upon), Mississippi, Tennessee, Arkansas, Kentucky, Ohio, Indiana, Illinois, Missouri, Iowa, and New Jersey, excepting, in Hudson and Essex Counties, and the city of Patterson, in this last State, *Seven* per cent is allowed, when either of the parties reside therein.

SECOND; *Seven* per cent. is the *Legal* rate in Michigan, New York, Minnesota, Wisconsin, South Carolina, and Georgia.

THIRD; *Ten* per cent. is the *Legal* rate in California; *Eight* per cent. in Alabama and Texas, and as strange as it may appear, in Louisiana only *Five* per cent.

Maine and Vermont allow no higher than legal interest to be collected, even if agreed upon. And if paid it can be recovered again, but no forfeiture.

In New Hampshire, three times the legal rate is forfeited, if unlawfully taken.

Rhode Island, has no forfeiture, but allows legal interest to be collected, even on usurious contracts.

In Connecticut, if usurious contracts are made, the principle only can be collected, to the lender, or, if collected, can be recovered, one-half to the informer, the other half to the State Treasury.

New York voids usurious contracts; but, if paid, only allows the excess over legal rates to be collected back.

New Jersey, also, voids usurious contracts, reserving half to the State, and half to the informer.

Pennsylvania allows only legal interest to be collected.

(352)

Deleware allows usurious contracts to be collected, half to the State and half to the prosecutor.

Maryland allows only legal rates to be collected.

Virginia voids the contract, and doubles the debt, half to the informer and half to the State.

North Carolina is the same as Virginia.

South Carolina, Florida, and Alabama, allow forfeitures of only the interest.

In Mississippi, although *six* per cent. is the legal interest on common debts, yet for money, actually borrowed, *eight* per cent is allowed, and although a rate may be agreed upon above what the law allows, simple interest may still be collected.

Louisiana, although allowing only *five* per cent. where no stipulation is made, permits *eight* per cent. in agreement, and Bank interest to be *six* per cent.

In Texas, although *eight* per cent. only is the legal rate, yet *twelve* may be contracted for, but if higher rates are agreed upon, none can be collected.

Arkansas allows as high as *ten* per cent. on contract, but voids usurious contracts.

Tennessee allows a fine to be collected not less in amount than is unlawfully taken.

Kentucky only voids usurious excesses.

Michigan and   allow *ten* per cent. to be contracted for, and void only excesses, if any are taken.

Indiana allows only her legal rates to be contracted for, and may be collected back, if, in any case, it should be obtained.

Illinois allows *ten* per cent. on money, actually borrowed, and only lawful rates can be collected.

In Missouri, *ten* per cent. may be contracted for, but forfeits *ten* per cent. to the common school fund, in cases where more than lawful rates are obtained.

Iowa permits *ten* per cent. to be agreed upon, and allows all illegal interest to be collected back

12

Wisconsin formerly permitted *twelve* per cent. to be agreed upon, and those who paid more than lawful rates might recover back three times the amount paid; but more recently allows only *sev* per cent., and makes all above that amount *usurious.*

California and Minnesota allow any rate agreed upon to be collected.

The interest which the State allows to be collected on notes drawn, "with use," not specifying the rate, is called *legal,* and that which some States allow to be contracted for, above the *legal* rate is *lawful;* but when a larger rate is taken, or agreed upon, it is called *usurious,* and subjects the person agreeing for it, or receiving it, to the *penalties,* or *forfeitures,* as given in the foregoing explanations.

Any Agent, or other person, who may know of any changes in *their* States from these rules, will confer a favor on the Author by communicating the same.

EXPLANATIONS OF THE INTEREST TABLES.

EXAMPLE:

Desired to obtain the interest on $1,111 00, for 1 year, 4 months, and 27 days, at 6 per cent.

Turning to the tables you will see that the *time* is given in the *left-hand* column, the *amounts* on which you desire to find the interest are given at the *heads* of the various *right-hand* columns, the *sum sought* is found at the meeting of the lines to the *right* of the time, and *down* from the amount, as follows:

The interest on $1,000, 1 year, at 6 per cent,...... $60,00
  "   "   "   100, " " " " " 6,00
  "   "   "   10, " " " " " 60
  "   "   "   1, " " " " 06
  "   "   "   1,000, 4 months, " " " 20,00
  "   "   "   100, " " " " " 2,00
  "   "   "   10, " " " " " 20
  "   "   "   1, " " " " " 02
  "   "   "   1,000, 27 days, " " " 4,50
  "   "   "   100, " " " " " 45
  "   "   "   10, " " " " " 05
  "   "   "   1, " " " " " 00

Whole sum of interest sought, $93,88

In the same manner, proceed with any other amounts, or any other time, or rate per cent.; and if for more than one year, multiply the interest for 1 year by the number of years for which the interest is sought; if for twenty, thirty, sixty, or any other amount between ten and one hundred dollars, multiply the interest on ten dollars, by the number of tens in the amount, which gives you the whole sum of interest sought; the same rule holds good on hundreds, between one hundred and one thousand, and also, on thousands.

To find interest at 5 per cent, take one-half of the 10 per cent rate.

And, of course, the principle works the same on all of the tables, for the different rates of per cent.

(355)

DR. CHASE'S RECIPES.

INTEREST TABLE.

SIX PER CENT.

TIME	$1	$2	$3	$4	$5	$6	$7	$8	$9	$10	$100	$1000
1 DAY	0	0	0	0	0	0	0	0	0	0	2	17
2 "	0	0	0	0	0	0	0	0	0	0	3	33
3 "	0	0	0	0	0	0	0	0	0	1	5	50
4 "	0	0	0	0	0	0	0	1	1	1	7	67
5 "	0	0	0	0	0	1	1	1	1	1	8	83
6 "	0	0	0	0	1	1	1	1	1	1	10	1,00
7 "	0	0	0	0	1	1	1	1	1	1	12	1,17
8 "	0	0	0	1	1	1	1	1	1	1	13	1,33
9 "	0	0	0	1	1	1	1	1	1	2	15	1,50
10 "	0	0	1	1	1	1	1	1	2	2	17	1,67
11 "	0	0	1	1	1	1	1	1	2	2	18	1,83
12 "	0	0	1	1	1	1	1	2	2	2	20	2,00
13 "	0	0	1	1	1	1	2	2	2	2	22	2,17
14 "	0	0	1	1	1	1	2	2	2	2	23	2,33
15 "	0	1	1	1	1	2	2	2	2	3	25	2,50
16 "	0	1	1	1	1	2	2	2	2	3	27	2,67
17 "	0	1	1	1	1	2	2	2	3	3	28	2,83
18 "	0	1	1	1	2	2	2	2	3	3	30	3,00
19 "	0	1	1	1	2	2	2	3	3	3	32	3,17
20 "	0	1	1	1	2	2	2	3	3	3	33	3,33
21 "	0	1	1	1	2	2	2	3	3	4	35	3,50
22 "	0	1	1	1	2	2	3	3	3	4	37	3,67
23 "	0	1	1	2	2	2	3	3	3	4	38	3,83
24 "	0	1	1	2	2	2	3	3	4	4	40	4,00
25 "	0	1	1	2	2	2	3	3	4	4	42	4,17
26 "	0	1	1	2	2	3	3	3	4	4	43	4,33
27 "	0	1	1	2	2	3	3	4	4	5	45	4,50
28 "	0	1	1	2	2	3	3	4	4	5	47	4,67
29 "	0	1	1	2	2	3	3	4	4	5	48	4,83
1 MONTH	1	1	2	2	3	3	4	4	5	5	50	5,00
2 "	1	2	3	4	5	6	7	8	9	10	1,00	10,00
3 "	2	3	5	6	8	9	11	12	14	15	1,50	15,00
4 "	2	4	6	8	10	12	14	16	18	20	2,00	20,00
5 "	3	5	8	10	13	15	18	20	23	25	2,50	25,00
6 "	3	6	9	12	15	18	21	24	27	30	3,00	30,00
7 "	4	7	11	14	18	21	25	28	32	35	3,50	35,00
8 "	4	8	12	16	20	24	28	32	36	40	4,00	40,00
9 "	5	9	14	18	23	27	33	36	41	45	4,50	45,00
10 "	5	10	15	20	25	30	35	40	45	50	5,00	50,00
11 "	6	11	17	22	28	33	39	44	50	55	5,50	55,00
1 YEAR	6	12	18	24	30	36	42	48	54	60	6,00	60,00

INTEREST TABLE.

SEVEN PER CENT.

TIME.	$1	$2	$3	$4	$5	$6	$7	$8	$9	$10	$100	$1000
1 DAY.	0	0	0	0	0	0	0	0	0	0	2	19
2 "	0	0	0	0	0	0	0	0	0	0	4	39
3 "	0	0	0	0	0	0	0	0	1	1	6	58
4 "	0	0	0	0	0	0	1	1	1	1	8	78
5 "	0	0	0	0	0	1	1	1	1	1	10	97
6 "	0	0	0	0	1	1	1	1	1	1	12	1,17
7 "	0	0	0	1	1	1	1	1	1	1	14	1,36
8 "	0	0	0	1	1	1	1	1	1	2	16	1,56
9 "	0	0	1	1	1	1	1	1	2	2	18	1,75
10 "	0	0	1	1	1	1	1	2	2	2	19	1,94
11 "	0	0	1	1	1	1	1	2	2	2	21	2,14
12 "	0	0	1	1	1	1	2	2	2	2	23	2,33
13 "	0	1	1	1	1	2	2	2	2	3	25	2,53
14 "	0	1	1	1	1	2	2	2	2	3	27	2,72
15 "	0	1	1	1	1	2	2	2	3	3	29	2,92
16 "	0	1	1	1	2	2	2	2	3	3	31	3,11
17 "	0	1	1	1	2	2	2	3	3	3	33	3,31
18 "	0	1	1	1	2	2	2	3	3	4	35	3,50
19 "	0	1	1	1	2	2	3	3	3	4	37	3,69
20 "	0	1	1	2	2	2	3	3	4	4	39	3,89
21 "	0	1	1	2	2	2	3	3	4	4	41	4,08
22 "	0	1	1	2	2	3	3	3	4	4	43	4,28
23 "	0	1	1	2	2	3	3	4	4	4	45	4,47
24 "	0	1	1	2	2	3	3	4	4	5	47	4,67
25 "	0	1	1	2	2	3	3	4	4	5	49	4,86
26 "	1	1	2	2	3	3	4	4	5	5	51	5,06
27 "	1	1	2	2	3	3	4	4	5	5	53	5,25
28 "	1	1	2	2	3	3	4	4	5	5	54	5,44
29 "	1	1	2	2	3	3	4	5	5	6	56	5,64
1 MONTH	1	1	2	2	3	4	4	5	5	6	58	5,83
2 "	1	2	4	5	6	7	8	9	11	12	1,17	11,67
3 "	2	4	5	7	9	11	12	14	16	18	1,75	17,50
4 "	2	5	7	9	12	14	16	19	21	23	2,33	23,33
5 "	3	6	9	12	15	18	20	23	26	29	2,92	29,17
6 "	4	7	11	14	18	21	25	28	32	35	3,50	35,00
7 "	4	8	12	16	20	25	29	33	37	41	4,08	40,83
8 "	5	9	14	17	23	28	33	37	42	47	4,67	46,67
9 "	5	11	16	21	26	32	37	42	47	53	5,25	52,50
10 "	6	12	18	23	29	35	41	47	53	58	5,83	58,33
11 "	6	13	19	26	32	39	45	51	58	64	6,42	64,17
1 YEAR.	7	14	21	28	35	42	49	56	63	70	7,00	70,00

INTEREST TABLE.

EIGHT PER CENT

TIME		$1	$2	$3	$4	$5	$6	$7	$8	$9	$10	$100	$1000
1	DAY.	0	0	0	0	0	0	0	0	0	0	2	22
2	"	0	0	0	0	0	0	0	0	0	0	4	44
3	"	0	0	0	0	0	0	0	1	1	1	7	67
4	"	0	0	0	0	0	1	1	1	1	1	9	89
5	"	0	0	0	0	1	1	1	1	1	1	11	1,11
6	"	0	0	0	1	1	1	1	1	1	1	13	1,33
7	"	0	0	0	1	1	1	1	1	1	2	16	1,56
8	"	0	0	1	1	1	1	1	1	2	2	18	1,78
9	"	0	0	1	1	1	1	1	2	2	2	20	2,00
10	"	0	0	1	1	1	1	2	2	2	2	22	2,22
11	"	0	0	1	1	1	1	2	2	2	2	24	2,44
12	"	0	1	1	1	1	2	2	2	2	3	27	2,67
13	"	0	1	1	1	1	2	2	2	3	3	29	2,89
14	"	0	1	1	1	2	2	2	2	3	3	31	3,11
15	"	0	1	1	1	2	2	2	3	3	3	33	3,33
16	"	0	1	1	1	2	2	2	3	3	4	36	3,56
17	"	0	1	1	2	2	2	3	3	3	4	38	3,78
18	"	0	1	1	2	2	2	3	3	4	4	40	4,00
19	"	0	1	1	2	2	3	3	3	4	4	42	4,22
20	"	0	1	1	2	2	3	3	4	4	4	44	4,44
21	"	0	1	1	2	2	3	3	4	4	5	47	4,67
22	"	0	1	1	2	2	3	3	4	4	5	49	4,89
23	"	1	1	2	2	3	3	4	4	5	5	51	5,11
24	"	1	1	2	2	3	3	4	4	5	5	53	5,33
25	"	1	1	2	2	3	3	4	4	5	6	56	5,56
26	"	1	1	2	2	3	3	4	5	5	6	58	5,78
27	"	1	1	2	2	3	4	4	5	5	6	60	6,00
28	"	1	1	2	2	3	4	4	5	6	6	62	6,22
29	"	1	1	2	3	3	4	5	5	6	6	64	6,44
1	MONTH	1	1	2	3	3	4	5	5	6	7	67	6,67
2	"	1	3	4	5	7	8	9	11	12	13	1,33	13,33
3	"	2	4	6	8	10	12	14	16	18	20	2,00	20,00
4	"	3	5	8	11	13	16	19	21	24	27	2,67	26,67
5	"	3	7	10	13	17	20	23	27	30	33	3,33	33,33
6	"	4	8	12	16	20	24	28	32	36	40	4,00	40,00
7	"	5	9	14	19	23	28	33	37	43	47	4,67	46,0
8	"	5	11	16	21	27	32	37	43	48	53	5,33	53,3
9	"	6	12	18	24	30	36	42	48	54	60	6,00	60,00
10	"	7	13	20	27	33	40	47	53	60	67	6,67	66,67
11	"	7	15	22	29	37	44	51	59	66	73	7,33	73,33
1	YEAR	8	16	24	32	40	48	56	64	72	80	8,00	80,00

INTEREST TABLE.

NINE PER CENT.

TIME		$1	$2	$3	$4	$5	$6	$7	$8	$9	$10	$100	$1000
1	DAY.	0	0	0	0	0	0	0	0	0	0	3	25
2	"	0	0	0	0	0	0	0	0	0	1	5	50
3	"	0	0	0	0	0	0	1	1	1	1	8	75
4	"	0	0	0	0	1	1	1	1	1	1	10	1,00
5	"	0	0	0	1	1	1	1	1	1	1	13	1,25
6	"	0	0	0	1	1	1	1	1	1	2	15	1,50
7	"	0	0	1	1	1	1	1	1	2	2	18	1.75
8	"	0	0	1	1	1	1	1	2	2	2	20	2,00
9	"	0	0	1	1	1	1	2	2	2	2	23	2,25
10	"	0	1	1	1	1	2	2	2	2	3	25	2,50
11	"	0	1	1	1	1	2	2	2	2	3	28	2,75
12	"	0	1	1	1	2	2	2	2	3	3	30	3,00
13	"	0	1	1	1	2	2	3	3	3	3	33	3,25
14	"	0	1	1	1	2	2	2	3	3	4	35	3,50
15	"	0	1	1	2	2	2	3	3	3	4	38	3,75
16	"	0	1	1	2	2	2	3	3	4	4	40	4,00
17	"	0	1	1	2	2	3	3	3	4	4	43	4,25
18	"	0	1	1	2	2	3	3	4	4	5	45	4,50
19	"	0	1	1	2	2	3	3	4	4	5	48	4,75
20	"	1	1	2	2	3	3	4	4	5	5	50	5,00
21	"	1	1	2	2	3	3	4	4	5	5	53	5,25
22	"	1	1	2	2	3	3	4	4	5	6	55	5,59
23	"	1	1	2	2	3	3	4	5	5	6	58	5,75
24	"	1	1	2	2	3	4	4	5	5	6	60	6,00
25	"	1	1	2	3	3	4	4	5	6	6	63	6,25
26	"	1	1	2	3	3	4	5	5	6	7	65	6,50
27	"	1	1	2	3	3	4	5	5	6	7	68	6,75
28	"	1	1	2	3	4	4	5	6	6	7	70	7,00
29	"	1	1	2	3	4	4	5	6	7	7	73	7,25
1	MONTH	1	2	2	3	4	5	5	6	7	8	75	7,50
2	"	2	3	5	6	8	9	11	12	14	15	1,50	15,00
3	"	2	5	7	9	11	14	16	18	20	23	2,25	22,50
4	"	3	6	9	12	15	18	21	24	27	30	3,00	30,00
5	"	4	8	11	15	19	23	26	30	34	38	3,75	37,50
6	"	5	9	14	18	23	27	32	36	41	45	4,50	45,00
7	"	5	11	16	21	26	32	37	42	47	53	5,25	52,50
8	"	6	12	18	24	30	36	42	48	54	60	6,00	60,00
9	"	7	14	20	27	34	41	47	54	61	68	6,75	67,50
10	"	8	15	23	30	38	45	53	60	68	75	7,50	75,00
11	"	8	17	25	33	41	50	58	66	74	83	8,25	82,50
1	YEAR.	9	18	27	36	45	54	63	72	81	90	9,00	90,00

INTEREST TABLE.

TEN PER CENT.

TIME		$1	$2	$3	$4	$5	$6	$7	$8	$9	$10	$100	$1000
1	DAY.	0	0	0	0	0	0	0	0	0	0	3	28
2	"	0	0	0	0	0	0	0	0	1	1	6	56
3	"	0	0	0	0	0	1	1	1	1	1	8	83
4	"	0	0	0	0	1	1	1	1	1	1	11	1,11
5	"	0	0	0	1	1	1	1	1	1	1	14	1,39
6	"	0	0	1	1	1	1	1	1	2	2	17	1,67
7	"	0	0	1	1	1	1	1	2	2	2	19	2,94
8	"	0	0	1	1	1	1	2	2	2	2	22	2,22
9	"	0	1	1	1	1	2	2	2	2	3	25	2,50
10	"	0	1	1	1	1	2	2	2	3	3	28	2,78
11	"	0	1	1	1	2	2	2	2	3	3	31	3,06
12	"	0	1	1	1	2	2	2	3	3	3	33	3,33
13	"	0	1	1	1	2	2	3	3	3	4	36	3,61
14	"	0	1	1	2	2	2	3	3	4	4	39	3,89
15	"	0	1	1	2	2	3	3	3	4	4	42	4,17
16	"	0	1	1	2	2	3	3	4	4	4	44	4,44
17	"	0	1	1	2	2	3	3	4	4	5	47	4,72
18	"	1	1	2	2	3	3	4	4	5	5	50	5,00
19	"	1	1	2	2	3	3	4	4	5	5	53	5,28
20	"	1	1	2	2	3	3	4	4	5	6	56	5,56
21	"	1	1	2	2	3	4	4	5	5	6	58	5,83
22	"	1	1	2	2	3	4	4	5	6	6	61	6,11
23	"	1	1	2	3	3	4	4	5	6	6	64	6,39
24	"	1	1	2	3	3	4	5	5	6	7	67	6,67
25	"	1	1	2	3	3	4	5	6	6	7	69	6,94
26	"	1	1	2	3	4	4	5	6	7	7	72	7,22
27	"	1	2	2	3	4	5	5	6	7	8	75	7,50
28	"	1	2	2	3	4	5	5	6	7	8	78	7,78
29	"	1	2	2	3	4	5	6	6	7	8	81	8,06
1	MONTH.	1	2	3	3	4	5	6	7	8	8	83	8,33
2	"	2	3	5	7	8	10	12	13	15	17	1,67	16,67
3	"	3	5	8	10	15	15	18	20	23	25	2,50	25,00
4	"	3	7	10	13	17	20	23	27	30	33	3,33	33,33
5	"	4	8	13	17	21	25	29	33	38	42	4,17	41,67
6	"	5	10	15	20	25	30	35	40	45	50	5,00	50,00
7	"	6	12	18	23	29	35	41	47	53	58	5,83	58,33
8	"	7	13	20	27	33	40	47	53	60	67	6,67	66,67
9	"	8	15	23	30	38	45	53	60	68	75	7,50	75,00
10	"	8	17	25	33	42	50	58	67	75	83	8,33	83,33
11	"	9	18	28	37	46	55	64	73	83	92	9,17	91,67
1	YEAR.	10	20	30	40	50	60	70	80	90	1,00	10,00	100,00

RULES FOR ADMINISTERING MEDICINES, HAVING REFERENCE TO AGE AND SEX.

For an adult, (a person of 40 years,) the dose of common medicines is allowed to be about 1 drachm, 60 grains.

Those, at	20	years,	2-3	"	40	"
"	13	"	1-2	"	30	"
"	7	"	1-3	"	20	"
"	4	"	1-4	"	15	"
"	3	"	1-6	"	10	"
"	2	"	1-8	" 7 to 8	"
"	1	"	1-12	"	5	"

For babes, under 1 year, the dose should go down by *months*, at about the same rate as by *years*, for those over a year.

Again, for persons in advanced life, say from 60 years, the dose must begin to lessen about 5 grains, and from that on, 5 grains for each additional 10 years.

Females, however, need a little less, generally than males.

The above rules hold good in all medicines, except castor oil, the proportion of which cannot be reduced so *much*, and opium, and its various preparations, which must be reduced generally, in a little *greater* proportion.

Explanations of Medical Abbreviations, Apothecaries Weights and Measures.

One pound (lb.) contains 12 ounces.
One ounce (oz.) " 8 drachms.
One drachm (dr.) " 3 scruples.
One scruple (scru.) " 20 grains, (gr.)

LIQUID MEASURE.

One pint contains 16 fluid ozs., 4 gills.
One ounce " 8 " drs., 1-4 "
One table-spoon " about half a fluid ounce.
One tea-spoon " " one fluid drachm.
Sixty drops make about one tea-spoon.

Whenever a tea, or table-spoon is mentioned, it means the same as it would to say spoonful; the same of cup, in fluid measures; but in dry measures, where a spoon, or spoonful is mentioned, the design is that the spoon should be taken up moderately rounding, unless otherwise mentioned.

EXPLANATION OF TECHNICAL TERMS FOUND IN
MEDICAL WORKS.

Abdomen..The lower front part of the body.

Aromatic..Spicy and fragrant drugs; used to prevent griping of drastic purgatives.

Aperient..A gentle laxative or purgative.

Acidity..Sourness. Acids neutralize alkalies.

Alkaline..Having the properties of alkali. Alkalies neutralize acids.

Antacid.Medicines which neutralize acids.

Anti..Being prefixed to any word signifies against.

Antiscorbutic..Alteratives for Scrofula; blood purifiers.

Antisyphilitic..Remedy for Venerial diseases.

Albus..White, hence whites; fluor albus.

Antisialagogue..Remedy for Salivation.

Antiseptic..That which will prevent putrefaction.

Antiphlogistic..Remedy for fever and inflammation

Antispasmodic..Remedy for Spasms, cramps, or convulsions.

Anodyne..A medicine which will allay pain and produce sleepiness.

Alterative..Medicines which will gradually restore healthy action.

Astringent..Medicines which constringe, draw up surfaces with which they come in contact; used in Flooding, Diarrhea, Whites, &c.

Abscess..A cavity containing pus.

Anemia..Without blood, more properly blood without its proportion of iron, which gives it the bright red.

Alvine..Relating to the intestines.

Aliment..Any kind of food.

Alimentary Canal..The entire passage through the whole intestines from mouth to anus; the passage for the aliment.

Albumen..An element found in both animal and vegetable substances, constituting the chief part of the white of eggs.

Antimonial..Medicines containing antimony.

(363)

inus..The external opening of the rectum, lower intestine.

Antiperiodic..That which cures periodic diseases, as Ague, Intermittent Fevers.

Antidote..An opposing medicine, used chiefly against poison.

Adult..A person of full growth.

Aqua..Water.

Aqua Ammonia..Water of Ammonia.

Amenorrhea..Absence of the menses.

Antiemetic..That which will stop vomiting; against emesis.

Arsenic..A metal, the oxide of which is arsenious acid, commonly called ratsbane.

Abortion..A premature birth, or miscarriage.

Abortives..That which will cause abortion.

Abrasion..Bruising the skin.

Acetate..A salt prepared with acetic acid.

Acrid..Irritating, biting.

Adhesive..Applied to sticking plasters, and to parts adhering from inflammations.

Balm..Aromatic and fragrant medicine, usually an ointment.

Balsam..Resinous substances, possessing healing properties.

Basilicon..An ointment containing wax, rosin, &c.

Belladonna..Nightshade.

Bergamot..Perfume made from the lemon peel.

Bile..A secretion from the liver.

Bilious..An undue amount of bile.

Bi-tartrate of Potash..Cream of tartar.

Blanch..To whiten.

Bowels..Intestines.

Bolus..A large pill.

Bronchia..Branches of the windpipe.

Bronchitis..Inflammation of the bronchial tubes, which lead into the lungs.

Bronchocele..Enlargement of the thyroid gland, enlarged neck.

Butyric Acid..An acid obtained from butter.

Calcium..The metalic basis of lime, (see fluor spar.)

Calimus..Sweet flag

Calcareous..A substance containing chalk or lime.

Calcined..Burned so as to be easily reduced to powder.

Calculus..Stone or gravel found in the bladder, gall ducts, kidneys, and ureters; ducts which lead from the kidneys to the bladder.

Callous..A hard bony substance or growth.

Capsicum..Cayenne pepper.

Catarrh..Flow of mucus.

Cathartic..An active purgative.

Catheter..Tube for emptying the bladder.

Carminative..An aromatic medicine.

Caustic..A corroding or destroying substance, as **nitrate of** silver, potash, &c.

Citric Acid..Acid made from lemons.

Chronic..Of long standing.

Collapse..A recession of the blood from the surface.

Coma..Stupor.

Constipation..Costiveness.

Contagious..A disease which may be given to another by contact.

Counter..To work against, as counter-irritant, Spanish-flies, draughts to the feet, &c.

Congestion..Accumulation of blood in a part, unduly.

Convalescence..Improvement in health.

Cuticle..The outer or first portion of the skin, which consists of three coats.

Datura Stramonium..Stink-weed, jimpson, &c.

Diaphoretics..Medicines which aid or produce perspiration.

Decoction..To prepare by boiling.

Dentifrice..A preparation to cleanse the teeth.

Defecation..To pass the feces, to go to stool.

Dentition..Act or process of cutting teeth.

Desiccation..To dry, act of drying.

Demulcent..Mucilaginous, as flax-seed and gum arabic.

Dermoid..Resembling, or relating to the skin.

Detergents..Cleansing medicines, as laxatives and **purga-** tives.

Diagnosis..To discriminate disease.

Diaphragm..Midriff.

Diarrhea..Looseness of the bowels.

Digest..Assimilation or conversion of food into chyme—to prepare medicines with continued, gentle heat.

Discutient..A medicine which will scatter or : *drive away* tumors.

Diuretic..That which increases the amount of urine.

Diluted..Reduced with water, as dilute alcohol, half alcohol and half water.

Digitalis..Fox-glove, a narcotic.

Dorsal..Having reference to the back.

Douche..A dash, or stream upon any part.

Drachm..Sixty grains, a tea-spoonful, or a tea-spoon of

Dulcamara..The bitter-sweet, or woody nightshade.

Dyspepsia..Difficult digestion.

Dysphonia..Difficulty in speaking.

Dysuria..Difficult or painful urination.

Eau..Water.

Eau de Cologne..Cologne water.

Ebulition..To boil.

Eclectic..To choose.

Eclectic Physician..One who professes to be liberal in views, independent of party, and who fa·or progress and reform in medicine.

Effervesce..To foam.

Efflorescence..Redness of the general surface.

Effete..Worn out, waste matter.

Elaterium..Fruit of the wild cucumber, a hydragogue.

Electuary—Medicine prepared at the consistence of honey.

Elixir..A tincture prepared with more than one article.

Emesis..The act of vomiting.

Emetic..Medicines which produce emesis, vomiting.

Emmenagogue..A medicine which will aid or bring on the menses.

Emollients..Softening and screening medicines, slippery-elm bark, flax-seed, gums, &c.

Emulsion..Mucilage, from the emolients.

Enema..An injection by the rectum.

Ennui..Lassitude, dullness of spirit, disgust of condition, &c.

Epi..Above, or over.

Epidermis..Outer skin

Epigastrium..Region of the pit of the stomach.

Epilepsy..Convulsion fits, with loss of sense for tne me foaming at the mouth, and stupor.

Epiglottis .Trap-door cartilage at the root of the tongue, preventing food, or fluid, from entering the wind-pipe.

Epistaxis..Nose bleed.

Ergot..Spurred rye.

Eructation..Raising wind from the stomach, belching.

Eruption..Pimples or blotches on the skin, or pustules from small-pox.

Eschar—A slough on the surface.

Escharotic..That which will destroy the flesh.

Essential..Having reference to essences made from essen tial oils and alcohol.

Ether..A volatile fluid.

Etherial Oil..Volatile oil.

Eustachian Tube..A tube leading from the side of the throat to the internal ear.

Eversion..Turning inside out.

Evacuation..To discharge by stool, to haste-away. [See the remarks in the body of the work, on "Costiveness.

Evaporation..To escape in vapor.

Exacerbation..Violent increase in disease.

Exanthemata..Eruptive disease, as small-pox, scarlet fever, measles, &c.

Excrement..The feces, that which passes by stool.

Excretion..That which is thrown off, become useless.

Excoriation..Abrasion, to bruise the skin.

Exhalents..Vessels which throw out fluid upon the external or internal surface of the body.

Expectorants..That which produces, or aids a discharge of mucus from the bronchial tubes, or from the lungs.

Excision—To cut off an extremity

Extremity..Applied to the arms and legs, called upper and lower extremities.

Exterpation..To cut out, or to remove a part.

Extract..To take out, as a tooth, to extract a ball or any foreign substance from a wound—an active principle obtained from vegetables.

Express..To press out juices.

Excresoence..An unnatural growth

Extravasation..A collection of blood into a cavity, or under the skin.

Facial..Belonging to, or having reference to the face.

Farina..Meal, or flour, from vegetables.

Farcy..A disease of the lymphatic vessels in the skin of the flanks of a horse.

Fauces..The pharynx and back part of the mouth.

Fascicular..A bundle, in bundles.

Feces..That which passes by stool

Febrile..Having reference to fevers.

Febrifuge..Medicines to drive away fever, producing perspiration.

Felon..A deep abscess of the finger, involving the bone, because under the periosteum, the membrane which covers the bone.

Femur..The thigh bone.

Femoral..Relating to the thigh.

Ferment..To oxidize, to effervesce, to work, as emptyings, beer, wine, cider, &c.

Fermentation..To sour, to decompose, both heat and moist ure being necessary to keep it up.

Ferri Limatura..Iron-filings, very valuable in female debility, and for males of a weak habit of body.

Ferrum..Iron.

Fever..That which "Old School Physicians" call a disease, whilst another class (the Thomsonians) say it is an effort of nature to throw off disease; but Eclectics take it as an indication that the circulating medium is not regular, and go to work at once to equalize the circulation, by the use of diaphoretics, combined with tonics and detergents, which soon sets all to-rights; for fever and perspiration cannot long exist together.

Filter..To strain through paper made for that purpose

Fibre..A very small, thread-like substance of animal or vegetable matter.

Fibula..The smallest bone of the leg below the knee.

Fistula..An ulcer.

Flaccid..Flabby, soft, relaxed.

Flabby..Loose and soft to the touch.

Flatus..To inflate the stomach or bowels with gas.

Fluoric Acid..A fluid obtained from the fluor spar cut with sulphuric acid.

Flatulence..Gas in the stomach.

Flooding..Uterine hemorrhage.

Fluor..An increased discharge, to flow

Fluor Spar..Fluoride of calcium.

Fluor Albus..White flow, leucorrhea, whites, &c.

Flux..To flow, diarrhea.

Friction..Rubbing with the dry hand, or dry coarse cloth.

Fumigate..To smoke a room, or any article needing to be cleansed.

Fundament..The anus.

Formula..Medical prescription.

Fulminating Powder..An explosive preparation, used in fireworks.

Function..The particular action of an organ, as the function of the stomach, liver, lungs, heart, &c.

Fungus..Spongy flesh in wounds, proud-flesh, a soft cancer, which bleeds upon touching its broken surface

Fusion..To fuse, to melt.

Furor..Very violent delirium, not accompanied by fever.

Galbanum..A resinous gum, from a genus of plants.

Genus..Family of plants, a group, all of a class, or nature.

Gall..Bile.

Gall Bladder..A bag which receives the gall, or bile, through ducts, from the liver, delivering it to the stomach, in health, through the duct called communis choledochus.

Gall Stones..Hard biliary concretions found in the gall bladder, and sometimes causing death, from not being able to pass through the ductus communis.

Galla..The gall-nut, an excrescence found upon the oak.

Gallic Acid..An acid from the nut-gall.

Galipot..A glazed jar, used for putting up gummy extracts.

Galvanic..Having reference to galvanism.

Gamboge..A drastic purgative, unless combined with aromatics.

Gangrene..Partial death of a part, often ending in entire mortification of the part, and sometimes of the whole body.

. —DR. CHASE'S RECIPES.

Ganglion..A knot, or lump on tendons, ligaments, or nerves.

Gaseous..Having the nature of gas.

Gastric..Of, or belonging to the stomach.

Gastric Juice..Secretion of the stomach.

Gastritis..Inflammation of the stomach.

Gastrodynia..Pain in the stomach, sometimes with spasm of the stomach.

Gelatine..Isinglass.

Gelatinous..Like jelly.

Genitals..Belonging to generation, the sexual organs.

Gentian..An European root, possessing tonic properties.

Genu..The knee.

Genuflexion..Bending the knee, kneeling.

Germ..The vital principle, or life-spark.

Gestation..To be pregnant.

Gland..Secreting organs having ducts emptying into cavities, which often become obstructed, causing them to enlarge; hence, the enlargement of the thyroid gland in the neck, causing bronchocele.

Glans..A gland.

Gleet..Chronic gonorrhea.

Globules..Small round particles, having special reference to particles of the red part of the blood.

Glossa .The tongue; a smooth tongue.

Gloss..To give a lustre; to comment; to write or make explanations.

Glossarist..A writer of glosses or comments.

Glossary..An explanation of words.

Glossarial..Containing explanations.

Glossitis..Inflammation of the tongue.

Glottis..The opening into the wind-pipe, at the root of the tongue, larynx, covered by the epiglottis.

Gluten..Coagulable lymph, white of an egg, a principle in wheat and other vegetables.

Glutton..One who eats excessively.

Gonorrhea..An infectious discharge from the genital organs.

Gout..Painful inflammation of the joints of the toes, or of the fingers.

Granule..A small particle of healthy matter, not pus

Granulation..Healing up of an ulcer or wound with healthy matter.

Gravel..Crystaline particles in the urine.

Green-Sickness..Chlorosis, debility requiring iron.

Griping..Grinding pain in the stomach, or bowels.

Gutta..One drop, drops.

Gutta Percha..Dried juice of a genus of trees Isonandra gutta.

Guttural..Relating to the throat.

Gymnasium..A place for sportive exercise, which is very valuable to those who cannot or will not take exercise for the sake of dollars and cents.

Gypsum..Sulphate of lime, more commonly called plaster of Paris, because first introduced from that place.

Habit..Good or bad habit, constitutionally, or prejudicially predisposed to do some particular thing; medically, as consumptive habit, rheumatic habit, &c.

Hema..Blood, prefixed to other words.

Hematemesis..Hemorrhage from the stomach

Hematuria..Hemorrhage from the bladder

Hemoptysis..Hemorrhage from the lungs.

Hemorrhoids..Piles, bleeding piles.

Henbane..Hyoscyamus.

Hereditary..Disease from parents.

Hernia..Rupture, which permits a part of the bowel to protrude.

Herpes..Disease of the skin.

Hiera Picra..A medicine containing aloes.

Humerus..The single bone of the upper arm.

Humeral..Pertaining to the arm.

Humors..The fluids of the body, excluding the blood.

Hydragogues..Medicines which produce watery discharges used in dropsy, as elaterium.

Hydrargyrum..Metalic mercury, quicksilver, Doctors' name for calomel.

Hydrocyanic Acid..Prussic acid, nothing more poisonous.

Hydrofluoric Acid..Same as fluoric acid.

Hygea..Health.

Hygiene..Preserving health by diet and other precautions.

Hypo..Signifies low, a low state of health, more annoying to the sufferers than to their friends, who are constantly boring them about it; called hysterics .n women, (from hysteria, the womb or uterus,) but blues only, when it gets hold of men; they come from the same cause, general debility · takes a strong remedy, iron, as medicine.

Hypoglottis..Under the tongue.

Hysteria..The uterus, (womb,) also disease, depending upon, or caused by uterine irregularities

Hysteritis..Inflammation af the uterus.

Ichor..An acrid, biting, watery discharge from ulcers, often corroding, eating the surface.

Icterus..Jaundice, a bilious disease, which shows itself by yellowness of the eyes and skin.

Icterus Albus..Chlorosis, whites, &c.

Ignition..To catch on fire, from Ignis, fire.

Ileus..Cholic in the small intestines.

Iliac..Situated near the flank.

Iliac Region..Sides of the abdomen between the ribs and the thighs.

Imbecile..One of weak mind, imbecility.

Imbibe..To absorb, to drink.

Imbricate..To over-lap, as tiles on a house

Immerse..To plunge under water.

Immobile..Immovable, as stiff joints.

Imperforate..Without a natural opening.

Impervious..Closed against water.

Impetigo..Tetter.

Imponderable..Not having weight, light or electricity.

Impoverished..Exhausted vitality.

Impotence..Sterility, not being able to produce

Impregnation..The act of producing.

Incision..To cut.

Incombustible..Incapability of being burned.

Incompatibles..Medicines which ought not to be mixed, or given together.

Incontinence..Not being able to hold the natural excretions.

Incorporate..To mix medicines together.

Incubation..To hatch eggs, slow development of disease

Indication..That which shows what ought to be done

Indigenous..Peculiarity of a country, or of a small section of country, applied to disease, plants, &c.

Indigestion..Dyspepsia.

Indolent..Slow in progress, applied to ulcers and tumors, which are slow and with but little or no pain.

Induration..Hardening of any part of the system by disease.

Infectious..Communicable disease, from one to another.

Infirmary..Where medicines are distributed gratuitously to the poor ; but more recently some physicians have got to calling their offices infirmaries

Inflammation..Attended with heat, redness, swelling, tenderness, and often with throbbing.

Inflatus..To distend, to blow up with wind, or to fill up with gas, as the stomach, bowels, &c.

Influenza..A disease affecting the nostrils, throat, &c., of a catarrhal nature.

Infusion..Medicines prepared by steeping in water, not to boil.

Inquinal..In the groin.

Ingredient..One article of a compound mixture.

Inhalation..To draw in the breath.

Injection..Any preparation to be introduced by the rectum

Inorganic..Matter not having organs, all alike, as metals.

Insanity..Derangement of the mind.

Insertion..The attachment of muscles and tendons to the bones, which they move by contraction.

Inspiration..The act of drawing in the breath.

Inspissation..To thicken by boiling, to make what is called the concentrated extracts, desiccation.

Instinct..An involuntary action, as closing the eyelids, breathing, &c., natural perception of animals.

Integument..A covering, the skin.

Inter..A prefix denoting between.

Intercostal..Between the ribs.

Intermission..Time between paroxysms of fever, or other disease.

Intermittent Fever..Fever which comes on at regular periods, between which periods there is little, and sometimes no fever, an interval.

Internal..Upon the inside.

Interosseous..Between the bones.

Interval..The period between the paroxysms cf periodi-al diseases, as ague, &c.

Intestines..The contents of the abdomen.

Intestinal Canal..Embracing the duodenum (the first di vision below the stomach,) the jejunum, (the the second division of the small intestines,) the ileum, (the third and longest portion of the small intestines,) the secum, (the first portion of the large intestine,) the colon, (the large in- testine,) and the rectum, (the lower trap-door.)

Intolerance..In medicine, applied to the eye, as intolerance of light; to the stomach, as intolerance of food.

Inversio Uteri..Inversion of the uterus.

Inversion..To turn the inside out.

Irreducible..Applied to hernia, and to joints which have been put out and cannot be put back to their place.

Ischuria..Not being able to pass the urine.

Issue..Sore made as a counter-irritant, to draw irritation from a diseased part.

Itch..Psora, scabies, a catching eruption of the skin.

Itis..An addition to a word denoting inflammation, as pleu ritis, pleurisy, &c.

Ivory Black..Animal charcoal.

Jaundice..A disease caused by the inactivity of the liver or ducts leading from it.

Jelly..Gelatine in a fluid state, as applied to medicine.

Jesuits Bark..First name of Peruvian bark, from its having been discovered by Jesuit missionaries.

Juglar..Applied to veins of the throat.

Jujube..An East India fruit, something like a plum, used in coughs, but of doubtful reputation.

Kali..Potash.

Kelp..Ashes of sea-weed.

Knot..Surgeons tie their knot by passing the thread twice through the loop, which prevents slipping.

Labia..Lips.

Labia Pudendi..Lips, or sides of the vulva

Labial..Of, or belonging to the lips.

Labor..Child-birth, parturition.

Laboratory..A place of chemical experiments, or operations, see Frontispiece.

Lancinating..Sharp, piercing, as lancinating pain.

Laryngeal..Of the larynx.

Larynx..The upper part of the throat.

Laryngitis..Inflammation of the throat.

Latent..Hidden, as latent heat, see the remarks connected with steam boiler explosion.

Lassitude..Weakness, a feeling of stupor.

Laxative..A very gentle cathartic.

Leptandrin..Powder made from the leptandria virginica, blackroot, Culvers physic.

Leucorrhea..Fluor albus, whites, chlorosis, &c.

Levigate..To reduce to a very fine powder.

Ligature..A thread, to ligate, to tie with a ligature

Located..Fixed, seated upon some organ.

Lingua..The tongue.

Linguist..A speaker, fluency, one who understands different languages.

Liniment..A fluid preparation to be applied by friction.

Lithontriptic..A medicine reported to dissolve gravel, or stone in the bladder.

Lithotomy..The operation of cutting, to take out stone of the bladder.

Liver..The largest gland, and largest organ of the body.

Livid..A dark colored spot on the surface.

Loins..Lower part of the back.

Lotion..A preparation to wash a sore.

Lubricate..To soften with oil, or to moisten with a fluid. The internal organs are covered with a membrane which throws out a lubricating fluid, enabling them to move easily upon each other.

Lute..A paste with which to close chemical retorts, the casein, curd of milk, is used for that purpose.

Lymph..A thin colorless fluid carried in small vein-like vessels called lymphatics.

Macerate..To steep, soften by soaking.

Mal..Bad, mal practice, bad practice, not according to science.

Malformation..Irregular, unnatural formation.

Malaria..Bad gases, causing disease, supposed to arise from decaying vegetable matter.

Malignant..A pestilential, and generally dangerous dis
case, as the Cholera of 1832.

Mamma..The female breast, which is composed of glands
that secrete the milk, upon the principle that
the liver secretes bile; each organ for its specific purpose; but secreting organs, or glands
are the more liable to get obstructed, thus producing disease.

Mastication..The act of chewing.

Masturbation..Excitement, by the hand, of the genital organs. The most injurious, health-destroying,
soul-debasing, of all evils introduced into the
world; because its frequent repetition draws
very heavily upon the nervous system, prostra-
ting the energies, destroying the memory, together with the life-principle, as well as the
principles of morality which ought to govern
every human being, between himself and his
Creator.

Maturity..To become ripe, to arrive at adult age, beyond
further growth.

Materia..Matter, healthy substance.

Materia Medica..The science of medicine, and medical
combinations.

Maturation..Formation of pus, unhealthy matter.

Matrix..The womb.

Meconium..The first passages after birth.

Medical..Relating to medicine.

Medicated..Having medicine in its preparation.

Membrane..A thin lining, or covering, skin-like, as the
peritoneum, which lines the cavity of the bowels and covers the intestines; and the periosteum, membrane, which covers the bones, &c

Medicament..A remedy; hence, medicamentum, the Welch
remedy for every disease.

Medicinal..Having medical properties.

Medullary..Like marrow, brain-like.

Mel..Honey.

Menstruation..Monthly flow.

Mentha Piperita..Peppermint.

Median..The middle.

Mellifluous..Flowing with honey, sweetness, delicious; akin to lucious, juicy mellowness.

Menorrhagia..Excessive flooding.

Micturition..To urinate, to pass the urine.

Midwifery..Art of assisting at child-birth.

Minim..About one drop, one-sixtieth of a fluid drachm

Minimum..The smallest, the smallest dose, the opposite of maximum.

Modus Operandi..The way in which medicines act, applicable also to any action, the way of doing it.

Morbid..Unhealthy.

Morbus..A disease ; hence, cholera morbus, disease of the bowels.

Mordant..That which fastens the colors in dyeing, as alum, cream of tartar, argal, vitriols, tin, liquor, &c.

Mucus..Animal mucilage.

Mucus Membrane..See remarks under the head of " Inflammation," in the body of the work.

Mucilage..A watery solution of gum, or elm bark, &c.

Muriatic..Having reference to sea salt.

Muriatic Acid..Marine acid, often called hydrochloric acid.

Muscle..A bundle of fibers.

Muscular..Having reference to the muscles, strong built.

Myrrh..A resinous gum.

Narcotic..Stupefying medicines, producing sleep.

Nares..The nostrils.

Nasal..Of the nose.

Nausea..Sickness of the stomach, may increase until vomiting takes place, or it may not.

Nauseant..That which produces nausea.

Navel..Center of the abdomen.

Necros..Death.

Necrosis..Death of a bone.

Nephros..The kidney.

Nephritis..Inflammation of the kidney or kidneys.

Nervous..Easily excited.

Nervine..That which will allay, or soothe nervous excitement.

Neuralgia..Pain in nerves

Nitre..Saltpeter.

Nocturnal..Occurring in the night

Nitrate...Nitric acid combined with alkalies or alkaline salts.

Normal..In a natural and health condition.

Nostrum..A medical preparation.

Nothus..Spurious, illegitimate, a bastard.

Nudus..Nude, without clothing.

Nutrition..Nourishment.

Nutritious..Nourishing.

Obesity..Corpulence, excess of fat, or flesh.

Obstetrics..The science of midwifery.

Ochre..An ore of iron.

Oculus..The eye.

Oculist..An eye-doctor.

Oleaginous..An oily substance.

Omentum..The caul, peritoneal covering of the intestines.

Opacity..To obstruct light.

Opaque..Not transparent, inability to see through it.

Opthalmos..The eye.

Opthalmia..Disease of the eye, inflammation of the eye.

Opiate..An anodyne.

Organ..A part of the body, which has a certain work to perform, called the function of organs, as the stomach, lungs, womb, &c.

Organic..Bodies made up of organs.

Organism..Vital organization.

Organized..Furnished with life.

Orgasm..The closing excitement of sexual connection.

Origin..The point of commencement.

Orifice..An opening.

Os Tince..Mouth of the womb, or uterus.

Osseous..A bony substance.

Ossification..To become bone; from ost, or osteo, a bone or like a bone.

Ostalgia..Pain in a bone.

Osteoma..Tumor, like bone.

Ostitis..Inflammation of a bone or bones.

Otic..Having reference to the ear.

Otitis..Inflammation of the ear.

Otorrhea..Discharge from the ear.

Ova..An egg, made up of little eggs

Ovaria..Testes; most generally applied to the female ; female testes, two egg-shaped bodies, (made up of little particles, or eggs,) having an attachment to the uterus in the broad ligaments, which support that organ, having tubes, or ducts, opening from them into the uterus, called Fallopian tubes, from the man's name who first gave a description of them. One of these particles is thrown off at each menstrual flow.

Oviparous..Birds, or any animals that produce their young from eggs, or by eggs.

Ovum..An egg.

Oxalic Acid..An acid found in sorrel, very poisonous.

Oxide..A combination of oxygen with a metal, or fluid, as oxygen combining with vinegar-fluid, forms vinegar, oxygen combining with iron, forms oxide of iron, rust of iron, &c.

Oxygen..One of the elements of the air, an acidifying (souring) principle, and an element (a particl or part) of water.

Oxymel..A preparation of vinegar and honey, from mel, honey.

Ozena..Feted ulcer of the nose, or fetid discharge from the nose.

Pabulum..Food ; aliment.

Pad..A cushion.

Palliative..To afford relief, only.

Palpitation..Unhealthy, or unnatural beating of the heart.

Pan..As a prefix, means all.

Panacea..Remedy for all diseases, consequently (speaking ironically) any patent medicine.

Paralysis..Loss of motion, numbpalsy.

Partus..Labor ; the young when brought forth.

Parturition..Child-birth.

Paroxysm..A fit of disease occurring at certain periods.

Periodical..Occurring at a certain time.

Petal..A flour leaf, as rose leaves, &c.

Phthisis..A wasting, consumption.

Pathos..A disease.

Pathology..The doctrine of disease.

Pectoral. . Pertaining to the breast.

Pedilurium . A foot-bath.

Pendulous. . To hang down

Penis. . The male organ of generation.

Pepsine A peculiar substance in the stomach. which aids di
    gestion.

Peptic. . Digestive; hence, dyspeptic, not digesting.

Percolation. . To run, or draw through some substance, straining

Premonitory. . To give a previous notice, as premonitory symp
    toms.

Peri. . Around, a covering.

Pericardium. . Around the heart, sac containing the heart.

Pericarditis. . Inflammation of the pericardium.

Perin. . A testicle, male organs, corresponding with testes, in
    females, with this difference, however, that with
    males they are upon the outside, whilst with females
    they are upon the inside of the body.

Perineum. . That part between the anus and organs of generation
    or genitals.

Perineal. . Relating to the region of the perineum.

Period. . A certain time.

Periodicity. . Returning at a certain time.

Periosteum. . The membrane which covers all bones.

Perspective View. . As it appears to the eye at a certain distance

Perturbation. . To disturb.

Perversion. . An unhealthy change; to change from its proper or
    natural course.

Pessary. . That which will support, or hold up the womb, in pro-
    lapsus; see our remarks on "Female Debility."

Phagedenic. . An eating and fast-spreading ulcer.

Pharmacy. . The art of combining and preparing medicines.

Phlegm. . Mucus from the bronchial tubes, and throat.

Phlogistic. . Tendency to inflammation.

Phosphorus. . An inflammable and luminous substance, prepared
    from urine and bones

Phosphate. . Phosphoric acid in combination with metals, as
    phosphate of iron, phosphate of lime, &c.

Piles. . Tumors at, or in the anus; sometimes protruding; often
    attended with hemorrhage, then called hemorrhoids.

Piperine. . A preparation from black pepper, considered valuable
    in ague.

Placenta. . After-birth, which has a connection to the womb, and
    to the child, during pregnancy: but is naturally
    thrown off by the violent contractions of the womb,
    at this period, there being no further use for it. Oh,
    the wisdom of our Creator, how glorious to contem-
    plate! Everything adapted to the necessities of the case

Plethora. . Over fullness; if healthy, causing obesity, corpu-
    lance.

Pleuritis. . Inflammation of the pleura, pleurisy

Pneumon. . The lungs.

Pleura..The serous membrane covering the lungs, and folded upon the sides.

Pneumonia..Inflammation of the lungs.

Podophyllin..A powder made from the podophyllum peltatum, mandrake root.

Pomum..The apple; hence, pomace, mashed apple.

Potassium..The basis of potash.

Potus..A drink; hence, potion, a medicated drink.

Predisposition..A tendency to a certain disease.

Pregnancy..Being with child.

Prognosis..The art of *guessing* how a disease will terminate.

Prolapsus..A falling

Prolapsus Ani..Falling of the anus.

Prolapsus Uteri..Falling of the uterus.

Prostration..Without strength.

Prussiate..A compound with prussic acid.

Prussic Acid..Hydrocyanic acid; one of, or the most virulent poison in existence.

Psora..The itch.

Pubes..The prominence at the lower front part of the body.

Puberty..Full growth; an adult; perfection

Pubic..Having reference to the region of the pubes.

Pudendum..The female organs of generation.

Puer..A boy, or child.

Puerpera..A woman who has just brought forth a child; hence, puerperal fever, fever at, or soon after child-birth.

Pulmo..A lung.

Pulmonitis..Inflammation of the lung or lungs.

Pulmonary..Relating to the lungs, as pulmonary balsam, pulmonic wafers, &c.

Pulvis..A powder; hence, pulverize, to make fine. All these words show how heavily we have drawn upon other languages, for our own, consequently, the necessity of studying the Latin and Greek, to properly understand ours.

Pupil..The dark circle in the eye.

Purgative..A gentle cathartic.

Pus..Unhealthy matter.

Pustule..A slight elevation, having pus.

Putrefaction..To decompose, by fermentation.

Putrid..Rotten; decomposed.

Pyroligneous Acid..An acid obtained from wood; the essence of smoke; if a little of it is put into a barrel with meat in the brine, it smokes it without trouble. I think gill to the barrel sufficient, perhaps a little less will do. It is obtained by inserting an old gun-barrel or other iron tube into a coal-pit, near the bottom, when burning; it condenses in the tube and drops from outer end into a dish, then bottled for use.

Quassia..A bitter tonic; the chips of the wood are used.

Rachis..The spin

Rachitis..Rickets, bending of the spine, and sometimes the long
   bones of the limbs; may be also enlargement of the
   head, bowels, and the ends of the long bones
Radius..The bone of the upper arm.
Radial..Having reference to the upper arm.
Radiated..Diverging from a centre.
Radix..A root.
Ramus..A branch.
Ramification..To branch out.
Rancidity..Rancid, stale; applied to oil, fat, butter, &c.
Rash..A redness of the skin, in patches.
Ratsbane..Arsenious acid, arsenic.
Rattle..Noise of air passing through mucus, as in croup.
Reaction..To return, after recession.
Recession..Striking in, the blood, or disease, going to the inter
   nal organs.
Rectum..The lower portion of the intestines.
Reduction..To set a fracture, or to return a hernia.
Refrigerant..A cooling medicine, or drink.
Regimen..Regulation of diet and habits, to preserve health, or
   to cure disease.
Relapse..Recurrence of disease after an improved appearance,
   which is generally worse than the first attack.
Relaxation..Losing the healthy tone of any part, or the whole
   system.
Repletion..Fullness.
Reproduction..Generation, procreation
Respiration..To breathe, including both inspiration and expira
   tion.
Resolution..To return to health, applied to inflammations.
Retching..An effort to vomit.
Retention..Delay of the natural passage of the urine or feces.
Revulsion..To draw away disease, as draughts, or blisters, irri-
   tating plasters, &c.
Rheumatism..Inflammation of the fibrous tissue, mostly con-
   fined to the large joints.
Ricini Oleum..Castor oil.
Rigor..Coldness, with shivering.
Rochelle Salts..A mixture of tartarate of potash and soda.
Rubefacients..Medicines which cause redness of the skin, as mus-
   tard, raddish leaves, &c.
Rupture..Hernia; by some, called a breach.
Saccharine..The properties of sugar.
Saliva..The secretion of the mouth, spittle; hence, salivation,
   an increased flow of saliva.
Salt..A compound of acid with an alkali, or metal.
Saltpetre..Nitrate of potash.
Salubrious..Climate favorable to health.
Sanative..A curative medicine.
Sanguis..Blood.

Sanguinious..Bloody—Sanguineous discharge, as bloody-flux

Santonin..A powder obtained from worm-seed.

Sarcoma..A fleshy tumor, generally of a cancerous nature

Scabies..The itch.

Scirrhus..A hard tumor, generally of a cancerous nature.

Scrofula..A constitutional tendency to disease of the glands

Scrotum..The sac which encloses the testicles.

Sedative..To depress, the opposite of stimulation.

Seidlitz..A village of Bohemia; hence, seidlitz powders, which originated at that place.

Sinapis..Mustard; hence, sinapisms, mustard plasters.

Slough..Death of a part, allowing it to come out from the healthy part.

Stimulant..A medicine calculated to to excite an increased and healthy action.

Styptic..To stop bleeding.

Snake-Root..Common or Virginia snake-root; but black snake-root is the black-cohosh.

Spasm..Cramp, or convulsion.

Specific..A remedy having a uniform action, producing health

Sperm..Seminal fluid, now more often called the semen, seed.

Spermatic..Having reference to the testicles, or ovaries.

Spina..The back-bone; hence, spine.

Stitch..A spasmodic pain.

Stoma..The mouth.

Stomatitis..Inflammation of the mouth.

Strangulation..To choke; also applied to hernia which cannot be reduced.

Sudor..Sweat; hence, sudorific, to sweat.

Sulphate..A combination with sulphuric acid.

Sulphuric Acid..Oil of vitriol.

Suppression..An arrest of a natural discharge.

Suppuration..To produce pus.

Sympathy..To be affected by the disease of another organ, as sick-headache from overloading the stomach.

Symptom..A sign of disease.

Syncope..To swoon, fainting.

Syphitis..Disease from sexual connection with those who have venerial disease.

Tannic Acid..An acid from oak bark, an astringent.

Tartaric Acid..An acid from cream of tartar, found in grapes.

Tenesmus..Difficulty and pain at stool, with a desire to go to stool often.

Tent..A roll of lint or cloth to keep wounds open until they heal from the bottom.

Testes..Testicles.

Therapeutics..Relating to a knowledge of treating disease, the curative action of medicine.

Thorax..The chest.

Tibia..The large bone of the lower leg

Tonsils. .Glands on each side of the throat.
Trachea. .The windpipe.
Translation. .Disease going to some other organ.
Triturate. .To rub into a powder.
Tumor. .An enlargement of a portion, usually of the external
    parts.
Ulna. .Small, or under bone of the arm.
Umbilicus .The naval.
Ureter. .Duct leading from the kidney to the bladder.
Urethra. .Duct leading out from the bladder.
Uterus. .The womb.
Vagina. .The passage from the womb to the vulva.
Venery. .Sexual indulgence.
Vermifuge. .Having the property to destroy worms.
Virus. .Contagious poison.
Vulva. .External opening of the female genitals
Whites. .Fluor albus
Yeast. .The principle of fermentation
Zinci Sulphas. .Sulphate of Zinc, white vitriol.

☞ LAWS OF COPYRIGHT.—The exclusive benefits of Copy-
rights extend to Twenty-Eight Years—then renewable for
Fourteen Years, if the Author is dead, to the Heirs, by re-re-
cording and Advertising the re-record for four weeks in any
Newspaper in the United States.

The forfeiture of all the books, and a penalty of Fifty Cents
on each Sheet, (16 pages), in the work, half to the United
States, and half to the Author, is the penalty for Publishing
or Importing any work Without the written Consent of the
Author; and the Printer is equally liable with the Publisher.

Entries can be made in any District Court of the United
States. The laws are found in Vol. 4, of the United States
Statutes, pages 436—439. The Clerk is entitled to a Fee of
Fifty Cents; and also Ffty Cents for each Copy of the Re-
cord, under Seal of the Office, that may be desired.

CPSIA information can be obtained at www.ICGtesting.com
Printed in the USA
LVOW10s2150081014

407962LV00001B/138/P